CODE NAME ARCADIA

Number 167
Williams-Ford Texas A&M Military History Series

CODE NAME ARCADIA

The First Wartime Conference of Churchill and Roosevelt

JOHN F. SHORTAL

Texas A&M University Press College Station

First edition

Library of Congress Cataloging-in-Publication Data

Names: Shortal, John F., 1951– author.
Title: Code name Arcadia : the first wartime conference of Churchill and Roosevelt / John F. Shortal.
Other titles: Williams-Ford Texas A&M University military history series ; no. 167.
Description: College Station : Texas A&M University Press, [2021] | Series: Williams-Ford Texas A&M University military history series ; number 167 | Includes bibliographical references and index.
Identifiers: LCCN 2020029255 | ISBN 9781623499327 (hardcover) | ISBN 9781623499334 (ebook)
Subjects: LCSH: United States. Joint Chiefs of Staff—History. | Combined Chiefs of Staff (U.S. and Great Britain)—History. | Washington Conference (1st : 1941–1942 : Washington, D.C.) | World War, 1939–1945—Campaigns—Congresses. | Combined operations (Military science)—Congresses. | World War, 1939–1945—Diplomatic history. | United States—Military policy. | United States—Politics and government—1933–1945. | United States—Foreign relations—Great Britain. | Great Britain—Foreign relations—United States.
Classification: LCC D734 .S46 2021 | DDC 940.54/0941—dc23
LC record available at https://lccn.loc.gov/2020029255

Cover: James A. Ernst sketch of the Arcadia Conference
(Courtesy of the George C. Marshall Foundation, Lexington, Virginia).

Dedicated to my wife, Pam, for a lifetime of constant inspiration, encouragement, and support

CONTENTS

ILLUSTRATIONS

ACKNOWLEDGMENTS

This book examines why the Joint Chiefs of Staff was created. The need for an organization to coordinate military strategy and staff work between services grew out of the first Anglo-American Chiefs of Staff Conference of World War II, code-named Arcadia, in December 1941–January 1942. During my research and writing, I benefited from the advice and assistance of many individuals. It is a pleasure for me to acknowledge the friends who provided help, guidance, and encouragement. I am indebted to Dr. Edward Drea for his unfailing support and reassurance. He took time from his own research and writing to read and comment on this manuscript and to answer my questions on the Pacific war. His insights on writing style and sources were invaluable. I am grateful to Dr. Steven Rearden who also read and commented on the manuscript and generously shared his vast knowledge and expertise on the formation of the Joint Chiefs of Staff. Both historians helped make this book a reality.

Special thanks go to Dr. Tim Nenninger and the staff at the National Archives, College Park, Maryland; Jeffrey Kozak and Paul Barron at the George C. Marshall Library and Archives, Lexington, Virginia; Colonel (Retired) Kenneth Foulks and the staff at the US Army Center of Military History, Fort McNair, Washington, DC; Molly Bompane and the staff at the Army Heritage and Education Center, Carlisle Barracks, Pennsylvania; Lisa Crunk at the Naval History and Heritage Command, Washington, DC; the staff at the Library of Congress, Washington, DC; and Dr. David Crist of the Joint History Office for his invaluable good will and belief in the need for this study.

I would also like to thank Dr. Jay Dew of Texas A&M University Press for his confidence and enthusiasm. His consistent passion for the book is greatly appreciated. I also want to thank Patricia Clabaugh and Dawn Hall for their superb editorial skill in improving the quality of this manuscript.

While I benefited from the assistance of those I mentioned and others, I alone am responsible for the text. The opinions expressed in this book do not represent the official views of the Department of Defense or Joint Chiefs of Staff. Any errors in fact or interpretation are mine alone, and they should not be attributed to anyone else.

My greatest debt is to my wife, Pam, who was my most encouraging and supportive advocate throughout the project. To her this work is dedicated.

CODE NAME
ARCADIA

INTRODUCTION

Three weeks after Japan's attack on Pearl Harbor, British Prime Minister Winston Churchill led a military delegation to the United States to coordinate the efforts of the two countries to defeat the Axis powers. This first international conference of the war, known as the First Washington Conference and code-named Arcadia, set the tone for Anglo-American wartime cooperation. During the conference, the American and British Chiefs of Staff met twelve times, in the Federal Reserve Building in Washington, DC, between 24 December 1941 and 14 January 1942. It proved to be one of the most successful international conferences of World War II and central to the development of the Anglo-American special relationship.

Winston Churchill headed the British delegation and moved into the White House for the duration of the conference. The British Chiefs of Staff were Admiral of the Fleet Sir Dudley Pound (Royal Navy), Air Chief Marshal Sir Charles Portal (Royal Air Force), and Field Marshal John Dill (the former chief of the imperial general staff). All three British chiefs showed remarkable patience, insight, and selflessness during the conference.

The United States was represented in the Chiefs of Staff talks by General George C. Marshall, the Chief of Staff of the Army; Lieutenant General Henry "Hap" Arnold, Chief of the Army Air Forces; and by two navy representatives, Admiral Harold R. Stark, the Chief of Naval Operations, and Admiral Ernest J. King, the Commander in Chief of the United States Fleet. They displayed innovativeness, adaptability, and unselfishness. The Chiefs of Staff of both nations set the standard for cooperation and compromise that, although tested later during the global conflict, was never severely challenged.

Yet the Arcadia Conference has never received the recognition it deserves. The official British history of World War II acknowledged some success in organizational development, such as the creation of the Combined Chiefs of Staff, but emphasized the failure to address the exact time, date, and location of the invasion of Europe. The conference also received harsh criticism for failing to reconcile the two philosophical approaches to defeating Germany, the peripheral strategy of Great Britain and the direct approach strategy of the United States. According to the British official history, "the strategic discussions at Washington were unduly one-sided since they proceeded based on papers written from the British point of view only. The agreements reached thus tended to be more formal than real; they were not the product of a full debate such as would have enabled either side to explore the principles on which the other wished to act."[1]

An official American history echoed this criticism, blaming the Americans' lack of unity of effort due to interservice rivalry between the US Army and Navy. "The actual measures indorsed by the President were specific military moves that did not necessarily reflect American commitment to any broad strategy or indeed to any particular operations, since the rather doubtful logistic feasibility of all the measures approved was largely ignored and no clear order of priority set for them. Partly as a result of these facts, though much more because of the unforeseen rapidity of Japanese advances in the Pacific, the Arcadia Conference as a whole was rather inconclusive except as a sound beginning of continuous, systematic British-American military planning in Washington."[2]

The only Chief of Staff to keep a diary, which he later published in 1957, was Field Marshal Alan Brooke, who replaced Field Marshal Dill as the chief of the Imperial General Staff. Brooke thought that the British Chiefs of Staff in Washington were too pliable and had conceded too much to the Americans. His assessment that the British chiefs at the Arcadia Conference "sold our birthright for a plate of porridge," has often been repeated.[3]

Brooke did not attend the Arcadia Conference, remaining behind in London to coordinate the war effort and chair the British Chiefs of Staff Committee. His understandable frustration over not being able to participate and influence decisions in Washington may account in part for his critical and sarcastic comments about the British chiefs' efforts at Arcadia. But they also suggest that he was temperamentally unprepared to work with the Americans at this critical juncture in the war. Nevertheless, Brooke made a decisive contribution to Arcadia; he convinced the prime minister to take Field Marshal Dill to the conference. This proved fortuitous because Dill forged a very close relationship with all the American chiefs, especially General Marshall.[4]

Brooke's skepticism about his new allies was hardly unique. Some American leaders also harbored a mistrust of the accommodations and accomplishments of the British and American Chiefs of Staff. Rear Admiral Richmond Kelly Turner, the lead planner for the navy at the conference, feared that after Arcadia, "British Officials would be given half the total authority on matters now solely under US control," and that "US interests would be subordinated to the interests of the British Commonwealth."[5]

Despite these naysayers' pessimism, the American and British Chiefs of Staff in Washington took on the most pressing issues confronting the two nations in an open-minded manner. They were willing to experiment, to take chances, and were broadminded enough to try to appreciate each other's perspectives.

National interests and attitudes manifested themselves initially in the relations between the American and British military planners. The British staff work was exceptional, allowing their well-crafted position papers intentionally to conceal British weaknesses. Unwilling to appear as a supplicant, Churchill sought to steer conferees to the British position, convincing American military participants that defeating "Germany First" really meant supporting "Britain First." The US military and naval staff officers who prepared the multiple topical papers responded to the British proposals. Together, the staff officers of both countries overcame prewar presumptions to translate lofty and often impractical goals into strategic and logistic reality.

It is unrealistic to expect that just three weeks after the United States entered a global war that a detailed combined strategy would be agreed on. Despite the comments by official historians on both sides of the Atlantic, the participants resolved the most pressing strategic issue confronting the Anglo-American Alliance on day one of the conference by confirming the "Germany First" strategy. While agreed on in theory before the US entry into the war, the British were dubious that it would become practice in the wake of Pearl Harbor. In retrospect, their fears were unfounded and the American Chiefs of Staff immediately confirmed this strategy. Historian Louis Morton termed this, "The most important single strategic concept of the war."[6]

President Franklin Roosevelt and Prime Minister Churchill planned and executed another important outcome during the Arcadia Conference. They jointly drafted and published, with the agreement and signatures of twenty-six countries, the Declaration of the United Nations that pledged the respective signatories to pursue the war to their maximum effort, military and economic, against the Axis. Furthermore, the charter committed the Allied nations not to sign a separate armistice or peace with the Axis enemies.

One participant, Lieutenant Colonel Paul Robinett, Assistant Chief of Staff for Intelligence War Department General Staff, served as the army secretary at the conference and enumerated several other important decisions made at the Arcadia Conference. First, was the creation of the Combined Chiefs of Staff, an apparatus the American and British Chiefs of Staff established for the conduct of combined operations. This organizational structure provided a framework for strategic coordination. The civilian leaders tasked the Combined Chiefs of Staff to recommend requirements based on strategic considerations, supervise the distribution of military supplies and equipment, and to prioritize overseas movements. Churchill considered the creation of this organization Arcadia's most important accomplishment.[7]

The establishment of the Combined Chiefs of Staff required the United States to develop an organization capable of meeting and collaborating on a continuing basis with the British Chiefs of Staff.

Previously, the United States lacked an official forum where the chiefs of the US Army, Army Air Force, and Navy could meet and prepare for their discussions with their British counterparts. The new system that replaced the existing ineffectual and outmoded interservice coordination mechanisms was the Joint Chiefs of Staff, an institution that continues to this day.

Still another significant accomplishment of the Arcadia Conference was the creation of a supreme commander for individual theaters who coordinated the army, navy, and air forces of multiple allies within his designated theater. The Allies initially applied the concept of a single unified theater commander who reported to the Combined Chiefs of Staff in the South West Pacific, and the results in an operational theater led to its repeated use elsewhere.[8]

During the conference, the British and American Chiefs of Staff not only engaged in a constructive dialogue but also made several key decisions on the movement of US troops to Iceland and Ireland to relieve British troops stationed there for operations elsewhere. The Combined Chiefs also agreed on the buildup of US forces in England in preparation for future operations against the Germans in northwest Europe. During the meetings, the British and American chiefs realized that not enough sea transport was available to accomplish all their requirements and accordingly developed a system to prioritize and coordinate the limited Allied shipping assets.[9]

The British and American chiefs also developed a general design for a strategy to check further Axis advances in Europe. The first step was to build up and secure the industrial base in the United States and Britain. They would follow this by securing key air and sea lines of communication between the United States and Great Britain and in the Mediterranean. The third phase would be to close the ring around Germany by providing military aid to Russia. Fourth, the chiefs agreed on the importance of wearing down the Germans by a strategic bombing campaign, a blockade of Europe, aid to resistance groups in occupied territories, and propaganda. Finally, the British and American chiefs acknowledged that after accomplishing all these goals an invasion of Europe would still have to occur, although without going into specific details. Critics subsequently faulted them for not having resolved the specifics of time, location, and method of attack. But the fact that they were able to agree on the other phases was a significant step forward, especially considering the United States was only a few weeks into the war.[10]

As for the Pacific, the American and British chiefs worked on plans to provide initial reinforcements to their forces fighting in the hard-pressed region. They realistically examined political and military needs of both nations and also agreed on common measures to provide material and organizational support to China. The unexpectedly rapid advance of the Japanese in early 1942 soon overcame some of these plans, but the foundation for organization and cooperative strategy was established.[11]

The American and British chiefs were successful in developing a concept for pooling and sharing war equipment. The Munitions Assignment Board, with American and British representatives, reported to and was an element of the Combined Chiefs of Staff, therefore guaranteeing that production was subordinate to and not independent of strategy. The board successfully set priorities and allocated equipment and war material to the multiple and diverse theaters of operation in support of the overall Allied strategy.[12]

Overshadowed by later conferences, the Arcadia Conference nonetheless firmly fixed the relationship between President Roosevelt and Prime Minister Churchill. Their bond of understanding and vision for the conduct of the war solidified during the conference. Likewise, the American and British chiefs developed a mechanism for the conduct of the war and agreed on an overall, if general, strategic blueprint. This conference established the bonds of Anglo-American cooperation and was the genesis of the "Special Relationship." What follows is a day-by-day account of the military chieftains' efforts at Arcadia that reveals their evolution during the sessions and, more importantly, their decisive contributions to this first great wartime summit meeting.[13]

1

Prelude to the Conference

The European war that began on 1 September 1939, took a dramatic turn in the spring of 1940 when Nazi Germany overran Western Europe, occupied France and the Netherlands, and pushed Great Britain to the brink of defeat. Japan saw the opportunity to move against the western colonies in Southeast Asia to secure raw material as well as to isolate China, at war with Japan since 1937, by cutting overland supply routes running through Burma and French Indochina. On 22 September 1940, the Japanese occupied northern French Indochina. Five days later Tokyo signed the Tripartite Pact with Germany and Italy. Berlin believed that the threat of a two-ocean war would keep the United States neutral; Tokyo expected that the pact would isolate the United States and deter Washington from war.[1]

The Japanese initially did not occupy southern French Indochina to avoid further alienating the United States. The Nazi invasion of the Soviet Union in June 1941 changed that equation. Japan's top strategists had to decide whether to move north against a weakened USSR or turn south against the weakened European colonial empires. Captured British documents previously had revealed to Tokyo the extent of British military debility in east Asia, and the Japanese did not anticipate a sharp American reaction. A 2 July 1941 imperial conference endorsed a move south, and on 25 July Japanese forces occupied southern French Indochina. The next day President

Franklin D. Roosevelt froze Japanese assets, and on 1 August embargoed the export of oil to Japan. These decisions left Japan unable to obtain raw materials and oil to keep her war machine running.[2]

The American reaction surprised the Japanese, whose bleak economic outlook was instrumental in Tokyo's decision for war. On the morning of 7 December 1941, Japanese carrier-based aircraft attacked the US Pacific Fleet then at anchor in Pearl Harbor. Japanese leaders expected to time the assault to follow immediately a declaration of war against the United States, but due to unanticipated delays the attack preceded the break in diplomatic relations. The air raid achieved complete surprise and caught US military forces in Hawaii literally half asleep. In ninety minutes Japanese warplanes sank or damaged nineteen US warships, including eight battleships. Almost six thousand American servicemen were killed or wounded and more than three hundred military aircraft were destroyed or damaged. Besides the sheer destruction, the Japanese ability to achieve total surprise and cripple the Pacific Fleet was especially demoralizing to the American public, who demanded accountability.[3]

Owing to a five-and-one-half-hour time difference, it was early afternoon in Washington, DC, when word of the attack arrived in bits and pieces. The secretary of the navy, Frank Knox, notified the president at 1340. Shortly after, Roosevelt informed Secretary of War Henry Stimson about Pearl Harbor. Stimson at seventy-four was an important advisor to the president. He was a moderate Republican who had served as secretary of war under President William Taft and as secretary of state under Herbert Hoover. He was a proponent of support to Britain and Russia in their fight against Germany. His was a strong voice for building the American military and he had opposed the isolationists in Congress. An hour later, the president met with his principal military leaders: Army Chief of Staff General George C. Marshall; the Chief of Naval Operations Admiral Harold Stark; and Secretaries Stimson and Knox, as well as Harry Hopkins, the president's top advisor.[4]

Roosevelt was at his best as a commander in chief, setting the example for others to emulate at a time of unprecedented stress and crisis. He was calm, and he was capable of taking a long view despite the grave situation. Hopkins said later that the meeting was "not too tense an atmosphere because I think that all of us believed that in the last analysis the enemy was Hitler and that he could never be defeated without force of arms; that sooner or later we were bound to be in a war and that Japan had given us an opportunity." Throughout the session the president personally handled calls from the navy that updated the damage at Pearl Harbor.[5]

The president also dictated a press release on the attack and held two additional meetings. The first was with his cabinet, which he pronounced "the most serious meeting of the cabinet since 1861." The second meeting with legislative leaders started at 2030 hours. In attendance were Vice President Henry Wallace, Senator Albin Barkley, Senator Charles McNary, Senator Tom Connally, Senator Warren Austin, Senator Hiram Johnson, Speaker Sam Rayburn, Congressman Sol Bloom, and Congressman Charles Eaton.[6]

It was a contentious meeting. Roosevelt updated the congressional leaders on Pearl Harbor's status. Senator Connally, an influential Democratic member of the Senate Foreign Relations Committee, asked Knox, "Well, what did we do?" As Knox started to answer, the Texas senator interrupted him. "Didn't you say last month that we could lick the Japs in two weeks? Didn't you say our navy was so well prepared and located that the Japanese couldn't hope to hurt us at all? When you made those public statements, weren't you just trying to tell the country what an efficient secretary of the navy you were?"[7]

As Knox struggled to respond, Connally again demanded, "Why did you have all those ships at Pearl Harbor crowded in the way you did?" Why, he asked, "did you have a chain across the mouth of the entrance to Pearl Harbor, so that our ships could not get out?" When Knox shakily responded, "To protect us against Japanese submarines," Connally demanded, "Weren't you thinking of an air attack?" Knox again had no answer. At this juncture, the ice was broken and the rest of the senators grilled Knox with pointed questions. Without knowing the full details of the Pearl Harbor attack, Knox could not rebut the accusations.[8]

Knox at sixty-seven was a former Rough Rider and moderate Republican who had opposed isolationists in his own party and advocated military preparedness in the face of Axis aggression. He was a professional journalist who had been the publisher of the *Chicago Daily News* before accepting the position of secretary of the navy. He was a forceful supporter and publicist for the US Navy. Now the hyperbole that oversold the capabilities of his service to secure congressional financing for prewar naval shipbuilding came back to haunt him. During a speech in Indianapolis just two months before the Pearl Harbor attack, Knox had ignited a firestorm by asserting that "the Navy was the nation's first line of defense" and denigrating the need to invest in land-based air forces. At the time, General Marshall wrote to Stimson, "The Secretary of the Navy's statement, relative to the decisive role the United States Navy might be expected to accomplish requires careful consideration especially in light of events transpiring in the European theater.[9] Sea power can no longer operate effectively without the strong support of air power. . . . Following the same premise, the effectiveness of the United States Navy as a first line of defense in the Western Hemisphere is directly contingent upon the strong support of land-based aviation."[10]

Senator Connally's interrogation of Secretary Knox launched the search for blame. Stimson believed that Connally was voicing the concerns of everyone in the room. The nation was stunned and angry that Japan would dare to attack the United States. Recriminations and rumors were widespread, as was the hunt for scapegoats. Congress and the American people would want to know who was responsible. Secretary Knox soon departed for Hawaii for an eye-witness appraisal of what happened.[11]

In London the reaction to the news was a relief. Prime Minister Churchill was at home dining with the United States Ambassador to Great Britain John Winant and the president's Special Envoy for the Lend-Lease program, W. Averell Harriman. Hearing the news on the radio, Churchill called Roosevelt to confirm that the Japanese indeed had attacked Pearl Harbor. During a conversation the president said, "It's quite true, they have attacked us at Pearl Harbor. We are in the same boat now."[12]

The next day, the president addressed a joint session of Congress. Less than twenty-four hours after the attack the president's memorable "Day of Infamy" speech established him as the wartime leader of the American people. He spoke for fewer than seven minutes but inspired confidence. He emphasized that he was in charge and that he had directed the military to use all measures to defend the nation; he asked Congress for a declaration of war against Japan. Congress authorized his request in under an hour.[13]

Churchill's first thoughts were of England and the impact Pearl Harbor would have on the war effort. He said, "No American will think it wrong of me if I proclaim that to have the United States at our side was to me the greatest joy. I could not tell the course of future events. I do not pretend to have measured accurately the martial might of Japan, but now at this very moment I knew the United States was in the war, up to the neck and in to the death. So we had won after all."[14]

Churchill's euphoria was short-lived. On that same day Stimson attended two meetings that would directly affect the British. He first met with Air Marshal Arthur Harris of the British Joint Mission in Washington and informed Harris that the British government would have to release some B-24 bombers that the United States had previously earmarked for Great Britain because these aircraft were needed to defend the US West Coast.[15]

Stimson later attended a meeting of the Supply Priorities and Allocation Board (SPAB), chaired by Vice President Wallace and requested a change in priorities. With the United States now at war, equipping the armed forces of the United States became the top priority. This would affect the Lend-Lease program. The Lend-Lease program dated from March 1941; it originally provided the British the military equipment that it desperately needed to fight Germany and later was extended to the Soviet Union. For almost a year the Lend-Lease military equipment enjoyed priority over American military requirements. One example of Lend-Lease's diversion of US-produced war equipment is found in a letter from Stimson to President Roosevelt. "Of our present tank production, roughly five-sixths is now going to Russia and Great Britain." Cutbacks in the Lend-Lease program to meet American priorities meant Great Britain, the USSR, and China would receive less military assistance.[16]

Two days after the Pearl Harbor attack the administration suspended some Lend-Lease shipments, mainly aircraft and aviation fuel. On the morning of 9 December, Stimson explained to the president that Lend-Lease depended on the navy's ability to defend America's West Coast, but wartime necessities forced the army to send B-17s to Hawaii to protect Pearl Harbor. Pursuit planes were deployed to the West Coast to defend aircraft factories in San Diego, Los Angeles, and Seattle. Continental defense was the priority, and the president approved Stimson's request to remove all the aircraft currently earmarked for Lend-Lease to augment the hurried formation of fifty-four Army Air Corps' groups designated to defend the United States.[17]

Stimson had not intended to suspend Lend-Lease completely, but in the confusion after Pearl Harbor directives were sometimes misinterpreted. One instance severely affected British operations in the Mediterranean. On 18 November British forces had launched Operation Crusader, a major ground operation in North Africa. For several weeks Crusader aimed to crush the German Army by recapturing Cyrenaica, destroying as much of German General Erwin Rommel's armor as possible, and seizing Tripolitania. Critical to this prolonged operation were thirty ships loaded with Lend-Lease tanks and other military equipment. They remained at anchor in American ports on the faulty assumption that the administration had suspended all Lend-Lease shipments.[18]

Churchill was concerned that this shipment would be diverted to the Pacific for the war against Japan. He worried not only about Crusader but also about the long-range wartime strategy. Did this signal a sweeping change from the previously agreed on "Germany First" strategy to a reorientation of American might against Japan? Churchill cabled Foreign Secretary Anthony Eden: "The United States have sustained a major disaster at Hawaii and have now only two battleships effective in the Pacific against ten Japanese. They are recalling all their battleships from the Atlantic and have laid an embargo on all exports of munitions for the time being. . . . Everything is in flux about the United States supplies and I cannot tell where we are till I get there."[19]

On 11 December the British asked Averell Harriman to contact Harry Hopkins, the president's chief troubleshooter, about the thirty ships idled in American ports to ensure that Crusader was not derailed by lack of tanks and materiel. Harriman did as requested and explained that Lord Beaverbrook (William Maxwell Aitken), the British Minister of Supply, would contact Hopkins that evening about the thirty ships. Harriman made Hopkins aware of the critical importance of these shipments to Crusader. "Much of these cargoes are vitally needed for the successful completion of the campaign here. I have such intimate knowledge of the needs that I cannot help but express to you the hope that you will find a way to get quick action on the release of these shipments which do not interfere with our own urgent needs."[20]

After speaking to Beaverbrook, Hopkins quickly cabled reassurances to Harriman. "Shipments to the United Kingdom and Middle East rapidly clarifying. Problem fully understood by the British here [British Joint Staff Mission which had been established in June of 1941]. Have just telephoned to you and wanted to assure you that almost everything except airplanes and 37 A.P. shot [the ammunition for the 37 mm antitank gun] has already been released. Tanks released this afternoon. Ships leaving regularly. No such delay as is indicated in Beaverbrook's wire."[21]

The flow of most Lend-Lease equipment resumed after a short delay. Harry Hopkins also informed Beaverbrook and Harriman that the United States was going to mobilize its industrial base to meet all wartime requirements. "British should be greatly encouraged rather than discouraged about our supplies from here. If Hitler thought he could stop materials going to Russia and British Empire by striking us he will be greatly mistaken. . . . Everyone here fully appreciates importance of not only getting back to our planned shipments but to increase them further. There is a big push here to go on a seven day week and many hundreds of factories are taking defense orders."[22]

Regardless of these reassurances, Churchill was still worried. Would the flow of war materials be stopped again? He could see the outrage of the American public from the press reports and wondered if this anger and energy might channel public opinion to demand that the United States abandon the "Germany First" strategy and strike back at Japan? Would the vast industrial engine of the United States gear up against Japan and not Germany? He expressed his fears to his physician, Lord Moran (Charles Wilson): "They may concentrate upon Japan and leave us to deal with Germany. They have already stopped the flow of supplies that we are getting."[23]

Churchill's fears that reduced American Lend-Lease portended grave consequences for the British economy were well founded. Unlike Germany, Britain had not invested in arms production in the 1930s. After the fall of France, Britain stood alone and had to rely on the United States for steel, aircraft, tanks, industrial equipment, and raw materials. Paying for all this had bankrupted London by December 1940. The Lend-Lease Act of March 1941, however, transformed Britain from a "bankrupt to a pensioner" by continuing the flow of food, raw materials, and military and industrial equipment from the United States via Lend-Lease, which in turn enabled the British to convert to a total war economy. Yet this system was fragile. According to one historian, Britain's economy was as "dependent on American strength as a patient on a life-support machine." In other words, Britain could not afford to have this lifeline interrupted.[24]

The United States had driven a very hard bargain for its Lend-Lease support. Churchill privately remarked, "We are not only being skinned but flayed to the bone." Certain repayment schedules and other details had yet to be finalized, and Churchill preferred to keep it that way. A particular sticking point was the American intimation that the British dismantle their Imperial Preference system, a discriminatory two-tiered arrangement with lower tariff rates for dominion members than for nonmembers. Churchill saw any overture to eliminate this system as an American attempt to gain international economic hegemony during the postwar years.[25]

Later, the prime minister also bemoaned Lend-Lease repayments: "Yes, by all means let us have an account if we can get it reasonably accurate, but I shall have my account put in too, and my account is for holding the baby alone for eighteen months, and it was a very rough brutal baby I had to hold. I don't know quite what I shall have to charge for it." Many in the United Kingdom shared his conviction and believed that one purpose of Lend-Lease was to fight Hitler to the last Briton.[26]

"Now that America was a belligerent," Churchill worried, "all existing agreements and priorities would be dislocated; and the problem was to ensure that we did not lose more than a minimum of the aircraft, weapons and munitions on which we had been counting." Great Britain desperately needed Lend-Lease continued and, just as importantly, Churchill needed access to the increased production of military equipment as the United States shifted to a belligerent status.[27] Having sacrificed so much, and having formulated their war plans on specific levels of supply from the United States, any post–Pearl Harbor diminution of resources had to be kept at a minimum.

Churchill determined that only a face-to-face meeting with Roosevelt could resolve his doubts. It would also offer the opportunity for the prime minister to bring his Chiefs of Staff Committee to Washington and allow the committee members to coordinate directly with their American counterparts. Time was of the essence, and on 8 December, Churchill formally requested King George VI's permission to travel to the United States because, "We have to be careful that our share of munitions and other aid which we are receiving from the United States does not suffer more than is, I fear, inevitable."[28]

With the king's permission, Churchill cabled Roosevelt the following day. "Now that we are as you say 'in the same boat' would it not be wise for us to have another conference? We could review the whole war plan in light of reality and new facts, as well as the problems of production and distribution. I feel that all these matters, some of which are causing me concern, can best be settled on the highest executive level." He continued, noting that he could leave in a day or two and would be accompanied by his military chiefs.[29]

President Roosevelt initially tried to delay Churchill's visit. Still reeling from Pearl Harbor, the president thought the American chiefs needed time to reassess policy before a visit. He expressed his concern for the prime minister's safety and recommended postponing a meeting for a month. Roosevelt's concern was both political and genuine. He worried that the inevitable and extensive press coverage of such a high-level meeting would alert the Germans, who in turn might intercept the prime minister's convoy during its return voyage. Churchill was adamant and dismissed any risks. "We do not think there is any serious danger about return journey. There is, however, great danger in our not having a full discussion on the highest level about the extreme gravity of the naval position as well as upon all the production and allocation issues involved. . . . I feel it would be disastrous to wait another month. . . . I hope to start tomorrow night."[30]

The following day Roosevelt officially invited Churchill to stay at the White House during the conference. While again voicing concern for the prime minister's safety, he was confident of a fruitful meeting because the production and allocation issues could be solved.[31]

The American chiefs of staff were not pleased when informed four days after Pearl Harbor that they would have to host the British military leaders at a conference in Washington. In the frenzied days following the Japanese attack the American chiefs were consumed by a myriad of responsibilities. Admiral Stark and General Marshall were scraping together scarce resources to defend the country. The Japanese had attacked the Philippines on 8 December and bombed Manila. Two days later Japanese troops landed in northern Luzon. Military efforts were underway to assemble planes, equipment, and troops to reinforce General Douglas MacArthur's forces in the Philippines.[32]

Furthermore, rumors of air raids, naval bombardments, and Japanese paratroops raced along the West Coast, causing alarm and confusion. Although most were unfounded, the military services wasted countless hours tamping down the "invasion fever" affecting the public. A rumor that a Japanese aircraft carrier was sighted off the coast, for instance, led to closing all the schools in Oakland on 10 December. The same day in San Francisco near panic ensued when radio broadcasts went off the air as part of an unannounced three-hour blackout test. Army units claimed that they tracked one hundred aircraft headed toward California from the sea. The navy, on 9 December, sounded alerts that thirty-four Japanese vessels were near Los Angeles. Upon investigation they turned out to be fishing boats. The same day navy warships responded to an alert of a Japanese cruiser near Catalina that turned out to be a whale.[33]

Every rumor had to be run to the ground because the security of the West Coast was paramount. Sizeable reinforcements, including antiaircraft artillery and warplanes, were diverted from planned missions to guarantee the West Coast's safety. The War Department reassigned troops initially sent to the West Coast for embarkation to Hawaii and the Philippines to coastal defense duties. Just sorting out the issues from California to Manila, it was no wonder the American chiefs had little time for a conference.[34]

The American chiefs also looked askance at the British penchant for demanding an inordinate share of US-produced war material. Before Pearl Harbor, they had resisted continual British requests for more and more arms and material and they did not look forward to further haggling. Their greater worry was that the British had a grand strategy while they did not, and they preferred more time to prepare for the meeting.[35]

Pearl Harbor was an American disaster, but the war in Asia was also going poorly for the British. The Japanese had bombed Hong Kong and Singapore and landed on the Malay Peninsula 400 miles from Singapore on 8 December. One week before the outbreak of hostilities Churchill sent two powerful warships to Singapore to boost morale (which they did) and to deter Japanese aggression (which they did not). On 10 December, Japanese naval aircraft sank the battleship the *Prince of Wales* and the battlecruiser *Repulse* off eastern Malaya. These critical losses handed Japan control of the seas from Hawaii to India.[36]

As the magnitude of the losses at Pearl Harbor became clearer, the bitterness over responsibility grew between the US Army and Navy. Both sides tried to shift responsibility for the disaster on to the other service. As early as 11 December friction and in-fighting between the services were apparent to Knox and Stimson. Both secretaries, as well as General Marshall and Admiral Stark, stayed above the fray, but other senior personages were not as circumspect. Backbiting and recriminations would prove counterproductive before and during the imminent conference.[37]

The fundamental issue was the absence of unity of command in Hawaii. No single person was in charge, leaving Lieutenant General Walter Short and the army responsible for the land defense of Hawaii, including the radar early warning system and the shore-based antiaircraft artillery guns and Admiral Husband E. Kimmel, the naval commander responsible for the defense of the fleet. The Commandant of the Fourteenth Naval District, Admiral Claude C. Bloch, was responsible for the defense of the Pearl Harbor Navy Yard. They each went their way, often without explaining how or what they were doing to their service counterparts, with predictable results. Interservice coordination was poor. Each assumed the other was doing its job. The navy assumed the army radar warning systems were operational. The army assumed the navy was conducting comprehensive long-range air patrols of the Hawaiian Islands. Admiral Kimmel assumed the harbor was too shallow for aerial torpedoes to be effective. Washington assumed that the commanders in Hawaii were receiving intelligence reports and sharing them. None of these assumptions was correct.[38]

The problem at Pearl Harbor was the "system, the setup both at Washington and Pearl, rather than individual stupidity or apathy, which muffled and confused what was going on. No one person knew the whole picture that the intelligence data disclosed; no one person was responsible for the defense of Pearl Harbor; too many people assumed that others were taking precautions that they did not take."[39]

Acrimony increased between the American Army and Navy during the first weeks of December. On 14 December in reply to MacArthur's repeated requests for aid and reinforcements, Admiral Thomas Hart, the commander of the US Asiatic Fleet, pronounced the Philippines doomed. This infuriated the army. Although the powerful Japanese Fleet controlled the maritime approaches to the Philippines, Admiral Hart's bluntness exacerbated the already tense relations between the services.[40]

Admiral Hart's view of the Philippines accorded with the navy's prewar thinking in case of war with Japan. The most recent revision of the war plan, code-named Orange-3, was completed in April 1941 and became part of the joint Army-Navy Rainbow color plans developed before the war. (Each color plan was prepared for a different emergency involving the United States. Orange was the plan for a war involving only the United States and Japan.) The plan's strategic flaw was the assumption that the US Navy would relieve the Philippine garrison within six months. Otherwise, the beleaguered garrison would fall. Navy planners, however, estimated that it would take two years, not six months, for the Pacific Fleet to relieve the Philippines. When war suddenly came to the islands, everyone hoped that some last-minute improvised plan would save the American and Filipino forces on Bataan. Consequently, Hart's remarks infuriated the army.[41]

The army was not willing to write off the Philippines just one week after Pearl Harbor. Stimson was upset by the navy's "defeatist" attitude. He saw a navy "shaken and panic stricken" after Pearl Harbor and thought that they were overly focused on defending Hawaii at the expense of the Philippines. While unfair, it well illustrated the deteriorating service relationships.[42]

Stimson shared his perturbations with the president, who agreed that the Philippines must be reinforced. Disappointed in the navy position, Roosevelt summoned Undersecretary of the Navy James Forrestal, who was the acting secretary of the navy while Secretary Knox was in Hawaii, and made it clear that he was bound to do everything in his power to help the Philippines and expected the navy's support to accomplish this.[43]

On 15 December, Knox returned from Hawaii and reported his observations to President Roosevelt. Stimson recorded Knox's remark, that "the responsibility for everybody being asleep seems to have been very clear." Stimson continued: "Knox agrees with me that there has been remissness in both branches of service—the Army and the Navy, and we both also are very anxious not to get into any inter-departmental scrap."[44]

The next day, Knox held a press conference to explain in general terms his findings about the Pearl Harbor attack. He did his best to defend the navy by highlighting individual acts of courage and heroism, but had to acknowledge that "the United States services were not on the alert against the surprise air attack on Hawaii. This calls for a formal investigation which will be initiated by the President." The press picked up on "not on the alert," ignoring almost everything else.[45]

Knox's press conference had unintended consequences. As one historian noted, "[The] Knox report did the Navy a disservice. It focused the spotlight of popular attention upon the Navy. To this day, discussion of the Pearl Harbor attack is likely to center on naval action and inaction, responsibilities, and failures, even though the Army had the prime mission of protecting the Fleet in harbor and also of guarding the islands."[46]

The army never submitted a comparable report. Immediately after Pearl Harbor, General Marshall had dispatched a trusted staff officer, Colonel Charles Bundy, Chief of the Plans Group, War Plans Division, to investigate. Bundy was killed in an airplane crash while en route to Hawaii, leaving the army dependent on Knox's report. Without an official army report, the press and the public tended to ascribe the disaster at Pearl Harbor to the Navy. The decision to send the navy secretary to look at Pearl Harbor rather than a staff officer had also produced the undue attention that service had hoped to avoid.[47]

On 16 December, after conferring with Knox and Stimson, President Roosevelt announced that a commission headed by Chief Justice Owen Roberts would investigate the Pearl Harbor attack. Committee members were Admiral William H. Standley, Admiral Joseph M. Reeves, General Frank R. McCoy, and General Joseph T. McNarney. The commission conducted interviews between 22 December 1941 and 10 January 1942, and on 18 and 19 December interviewed Stark and Marshall, drawing both service chiefs away from frenetic preparations for the upcoming conference with the British Chiefs of Staff in Washington.[48]

The Roberts Commission's report only increased the already bad feelings between the services. Admiral Ernest King remained bitter toward the army long after the war. "By an arrangement of many years standing the Army was responsible for the land defense of the islands. The failure to discharge their responsibilities was the Army's and especially the Air Corps'. They carefully said nothing about this during the investigation—something for which I will never forgive them, for they could at least have taken part of the blame."[49]

This blame game trickled down through the services. Lieutenant Colonel Paul Robinett, the army's assistant chief of staff for intelligence, complained about poor coordination between the army and navy, especially the navy's repeated refusal to share information with the army staff. Basic matters of joint concern such as a common code to transmit meteorological data or a standardized system for recognition signals for the army, navy, and merchantmen should have been developed before the outbreak of war. They were not, and only on 15 December did army and navy signal experts start to develop such joint systems. The finger-pointing over Pearl Harbor threatened to derail even these fundamental efforts.[50]

On 17 December, the army staff finally received a detailed report on Pearl Harbor. The same day General Marshall relieved General Walter Short and Major General Frederick Martin from their commands in Hawaii. The navy relieved Admiral Husband Kimmel. The implication was that they bore responsibility for the disaster. Who would be relieved next?[51]

In contrast to the hectic tempo of wartime America and the interservice dysfunction, the unified British Chiefs of Staff boarded the battleship *Duke of York* on 13 December for a nine-day trip to America. Churchill assembled his best people. Admiral of the Fleet Dudley Pound, the First Sea Lord, represented the Royal Navy, and Air Chief Marshal Charles Portal, Chief of the Air Staff, represented the Royal Air Force. Field Marshal John Dill represented the army even though Churchill had recently fired him as the Chief of the Imperial General Staff and replaced him with General Alan Brooke.[52]

The sixty-four-year-old Pound was the senior member of the British Chiefs of Staff and had been the First Sea Lord for more than two years. Pound was charming and courteous and, more importantly, enjoyed a close relationship with Churchill. His exceptional intelligence and reputation for hard work preceded him, but he was suffering from a brain tumor. Still, he chaired the British chiefs meetings during the day and spent evenings at the Admiralty working on U-boat issues. His age, illness, and the wartime strain showed when he dozed off in staff meetings. A reticent person, when he did speak it meant something.[53]

Portal had been the Chief of the Air Staff for over a year at the time of the Arcadia Conference, and at forty-eight was by far the youngest member of the British Chiefs of Staff Committee. Intelligent, with a calm demeanor, he was a good listener able to articulate the most complex topics in an easily understood fashion. His openness and good sense conveyed the impression that he was honest and open-minded. General Frederick Morgan, who later served as Eisenhower's Deputy Chief of Staff, said Portal was the "leading spirit of the British Chiefs of Staff. Seemed to be a different breed. Thoroughly competent in his own sphere, also knowledgeable on any topic. . . . Remembers not a single case with [British] Chiefs of Staff in which Portal was not the first to see and appreciate my point."[54]

Field Marshal Dill was different. Unlike Portal and Pound, he was a lame-duck member of the Chiefs of Staff Committee, his resignation announced on 18 November had an effective date of 25 December. His replacement, General Brooke, was the acting Chief of the Imperial General Staff. Dill and Winston Churchill did not get along, and the two repeatedly butted heads over strategic priorities. Britain stood alone after the fall of France, and Dill insisted that scarce resources had to be devoted to protecting the homeland not penny-packeted into campaigns of dubious value. He regarded Churchill's demands for operations in Egypt, Crete, and Greece as folly because all that mattered was the nation's survival. Churchill naturally resented Dill's criticisms.[55]

For his part, Churchill often dealt rudely with his military advisors. He remarked that "we don't get paid to be polite to each other," and he openly complained about military leaders. "Can't I get commanders who will fight? You don't care if you lose this war. You just want to draw your pay and eat rations." Dill resented the badgering and stood up for the army and its senior commanders. General Morgan remembered, "Churchill, having always regarded himself as reincarnation of his great ancestor [Duke of Marlborough], was impatient almost to intolerance of his advisors. Had it not been for the devotion of his Chiefs of Staff in curbing his wild flights of imagination there are no limits to the wildcat disasters in which he would have involved our forces." From Churchill's perspective, Dill was worn out (true he was worn down) and he pejoratively referred to him as "Dilly-Dally." As tensions mounted, Churchill openly ridiculed Dill, once referring to him in a cabinet meeting as "the dead hand of inanition," and telling Anthony Eden, then-Secretary of State for War, "I do not think we are having the help from General Dill which we hoped for at the time of his appointment . . . he strikes me as being very tired, disheartened and over-impressed with the might of Germany."[56]

Field Marshal Dill was scheduled to be the governor of Bombay, a sinecure that came with a nice title, few responsibilities, and would get him out of sight and out of mind of Churchill. Shortly before Churchill boarded the *Duke of York*, however, Brooke convinced him to take Dill along to America. Brooke had worked for Dill on several occasions, greatly admired him, and knew that Dill's knowledge of strategy and the inner workings of the British Chiefs of Staff Committee would be invaluable in Washington. Churchill was reluctant, but Brooke was adamant, and the prime minister finally acquiesced. Brooke later characterized "that half hour's discussion with Winston at 10 Downing Street on December 11th as one of my most important accomplishments during the war." Dill was pleasantly surprised, telling a friend, "It is odd that Winston should want me to represent him here when he clearly was glad to get me out of the CIGS [Chief of the Imperial General Staff] job."[57]

Churchill wanted Portal, Pound, and Dill to focus their attention on the negotiations with their American counterparts during the conference. To accomplish this he left Brooke in London to chair the Chiefs of Staff Committee. Brooke was supported in London by Pound's and Portal's deputies. Together they were responsible for coordinating the war in Libya, the Atlantic, the Mediterranean, and the Far East. They could maintain contact with the prime minister by cable. Throughout the Arcadia Conference, Brooke resented not being present in Washington and being able to press his strategic views for the war effort. He also believed that his presence could curb Churchill's penchant for undertaking new commitments that the British lacked resources to execute.[58]

Also aboard the *Duke of York* were Ambassador Winant, Harriman, and Beaverbrook, the last to assist with production and supply issues. The British Chiefs of Staff brought several top staff planners to prepare position papers and coordinate specifics with their American counterparts. They were the veritable backbone of the British Chiefs of Staff Committee and included Captain Charles Lambe (deputy director of Naval Plans), Major General Gordon Macready (assistant CIGS), Brigadier Vivian Dykes (director of Army Plans), Air Commodore William Dickson (director of Air Plans), and Brigadier Leslie Hollis and Colonel Ian Jacob (the British secretaries for the conference).[59]

A Committee of Imperial Defence, chaired by the prime minister and consisting of the three chiefs of staff, advised the cabinet. A secretariat maintained a record of meetings and decisions for future action and reference. In 1923 the newly established Chiefs of Staff Committee (COS) provided a venue for regular meetings of the three service chiefs to discuss issues, prepare plans, and provide advice to civilian leaders. Planners assigned to joint subcommittees assisted the COS. The system enabled the British military chiefs to review various relevant factors systematically and thoroughly before making a consensus-based decision. British staff officers and service chiefs alike came of age in this system during the interwar years. They were familiar with its staff structure and its place in the decision-making process. By way of contrast, the American army and navy staffs worked independently of each other, had no secretariat to keep or organize records, and only reluctantly shared information with each other.[60]

Another feature of the British staff system was unanimity. No matter what the British military chiefs thought, they officially supported their political leaders' decisions, even when it seemed to American military professionals that some premises ignored military realities, logistic constraints, or common sense. During Arcadia the American military leaders discovered that their counterparts privately shared US concerns and worked within their staff system to address such issues. In other words, the British chiefs paid lip service to Churchill's overly ambitious, and unrealistic, strategies while working to improve and execute what was realistically possible.

Aboard the *Duke of York* the British had nine uninterrupted days to prepare for the Arcadia Conference. Churchill was determined to have everything in order before the delegation reached Washington so that he might drive the conference agenda to secure British objectives. First, and most important, he wanted the United States to honor all previous Anglo-American arrangements, that is, the "Germany First" strategy. Second, they wanted to minimize any near-term diversion of weapons and equipment, for example, the recent Lend-Lease contretemps. Third, they wanted a larger share of US war production that would increase tremendously with America in the war. Previous meetings had made them skeptical of the quality of US strategic thinking, and the British wanted to guide the Americans to support their vision for the conduct of the war against Germany and Japan.[61]

As Churchill and the British Chiefs of Staff approached the United States, they had to wonder about their American counterparts. The announcement of the establishment of the Roberts Commission to investigate the debacle at Pearl Harbor reached them en route and prompted speculation about Marshall's and Stark's futures. They had seen Churchill sack senior military officers for far less. Would Roosevelt do the same? Did the Pearl Harbor catastrophe undercut Stark's and Marshall's credibility with the president? How much credence could the British give to their decisions?[62]

The United States and Great Britain had met on two previous occasions to discuss strategy; in February and March 1941 at the American-British Conversations (also known as ABC-1) held in Washington, and in August during the Atlantic Conference held in Placentia Bay, Newfoundland. At both sessions the British and Americans found much to agree on, but still they diverged about the strategy and the approach to defeat Germany.

The American British Conversations (ABC-1) were a series of fourteen meetings held between 29 January and 29 March 1941 that also included a Canadian delegation. Although the secret meetings were held in Washington, neither Marshall nor Stark attended; at this stage both the British and the American chiefs preferred sending representatives to present their respective positions. It was in that regard a missed opportunity to interact personally with one another, assess their counterparts' basic concerns, and develop a rapport.

The American British Conversations constituted a basis for Anglo-American coalition grand strategy. The most important outcome was that both agreed that a broad strategic objective "will be of the defeat of Germany and her allies." To accomplish this goal the British advocated economic pressure and a blockade of Germany accompanied by a strategic bombing campaign. They proposed supporting neutrals and resistance groups in occupied areas and small raids as well as minor offensives, but they did not discuss the contours defining a final offensive against Germany. At this stage of the war it was all both nations could support.[63]

On 25 March 1941, Stimson, Knox, Stark, and Marshall joined British representatives to hear the British perspective on the conference. The British were gratified by the "Germany First" strategy and Europe as the decisive theater. They endorsed the exchange of information, continued planning coordination, and recommended a Joint Staff Mission be created to assist with Lend-Lease. In case of war simultaneously against Germany and Japan, the British concurred with a strategic defense that contained Japan while focusing the main effort against Germany. But there was disagreement when the British brought up the importance of Singapore.[64]

The British developed their "Singapore Strategy" shortly after World War I. Australia and New Zealand had sacrificed a generation of young men in support of the British war effort and looked to Britain to protect them. The dominions wanted Britain to provide a powerful fleet to defend them from any economic or military threat in the Far East. In 1921, Britain agreed and assured the dominions that they would build a major naval base at Singapore for this purpose. The problem was money. After the war, Britain was economically strapped. With the rise of Japan, they could no longer rely on the prewar paradigm that maintaining a single fleet in the Atlantic would protect the Far East by deterring European aggression. Now, to properly protect the eastern dominions they would have to maintain two fleets, one in the Atlantic and the other in the Pacific. However, Britain could not afford to build and maintain two large fleets. The British, therefore, decided to maintain a single fleet in the Atlantic and to also build the naval base at Singapore with the assurance to the dominions that in a time of crisis they would dispatch the fleet to the Far East base within seventy days. Throughout the interwar period Australia and New Zealand took this guarantee very seriously.[65]

The promise to the dominions was predicated on the assumption of stability in Europe. After 1939 and the start of World War II, the British needed their only fleet in the Atlantic and Mediterranean. They did not possess the means to fulfill their guarantee to Australia and New Zealand. In 1940 and 1941, the British hoped to solve this dilemma with a commitment from the United States to send an American fleet to Singapore. They tried to convince the Americans that Singapore was the key to the defense of the Far East and should take precedence over everything else, including the Philippines. The American military never accepted this premise. They had their own naval base at Pearl Harbor and believed that the Philippines were more important than Singapore.[66]

Stimson and Knox were aware of the place that Singapore occupied in British strategy. During the ABC-1, opinions diverged between delegations and almost ended the conversations prematurely. The British wanted a US guarantee that in the event of war with Japan the United States would send an aircraft carrier, heavy cruiser division, and necessary supporting naval craft to defend Singapore. Moreover, the US Pacific Fleet would reinforce the British Asiatic Fleet (which existed in name only) at Singapore and begin operations against Japan. The Americans dismissed as absurd an Asia-Pacific naval strategy premised on the defense of Singapore. After all, the previous November Admiral Stark's draft strategy proposal ruled out any Singapore deployment because the Pacific Fleet could better support the allies by holding Southeast Asia and threatening Japan's line of communication from Hawaiian bases.[67]

The British continued to press their counterparts, disregarding Churchill's guidance not to upset the Americans with the "Singapore strategy." US military planners resented British bullheadedness and reported on 13 February 1941, "that a concerted drive was being made by the British to influence the United States into accepting the British point of view in reference to the Far East situation. That the United Kingdom, while accepting the United States' Staff Committee's decision not to send the Pacific Fleet to the Far East, continued to push their requests for the United States' commitments of force in that theater." The two sides hardened their positions on the Singapore issue and drafted supporting papers.[68]

The British military delegation, desperate for an American commitment, emphasized the strategic importance of Singapore's role in defending the Far East from Japanese aggression. American participants, however, questioned Singapore's priority concerning the main objective, namely, the defeat of Germany. The British chiefs provided answers of a sort. First, Britain was a maritime commonwealth and as such depended on Singapore to protect its oceanic trade routes that ensured the uninterrupted flow of foodstuffs and raw materials such as rubber and oil to the homeland. The second was a frankly racist argument that the loss of Singapore entailed a fatal loss of face for the British. "Our morale and prestige, especially among the peoples of the East, would suffer a resounding blow, and those of the Axis powers and Japan would be correspondingly enhanced, with almost incalculable consequences both during and after the war." Third, the British appealed to grand strategy, highlighting the difficulty of supporting Chinese resistance against Japan (which they had heretofore ignored) and the threat that Russia might make a separate peace with the Axis if Singapore fell (although what the connection might have remained vague). Consistent with their defensive strategy, they stressed that priorities were necessary because the allies could not defend the entire Far East against the Japanese. Why they believed the Americans would sacrifice the Philippines for Singapore was never explained, perhaps because there was no sound explanation. They concluded with the claim that holding Singapore was the key to defending Australia and New Zealand, hearkening back to the original rationale for the Singapore base that dated from the early 1920s. What the British chiefs did not and could not say was that Singapore was indefensible without American military assistance.[69]

The Singapore question exploded on 17 February when the British notified the Americans that they were referring all conference discussion papers to the British ambassador, Lord Halifax. Furthermore, Halifax had used these documents to try to convince Secretary of State Cordell Hull to agree to Britain's Singapore strategy. The

American military resented the British attempt to circumvent them by appeal to higher authorities. Besides the ill will, the Americans lodged an official protest, suspended the conference, and forwarded a formal protest to London. It plainly expressed the US position. First, that the American people wanted to stay out of the war. Second, the United States was prepared to provide material and economic aid to the British but could make no commitments other than on technical means of cooperation. Third, military plans were contingent on future political developments in both countries. Both sides had agreed to all these points at the beginning of the conference. The Americans believed that Halifax violated the conference protocols that the discussions were to be between military authorities and that the participants' agreements were subject to later approval by political leaders.[70]

The British written response agreed that the staff conversations should remain between the military authorities of the respective nations. They condescendingly added that the US delegation needed to understand the British Chiefs of Staff Committee reported to the War Cabinet and that Lord Halifax was a member of the War Cabinet. Singapore was a political issue, and that committed Halifax to work with his counterparts in the State Department. Despite their rationalizations, the British delegates realized they had overstepped their brief and angered the only people who mattered to their survival. They promised not to forward any more delegation papers to London. Rear Admiral Roger Bellairs, the British Navy delegate, sent a note of apology to the American delegates and assured them it would not happen again. This mollified the Americans and the talks continued, but with an undercurrent of suspicion that the British would exploit any perceived American weakness to strengthen their strategic policies.[71]

Churchill quickly realized that Roosevelt had no desire to support British Imperial aspirations. To ensure the conference's success, Churchill ordered the British chiefs not to press the Americans for a commitment to reinforce Singapore. He cabled Admiral Pound: "I very much deplore Admiral Bellairs spreading himself in this way. . . . I particularly depreciated the raising of this controversy. Our object is to get the Americans into the war, and the proper strategic dispositions will soon emerge when they are up against reality, and not trying to enter into hypothetical paper accords beforehand." During a 25 March meeting with Secretaries Stimson and Knox, the British again surfaced the Singapore strategy, arguing in effect that the Americans did not understand the importance of Singapore to the United Kingdom. They attributed the attitude to political and administrative difficulties of American chiefs of staff, rather than their ineptitude in clinging to an outmoded and unrealistic Singapore strategy that they lacked the political will to implement. Although the ABC-1 agreements were nonbinding, there were lingering feelings of ill will on both sides over the Singapore question. The British dismissed the Americans as lacking strategic insight and sophistication. The Americans pronounced the British condescending and pompous. This was not a firm foundation on which to build a grand coalition.[72]

The second strategy meeting between the United States and Great Britain occurred 9–12 August 1941 at the Atlantic Conference in Placentia Bay, Newfoundland. American and British Chiefs of Staff attended as it was their first opportunity to get to know one another face to face and to discuss issues without going through a third party. The chiefs were there primarily as advisors. The most important accomplishment of this conference was, of course, the Atlantic Charter, which outlined "common principles" both nations were fighting for and would support in the postwar world. The president and prime minister issued the "Joint Declaration" on 14 August, framing the Allies' objectives in terms of democratic principles. It promised that the United States and Great Britain would seek no aggrandizement, territorial or otherwise; that they would respect the rights of all people to choose their own government; and that they would restore self-government to nations under German occupation. The signatories defended the rights of all people to freedom of speech and freedom of thought, the full economic collaboration between nations, and expressed the hope that all nations might abandon the use of force to solve differences.[73]

Roosevelt also promised Churchill that he would get tougher diplomatically with Japan, and subsequently informed Tokyo that "any further encroachments by Japan in the South West Pacific would produce a situation in which the United States Government would be compelled to take countermeasures, even though these might lead to war." He also promised to increase Lend-Lease, but this was intended for the Soviet Union then engaged in a fight to the death against the advancing Germans.[74]

During the Argentia (Placentia, Newfoundland) meeting Admiral Dudley Pound spoke to the American and British Chiefs of Staff about global strategy. Generals George C. Marshall and Henry "Hap" Arnold, Admirals Harold Stark and Ernest King, General John Dill, and Air Chief Marshal Charles Portal attended. British strategy to defeat Germany stressed the destruction of the German war machine by attacking its economy, morale, and supplies. It would accomplish this by three means. First, a blockade to deny imports to Germany. The present blockade was ineffective, and Germany continued to receive war material via the French colonial empire. A stronger blockade of French colonies and military operations against France's African colonies would dry up these sources. It also justified current and proposed British operations in North Africa.[75]

Strategic bombardment was the second method. The British proposed a bombing campaign targeting Germany's transportation systems as well as cities to break German morale. They needed more bombers to accomplish this mission and they needed them from the United States. Third was subversion. Sabotage of key factories and distribution centers would complement the night bombing campaign by destroying targets that were too difficult or small to distinguish from the air. This again required US produced aircraft to expand the Royal Air Force. American entry into the war would, of course, greatly enhance all three approaches. The US Navy could tighten the blockade while the US Army Air Forces (USAAF) would swell the bombing campaign against Germany.[76]

British strategy was vague about land operations against Germany, but the fundamental American conviction was that ground forces had to defeat Germany in Western Europe. The British acknowledged that if blockade, bombing, and subversion failed to compel Germany to sue for peace, land forces might become necessary. But there was no plan for their employment, except a vague and optimistic assumption that ground forces would assist local populations in defeating the remaining elements of the German Army: a case that consigned regular forces to the role of auxiliaries. Saying that "United States intervention would not only make victory certain, but also make it swift," the British placed the heavy burden of ground operations on the Americans' shoulders. The American chiefs said little, periodically criticized some points in the British strategy, but generally accepted the strategic approach, which was similar to the ABC-1 strategy. They did not produce an alternative strategy because the United States was not at war and was just beginning to mobilize for that possibility. The British regarded this as evidence that "strategic planning in the United States was in a primitive stage which scarcely looked beyond the defense of the American continent." This condescending attitude permeated British staff work preceding the Arcadia Conference.[77]

Admiral Pound did address the Singapore strategy, insisting that holding the secure base at Singapore was vital to both nations because it protected the lines of communication to Australia, New Zealand, and India. Singapore's defense was essential for the successful continuance of the war effort. The Americans were not swayed to change their position and send a force to Singapore.[78]

Perhaps the most important result of this conference was the relationship developed between Generals Marshall and Dill. The two established a rapport as they exchanged ideas and were receptive to each other's challenges and viewpoints. They stayed in touch after the conference. On 13 October, Marshall invited Dill to come to the United States to observe training. Dill, consumed with Crusader, could not attend. After hearing of his retirement, on the Tuesday before the Pearl Harbor attack, Marshall invited Dill to travel to India via the United States and stay with the Marshall's before going to Bombay.[79]

Aboard the *Duke of York* Churchill had some reason for optimism. British fortunes seem to have turned in North Africa. Operation Crusader had pushed back Rommel's forces, relieving the threat to Egypt and the Suez Canal. He received a series of optimistic cables from General Claude Auchinleck, the Commander-in-Chief Middle East, who reported on 17 December that "our troops are in full pursuit and have already made considerable progress, while our armored forces and mobile field columns are moving against enemy lines of retreat." The next day Auchinleck reported that "pursuit of retreating enemy continued throughout yesterday, being pressed relentlessly by our forces, which advanced 30 miles." An ecstatic Churchill told Harriman, who was traveling with him, "If it were not for the momentous things that are happening elsewhere there would be great rejoicing in Libya. It is no mean accomplishment, an army of 150,000 men destroyed—totally destroyed—none of them will escape." This was rhetorical hyperbole and did not accurately reflect the reality of the operational situation in Libya.[80]

On 18 December Churchill sent Roosevelt a proposed conference agenda covering five topics. First, the two nations needed to develop a common basis of joint strategy; second, they hoped to identify immediate military measures and operations to implement the strategy; third, they sought agreement on how to redistribute forces to execute the strategy; fourth, they wanted a plan to raise and equip the forces required; and finally, fifth, they recommended creating a joint organization for collaborative planning and implementation of the strategy.[81]

Churchill also had an unspoken agenda that was not included in the 18 December cable to FDR. Churchill was a symbol, at least in the eyes of many Americans, of British indomitability against long odds. Newspaper and magazine photographs captured his bulldog determination while radio broadcasts brought his soaring rhetoric into American living rooms. His resolution stamped him as a wartime leader—a leader who could endure adversity and defeat but who would never surrender. These attributes combined with Churchill's seemingly boundless ambition convinced the prime minister that he was the obvious choice to lead the emerging Anglo-American coalition. He arrived in Washington determined to do just that. He not only wanted to defeat the Axis, he also desired to maintain the status and prestige of the British Empire. He hoped to accomplish both by controlling the strategic direction of the war. This could be accomplished by guiding Roosevelt on the appropriate strategic objectives and resource allocation necessary for winning the war.[82]

Over the next few days, as the *Duke of York* approached the US East Coast, Churchill worked feverishly with his military advisors to coalesce their thoughts and prepare strategic appreciations for the Atlantic and Pacific theaters with recommendations for future operations that he personally intended to hand to President Roosevelt. Shortly before arriving in America, Churchill's optimism suffered a blow. On 19 December an Italian submarine penetrated Alexandria Harbor and launched human torpedoes, who affixed time bombs on the British battleships *Queen Elizabeth* and *Valiant*, badly damaging both capital ships. This was the culmination of the Royal Navy's disastrous December when it lost five battleships in nineteen days. A German U-boat sank the battleship *Barham* in a terrific explosion off the Egyptian coast on 9 December, and Japanese naval aircraft sank the *Prince of Wales* and *Repulse* off the eastern Malaya coast the next day. That same day three heavy cruisers and four destroyers escorting a convoy headed to Tripoli to support Operation Crusader; they entered a minefield and suffered serious damage. Suddenly the tide had shifted in the Mediterranean, enabling Axis resupply convoys to reach Rommel's forces in North Africa. Early optimism over North Africa was fading.[83]

President Roosevelt had his own agenda, including input from China and the Soviet Union. He asked Halifax, Soviet Premier Joseph Stalin, and Generalissimo Chiang Kai-shek, the leader of the Republic of China, to host military conferences in Singapore, Moscow, and Chungking. Roosevelt anticipated that the forums would encourage the Australians, British, Chinese, Dutch, New Zealanders, and Russians to share their views, estimates, and recommendations of the current situation, which he planned to use to steer the upcoming conference with the British. He was also searching for advice on some kind of joint military organization to direct the war effort, although he was considering a multinational inclusive war council whereas the British were promoting a bilateral United States and Great Britain arrangement. Roosevelt's idea was somewhat similar to the Supreme

War Council of World War I. But the global war he faced had neither one continuous linear front nor single theater.[84]

Nothing of any significance emerged from either the Chungking or the Moscow meetings. The Singapore Conference did prove fruitful. Lieutenant Colonel Francis Brink, US Army, was the US representative. He reported that the British remained adamant that the defense of Singapore took precedence over the Philippines. With nations naturally giving preference to protecting their national interests and seeking a larger share of limited resources to ensure that result, someone had to set priorities. Brink's 21 December note to the president recommended unity of command, that is, a single theater commander empowered to make such decisions. "Singapore conference clearly indicates an immediate need for one supreme head over a combined Allied staff for detailed coordination of USA, British, Australian, and Dutch measures for movement to their designated locations, institution and maintenance of air and sea lines of communication and strategic direction of all operations in the Pacific area." Brink's assessment greatly influenced both General Marshall and the president.[85]

On 20 December, the president appointed Admiral Ernest King as the commander in chief of the United States Fleet. Admiral Stark remained as the Chief of Naval Operations, but with diminished responsibilities, mainly logistics and administration. King took over operations. Although both admirals would represent the navy and participate at the Arcadia Conference, the writing was on the wall that Stark was being eased out because of the disaster at Pearl Harbor.[86]

On the eve of the British delegation's arrival, Roosevelt met with both service secretaries, Harry Hopkins, Admirals King and Stark, and Generals Marshall and Arnold at the White House. The president informed them of the imminent arrival of Churchill's entourage, which included eighty-two officers and other staff personnel. He would meet separately with the prime minister the evening of the twenty-second, but the next afternoon all present would meet with the British at the White House to discuss general strategic problems. Roosevelt reviewed two papers from the Joint Board, "Tentative Views on Subjects of British Memorandum, Dec. 18," and "Broad Military Positions," and a memo from Secretary Stimson. The president asked Marshall to give an estimate of the situation and outline procedures for the conference. The navy did not brief because both admirals had already reviewed the army paper and liked it more than their own.[87]

Marshall reaffirmed the "Germany First" strategy, maintenance of air and sea lines of communication, an initial strategic defensive with local offensives as appropriate, and assistance to China and Russia with weapons and material. In the Pacific, the United States would reinforce the Philippines and the British would do the same for Singapore. The army would adjust its so-called Victory Program—the blueprint to mobilize, train, and equip the expansion of the armed forces to defeat the Axis. This program included production requirements for weapons and equipment that Marshall recommended increasing. The president approved the presentation.[88]

Secretary Stimson regarded the session as especially harmonious and one of the best wartime meetings he had ever attended. The president, as commander in chief, solicited input from his key military and civilian advisors and made clear his priorities. In Europe and the Atlantic it was critical to strengthen the defenses of the British Isles by deploying American air forces, dispatching US troops to Northern Ireland to relieve British forces, and establishing unity of command over the US and British forces stationed in Iceland, a vital strategic location that guarded the northeastern passage of Atlantic convoys. The US Navy would submit its requirements to protect Atlantic convoys from German U-boats. In the Pacific region, the preservation of the lines of communication was paramount. The competing Anglo-American interests in Asia created questions of strategic priorities—Churchill would reinforce Singapore, Roosevelt the Philippines—which suggested unity of command was required, perhaps in the form of a supreme Allied war council that would convene in Washington, DC, to plan strategy and allocate resources and the establishment of a joint planning committee and a joint supply committee to implement the council's decisions. With this broad outline the chiefs of staff adjourned to finalize preparations for the conference.[89]

2

The Conference Commences

First Impressions

22 December 1941

As the Americans prepared for the British arrival, Admiral King made his presence felt on his first full day as commander in chief of the US Fleet. King may have lacked interpersonal skills, but his vision and decisiveness were never in doubt. He immediately impressed Secretary Stimson with his desire to take the fight to the Japanese, fully supported reinforcing the Philippines, and wanted every available resource for the Pacific. More important, he reinvigorated Admiral Hart's and the US Navy's aggressive spirit—a change Stimson welcomed.[1]

King's personality and leadership style contrasted sharply with that of the Chief of Naval Operations, Admiral Harold "Betty" Stark, whose approach was low key and unobtrusive. Stark was brilliant and a born diplomat familiar with the workings of Washington, enjoyed excellent relations with Congress, and always had the best interests of the navy at heart. If he had a fault, it was his overly deliberate and slow approach to decision-making, although once committed he was relentless.[2]

President Roosevelt, a former assistant secretary of the navy, also had a soft spot for his favorite service. He knew many admirals and was much closer to the navy than the army. Consequently, he took the navy's losses at Pearl Harbor personally, an attitude that equated Stark's performance in the president's mind with defeat. Roosevelt wanted someone willing to make difficult decisions rapidly. King was that man. He could make hard decisions quickly and with minimum consultation. He refused to tolerate inefficiency. Roosevelt liked to joke that King was so tough he "shaved with a blowtorch." He wanted that toughness in charge of the navy. The navy respected him and feared him.[3]

Captain McCrea, the US Navy Department's secretary for the Arcadia Conference, described King as "everything a naval officer should be. He was ramrod straight and carried himself with dignity. He was strictly business and a man of few words. While his manner was cold and forbidding, he had a service reputation for being quick tempered, I always found it a pleasure to work with him. He was a no-fooling guy, and I preferred a no-fooling officer to a wishy-washy type." During the conference he constantly displayed this business-like approach to negotiations with the army and the British.[4]

King's arrival coincided with the Japanese landings on Luzon, Philippine Islands, on 22 December 1941. The sizable landing force moved rapidly toward Manila. Stimson understood MacArthur's perilous situation and counted on the navy to get reinforcements and supplies to the embattled defenders.[5]

King had his hands full that day when a separate action diminished the navy's reputation for aggressiveness. The outnumbered Wake Island garrison's heroic resistance captured the American public's imagination, and the beleaguered garrison's repulse of a Japanese landing on 11 December shone brightly as a much-needed boost to US morale and as the only victory in a cascade of military defeats in the Pacific. Newspapers made heroes of the island's defenders, and the *Washington Post* compared their pluck and gallantry to the heroes of the Alamo, perhaps forgetting the fate of that doomed garrison. A fleet, organized around the aircraft carrier USS *Saratoga*, dispatched to relieve the Wake defenders, moved slowly and hesitantly. At the last moment, taking counsel of his fears, the Pacific Fleet commander ordered the task force to reverse course and return to Hawaii. The president was disappointed, Knox took it as a personal affront, and King as the need to get a fighter to take charge in the Pacific.[6]

That stressful morning Stimson and General Marshall discussed the Philippine situation and the upcoming meetings with the British Chiefs of Staff. Both expressed great concern over MacArthur's situation in the Philippines and their annoyance at having their attention diverted to deal with expected British demands for limited American resources. Unlike the British chiefs in the upcoming conference, Marshall realized that the Americans could not focus solely on the meeting with their counterparts because they would have to handle the day-to-day operations of the war. Two days earlier, Marshall had the head of his War Plans Division, Brigadier General Leonard Gerow, meet with the British Mission in Washington to discern British intentions for the conference. While Marshall and Stimson could anticipate some of the British requests, others were surprising and contentious.[7]

The British Mission believed that their Chiefs of Staff wanted to discuss general strategy based on the ABC-1 discussions as a departure point to allay British fears that a Pacific campaign against Japan might force the United States to deviate from the Germany First strategy. As the Americans expected, the British would want the United States to deploy forces to Ireland and Iceland to relieve British troops stationed there for future operations against Germany. A predictable British Chiefs of Staff request for a review of the Victory Program given recent reductions in Lend-Lease aircraft shipped to England placed the Americans in the bizarre position of arguing for access to their own equipment. The British Mission then surfaced two unforeseen issues that would prove contentious during the upcoming conference and that were driven by the prime minister. Both were unexpected and irritating to the Americans. First, the British chiefs would request US troops for operations in North Africa, a mission the Americans thought was a diversion of limited resources. Second, the British wanted to revisit the Singapore strategy, believing that Singapore was more important than the Philippines. On three separate occasions in that meeting Gerow reported the British Mission brought up the need to reexamine US support to Singapore. Stimson and Marshall were focused on Luzon and had little patience for even discussing, let alone providing, military assistance to Singapore.[8]

The *Duke of York* arrived in Chesapeake Bay late on the afternoon of 22 December 1941. Rough weather had delayed the battleship's arrival, left many staff officers aboard ill or queasy from the choppy seas and postponed preliminary meetings scheduled for that afternoon. After arriving at Norfolk, the prime minister, Portal, Beaverbrook, Harriman, and Charles Wilson departed with their hand luggage for the Norfolk Naval Air Station and flew to Washington. The rest of the British party embarked by train, on the specially equipped railroad car of the vice president of the Baltimore and Ohio Railroad.[9]

The train ride to Washington, DC, offered the British planning staff a pleasant surprise. They had a chance to relax, forget the rolling seas of the past few days, and enjoy the special car's amenities, especially the variety and quantity of good food. Colonel Ian Jacob and Brigadier Vivian Dykes were astounded by the picnic baskets arranged for each member of the British party. The chicken, hard-boiled eggs, and large quantity of fruit were an unexpected treat for officers grown used to the privations of food rationing back home. Despite their early morning arrival in Washington, all were in good spirits.[10]

Jacob and Dykes were brilliant staff officers who both maintained personal diaries that provide insight and texture to the sterile minutes of the conference. Both were engineer officers with impeccable reputations. Jacob, the son of a field marshal, had graduated fourth, out of ninety-eight, in his class at the Royal Military Academy. He was selected as Assistant Military Secretary to the Committee of Imperial Defence by General Hastings Ismay in 1938. Jacob was aloof and austere. He worked hard and expected everyone else to do the same. Senior British leaders respected his intellect and talent for accomplishing difficult assignments. A no-nonsense officer, he was all business and did not "suffer fools gladly" or waste time on pleasantries. He was handpicked to attend the conference as one of the two British secretaries responsible for developing the agenda and maintaining the minutes of the meetings.[11]

Dykes had a similar career to that of Jacob. He had been the Military Secretary to the Committee of Imperial Defence before Jacob. He was equally brilliant and was respected by both the American and British delegations throughout the Arcadia Conference. Unlike his close friend Jacob, he was charming and had an infectious sense of humor. His personal style won many admirers among the Americans. He attended the conference as an army planner, but when the conference ended he was selected as the British Secretary to the Combined Chiefs of Staff in Washington. Tragically, his life was cut short in an aircraft accident in 1943.[12]

Churchill was in high spirits. Roosevelt personally met his plane and then rode with Churchill to the White House. The prime minister thrived during the sea voyage and arrived happy, energized, and determined not to lose a moment with the American president. Over drinks the prime minister briefed the president on the success of his Operation Crusader. Present at the meeting were Secretary of State Hull; the Assistant Secretary of State for Latin American Affairs, Sumner Welles; Harry Hopkins; Lord Beaverbrook; and Lord Halifax. Churchill oozed enthusiasm and confidence. Optimistic that he could crush Rommel's Afrika Corps, he waxed eloquent on the opportunities for joint ventures in North Africa.[13] According to Churchill, "The impending victory of General Auchinleck in Cyrenaica [eastern Libya] is an injury to the German Powers. We may expect the total destruction of the enemy forces in Libya to be apparent before the end of the year. This not only inflicts a heavy blow upon the Germans and Italians, but frees our forces in the Nile Valley from the major threat of invasion from the west under which they have long dwelt." This would, the prime minister expected, end the Axis threat to Middle East once and for all.[14]

Churchill's expansion of the North Africa campaign established at the conference's outset a tone of confidence and leadership that would guarantee the uninterrupted flow of Lend-Lease material required for his strategic bombing and Middle East plans for 1942. It all depended on Auchinleck's "continuous victorious advance." As Churchill confided to his wife, "Before the end of the year he [Auchinleck] will be at Benghazi and well on the road farther West. . . . It is very important for the Americans that we should have proof that our soldiers can fight a modern war and beat the Germans on even terms, or even at odds, for that is what they have done. This lends weight to our counsels and requests."[15]

Churchill's chimerical strategy sought American support to isolate Germany from French colonies in Africa. He believed German reverses in the Soviet Union and the British victory in Libya created an opportunity for the Allies to convince the Vichy government that the tides of war were running against Germany. A pro-Allied Vichy regime would invite the Anglo-Americans to take control of their African colonies and commit France's colonial army to help them. He fancied the United States persuading the Vichy government to move the still-powerful French Fleet from Toulon to Oran or Bizerta to deny its use to Germany. Why Vichy would do so with the German military occupation of France extending to Vichy's borders, he did not explain. The "success" in Libya was ephemeral. The Germans were pushed back but hardly crushed. Churchill's strategy was wishful thinking whose ethereal assumptions were based on hopes not reality.[16]

Unlike Britain, the United States did recognize the Vichy regime, and the former Chief of Naval Operations, Admiral William Leahy, was the US ambassador. Leahy, a Roosevelt confidant, had developed a good rapport with Marshal Philippe Petain, Vichy's Chief of State, and was respected in France. That February, his chargé d'affaires Robert Murphy signed an agreement with the French General Maxime Weygand that allowed the French to use funds currently frozen in US banks to buy nonstrategic American goods needed in North Africa. Known as the Murphy-Weygand Accord, the British permitted these cargoes to pass through the naval blockade they enforced since the rupture of relations with Vichy France in July 1940. Churchill hoped to capitalize on the positive Franco-American relations to propel his adventures. But he was never a Pollyanna. Should Vichy refuse to welcome the Anglo-American allies into their African colonies, Churchill would enter by force of arms.[17]

Roosevelt was a congenial host and a consummate politician. He enjoyed the wide-ranging discussions of global strategy with his entertaining new houseguest and was impressed by the prime minister's glowing accounts of British military victories in Libya. Churchill at this point thought that he was making progress in guiding the American president into following his strategy for fighting the war and protecting the British Empire. Roosevelt, however, was an enigma and impossible to read. Even his friends admitted that he was hard to understand and discern. Frances Perkins, his secretary of labor, described him as "the most complicated human being I ever knew." Henry Morganthau, his secretary of the treasury, agreed and said, "Roosevelt is an extraordinarily difficult person to describe . . . frivolous as well as grave, evasive as well as frank . . . a man of bewildering complexity of moods and motives." He had been president for nine years and was adept at keeping his thoughts and intentions to himself. He agreed with Churchill's sentiments and told the prime minister that he would like to get American forces into the fighting to show the American people that they were at war. He needed to show the Soviets that Americans would fight Germany. He also needed a victory. Where did not matter, so North Africa was as good a place as any. Both leaders agreed that during the conference there would be staff studies for a joint expedition to North Africa. The president also told Churchill that he supported sending American forces to Northern Ireland to relieve the British and would so direct his chiefs. He did not think this troop movement would affect any potential North Africa endeavor. Both were satisfied with the opening discussion.[18]

While Roosevelt hosted Churchill and his party, another meeting took place that evening between Lieutenant General Arnold and Air Chief Marshal Portal. The two had met the previous April and developed a good rapport, regardless of the significant difference in rank. The US Army Air Forces (USAAF) were under Army Chief of Staff Marshall's control, making Arnold subordinate to Marshall, but in practice, the USAAF operated as a separate command. At Arcadia, however, Arnold was Portal's American counterpart, and to reinforce that point the president and Marshall wanted Arnold to represent them at the session whose overall purpose was to develop a common appreciation of the Allies' air forces. Portal was unpretentious and treated Arnold as his coequal from that evening on. The British delegation was discernably anxious about the suspension of Lend-Lease aircraft and the current buildup of the American Air Force to fifty-four groups. London was due to receive more than 8,200 various aircraft between October 1941 and July 1942. A continued interruption of Lend-Lease would seriously jeopardize both their strategic bombing offensive and the North Africa campaign. It was imperative that the British know when, and if, the flow of US-produced aircraft to Britain would resume. Portal's interests ranged from American plans for stationing and employing its air units and the future relationship with the British. Arnold was noncommittal, willing to abide by the chiefs' decisions during the conference.[19]

Arnold, at fifty-five, was smart, tough, and even-tempered. He was the US Army's aviation expert par excellence. A pilot since 1911, he had held and broken numerous aviation altitude and speed records, but his true genius lay in organization. An air power champion, his ingenuity with Congress enabled him to improve combat readiness in an era of bare-bones military budgets. Between 1939 and Pearl Harbor he engineered a sixfold growth in aircraft production and pilot training. He got on well with Portal, who characterized Arnold as a man who spoke little, except about air. General Morgan described Arnold as outstanding in every way, a man of unique caliber. His extraordinary drive had built the American air force from scratch, and the British doubted that anyone else could have accomplished it.[20]

Portal steered the conversation to the American strategic employment of air units, confirming earlier reports by the British Mission. He opened the meeting by presenting Churchill's position on the importance of reinforcing Singapore and in so doing protecting the British Empire. Portal announced that the "British could not afford to see Singapore pass by the Board." Arnold expected this and shot back that the United States "could not afford to see the Philippines pass by the board" and followed up informing Portal that the American Air Force had a plan for getting airplanes to MacArthur. General George Brett would command an organization in Australia tasked to assemble aircraft for use in the Philippines and Dutch East Indies against the Japanese. The concept was to immediately get Brett eighty heavy bombers and 160 to 200 pursuit planes in an attempt to regain air superiority in that theater. Arnold was clear that this near-term strategy dictated the Philippines, not Singapore, had priority for aircraft deliveries from the United States.[21]

General Colville Wemyss, the head of the British Military Mission to Washington, later summarized the British position in a note to General Marshall: "the policy is that the security of Singapore and Burma and sea communications to the Indian Ocean are second in importance only to the security of Great Britain and her sea communications." But Portal failed to gain Arnold's support for this strategy. He had dutifully supported the prime minister and broached the subject of Singapore, but the American position on Singapore remained unchanged, and, as Arnold emphasized, the United States had no intention of reinforcing Singapore.[22]

Portal continued to press Churchill's position and then suggested that attacking Japan was really the navy's job and proposed that American carrier-based aircraft launch surprise attacks on Japan in a manner similar to Pearl Harbor. Any risk was minimal because the fast carriers would be difficult to locate in the vast Pacific Ocean. Portal asserted that such raids would force the Japanese to withdraw their fleet from the southwestern Pacific to protect their home islands. The US Navy should handle Japan, and any resources sent to the Far East should go to Singapore. This made no strategic sense, and Arnold was dismissive. "Portal mixed wishful thinking in with his reasoning concerning the Pacific aerial strategy." The nub of the air marshal's argument was that any aircraft sent to the Philippines was one less aircraft sent to the RAF in England.[23]

On another aspect of the Far East, Portal was more prescient than Arnold on the political realities of the region. Arnold told Portal that the United States would soon get permission from the Russians to operate air forces from bases in Vladivostok. Portal expressed doubt because the Russians had their hands full with the Germans and did not want to antagonize Japan. Arnold said later, "It turned out that Portal knew the Russians and their way of doing business far better than I . . . for we never did get such bases."[24]

Portal continued to expound Churchill's strategy as rehearsed aboard the *Duke of York*. Since Arnold was not receptive on Singapore, he shifted the discussion to another part of the Empire. He pointed out that North Africa offered a splendid opportunity for the Americans to negotiate with Vichy to operate air bases in French Morocco. Airfields along the North African coast would enable the allies to interdict Axis resupply convoys and control shipping in the Mediterranean Sea. Simultaneously, the United States should station bomber groups in Britain to participate in the RAF-directed strategic bombing campaign against Germany as well as more heavy bombers because the British had an excess of pilots awaiting aircraft. Fighter planes and pilots were needed for North Africa. All these requirements suffered due to recent reductions in Lend-Lease that exacerbated the shortages. As the RAF saw it, America should produce more planes for British use. Churchill had brought Lord Beaverbrook, his minister of supply, to the conference to help expand American war production and thereby increase the allocation of aircraft and other weapons earmarked for Britain.[25]

Portal, acting as Churchill's cat's paw, was unabashed about his outrageous demands. Britain wanted planes for North Africa and for their strategic bombing campaign. American bomber and fighter units should be deployed to Britain and North Africa. The British had requirements and a strategic plan to justify their demands, in effect committing the United States to a junior partner in the grand alliance. This set the tone for the conference and, despite Arnold's firmness, put the Americans on notice.

Arnold had weathered countless congressional fights over USAAF budgets and had learned to listen. He did not challenge Portal's assertions; after all, the president's guidance was to get along with Portal as a coequal. The two did concur about the purpose of the conference—develop an agreed-on grand strategy, identify the forces and equipment required to accomplish that strategy, prepare a plan to build the facilities to produce that equipment and to raise and train the required forces, and produce a plan and system to allocate the material. This outline comported with Stark's and Marshall's guidance.[26]

23 December 1941

The following morning, Stimson hosted Marshall, Gerow, Arnold, Portal, and Dill in his office. The informal session was congenial as each side acquainted the other with its respective overall strategic situation and desired goals for the upcoming conference. The gathering allowed the respective army and air force chiefs to assess their counterparts one on one and to establish both a working and a personal rapport. War news from Asia and North Africa was grim that morning. Wake Island, without reinforcements after the fleet was recalled, had been overwhelmed. MacArthur had evacuated Manila and retreated to the Bataan Peninsula. In Malaya, the Indian III Corps had withdrawn all forces on the west coast behind the Perak River. Japanese bombers struck Rangoon and Burma, sowing destruction and panic. Supply shortages in Libya slowed the British Eighth Army's offensive.[27]

After meeting with Stimson, the British chiefs and their staffs finalized their strategy paper for the next day. It was an uneventful, not to say boring, ninety minutes that ended with no important revisions. The British chiefs next got ready for a meeting with the president and prime minister at the White House.[28]

Meanwhile, Churchill continued to work on the president to persuade him to accept his strategic view of the war. Roosevelt and the prime minister continued to debate North African strategy. H. Freeman Matthews, the recently returned first secretary from the US embassy in Vichy, was not optimistic about the likelihood of inducing Weygand to join the Allies. He thought that Weygand was in Petain's pocket and said that if the Allies approached Weygand he would immediately inform the marshal, whose collaborationist Vichy government in turn would alert the Germans, who would act. Churchill, undeterred, insisted that it did not matter even if the Germans knew of the plans. Churchill's flippancy stunned Matthews, who only recently had returned from Vichy. Hopkins supported Matthews, agreeing that the Weygand ploy was a bad idea. The prime minister remained adamant. He was prepared to go with or without French support and was willing to risk tipping his hand by talking to Weygand. Churchill's stubbornness prevailed, and although it took a month, the Americans got a message to Weygand. Roosevelt committed nothing to paper. He verbally instructed Ambassador Leahy, who sent his third secretary in the American embassy, Douglas MacArthur (the nephew of the general in the Philippines), to inform Weygand in person. MacArthur asked the general to take a leadership role in North Africa and to rally the military to support the Allies' cause. Weygand was polite but declined "even to consider the possibility of his playing an active role in French North Africa."[29]

Churchill also handed Roosevelt three carefully crafted strategy papers that he originally had developed aboard the *Duke of York*. The prime minister hoped to use these papers to steer Roosevelt into acquiescing to his lead on protecting the British Empire and defeating the Axis. He walked a fine line of pushing the Americans to his strategic vision for victory without alienating Roosevelt. The first paper dealt with the Atlantic theater and summarized the previous evening's discussion, emphasizing the opportunity the British success in Libya presented to the Allies. Northwest Africa offered the best prospect for near-term success, and after the British troops destroyed German and Italian forces in Libya, the way would be open to the Tunisian border. Regardless of the Vichy government, Churchill advocated Operation Gymnast, a plan to land 55,000 troops in French North Africa just three weeks hence. They would quickly capture the port of Bizerte, the northernmost city in Africa and a key German anchorage in the Mediterranean. Churchill almost offhandedly requested the United States deploy three infantry divisions and one armored division to Northern Ireland to protect the British Isles.[30]

While Gymnast was entirely a British operation, Churchill promised total victory in the Mediterranean if the Americans sent 150,000 troops to Casablanca within six months, thereby occupying the entire North and West African coasts. This ensured total control of shipping in the Mediterranean and access to oil in the Levant via the Suez Canal. The bold, sweeping concept appealed to Roosevelt, just as Churchill knew it would. FDR was searching for a location to involve American troops because he wanted a victory within the year to rally public support for the war effort.[31]

Auchinleck's success intoxicated Churchill. The Eighth Army had driven the Germans back, inflicted heavy losses, and lifted the eight-month siege of Tobruk. Churchill paradoxically had undermined the campaign when on 12 December, he diverted two divisions, four bomber squadrons, and a shipment of antitank guns destined for Crusader to the Far East. Without these reinforcements, Eighth Army could neither advance to the Tunisian border nor sustain its momentum against Rommel. Recent British fleet losses in the Mediterranean had allowed the Germans to reinforce the Afrika Korps, and the new military balance of forces rendered the entire North African discussion spurious.[32]

Back in London, General Alan Brooke grasped the strategic picture more realistically than either the more narrowly focused Auchinleck or Churchill. According to Brooke's diary entry, "Auchinleck struggling along with the forces at his disposal and sending optimistic personal and private messages to PM, little knowing that his activities must shortly be curtailed owing to transfer of air and sea reinforcements from Middle East to Far East."[33]

Churchill's second paper dealt with the "Pacific Front" and carefully avoided asking for US troops for Singapore. He still intended to push for his "Singapore-first" strategy, but after being burned during the ABC-1 discussions he did not want to overplay his hand in writing at the outset of the conference. Instead, Churchill requested American thinking on Japanese intentions to occupy Hawaii and on how long MacArthur could hold out in the Philippines. He expressed confidence that the Singapore fortress could withstand Japanese assaults for six months. His real interest was warships. The British Fleet was overstretched by commitments in the Atlantic and Indian Oceans and could spare no ships for the Pacific, leaving the American Navy to fend for itself. He worried that the Americans might reposition warships from the Atlantic Fleet to the Pacific, and that would open the Atlantic sea lanes to the German battle fleet and increasingly vicious U-boat attacks. He asked Roosevelt to maintain enough destroyers in the Atlantic to escort convoys and keep open the sea lines of communication between the United States and Great Britain.[34]

Churchill's concern, which he relayed to the British Defence Committee shortly after the conference, was that the United States would build up a large force for the reconquest of the Pacific and the defeat of Japan. He feared that this force "for at least two years while it was training" would consume all American resources and "stand idle defending the American continent." Churchill wanted the United States to quickly "regain their naval power in the Pacific." He did not want America wasting too much time and resources on Japan. His goal was to ensure that the bulk of American forces and supplies were available for the European theater of war. Specifically, he advocated for a European landing in 1943 but was vague on where the landing should occur.[35]

Churchill's final paper offered his vision for 1943 and illuminated the prime minister's strategic thinking on Germany. Only the defeat of the German Army or the collapse of popular morale would induce surrender. Building on the expected success during 1942, Churchill sought to weaken German home-front support for the war effort by an economic blockade and urban bombing campaign. If the Nazi's internal political structure still survived, Allied ground troops would invade the continent. Rather than rely on numbers of troops and a massive invasion force to engage the German Army directly, Churchill proposed landing small forces in Norway, the Low Countries, Belgium, the French Channel Islands, Balkans, or Italy to assist indigenous resistance groups throughout the occupied nations in Europe to rise up and oust the Germans. The German Army would be forced to disperse its armies to all corners of its conquests, leaving it vulnerable to localized defeats by an aroused and armed populace.[36]

Here was the crux of the strategy debate: if the blockade, bombing, and aid to subversive groups would weaken Germany but the Nazi regime did not collapse internally, how was their army to be defeated? Even if multiple landings at various locations caused the German Army to spread its legions thin, it did not follow that the occupied countries could overthrow their conquerors without massive external military might. At some point Allied forces would have to confront and defeat the German Army.

In postwar remarks Portal insisted that this strategy paper "proposed to sell to the American chiefs" that Churchill had "plans for encircling Germany. [It] was meant to include the need of going into the continent, but also first needed to hit the Germans through the Mediterranean . . . he [Churchill] did want to hit at the Germans and weaken them before going into Europe." Portal was candid about the prime minister's equivocation and allowed that Churchill hated the thought of the losses that would result from an invasion of northern France. "You must remember that our Army had met the Germans at their height, and after they had been pushed around, they began to feel in their heart that they weren't the equals of the Germans." Churchill's quixotic strategy matched his vaporous guidance to his chiefs. His ambiguity made it irrelevant to even attempt to define the where, when, and how of invading Europe and defeating the German Army.[37]

Shortly after the meeting adjourned, Churchill encountered the secretary of the navy at the halls of the White House. Knox had just learned that the Japanese had overrun the Wake garrison. Particularly galling to Knox was the relief fleet's failure to attempt the reinforcement of the island the previous day. An angry and frustrated Knox vented to Churchill: "We ordered our fleet to fight a battle with the Japanese to relieve Wake Island, and now within a few hours of steaming the Admiral has decided to turn back. What would you do with your Admiral in a case like this?" Churchill responded diplomatically, careful neither to criticize the military performance of the ally he was courting, nor to give the United States the impression that he was somehow instrumental in an admiral's relief for cause. He replied, "It is dangerous to meddle with Admirals when they say they can't do things. They have always got the weather or fuel or something to argue about."[38]

Some responsibility for the Wake defeat belongs with the president and Knox himself. In their haste to appear decisive, they had relieved Admiral Kimmel before his replacement, Admiral Chester Nimitz, reached Hawaii. The Pacific Fleet, operating under an acting or temporary commander, was naturally hesitant to make major campaign decisions. Kimmel had designed and assembled the relief for Wake Island, but his forceful and controlling hand was gone and yet to be replaced. When the relief force was slow in moving, no one called them to task. Navy leadership at Pearl Harbor remained cautious until Nimitz took over.[39]

At 1700, Churchill and Roosevelt gathered the British and American Chiefs at the White House to give guidance for the conference. Also present were Secretaries Stimson and Knox, Hopkins, Beaverbrook, Major General Edwin Watson (senior aide to the president), Captain John R. Beardall (naval aide to the president), Brigadier Hollis (British Secretariat), and Colonel Jacob (British Secretariat). This was an informal meeting, and the two heads of state did most of the talking. Although uninvited, Brigadier Hollis and Colonel Jacob of the British Secretariat talked their way into the session to keep an official record of the discussion for British reference. This allowed Portal, Dill, and Pound freedom to focus all their attention on the discussion. The Americans had no note takers, in accordance with Roosevelt's desire not to have records of his meetings, and no organized secretariat, forcing Stark, Arnold, and Marshall to take their own notes of the discussion.[40]

This was the first time that the two heads of state met together with the chiefs at this conference. Roosevelt, as the host, wanted to meet everyone face to face and to hear his thoughts on the way ahead. He also enjoyed an opportunity to take the measure of the British chiefs' talents and personalities. For Churchill, it was a chance to determine who among the American chiefs Roosevelt relied on and trusted. Roosevelt started by formally reassuring the British chiefs, as he had Churchill, that the United States remained committed to the Germany First strategy. Churchill was greatly relieved, but this strategy was never in doubt. Stark said after the war that the American chiefs never even considered any other strategic policy.[41]

The president's overview included the previous evening's conversation with Churchill on the current situation and relationship with the Vichy government. He explained Churchill's view of the potential opportunity that existed in North Africa, but it seemed apparent that

Roosevelt had cooled on this strategy. Perhaps advice from Hopkins and Matthews had dampened his enthusiasm. Roosevelt took pains to reassure his chiefs that there was no agreement on North Africa. In the next breath he instructed the British and American Chiefs and their staffs to work together on the specifics of such an operation and make a recommendation. Roosevelt's equivocation left Arnold puzzling about exactly what Churchill and the president were thinking on doing with Vichy.[42]

Roosevelt, much to Stimson's surprise and pleasure, went point by point through the list the secretary gave him two days earlier. The topics covered the globe: The United States stationing bombers in Britain; a decision to move American divisions to Northern Ireland; unity of command in Iceland; the need for air bases in China; Russia's decision not to attack Japan; a decision not to send troops to the Near East; the importance of the air route across Africa; the need to protect the sea lines of communication in the Atlantic from German U-boats; the shortage of transport ships to move troops; and a need to relook the production plan to increase tanks, planes, antiaircraft guns, and ammunition.[43]

Roosevelt and Churchill set priorities for the respective staffs to address. First, develop a plan to ship three American infantry divisions and one armor division to Northern Ireland to free the British units currently stationed there for use in North Africa. Second, prepare plans to station American bomber groups in England to encourage the French people that the Americans were active participants in the war and simultaneously discourage the German people. (Why a few bomber groups would have such a great effect was not discussed. This was another example of Churchill's rhetoric. He really wanted to get bombers sent to England and not the Far East.) Third, develop a plan for unity of command that integrated the joint organization in Iceland.[44]

Roosevelt told the chiefs that he and Churchill agreed that the British assumed responsibility for Singapore and the Americans for the Philippines. The United States would also build a base in Australia from which to launch future offensive campaigns against Japan.

Although Churchill had pledged support to the president on these issues, the American chiefs were hearing different lyrics from their British counterparts.[45]

The president notified the chiefs that he and Churchill were drafting a joint declaration based on their understanding that "there must be an agreement between all nations; that hereafter there would be no peace without the concurrence of all until we had complete victory; that they were taking the necessary steps to insure this." Both believed this important commitment to the international community would reassure Allies and signal Allied determination to Germany and Japan. The two heads of state polished the draft over the next few days.[46]

Roosevelt delighted Churchill by inviting Beaverbrook to join discussions about a new program for the production of weapons and war material for 1942 and 1943. The president told the group that he would announce a new budget and production plan during his 5 January 1942 State of the Union Address. In other words, Churchill, via Beaverbrook, would enjoy an inside view of American industrial mobilization and the potential allocation of war material for the next two weeks.[47]

After Roosevelt finished, Churchill thanked the president and with his usual eloquence expressed his gratitude for the American principle that their primary concern was "the preservation of our communications across the North Atlantic with our fortress in the British Isles covering the British fleet." He reiterated much of what Roosevelt had said, adding greater details about North Africa and French Morocco. He employed all his charm, eloquence, and persuasiveness to try and convince the American chiefs of the opportunity awaiting the Allies when the British captured Tripoli and reached the Tunisian the border within the month. The crushing blow to German morale coupled with the American entry in the war would greatly influence Vichy France leaders, and "it should serve to boost up the morale of the French so as to make them want to regain their lost prestige and put up a fight for their rights." Churchill recommended a combined US-British task force invade French Morocco.

French colonial authorities might welcome the Anglo-Americans, but if not, the staffs should study the feasibility of invading anyway. A less enthusiastic president demurred slightly but agreed that it was worthy of staff study.[48]

Churchill, alert to Roosevelt's nuances, urged the United States to launch offensives against Germany and Japan because battlefield successes would boost American and Allied morale. Churchill encouraged the American chiefs to dispatch troops to Northern Ireland, Iceland, and Australia without delay and stressed that the United States must unleash the potential of its enormous economic, industrial, production, and manpower might against Germany and Japan immediately.[49]

As for the Pacific, he dismissed the US Navy's worries about keeping open the supply lanes to Hawaii and then launched into a convoluted, but implicit, plea to reinforce Singapore. According to the prime minister, Hawaii's ability to defend itself allowed the Pacific battle fleet to be used elsewhere. Since the fleet would be elsewhere, Hawaii was no longer an important naval base and the fleet could be based elsewhere (read Singapore). These ambiguous remarks confused Arnold, and no doubt other American chiefs, but Churchill insisted the staffs discuss it.[50]

After the ninety-minute meeting, the American and British chiefs and their staffs dined with Knox and Stimson at the Carlton Hotel. Stimson, who was dreading the affair, made a brief speech that recalled a similar British Mission that came to Washington in 1917, and how it fulfilled his life's dream of cooperating with the British. The British seemed more impressed with the sumptuous spread and American largesse. Dykes said, "The whole dinner was quite in the Hollywood style but certainly very well done." The affair also provided another social occasion for the military leaders to get to know one another. Dykes, for example, discussed unity of command issues with his tablemate Lieutenant General Lesley McNair (Marshall's deputy responsible for training, organization, and mobilization), confiding to his diary that evening, "We had a great chat about unity of command which is like a King Charles head with the Yanks."[51]

24 December 1941

Arcadia convened at 1030 in the Federal Reserve Building on Constitution Avenue just a short distance from the White House. It began as an unmitigated disaster that confirmed British preconceptions of American ineptitude.

General Marshall instructed Brigadier General Raymond Lee to arrange the conference room for the meeting of the Combined British-US Chiefs of Staff. As the former military attaché at the American embassy in London, Lee's experience with the British made him an obvious choice. Lee in turn delegated the set-up arrangements to Lieutenant Colonel Lawrence Higgins, his administrative assistant. For whatever reasons, Higgins ignored the imposing buildings' main conference room for the venue. The large, formal setting was ideal for impressive formal arrangements and offered participants the chance to move to talk to their counterparts. Higgins chose a smaller 20 × 30 foot room that could barely hold the Chiefs of Staff, much less their entourages. Lieutenant Colonel Paul Robinett, the army secretariat for the conference, was appalled by the "rather unpretentious room in a very pretentious building."[52]

Robinett was an astute observer throughout the conference who kept a diary that revealed insights into American attitudes and concerns. An excellent athlete, he was a crack shot and had been a member of the US Olympic equestrian team. He was a small man, only five feet four inches, but was the stereotypical American Cavalry officer. Confident, cocky, and arrogant. He also was smart and trusted by Marshall. He had great attention to detail and annoyed people with his fussy nature.[53]

This lackluster room was not Higgins's only blunder. He failed to coordinate with the British and the American Navy and never assembled a list of attendees. The number of aides, note takers, assistants, and observers accompanying the chiefs surprised him and overwhelmed the room. For arguably the most important wartime conference, participants found themselves working in little more than a broom closet. The overflow from the tiny room forced the American and British chiefs to mill around in the hallway, awaiting another venue. This wasted precious time and embarrassed Marshall. More time was lost moving everyone to the board room where harassed staff officers culled nonessential assistants and observers inside while others set up administration and security outside. Finally, the chiefs took their seats facing one another across the boardroom table. Admiral Stark as the senior chief of the host nation presided and sat in the middle of the American delegation.[54]

The Americans had no agenda for the meeting. Stark simply read from his notes on the discussion the previous evening, rehashing information that the British had already typed up and distributed to their members before the meeting. The only ones who had not heard this before were the American assistants and secretariat. Brigadier General Thomas Handy acknowledged the Americans were "more or less babes in the woods in this planning and joint business with the British. They'd been doing it for years. They were experts at it and we were just starting. They'd found a way to get along between services, that they had to get along." Captain John McCrea, the navy recorder, echoed this assessment and said, "They [British] knew their stuff. They all talked exceedingly well and made much sense. The staff organization was superb, as well. Three brigadiers did the bulk of the work, and their reports of the meetings were masterpieces." Robinett was underwhelmed by Stark, who talked a lot but "none of it was very illuminating."[55]

The British secretariat echoed Robinett's impression and was disturbed by the Americans' disarray. "To our eyes, the American machine of government is hopelessly disorganized. To illustrate this from the first meeting . . . the US Chiefs of Staff met ours in their first formal meeting at the Federal Reserve Building. There was no Agenda and the first thing Admiral Stark, who was in the Chair, did was run through the notes he had made on the previous day's meeting. General Marshall had also dictated, on his return to his office, his idea of what had happened. We of course had our minutes prepared, and it was a complete waste of everyone's time to go all over the ground again. Not to mention the waste of effort on the part of those Chiefs of Staff who had themselves to put down an account of the meeting. We found this lack of system extended right throughout."[56]

Stark reaffirmed the Germany First strategy, officially putting the primary British concern to rest with his opening remarks. He continued, "The British Isles was the fortress which must be protected at all costs," reiterating what was agreed to the previous evening. Any swelling goodwill evaporated when Stark responded to a question by stating that reports from two US Marine Corps observers indicated that the British defenses "left much to be desired." He offered a copy of these reports to the British to use as they saw fit. Dill, until recently responsible for those defenses, replied laconically that they were "constantly being improved." Pound, the senior British member, stepped into the breach and smoothed over the gaffe by saying he "welcomed Admiral Stark's proposal" to send the report to the British.[57]

Later in the discussion the British presented an assessment of the defenses of the American West Coast. This was the first the American side knew of a very controversial position paper. It identified four possible Japanese threats to the United States: seaborne expeditions, naval bombardment, carrier-borne air attacks, and mine-laying or human torpedo attacks on American ports, and it quickly dismissed all four. The tone and tenor was condescending and yet another appeal to reinforce Singapore, a topic the Americans considered closed. It concluded by stating the obvious: "So long as the United States maintained a battle fleet in the Pacific, large scale seaborne expeditions against the western seaboard of North America and the employment of capital ship forces in this area are considered impractical." The British argued that because the Japanese had to move across the vast ocean distances to reach American shores, it should be unnecessary for the United States to provide a strong West Coast defense except at selected important locations, which, in their opinion, existing coastal and air defense units supplemented by the army ground and air forces could adequately protect. The British assessment was carefully designed to minimize the Japanese threat to the continental United States to forestall massive air, ground, and naval reinforcements to the West Coast when they could be better used in Singapore or the RAF's strategic bombing effort.[58]

Stark's comment about the state of British defenses and the British appreciation of the threat to the US West Coast were parochial and self-serving, but as the conference progressed the chiefs consciously worked to get along with one another and rise above petty suspicions and prejudices.

Still the well-crafted British initiatives were difficult to refute due to the lack of US Army and Navy cooperation. One reason was that the American services had not coordinated with each other before the meeting. Each had its independent secretariat and neither spoke to the other. The British discovered that "papers sent to the US Army secretariat did not get to the US Navy." Jacob observed, "The American ideas on organization and ours are wide apart, and they will have first to close the gap between their Army and Navy before they can work as a real team with us."[59]

The criticism of Stark's tedious three-hour point-by-point restatement of the previous evening's discussion is legitimate to a point. What Stark made apparent was that the British, the US Army, and the US Navy all interpreted Churchill's and Roosevelt's guidance differently. During Stark's recitation, which was more tactical than operational, participants identified and rectified three misconceptions.[60]

Stark had announced that the heavy bombers sent to England would be manned by American crews. This upset Portal, who immediately interjected that this was not the agreement. Arnold, who was also surprised, explained that British crews would fly the Lend-Lease aircraft while the organized US bomber groups would have American crews. He agreed to work on the details with Portal on the still unresolved role of these aircraft.[61]

As for the relief of British forces in Northern Ireland, Stark noted Churchill's comment that the United States would relieve the three British divisions. Dill interjected and Marshall agreed that the Americans would replace this force with four divisions. Both sides concurred on the force structure in Iceland, contingent on available merchant shipping. The chiefs instructed the joint planning committee to study the matter.[62]

Churchill raised the possibility of getting more American destroyers to counter the U-boat threat. This off-the-cuff remark just assumed that the Americans had sufficient destroyers for the mission. This assumption that the United States possessed unlimited resources that Britain could draw on was to become a recurring theme and sore point over the next three weeks. Stark rejoined that the United States had no destroyers to spare and current shipbuilding schedules assigned a low priority to destroyers. Indeed, Stark asked the British to spare any available small craft to augment US coastal patrols. Pound was surprised and proposed that the two navies review the respective naval dispositions.[63]

Stark also reiterated Roosevelt's instructions regarding North Africa, that it was undesirable for the United States to send troops to Egypt or Libya. From his notes, Marshall read Churchill's claim that if British troops reached the Tunisian border a possibility existed that the French might invite the allies into Morocco. Dill had a slightly different interpretation. The 55,000 troops in England could land in North Africa in twenty-three days. If that happened, the Americans could land in Morocco, possibly preceding the British landings. Marshall insisted that this could only be accomplished if the French provided free passage for the Allies because the American forces, short planes, antiaircraft guns, and ammunition, were incapable at the time of making a forced landing. He also made clear that the United States could not deploy such a force in twenty-three days. He did so to acquaint the British with his shortages, not to criticize the diversion of the resources to Britain during the past year.[64]

The defense of the islands of Curaçao and Aruba was a greater concern to the Americans than the British, who had many higher priorities. Stark, however, pushed the British to reinforce these island defenses because 95 percent of all the oil used on the American East Coast and 50 percent of the Lend-Lease oil to England came via Curaçao and Aruba. He requested British permission to station US air units on the islands, and Pound, now convinced of their importance, promised to look into this immediately following the meeting.[65]

The Pacific remained a region of conflicting strategies; the British concern was Singapore and the Americans' the Philippines. Stark's joint goals were: security of the Burma Road, aid to China, hold Singapore, hold the Philippines, and develop a base in Australia. Attendees, like Robinett, thought these aims were unrealistic. But these objectives were accepted with much less discussion than about German-related issues, probably because participants realized there were no good answers to questions about what to do in Asia. The British were interested in the situation in the Philippines, and after Stark and Marshall updated them and in response to their request, Pound and Dill provided an update on the Singapore campaign. The British side was much more sanguine about Singapore's defenses than the Americans were about the Philippines.[66]

Marshall realized that shipping was the bottleneck restricting troop deployments and asked where the British most wanted US troops. Dill's surprising priorities were: first, Africa; second, Iceland; third, Northern Ireland. Marshall then asked the British plan for the 55,000 troops if the French initiative failed. Dill's rambling nonanswer proposed putting them in the Canary Islands if Germany invaded Spain (although why Germany would do so was vague at best). This convinced Marshall that British assumptions about French cooperation in Morocco were wildly optimistic. Overall, the discussion of previous guidance from Roosevelt and Churchill identified misconceptions, allowing the chiefs to clear the air among themselves and enable the joint planning committee to cooperate on a number of projects.[67]

Grand strategy discussions occurred at the end of meeting with the British taking the lead. Marshall would later praise them for doing so. He believed the Americans were still shell-shocked after Pearl Harbor, and instead of looking at the big picture were too focused on the Philippines and other beleaguered American garrisons. At Arcadia, the British chiefs woke them from their stupor and refocused their perspective on global strategic matters.[68]

Admiral Pound reiterated much of previous British strategic thinking already familiar to the Americans, the Germany First strategy. He said that Germany was the "predominant member of the Axis Powers" and the "prime enemy." Germany's defeat was the key to victory. The Allies must focus the majority of their resources to this end and devote "only the minimum force necessary for the safeguarding of vital interests in other theaters [Pacific]." American civilian and military leaders made the pivotal strategic decision of the war at a time when the United States had its back against the wall and American public opinion clamored for revenge against Japan.[69]

Pound's proposed strategy had six parts. First was to secure their industrial base areas to guarantee war production. This implied that the United States shift from a peacetime economy to a fully mobilized total wartime one to produce the sinews of war that would outfit the expanding American military machine and provide additional Lend-Lease equipment to Britain, China, and Russia. (Later in this conference, the Allies established dramatic new production goals and created a system to manage it.) Securing the mobilized industrial bases required the United States to protect the new production facilities for planes, tanks, guns, and ammunition along the West Coast against Japanese attack. It required the British to maintain forces to defend the homeland against a German invasion.[70]

Second, to insure the delivery of war material around the world, the Allies had to maintain sea and air lines of communication. Essential naval bases had to be held or captured to guarantee merchantmen safe passage across six vital sea routes. U-boat attacks were extracting a terrible toll of Allied shipping, sinking 1,419 merchant ships (including neutrals) and 4,693,000 gross tons during 1941. A contemporary US Navy training manual placed these figures in perspective. "If a submarine sinks two 6,000-ton ships and one 3,000 ton tanker, here is a typical account of what we have totally lost: 42 tanks, 8 six-inch howitzers, 88 twenty-five pound guns, 40 two-pound guns, 24 armored cars, 50 Bren carriers, 5210 tons of ammunition, 600 rifles, 428 tons of tank supplies, 2000 tons of stores, and 1,000 tons of gasoline." Shipping losses forced the British to reduce the import of dry cargo by more than half.[71] Cutting foodstuffs in favor of military cargoes exacerbated food rationing in Britain and accounts for the British officers' fascination with American culinary abundance.[72]

Seven important air routes had to be secured and air bases built along these routes to insure the safe air transit of men and material. Within a few days, the Americans agreed to the air and sea route proposals with minor adjustments.[73]

Third, the British expected to close and tighten a ring around Germany—north through Archangel, east through the USSR, south through the Mediterranean, and west through the European continent. The Soviet Union was the critical piece because the eastern front tied down the majority of German air and ground forces. The Soviets had stopped the German advance, but the Russians still needed planes, tanks, war equipment, and food to continue the struggle, tie down Hitler's legions, and eventually go over to the offensive. Allied aid to Russia meant increasing the Lend-Lease support to enable them to hold Leningrad, Moscow, and the oil fields of the Caucasus. As the Soviets blocked Germany in the east the Anglo-Americans would occupy North Africa and cut off German and Italian access to the Mediterranean, the ring around Nazi Germany would tighten and slowly strangle the regime to death.[74]

Fourth, a strategic bombing campaign targeting German industries and cities, a naval blockade restricting imports, and aiding resistance groups in the occupied countries would wear down German resistance and undermine willingness to continue the war. Fifth, at that point, the Allies would invade northwest Europe to conduct a ground offensive on the continent. Exactly when, where, and how remained nebulous. The British realized that invasion would not happen in 1942, but later offensives considered for 1943 depended on taking advantage of short-range success in 1942 to determine when or how to return to the continent.[75]

The situation in the Far East and the war with Japan was the final (sixth) topic. The Allies had to defend Australia, New Zealand, the Philippines, and India against Japan and support and encourage China to continue to resist Japanese aggression in order to tie down Japanese ground and air forces. Only limited offensives against the Japanese were foreseen because only minimum forces would be deployed to the South and East Asia.[76]

Pound's presentation elicited few questions from the Americans and was de facto accepted the same day. Over the next few days the American chiefs made minor superficial edits, mostly to the air and sea lines of communication. In the words of the official British history, "The British [Strategy] paper therefore had an easy, almost too easy, passage."[77]

Pound's paper was not a detailed blueprint for waging global war against Germany, Italy, and Japan. It was an outline or guide to a way ahead, which was a significant accomplishment given the grim situation facing the Allies in late December 1941. Pound got the Allies moving in the right direction. The strategic details would be filled in as the situation developed.

The British had neither selected a time nor a place for an invasion of Europe, which later became a major source of criticism. The official British history lamented, "A form of words had been found to which both parties could assent, but that did not necessarily mean they had yet discovered a common strategy." The British-proposed war of attrition, relying on air and sea power to weaken Germany, sought to minimize cost of victory in Allied lives. The ground forces would fight on the margins in expectations of triggering a chain reaction that would bring about Germany's internal collapse. The Americans acquiesced, preferring to place their own interpretations on the vague, if eloquent, plan. General Marshall interpreted the strategy as a return to northern France and the destruction of the German Army. If the attrition made this easier, so much the better. The full extent of this difference of opinion did not manifest itself during the Arcadia conference. It was to be a major topic of bitter discussion in the future.[78]

While the chiefs met, Churchill and Stimson discussed the Philippine situation at the White House. Stimson brought newly promoted Brigadier General Dwight D. Eisenhower with him. Eisenhower headed the War Department's Far East desk, but had only been in Washington ten days. He had, however, served under MacArthur for seven years both in the Philippines and in Washington and was intimately familiar with defense planning for the islands. Churchill, casually dressed in a pajama jumpsuit, had a map room set up near his bedroom in the White House. He asked that Eisenhower plot the exact American and Japanese dispositions so that he might better visualize what was happening. He asked about the campaign and expectations about the outcome of the retreat to Corregidor. What really interested him was the diversion of American resources and reinforcements to the Philippines. Eisenhower then departed, leaving

Churchill to press Stimson one-on-one to support the North Africa operation.[79]

British and American staff planners were working out the details of the multiple tasks assigned to them during the previous day's session. Rear Admiral Richmond Kelly Turner and Brigadier General Leonard Gerow led a team of twenty officers. Brigadier Dykes and Captain Richard Coleridge, the British Staff Mission secretary, headed a much smaller group. It was an unpleasant meeting. Turner, as chair, had a long list of tasks, but Coleridge disagreed with them. Both sides brought differing interpretations of their chiefs' instructions. Both disagreed about how to approach the assigned tasks or whether subcommittees were necessary. Much of the discord traced to the differing military cultures and staff methodologies, but American Anglophobia and British condescension made matters worse. Unlike their respective superiors who tried to see the other's point of view, the planners lacked collegiality. The British viewed the Americans as naive, disorganized, and amateurish. The Americans disdained British arrogance as overcompensation following a long string of defeats in Norway, Crete, Greece, North Africa, and France. After bickering back and forth, the two sides cleared unneeded staff from the room and went to work on Gymnast.[80]

Throughout the conference the British had to deal with the diverse personalities of the American Army and Navy planners. Richmond Kelly Turner was the director of the Navy War Plans Division since October 1940. He was sensitive to the destruction of the Pacific Fleet at Pearl Harbor and was disdainful of operations that distracted from the defeat of Japan. He was, in the words of one subordinate, "the meanest man I ever saw, and the most competent naval officer." His nickname in the navy was "Terrible Turner." He was a genius who drove himself hard and expected his subordinates to follow his lead. He was merciless with those who did not measure up.[81]

Leonard Gerow, the chief of Army War Plans, was a different personality. He was junior to Admiral Turner. An experienced combat veteran, he had served in both the occupation of Veracruz, Mexico, in 1914 and in France in World War I. A first-rate intellect, General

Marshall respected him and selected him as the head of the War Plans Division. Gerow was a less quarrelsome personality than Turner, and the British found him easier to deal with. As the conference progressed relations between the British and American Navy planners remained strained.[82]

During the day's meetings a crisis developed over the oldest French colony in North America, the islands of Saint Pierre and Miquelon off the coast of Newfoundland. The US State Department and the Vichy government had agreed to maintain the status quo on all French possessions in the Western Hemisphere. The British and Canadians, however, warned that a wireless station on the islands could transmit critical convoy information to U-boats lurking offshore. The British would shut the transmitter down, but the Canadians, conscious of their large and potentially volatile French Canadian population, were sensitive about antagonizing Vichy. On the morning of 24 December, Free French Forces broke the impasse by occupying the islands. Their timing was also inauspicious because at that very moment Churchill and Roosevelt were drafting the "Declaration of the United Nations" that promised such land grabs would be outlawed. The Free French decisiveness pleased the British, relieved the Anglo-Canadians, and angered Secretary of State Cordell Hull, who did not want to jeopardize the good relations that the United States enjoyed with Vichy. Hull wanted the Free French out and made the occupation a cause célèbre that attracted disproportionate attention over the next week.[83]

Roosevelt and Churchill celebrated Christmas Eve together. A Christmas tree was set up in the Rose Garden for the festive occasion, and a large crowd gathered outside the White House. At 1700 hours the tree was lit and both leaders addressed the crowd from the White House South Portico. Churchill waxed eloquent as he endeared himself to the American public and press. He told the audience that stood in the cold that evening that despite being separated from his own family, he felt he was close to home. "Whether it be the ties of blood on my mother's side, or the friendships I have developed here over many years of active life, or the commanding sentiment of comradeship in the common cause of great peoples who speak the same language, who kneel at the same altars, and, to a very large extent, pursue the same ideals. I cannot feel myself a stranger here in the centre and at the summit of the United States. I feel a sense of unity and fraternal association which, added to the kindliness of your welcome, convinces me that I have the right to sit at your fireside and share your Christmas joys." He then turned to the war and told the audience that although "almost the [entire] world is locked in deadly struggle. Armed with the most deadly weapons which science can devise." That the United States and Britain were not fighting for "greed for the lands or wealth of other people," nor "morbid lust for material gain at the expense of others." He exhorted the audience to resolve that "by our sacrifice and daring" our children "shall not be robbed of their inheritance or denied their right to live in a free and decent world."[84]

Shortly after the tree lighting ceremony Churchill and Roosevelt met with Secretary of the Navy Knox and Admiral Pound to discuss the Pacific and Southeast Asia. Around 1800 hours, Churchill received a message from the British commander in chief in the Far East, Lieutenant General Henry Pownall, requesting that the USS *Mount Vernon*, an American transport carrying a British infantry brigade, be immediately diverted from its original destination at Colombo, Ceylon, to Singapore. Roosevelt told Knox, who was at the White House, to notify the *Mount Vernon*'s captain to change course. Roosevelt also remarked off-handedly that because of the slim hope that reinforcements now en route from America could break through the Japanese blockade of the Philippines, they could be diverted elsewhere in Asia in the interest of cooperation. The prime minister saw this as an opportunity to guide the Americans into following his strategy for protecting the Empire in the Pacific. Churchill immediately seized on Roosevelt's off-the-cuff comment and requested that the American and British chiefs discuss the possibility the following day and work out the details of diverting US forces due to arrive in Australia to reinforce the Philippines to Singapore instead. He directed Brigadier Hollis, the British secretariat, to notify the British chiefs of this agenda change. The prime minister was ecstatic and informed Australian Prime Minister John Curtin, "Not only are they impressed with the importance of maintaining Singapore, but they are anxious to move a continuous flow of troops and aircraft through Australia for the relief of the Philippine Islands, if that is possible. If the Philippine Islands fall the President is agreeable to troops and aircraft being diverted to Singapore." He believed that Roosevelt was following his guidance on how to win the war and had bought into his Singapore strategy.[85]

Churchill had an unrealistic perception of the strength and fortifications at Singapore. He believed it an impregnable fortress that could hold out for months. In reality its defenses were incomplete and the naval base was of limited utility. It had more political value than strategic value and had become in the words of one historian a "British virility symbol." It displayed British resilience in the face of adversity and served as proof to New Zealand and Australia of British good faith during the interwar years. However, Churchill was poised to repeat the mistake he had made in Greece. He had pulled limited resources from a successful operation in North Africa and wasted them on a doomed enterprise in Greece. Now he was prepared to throw away limited resources on another doomed enterprise of no strategic value. This time he wanted the Americans to support him in this initiative.[86]

Churchill dined that evening with the president, the Crown Prince and Princess of Norway, and Bernard Baruch, an advisor to the director of the office of War Mobilization. Roosevelt and Churchill then moved to the Monroe Room to meet with Hopkins and Baruch on mobilization issues for almost two hours. The two political leaders retired shortly after this meeting. Churchill went to bed on Christmas Eve a happy man. He had received good news from Libya. General Auchinleck cabled that the "Royal Dragoons occupied Benghazi this morning. The Army of the Nile sends you hearty greetings for Christmas." The Americans had agreed to Germany First. The British strategy paper had been accepted. The increase in American production was under review. The North Africa operation was advancing; reinforcements for Singapore were open to review. Everything had gone Churchill's way. But as Field Marshal Sir William Slim later remarked, allies could be frustrating. "Allies are the most aggravating people. They are so difficult to understand, so unreasonable; they approach such straightforward problems from such extraordinary angles. Even when one agrees with them on common objectives their methods toward obtaining them are so queer, so very queer. They even introduce considerations of their national politics and hangovers from their history, none of which have the faintest bearing on the matter of immediate issue. Their most annoying characteristic, however, is that among all the arguing and haggling is the astonishing way they seem incapable of recognizing how sound, how wise, how experienced are our views; how fair, indeed how generous, how big-hearted we are. They even at times credit us with the same petty jealousies, narrow nationalistic outlook, selfish maneuverings, that obviously sway them."[87]

Churchill would discover the veracity of Slim's admonition and the fickleness of friends when he awoke on Christmas morning.

3

Marshall Makes His Presence Known

25 December

Christmas Day brought grim news from the Pacific. Roosevelt's daily situation report foresaw no letup in the vicious fighting on Luzon. More Japanese troops had landed just sixty miles south of Manila and were moving relentlessly toward the capital under cover of sustained air raids. MacArthur was hard-pressed and cabled his intention to withdraw slowly down the Bataan Peninsula toward Corregidor Island, evacuating the Philippine government and declaring Manila an open city. The British received equally bad news. Hong Kong's garrison had surrendered, and the rapid Japanese advance in Malaya had reached the Perak River line, threatening to open the way to Singapore. The final lump of coal for Christmas came when the US Navy announced the fall of Wake Island.[1]

The unexpected suddenness of Hong Kong's fall stunned Churchill. "The worst that has happened is the collapse of resistance of Hong Kong: although one knew it was a forlorn outpost, we expected that they would hold out on the fortified island for a good many weeks, possibly for several months." Instead, capitulation came after a "fortnight's struggle."[2]

Churchill did get one piece of good news. Eighth Army had captured Benghazi, an important port and transportation hub on the

Mediterranean coast. The much-needed success bolstered Churchill's arguments for Gymnast. Unfortunately, his enthusiasm over North Africa caused Churchill to direct General Auchinleck to transfer four fighter squadrons and one hundred Stuart Tanks from Libya to the Far East. This impetuous decision, as Brooke had foreseen, ended any chance of Eighth Army advancing to Tripolitania and destroying Rommel's Afrika Korps. Churchill's zeal inadvertently undercut his Gymnast proposal.[3]

Regardless of Christmas, the British planners began work early and were busy all day. Brigadier Dykes, the army planner, met with his Royal Navy and Royal Air Force counterparts. Brigadier Hollis had notified them of the previous evening's discussion between the president and prime minister, but the staff could do nothing until the American and British chiefs met later that afternoon. To fill in the time, they drafted a paper on Gymnast. At 1045, the British planners discussed their draft with Brigadier General Gerow and the US Army staff officers, aiming for an agreed-on approach to submit to the respective chiefs. The session was cordial and productive. Although both sides reached a general accord, they could not agree on forces required for victory in North Africa. The Americans would double the number of troops proposed by the British who, accustomed to operating on a shoestring, could not produce additional forces and demurred. The American side, wanting a guaranteed victory, insisted on a larger, overwhelming force. No agreement was reached.[4]

Hollis also informed the American chiefs of Churchill's and Roosevelt's conversations of the previous evening about the diversion of US forces to Singapore. Before Christmas services with the president, Marshall and Arnold met with Stimson. They brought Eisenhower, the head of the War Plans Division Far East desk, with them. All three officers were agitated. At a special meeting that morning, they showed Stimson a copy of Hollis's memo, which directed the British and American Chiefs to consider diverting reinforcements from the Philippines to Singapore.[5]

The memo shocked Stimson. MacArthur was fighting for his life in the Islands, and American newspaper readers closely followed the well-publicized campaign in the daily papers. Stimson was at a loss to understand how Roosevelt, the consummate politician, could ever agree to "turning over to the British of our proposed reinforcements to MacArthur." He told Arnold and Marshall that he would handle it, and the generals went off to church services. Stimson fumed because his worst fear had come true, that without advisors present Churchill might cajole Roosevelt into agreeing to a British agenda. He went home for lunch to gather his thoughts.[6]

Churchill and Roosevelt attended the 1100 service at the Foundry Methodist Church on Sixteenth Street, just eight blocks from the White House. Numerous British and American dignitaries participated, including Vice President Wallace, Lord Beaverbrook, and the American chiefs. Churchill remembered, "I found peace in the simple service," apparently a combination of gaining Roosevelt's approval on Malaya and singing hymns. Arnold and Marshall remained fixated on the Hollis report, uncertain how the president could justify abandoning American troops in the Philippines.[7]

After services, the Marshalls hosted a midday Christmas dinner at their Fort Myer, Virginia, residence, a scenic setting overlooking Washington, DC, just across the Potomac River. Lord and Lady Halifax, Lord Beaverbrook, Admiral and Mrs. King, and the British chiefs—Portal, Pound, and Dill—attended, and the Christmas celebration took on additional meaning when the Marshalls' discovered it was also Dill's birthday. Mrs. Marshall, despite short notice and bakery shops closed for the holiday, still managed to serve a birthday cake topped by candles and US and British flags. Everyone had a good laugh when they discovered the flags were made in Japan. Hilarity aside, the intimate gathering emphasized the close personal relationship developing between Dill and Marshall.[8]

Stimson was still seething, and the more he thought about the diversion of US forces, the angrier he became. In a fit of temper he called Hopkins at the White House and told the president's advisor of the Hollis memo and the chiefs' special session scheduled that afternoon. Hopkins, the insider who supposedly knew everything that went on in the Oval Office, was caught short, totally unaware of the Churchill-Roosevelt initiative. Stimson told him that if the president decided to divert forces from the Philippines, then "the President would have to take my resignation." Such intense vehemence from Stimson shocked Hopkins.[9]

Hopkins was rarely so far out of the loop, but he had not been present the previous evening during the two civilian leaders' discussion. Consequently, Hopkins was as amazed and shocked as Stimson, unable to believe the president could do such a thing. He asked Roosevelt in the presence of Churchill about the directive. Hopkins's tone and demeanor alerted the president to the potential political ramifications, and he cavalierly reassured Hopkins that Stimson was misinformed. When Hopkins reported this to Stimson, the secretary of war exploded. Stimson read from the Hollis memorandum verbatim to Hopkins, who realized the president really had blundered. If American reporters got wind of this story, newspapers across the country would headline, "Roosevelt Abandons Philippines." Hopkins again met with the president and more forcefully discussed the situation. Roosevelt understood that he had to nip the notion of troop diversions in the bud before it became a political hot potato. Shortly after, Hopkins notified Stimson that the president would meet with his military advisors later that evening at the White House.[10]

The American and British chiefs were scheduled to meet at 1600 that afternoon. Marshall had no details of the Roosevelt-Churchill discussion of the previous evening, other than the Hollis memo. However, priorities for Singapore and the Philippines were issues that constantly cropped up as the British doggedly sought reinforcements for Singapore and the Americans did the same for the Philippines. Marshall had to resolve the divisiveness because so long as it festered the Anglo-American allies would never agree on the Far East strategy.

Marshall's solution was to create a structure to ensure unity of command in the Far East. Three factors influenced his thinking. First, the debacle at Pearl Harbor resulted from a divided command structure. The army thought the navy was conducting protective reconnaissance with the fleet in port while the navy thought that because the army was responsible for defense of the Hawaiian Islands the fleet was secure. Each service had assumed the other was coordinating the overall defense of the islands. Marshall's lesson was that a single commander with a coordinating joint staff could have supervised the army and navy and held both services to account. Such a structure would eliminate facile assumptions because a coordinating staff would provide unified guidance to both services and verify what needed to be done.[11]

Second, Marshall realized that this was not a problem unique to US military forces. British military operations in the Middle East also suffered from a lack of unity of command. In the months before Pearl Harbor, Marshall read reports by the military attaché in Egypt, Major Bonner Fellers, on the lack of coordination among the British Army, Navy, and Air Force. Fellers commented as early as June that the absence of a unified command hobbled British Middle East command. Following the loss of Crete, Fellers cabled the War Department: "This battle was the fourth disastrous setback to British and on account of the divided responsibility which is a part of her command system, she has not yet the faintest conception of where the blame lies. The facts remain that no blame attaches to any one person. By dividing the responsibility a convenient system is built up which protects all commanders, reduces all blame, whitewashes every defeat, furnishes hole proof excuses, but will not manufacture victories." He foresaw that "it is fundamental that there be a single general commanding in the Middle East Theater, alone responsible for the conduct of operations."[12]

Through the summer and fall of 1941, State Department observers echoed Fellers's reports that a lack of unity of command in the Middle East hampered British military effectiveness. In September, for example, the US minister in Cairo informed the secretary of state that "the accomplishments of the British armed forces in the Middle East have been limited and the efficiency of their military effort has been lessened by the lack of a unified command." The Americans were frustrated that much of the equipment they sent to the region was "squandered." Simply too many agencies believed they were the number one priority, making effective interagency coordination impossible. No single organization managed theater communications, transportation, and logistics. A State Department official in Egypt reported, "We are sending into this region equipment that we have produced with difficulty and that cannot easily be spared from other regions." State called on the British to reorganize the command structure and to remedy the "inefficient organization." Without reform, the State Department thought American military assistance was "completely wasted."[13]

Fellers's astute observations impressed Marshall. He succinctly explained the divided command structure in the Middle East, enumerating three separate commands, with competing agendas, that slowed coordination. General Henry M. Wilson was in command in Syria and reported to General Auchinleck. General Wavell commanded the forces in Iran and Iraq and reported to the War Office in London. Air Marshal Arthur Tedder, who commanded air forces in the Middle East, reported to the Air Ministry. All three competed for limited resources. Each naturally assumed their command was the most important, and no system existed to coordinate and prioritize their respective requests. A US Army Air Force observer, Major General George Brett, declared this system unworkable because the air commander could not support concurrent requirements. Tedder glibly retorted that issues could be resolved face-to-face. Brett dismissed such an approach as a total waste of time.[14]

That September Brett expounded his views in an eyes-only cable to Marshall. British operations were "haphazard" because they lacked a unified command organization. "Three separate commanders with three separate staffs, each endeavoring to secure the most for their command and to prove the other two wrong." He continued that "confusion" occurred when different services had to coordinate with one another because without a centralized command, it was tough to obtain a decision that affected various services. In brief, British military operations in the Middle East could not succeed until they recognized that "defeat of the enemy must be founded on centralized, unified supreme control by only one authority."[15]

British forces were very much aware of the problems the absence of a single theater commander created. According to Fellers, "British Army very disgruntled that it must request, each time, close air support for its troops, rather than actually command such support." His solution reiterated Brett's belief that the situation could only be resolved by appointing a single commander in charge of all the air, sea and land assets in theater.[16]

The lack of unity of command in the Middle East also concerned Admiral Stark. After reading Fellers's reports, on 8 October Stark recommended that Marshall discuss setting up a single commander in the Middle East with the British. Stark, however, was opposed to a single commander for US forces and regarded the Middle East question as an army issue to be settled by soldiers, not sailors. "It does seem to me that Fellers reports contain so much common sense that it would be well if the British could see for themselves as others see them." General Gerow, chief of the army's War Plans Division, advised against bringing up the matter with the British because at the time the United States was not at war and the British might resent gratuitous observations about their veteran command structure. Still, Gerow was concerned that the defective command structure nullified American logistical support in the Middle East. Marshall originally heeded Gerow's advice, but on Christmas Day 1941, with the United States at war, he realized that the moment had arrived to recommend a unified command structure in Asia to avoid repeating British errors in the Middle East.[17]

The third influence was a report Marshall received Christmas Day from Lieutenant Colonel Francis Brink, who had attended the Inter-Allied Conference in Singapore the previous week. His report arrived while Marshall mulled over his approach to the Hollis memo in preparation for that afternoon's meeting with the British chiefs. Brink noted that the British, Dutch, and Americans had differing strategic appreciations of the war in Asia and the Pacific and seemed unable to rise above nationalistic parochialism. He was certain that the Allies were incapable of developing a coordinated plan to fight the Japanese. "The fact that the commands and staffs of the several governments represented think and operate along different lines was an added disadvantage and the necessity for coordinating staff action between the governments was clearly indicated."[18]

Brink concluded that the Singapore conference demonstrated the "need for a unified command to secure direct and immediate action both from the administrative and the operational standpoint." The challenge went beyond synchronizing multinational operations and extended to national interservice coordination problems. He pointed out that theater commanders, such as the Commander in Chief Far East (ground forces) and the Commander in Chief Eastern Fleet (naval forces), reported to different masters. Their limited command authority forced them to refer major issues to the different higher headquarters for adjudication. Differences of opinion between services resulted in slow and unwieldy decision-making, hindered operations, and underlined the requirement for the "direction and coordination of those services by one head to carry out any combined service mission."[19]

Marshall grasped that the real issue was not support either to the Philippines or to Singapore. Finite resources compelled a unified plan and unified command structure to ensure that the Allies used resources effectively and efficiently. Churchill, however, pursued a short-term logistic solution favorable to Britain. Marshall wanted the Allies to develop an organization capable of planning, coordinating, and working together. Marshall garnered his thoughts in church, during the Christmas meal, and in quiet reflection, then he carried his resolve to the afternoon meeting of the Anglo-American chiefs at the Federal Reserve Building.

Admiral Richmond Kelly Turner, the senior American planner, opened the second chiefs' meeting with an update. The British and American Joint Planning Committee had outlined a plan for a peaceful occupation of North Africa and proposed priorities in the Atlantic (relief of British forces in Iceland and Northern Ireland by US troops and possibly other locations if invited by host nations). Neither plan was complete, but he expected both would be soon. In fact, the planning committee was meeting concurrently and working on these projects. Turner was optimistic that both would be completed shortly.[20]

The chiefs then addressed the Hollis memorandum. The first item was the *Mount Vernon*, one of the US Navy's three largest American troop transports originally en route from Halifax, Nova Scotia, to Basra carrying twenty thousand British troops.[21] After Pearl Harbor, the British diverted the convoy to Asia. Churchill requested that the

Mount Vernon, with one brigade, leave the convoy and head immediately to Singapore. (The remaining two transports would follow and arrive in Singapore several weeks later with the rest of the division.) It quickly became apparent that the US Army and Navy had again failed to coordinate before the meeting. Marshall, uninformed by the navy on the actions already taken to divert the *Mount Vernon*, asked the British if they wished to change the ship's destination. He was surprised and embarrassed when Stark quickly interjected that the navy had already issued the order, although without directives for an escort. Admiral Pound, who was present with Roosevelt and Churchill the previous evening, reassured Stark that the Royal Navy accepted full responsibility for protecting the transport ship. This latest American miscommunication frustrated the British, who came to meetings fully prepared and united on all issues.[22]

Marshall next turned to the meeting's main subject, the diversion of US reinforcements from the Philippines. Because he had only received Hollis's memo that morning, Marshall had yet to coordinate a response with Stark. Instead, in the time available, he had prepared a detailed list of troop and equipment shipments from the United States and their anticipated arrival time in Australia, from whence the reinforcements would move to the Philippines. He handed the British a copy that detailed all land, sea, and air reinforcements intended for MacArthur's defense of the Philippines. Marshall also reiterated that General Brett was going to Australia to coordinate support to MacArthur.[23]

The British chiefs were put in an embarrassing position. This was only the second meeting of this important conference and individual relationships and rapport between the chiefs was still in the embryonic stage. Yet the British had to have realized how this looked to their American counterparts. If the situation were reversed they would not have sacrificed Singapore for the Philippines. Their Singapore plan similarly made no strategic sense for the Americans. Conformance to Churchill's designs forced them to push an agenda that could potentially end the conference on the second day. Portal gamely pressed the topic, as directed, of diverting the American resources to Singapore.

Portal immediately questioned the air portion of this report by insisting that not enough octane gasoline was in Australia to fuel the American aircraft, so the United States would also have to send domestically produced aviation fuel as well. Arnold dismissed the suggestion, citing limited shipping resources and the proximity to the oil fields of Sumatra, Dutch East Indies. Portal insisted that oil from Dutch stocks was unsatisfactory and that only US produced aviation gas would work. Arnold explained that the Dutch fuel was acceptable, allowing that it was noxious and destroyed the leak-proof lining of the current fuel tanks. Arnold was sending new tanks to remedy the problem.[24]

Marshall told the British that he would not precipitously reduce reinforcements destined for the Philippines. He had contacted MacArthur and awaited an update on the tactical situation on Luzon, estimating twenty-four hours to determine the speed of MacArthur's withdrawal and Brett's ability to support him with pursuit planes. Portal again pressed the Americans to send these aircraft to Singapore. What instructions were sent to MacArthur for the planes if they could not operate in the Philippines? American bombers were already operating from Australia, Arnold replied, and MacArthur's air officer would determine the disposition of the pursuit planes. Portal was not satisfied and sought a commitment to send these pursuit planes to Singapore. He bluntly told the Americans that this was too important a decision to be left to MacArthur's air officer and had to be made by a more senior authority, that is, the chiefs in the meeting.[25]

Portal argued for an immediate vote on the deployment of the aircraft and advocated establishing a committee in Washington to select the missions for the air, land, and sea forces of the various allies fighting in Asia. The committee would not only approve operations but also allocate the resources to support its choices.[26]

Marshall rarely took a radical position and sought to develop a good working and friendly personal relationship with the British. He had the utmost respect for Portal, who "had the best mind of the lot." This time, however, Portal's recommendation was nonsense. A central organization in Washington trying to plan and control the fighting in a theater was a recipe for failure.[27]

Marshall's approach was entirely different. Rather than micromanage the air, sea, and land forces of multiple nations from afar, he introduced the idea of a unified command within a designated theater. He believed the British approach too narrow. It was premature to divert resources from the Philippines to Singapore, and the allocation of resources among allies was bound to reoccur without a single theater commander. Marshall was loath to referee endless arguments about distributing forces and equipment and insisted the commander on site could make the best determination of the best way to defeat the enemy.[28]

Marshall spoke eloquently without notes. "I express these as my personal views and not those as a result of consultation with the Navy or with my own War Plans Division. As a result of what I saw in France and from following our own experience, I feel very strongly that the most important consideration is the question of unity of command. The matters being settled here are mere details which will continuously reoccur unless settled in a broader way. With differences between groups and between services, the situation is impossible unless we operate in a frank and direct basis. I am convinced that there must be one man in command of the entire theater—air, ground, and ships. We cannot manage by cooperation. Human frailties are such that there would be emphatic unwillingness to place portions of troops under another service. If we make a plan for unified command now, it will solve nine-tenths of our problems."[29]

Marshall's recommendations were unprecedented and cut to the heart of the issue. Field commanders could not see the big picture and consequently would always be influenced by their personal requirements. A single theater commander, however, could rise above service and national demands and decide conflicting directives and requests, thereby formulating a cohesive and effective operational strategy. Never before had the army, navy, and air forces of multiple nations been fused under a single commander. In fact, the US Army and Navy had never subordinated service rivalries to operate under a single commander.[30]

The response was muted. Stark was noncommittal, and the navy offered little support. King accepted the concept's merit but thought that there were limits to the amount of influence a commander could exercise on issues of national sovereignty. Portal, following the guidance he had received from the prime minister, wanted to skip a discussion of unified command and return to the topic of diverting reinforcements from the Philippines to Singapore. Marshall steered the discussion back to the creation of a unified command, insisting that a broader solution was necessary.[31]

The meeting reached an impasse. Marshall refused to discuss diverting US reinforcements until unity of command was settled. Portal was unwilling to discuss unity of command without further guidance from Churchill and recommended that the Joint Planning Committee develop a study on the disposition of the reinforcements using two scenarios: first, if the Philippines held; and second, if the Philippines did not. The British should not have been surprised by the American response even if they were taken back by Marshall's unyielding insistence to the Singapore concept and his sweeping recommendations for unified command. Pound defused the tense moment by interjecting that the Joint Planning Committee make this study of the utilization of reinforcements its top priority. The second day's Anglo-American Chiefs' talks ended on that sour note, and the American chiefs left for a 1730 meeting with the president.[32]

Marshall's proposal for unified command surprised the British delegation. In an attempt to discern Marshall's motives, Pound cornered Lieutenant Colonel Robinett, serving as head of the US Army Secretariat, after the meeting, and asked his views on the issue. Pound was intrigued but admitted he feared the idea. Robinett explained that Marshall's passion reflected his belief that the Pacific Fleet was destroyed because no single commander was in charge at Pearl Harbor.[33]

Pound mulled this over and told Robinett that the British did have unity of command in Alexandria. Robinett, who was familiar with Fellers's reports, asked if this was universal throughout the British armed forces, and Pound acknowledged that such was not the case. Marshall's plea for unity of command had influenced one member of the British chiefs as Pound gradually saw its value.[34]

Marshall admitted his mistake in not preparing his audience in advance for his bold proposal. He thought he had failed to convince either the US Navy or the British chiefs on the utility of unity of command. As he left the conference room, he instructed Eisenhower to draft a letter that defined the specifics of unity of command in the southwestern theater. Marshall envisioned a letter of instruction to the new theater commander, "giving him his mission, defining his authority and placing upon his authority specific limitations so as to exclude his interference from anything that was strictly the business of any particular government." He insisted on this degree of specificity to convince the British and the US Navy that unified command posed no risk to the national prerogatives of any country and sought to convince them of the benefits of such a command structure in the South West Pacific.[35]

The American chiefs then rushed to the White House for their late afternoon meeting with the president. Hopkins, Knox, and Stimson also attended. Roosevelt reviewed the situation in the Far East, detailing various suggestions on providing assistance to the beleaguered Allied campaigns in Asia and the Pacific. Almost as an afterthought, he casually mentioned "that a paper is going around which was nonsense and which entirely misrepresented a conference between him and Churchill." He directed his remark at Stimson, to make clear that the subject of diverting MacArthur's reinforcements to Singapore was dead. Whether Roosevelt had seriously entertained the idea or not was moot, but no more would be heard of it.[36]

The incident had embarrassed Roosevelt, who felt "he had pretty nearly burnt his fingers." Stimson and the American chiefs saw the episode as illustrative of the danger of Roosevelt discussing military matters with other Allied leaders without his military advisors present. Hopkins agreed completely with Stimson and urged the president to be more "careful in the formality of his discussions with Churchill." There was also the danger of political fallout to consider because press reports of the Hollis memo would have created a public uproar.[37]

The meeting cleared the air, but unfortunately the decision not to divert reinforcements from the Philippines came so late that the

British secretariat wasted most of the day finalizing a directive on the South West Pacific Area that was already overtaken by events. The Joint Planning Committee endured four hours of acrimonious exchanges that afternoon and evening. "We went at it hammer and thongs," Dykes recalled, "with the size of the committee and the bedlam increasing all the time." Participants argued over Iceland, Northern Ireland, and Gymnast. Admiral Turner had attended the Anglo-American chiefs' meeting and came late to the planners meeting. His arrival did not help as the British found Turner "increasingly difficult." After more than four hours, he tabled the British draft on project priorities, leaving planners with an "emasculated version" of the implications of conducting Gymnast.[38]

While the planners argued, Roosevelt hosted Christmas dinner at the White House. The state dinner for sixty people included Churchill, the prince and princess of Norway, and members of the British delegation. After a sumptuous dinner the Roosevelt's hosted the popular movie, *Oliver Twist*, and led in singing Christmas carols.[39]

Finally, at 2340, Roosevelt and Churchill conferred privately on the events of the day. Churchill was present when Hopkins had confronted Roosevelt about diverting reinforcements from the Philippines and finally recognized the lay of the American military and political landscape. Roosevelt could not simply divert American resources to Singapore. Churchill began to see that guiding Roosevelt to his strategy might be more difficult than he first expected. Roosevelt kept his own counsel and sought advice from advisors he trusted. In the end, he always made his own decision after weighing all available information. The prime minister also started to grasp that others besides Hopkins and Stimson influenced the president. He concluded that Marshall was a key advisor and someone that Churchill definitely needed to get to know.[40]

26 December 1941

Japan's southern advance continued remorselessly on 26 December. MacArthur continued a disciplined and orderly retreat toward the Bataan Peninsula. (However, in his haste to save his forces a large quantity of equipment and stores, especially food, were left behind.)

In Malaya, the Japanese continued to press attacks along the Perak River and bombed critical British military communication hubs.[41]

Secretary Stimson, a former governor-general of the Philippines, enjoyed close relations with many Filipino leaders, including Manuel Quezon, the president of the Commonwealth, and was determined to reinforce the islands. On Christmas Eve MacArthur had cabled him from Corregidor where the general had withdrawn with his family and staff. On the morning of 26 December, Stimson met Marshall to discuss additional relief for MacArthur and possible aid to the Dutch East Indies. Marshall used the occasion to familiarize Stimson with his single commander concept, explaining that the air, land, and sea assets of the Americans, British, and Dutch would work together under an integrated command, rather than squabbling among themselves over limited resources. Marshall realized that he needed support from Stimson and the president to convince the US Navy and British of the soundness of the proposal.[42]

Stimson proved sympathetic and was impressed by Marshall's presentation. He judged the concept was "timely" and Marshall's recommendation that a British general, Archibald Wavell, be appointed as the single commander in the theater politically astute. The Americans respected Wavell's tactical skill and command ability. Since 1939, he had campaigned in Libya, British Somaliland, Eretria, Italian Somaliland, Abyssinia, Greece, Crete, Iraq, Syria, Iran, Malaya, and Burma. No American general had that breadth of operational experience. Marshall knew that Wavell was "used to moving troops" and as a commander had experienced both victory and defeat. His appointment would reassure the British that the American's had no intention of diverting Empire forces from the defense of Singapore to fight elsewhere in the Asia-Pacific region. Stimson wholeheartedly supported Marshall but cautioned him to make the principles of command absolutely clear in the commander's written guidance. Marshall then returned to the War Department and conferred with Eisenhower on the draft unity of command paper.[43]

Shortly after noon Churchill delivered a tour de force performance to a joint session of Congress designed to secure the support of the US Congress, and the American people for the Germany First strategy as well as continued material support for his country. He began on a humorous note. "I cannot help reflecting that if my father had been American and my mother British instead of the other way around, I might have got here on my own. In that case this would not be the first time you would have heard my voice. In that case I should not have needed any invitation. But if I had it is hardly likely that it would have been unanimous. So perhaps things are better as they are."[44]

Churchill praised and thanked the American people. When "attacked and set upon by three most powerfully armed dictator states," he found no trace of fear, only "Olympian fortitude" and confidence in final victory. He emphasized the recent British military success in Libya and thanked the American people for the generous support in tanks and planes. (He was simultaneously sowing the seeds for US support of his future North Africa schemes.) Churchill pleaded for more war material, "The broad flow of munitions in Great Britain has already begun. Immense strides have been made in the conversion of American industry to military purposes. And now that the United States is at war, it is possible for orders to be given every day which in a year or eighteen months hence will produce results in war beyond anything which has been seen or foreseen in the dictator states." His fiery peroration directed at Japan brought his legislative audience to its feet. "What kind of people do they think we are? Is it possible they do not realize that we shall never cease to persevere against them until they have been taught a lesson which they and the world will never forget."[45]

It seemed, however, that the American chiefs needed a lesson in coordination. The third session of Anglo-American staff discussions witnessed the same ineptitude that characterized the Americans' previous performances. Stark again opened the conference in a rambling fashion. According to Robinett, "He talks and talks in an ambling sort of way, never speaks concisely." The British chiefs in contrast spoke very little, but Pound "strikes straight to the point" when he does speak. More significant was the American services' inability to coordinate and administer the interdepartment, much less the international, exchange of information. Stark asked Admiral Turner of the Joint Planning Committee for an update. The navy and the British had copies of Turner's update, but Marshall and the army planners did not. It became all the more embarrassing for Marshall when the British, who had extra copies, offered to share them with the army representatives.[46]

For Robinett the episode summed up the conference. The British staff system was far more organized and institutionalized than the American. The British services spoke with a single voice while the Americans fumbled efforts at basic interservice cooperation. The British chiefs kept their planners abreast of the decisions made in all the meetings. Neither Stark nor Marshall ever told their planners or secretariat what went on in meetings. The British Section "functions beautifully" and the Americans "just struggle along," always one step behind in their planning. This forced them to attend all the meetings they could in an effort to find out what was happening while their well-informed British counterparts looked ahead to matters of specific interest to Churchill and Roosevelt. As a result, "the British seem to determine the course of the conference. US representatives just follow and contribute what they can, or nothing at all."[47]

Admiral Turner's overview of the US-UK overseas expeditions in the Atlantic Ocean involved the movement of American troops to Iceland, Ireland, and North Africa. That morning British staff officers had filled the British chiefs' ears with a litany of complaints about Turner's polarizing personality. Samuel Eliot Morison, the official navy historian, who said something nice about almost every admiral, described Turner as "highly opinionated and difficult to work with." The British planners were more candid. Jacob described Turner as a "discontented camel. . . . His utterly rigid mind was most unsuited to working in a Joint Planning Committee, of which by virtue of his rank and position he was Chairman. 'Take' he could understand, 'give,' was not in his vocabulary."[48]

US Army planners also detested Turner. For example, sometime before the Pearl Harbor attack, Arnold had extended an air route to Australia without consulting the navy. A furious Turner ordered Commander Forrest Sherman to write a letter of protest for Stark to send to Marshall. Tempers ultimately cooled and no letter was sent, but the episode illustrated Turner's hair-trigger temper and contempt for the army. Robinett found Turner "flighty and non-receptive to new ideas. He always had to have all the ideas himself and was a tough customer to deal with." His treatment of the US Army and the British in the Joint Planning Committee was more of the same.[49]

Personalities aside, Turner did know his craft. He lacked tact, but that did not invalidate his proposals and forced the British to confront hard facts. The British, for instance, wanted the Americans to conduct three operations in the Atlantic, involving relief of Empire forces in Iceland and Northern Ireland as well as participate in Gymnast, the North Africa operation. The United States did not have enough transport ships and escorts to conduct these simultaneous missions. Turner gave the chiefs the bad news that the Anglo-Americans were woefully short of troopships and the Americans had already committed their three largest vessels (USS *Mount Vernon*, USS *Wakefield* and USS *West Point*) to carry British troops to East Asia. Someone had to establish priorities or sequence for the three proposed operations. That was a role for the Chiefs of Staff, not his planning committee.[50]

Turner bluntly laid out the current shipping situation and its effect on planned operations in the Atlantic. The Anglo-Americans were woefully short of troopships. The British were also short troopships, as shown by pressing the *Mount Vernon*, *Wakefield*, and *West Point* into service to transport British troops to Asia. Turner had quickly realized that when Arcadia began, the British were unaware of these American shortages in shipping. On 26 December a formal US report on available shipping and capabilities pegged 200,000 troops as the most the United States could move at any one time. Even this figure was misleading because major resources were already committed to maintaining the American forces overseas and to responding to requests for reinforcements in the Pacific. Thus American planners calculated that by mid-January 1942 available shipping could transport just 25,000 troops for new operations in the Atlantic. Over time, of course, more transport ships would become available; an additional 18,000 troop capacity by 1 February, 15,000 additional by 1 March, and 24,000 additional by 1 April, which was still short of 200,000.[51]

To move three US divisions with air and support units (the planners estimated force) required seaborne transportation for more than 60,000 troops. Based on this requirement, planners determined that if the allies invaded North Africa, no other maritime transport would be available for at least three months. The British could not supplement shipping needs because they had fully committed their transports for projected troop movements from Britain to the Mediterranean and Far East. The shipping shortage precluded immediate American relief of British forces in Iceland and Northern Ireland. Furthermore, deploying British troops to North Africa without replacement American divisions would increase the vulnerability of the British Isles to attack. Turner was clear. The issue was not troops; these the American Army could provide. The problem was shipping: there was only enough to conduct one operation at a time. Turner put it back on the chiefs. Dill had said that North Africa was the priority. If the Allies launched Gymnast, Iceland and Northern Ireland could not be relieved. Moreover, the shipping requirements for Gymnast would delay the flow of the British reinforcements to the Middle East and Asia because the Americans would have no excess shipping available for British use.[52]

Turner leveled his sights on Gymnast. Planners assumed that because the French invited the allies into their colonies the landings would be unopposed and speculated that the Germans would need three months to react. Anglo-American planners did disagree about the size of the forces required for this operation. The British favored a smaller one (one US and four British divisions), while the Americans wanted a larger one (six US divisions and one British division) for the first three months. The primary British emphasis was on the initial landings near Algiers; the main American emphasis was on the postlanding expansion of their base at Casablanca. As American forces moved from Casablanca, US planners anticipated that they would need more and more troops and substantially larger air forces, underlining the American attitude that "if the operation is worth undertaking it should be done in sufficient strength to give a reasonable chance of success." The British insisted that the German air force was spent and a nonfactor. Both sides compromised by assigning upper and lower limits to troop numbers needed and deferred the final determination to the chiefs.[53]

The meeting then adjourned to allow the British and American Chiefs to meet at the White House with Churchill and Roosevelt. The two heads of state sought a sense of Arcadia's progress and accomplishments to date and an assessment of the personal and professional interactions of the chiefs. Stimson, who along with Knox and Turner, also attended, seemed impressed by the harmony and close working relationship among the chiefs. The acrimony and disagreements present among the planners had not bled over into the chiefs discussions.[54]

Roosevelt asked Dill for his opinion on Gymnast. He intuitively realized Dill's objectivity would provide an unbiased assessment. Marshall's opinion of Dill was already high, but now others like King got to observe his conduct and demeanor during this critical session. Dill highlighted the assumption that the landings would be by invitation of the French and unopposed, but he glossed over the differences in force sizes since they were still under review. He synopsized Turner's earlier presentation regarding the lack of shipping.[55]

Roosevelt clearly and patiently drew the chiefs out about shipping shortages. Did they affect material and equipment (Lend-Lease) that the United States was sending to Britain? That, Marshall interjected, was not a problem, but because the United States lacked the shipping tonnage to simultaneously conduct the Iceland, Northern Ireland, and North Africa missions, civilian leaders had to prioritize objectives. Roosevelt agreed, remarking though that Northern Ireland should be the priority and if the situation changed in the future the priority could shift to North Africa.[56]

Churchill was not as flexible. As General Wavell once commented, "Winston is always expecting rabbits to come out of empty hats." Now Churchill tried to work his magic, telling Marshall that because he "placed tremendous importance" on Iceland and Ireland relief missions they had to be executed concurrently with Gymnast and the Far East reinforcement. He drew on a specious historical analogy to "prove" his contention. During World War I, he recalled, America shipped two million men to France in a short period of time. Where were all those troop transports now? How could there be a shipping bottleneck? The Americans simply had to work harder or else he would be "frightfully unhappy" to have to choose between missions.[57]

The American chiefs got a front-row view of Churchill's leadership style that relied on not listening and insisting on doing everything at once. He acted as if the United States, which had only been at war for nineteen days, had unlimited resources to draw on. The prime minister was not interested in the facts, he was upset because he was not getting his way. His demands were sometimes outlandish, sometimes overbearing. For example, he proposed transporting troops on battleships and argued that American soldiers did not need artillery (which took up cargo space) because they could use British guns, even though the British Army lacked its full complement of artillery pieces. He recommended conserving tonnage by having American troops in Ireland eat local food, thereby increasing cargo space by decreasing food shipments. Tiring of flights of fancy, Marshall reminded the prime minister that the Allies had unsuccessfully tried a similar food policy during World War I. Undeterred, Churchill pushed ahead, insisting that it was not "too great a problem to be solved." He restated Gymnast's importance and demanded the Americans relieve Ireland as soon as possible.[58]

Churchill's reaction was surprising. General Brooke had cabled the prime minister that day to advise against the operation (Gymnast) and bluntly informed Churchill that "first of all in importance comes security of this country and its communications." As Brooke analyzed it: "Problem complicated by the fact that it does not look as if we are likely to be called in, and secondly that PM now is toying with the idea of carrying out such a plan against resistance, and finally owing to the fact that shipping available does not admit of both occupying North Africa at request of French and reinforcing Far East sufficiently to secure Singapore, Burma, and Indian Ocean communications." Regardless, Churchill continued to insist on a North Africa operation.[59]

The British chiefs' attitude regarding Churchill's more impractical proposals puzzled their American counterparts. Logistic deficiencies, manpower shortages, and insufficient equipment all augured against success. How, the Americans wondered, could seasoned British officers unanimously support such untenable recommendations? Churchill's position on North Africa reflected his personal opinion and not the professional advice of his own military advisors. The British chiefs privately had concerns. In London, Brooke and the British Cabinet thought this operation premature and risky. Brooke's diary was full of angst. He realized resources were limited and the assumptions were not realistic. He thought, "The situation was evidently fraught with many dangers and a false step at this stage might well lead to the worst of catastrophes. Operations in North Africa were evidently dependent on many factors, and we were not in a position at the moment to undertake further commitments until we could see more clearly how we stood." Brooke worried because Churchill was difficult to argue with. "Winston was never good at looking at all the implications of any course of action which he favored! In fact he frequently refused to look at them." Brooke feared that Churchill would commit the military to a mission that they believed lacked strategic sense.[60]

Roosevelt tactfully shifted the conversation to the Far East by asking Marshall about the status of reinforcements to the Pacific. Marshall's reply that aircraft and personnel were moving as quickly as shipping became available carried the implication for Churchill that the Americans were not withholding transports from the British. Roosevelt subtly shifted the topic to unity of command by asking if the matter was resolved. In typical fashion, the president casually remarked that "this would seem to be most desirable, since there are four forces involved in the Far East."[61]

More for Churchill's benefit than Roosevelt's, Marshall related that the chiefs discussed unity of command yesterday but it was not on today's agenda. Roosevelt reiterated that it should be considered because the current fragmented command structure failed to maximize the power of allied forces in the Far East. This caught Churchill short. He opposed the idea, arguing that the extreme distance between theaters was too great for a single commander to control. Churchill resurfaced Portal's earlier recommendation that a Washington headquarters act as a clearinghouse for orders and the allocation of resources to the separate commanders fighting in the Far East. But the prime minister had neither reckoned with Marshall's adroit bureaucratic maneuvering nor with the general's influence on his president.[62]

Roosevelt was not impressed with the clearinghouse proposal. He told Churchill that the information he was receiving from the Pacific was sketchy at best and thought a single commander overseeing the various operations could rectify the deficiency. Churchill tried to reassert his role as mentor to the president, and he again resorted to a geopolitical history lesson. During the First World War, unity of command, he claimed, was only possible because there was a single front with "a continuous line of battle." In Asia and the Pacific the operating areas were widely separated and consequently difficult for one person to control. Churchill stubbornly reiterated the need for a Washington headquarters to exercise command over the Far East.[63]

Shifting the subject slightly, Roosevelt asked for King's opinion about cooperation among the various national naval commanders in the region. The system was working well, King said, divided into spheres of action between Dutch and British around Singapore and the Americans in the western Pacific. Heretofore King was silent on the subject of unity of command, neither actively supporting Marshall nor openly opposing him. It was a new, untried concept, and King was still thinking through the ramifications or advantages for the US Navy. Secretary Knox, who, like Roosevelt, was acutely aware of the unity of command issues at Pearl Harbor, was a strong supporter. Pound politely interjected that the cooperation between naval forces in Asia could stand improvement. After listening to the various comments, Roosevelt instructed the chiefs to study unity of command. A visibly unhappy Churchill wished to discuss the issue later with Roosevelt. He hoped to persuade the president to his viewpoint in private.[64]

Roosevelt had made time for a short meeting with Lord Beaverbrook, the British Minister of Supply. Churchill was interested in obtaining greater access to the war equipment produced in America and hoped Beaverbrook could convince the president to agree. Hopkins monitored the discussion to prevent a recurrence of the president making unilateral commitments, as had happened contretemps during Roosevelt's Christmas Eve meeting with Churchill. Its brevity belied the importance of the meeting to the allied war effort. Beaverbrook understood weapons production. His conference presentation relied on the metaphor of British industry as a three-legged stool: first, the industrial plant of the United Kingdom; second, raw materials from the commonwealth; and third, American production to bridge the gap between British output and requirements. Britain needed all three legs for balanced industrial mobilization, and, to make sure the Americans understood, he passed out detailed lists of support that the United States would be responsible for supplying. Beaverbrook had carefully examined the Americans' programmed output of tanks, artillery, and aircraft enumerated in their so-called Victory Program and judged it grossly inadequate. Projected goals seriously underestimated the nation's industrial mobilization potential. As implemented, during 1942 the United States would produce the same number of planes, tanks, antitank, and antiaircraft guns as Great Britain. That was insufficient, and if the president agreed to it the Allied war effort would fail. Beaverbrook relied on all his eloquence to persuade Roosevelt to increase production goals.[65]

Beaverbrook emphasized that Britain and the Soviet Union depended on receiving increasing numbers of these weapons from the United States. He contended that America should be the arsenal for arming and supplying all nations fighting for democracy, not coincidentally one of Churchill's major objectives at Arcadia. This idea also appealed to Roosevelt, and the next day Beaverbrook sent him a chart that outlined the requirements of Britain, the USSR, and the United States for tanks, aircraft (bombers and fighters), artillery (antiaircraft, antitank, and field), and rifles. Comparing Beaverbrook's figures to the 1942 production plan revealed the startling deficits. Without expanded US war production, the Allies would be short more than of 10,500 tanks, 26,700 planes, 22,600 artillery pieces, and 1,600,000 rifles. This was a sobering document. He urged the president to place Hopkins in charge of a production committee to distribute raw materials, determine production requirements, and mobilize American industry.[66]

After meeting with Beaverbrook, Roosevelt had already directed Vice President Wallace to work with logistics experts to develop enhanced production goals. The president also planned to take his case to Congress and publicly lay out new production goals for tanks, planes, and artillery. He felt that this would reassure US allies of the American commitment and put the Axis powers on notice that America was gearing up its dynamic industrial might to crush them.[67]

At 1900 hours Churchill had a short meeting with the British chiefs before meeting with the president. Churchill informed them that he was thinking of drafting an Anglo-American agreement based on three points: first, Germany was to be recognized as "the main enemy"; second, the general direction of the war against Japan would be run from Washington; and third, the general direction of operations in the "Atlantic and European theater" would be run from London. Maintaining control of the war with Germany was an unstated objective of the Arcadia Conference, and he was hopeful that the Americans would accept his plan. He intended to broach it in discussions over the next two days.[68]

Later that evening Churchill and Roosevelt discussed unity of command over dinner with Hopkins and Beaverbrook. Churchill still opposed a single commander in chief in the Far East. He preferred to centralize the distribution of troops and material and believed such decisions rested with civilian governments, not theater commanders. The respective services of the four allies fighting in the Pacific would operate under their own individual commanders, who would in turn report to Washington to receive strategic guidance and resource allocations. Churchill's ulterior motive was to establish a similar headquarters in London to run the Atlantic theater. That way the Americans would direct the war against Japan and the British would direct the war against Germany. Roosevelt was unenthusiastic. He was not prepared to subordinate American to British thinking on grand strategy.[69]

Churchill oscillated between realism and romanticism. He was demanding and enamored by risky, adventurous operations. He was also a realist and politician. He disliked a single service handing autonomy over to another, much less all services handing over command prerogatives to a foreign commander. Churchill was canny enough to see that Roosevelt vigorously supported unity of command, and the president's suggestion that Wavell command the enterprise left the prime minister with a conundrum, he did not like unified command but he needed to reach an agreement with Roosevelt on command organization. Beaverbrook passed Hopkins a note and said: "You should work on Churchill. He is being advised. He is open minded and needed discussion." Hopkins later arranged for a private meeting the following morning between Churchill and Marshall to discuss unity of command in the Far East.[70]

27 December

Marshall met Churchill at the White House on 27 December to discuss unity of command. Churchill's habit of staying up late and sleeping in late found him still in bed when Marshall arrived. The prime minister though was full of energy and ready to convince Marshall on the proper way to run the war in the Pacific. He had failed, however, to reckon with the character and conviction of the Army Chief of Staff.[71]

Marshall was unlike any general Churchill had ever dealt with. The prime minister knew of Marshall's sterling reputation, iron discipline, and self-control. He knew the soon-to-be sixty-one-year-old general was modest and assiduously avoided publicity. He knew Marshall was a superb organizer with a jeweler's eye for talent who, although not effusive, was inspirational and had enjoyed the confidence of Congress and the president. These attributes were common knowledge. What Churchill did not know was how Marshall became Chief of Staff.[72]

Marshall had been a prominent figure in the US Army since World War I. He rose through the command structure and in November 1938 was a major general and Deputy Chief of Staff when he attended a White House meeting. There Roosevelt announced his intention to ask Congress for money to build 10,000 planes a year, although without funding for air or ground crews, spare parts, or bases. Ten thousand aircraft sounded good, but with no one to fly or maintain them the planes alone were worthless. Marshall was surprised when everyone at the meeting agreed with the president, apparently being reluctant to criticize his plan. Enjoying the acclaim, Roosevelt noticed that Marshall was quiet and asked for his opinion. Marshall responded, "Mr. President, I am sorry but I do not agree with that at all." This frankness impressed Roosevelt, who admired the integrity of people who were willing to speak their minds.[73]

A few months later, Roosevelt offered Marshall the post of US Army Chief of Staff. Marshall naturally aspired to the position but warned the president that he "wanted the right to say what I think and it would often be unpleasing." Roosevelt joked that Marshall said "yes" pleasantly enough. Marshall reiterated that if appointed "it may be unpleasant." Roosevelt selected him anyway and he was sworn in on 1 September 1939, the day Germany invaded Poland.[74]

On the morning of 27 December, Churchill got a firsthand taste of Marshall's forthrightness. Churchill fired the opening salvo, addressing Marshall in the condescending fashion he used on his own chiefs. He opposed putting the navy under an army commander because command of a ship was unique and what did an army officer know about handling a ship. Marshall fired back, "What the devil does a naval officer know about handling a tank?" He told Churchill he wasn't trying to get sailors to drive tanks; he desired a unified command structure.[75]

Churchill resorted to a lecture on British naval history, but Marshall stood firm. He interrupted the prime minister's soliloquy, reminding Churchill that he was "not interested in Drake and Frobisher, but I was interested in having a unified front against Japan, an enemy which was fighting furiously." He then told Churchill that if something was not done quickly, "we were finished in the war." The interruption surprised Churchill, who admonished Marshall as he left that he would have to take "the worst with the best."[76]

Marshall next met with Roosevelt, Stimson, and Arnold on the same subject. Roosevelt expressed interest in Marshall's meeting with

Churchill. Marshall told him that Churchill was "dead set against" unity of command because it violated British historical thinking on the navy as the "Queen of the Sea" and that nation's principal branch of defense. He had misjudged Churchill's reaction because the prime minister was impressed by Marshall's spirited articulation on the need for unity of command. His physician, Lord Moran, later confided in his diary, "Marshall remains the key to the situation. The P.M. has a feeling that in his quiet, unprovocative way he means business, and that if we are too obstinate he might take a strong line."[77]

Stimson supported Marshall and told Roosevelt (incorrectly) that the Japanese had unity of command in the theater and were more coordinated in their efforts. The secretary favored a powerful base in Australia from which to counterattack the Japanese, but this was impossible if units were piecemealed to Singapore, Burma, and the Philippines without an overarching strategy. The president proved a willing audience. He shared his feelings on unity of command and asked the trio for their thoughts on Churchill's idea of running the war in Asia from Washington.[78]

All opposed, regarding it impossible to overcome the time lag which was too great between a commander requesting a decision from Washington and receiving a reply. To maximize the effectiveness of air power, for instance, targets susceptible to surprise raids appeared quickly and needed immediate authorization. Even a delay of twenty-four hours would deny American air power an advantage.[79]

Roosevelt next asked who should command this theater in the Far East. He was inclined toward MacArthur and thought that the Dutch and Australians would find an American commander more acceptable than a British one. Stimson, Marshall, and Arnold were reluctant to pull MacArthur from the Philippines, fearful of unhinging the Islands' defense. No other American officer came to mind, so after further discussion, they agreed on Wavell. This was just as well considering that Roosevelt had proposed Wavell to Churchill the previous evening. They adjourned unanimously convinced that unity of command was essential.[80]

As the participants disbanded, Roosevelt asked Arnold to remain to discuss Beaverbrook's earlier comments. Beaverbrook had forced the president to consider the nation's enormous industrial might in relation to the Victory Program's goals. What was Arnold's opinion of Beaverbrook's comment that Great Britain, a nation of forty million people that imported all its raw materials, could still produce more airplanes than the United States, which had three times the population and access to apparently unlimited natural resources. Arnold expressed confidence that the United States could dramatically increase aircraft production, if "we had the will to do so." Boeing's goal, for example, was thirty-seven B-17s a month; they already produced fifty and would reach seventy-five by the end of January. Raising production goals would motivate industry to meet them.[81]

Afterward Marshall visited Admiral Stark's office to make his case for unity of command. The services had to present a unified front if he was to convince the British of its value. The navy's main objection, like Churchill's, was having a commander from another service in operational control of naval forces. Who was Marshall considering for command? Marshall acknowledged that the Australians wanted MacArthur, but in keeping with presidential wishes, Wavell. Stark listened quietly, other admirals in the room seemed hostile, but King, apparently swayed by what one participant described as Marshall's persuasiveness, did agree, and once he threw his considerable weight behind unified command everyone else fell into line. One observer neatly summed up Marshall's presentation: "His grasp and understanding of the entire situation is way in front of the others."[82]

Asked his decision after the war, King explained: "The idea of setting up a unified command in the Southwest Pacific was a 'natural' since there were at least three countries that had to be considered under one command. . . . I think under the circumstances it was correct to set up a unified command in the Southwest Pacific." As for the commander, King admitted that the navy favored MacArthur. "But, as we know, he had a job to do against the Japanese in the Islands and wasn't available, and the Allies had no time to lose."[83]

The Anglo-American chiefs' fourth meeting of began at 1500 that afternoon. Marshall was ready. He had gained the support of Roosevelt, Stimson, Knox, and the navy. He had faced down Churchill. He had ordered Eisenhower to draft detailed instructions to frame the dialogue. Before Marshall could even broach the subject, however, American staff ineptitude and miscommunication again reared its ugly head. Stark summarized the Joint Planning Committee's priorities for the Atlantic. No sooner had he started than Pound interrupted. The British had not reviewed a copy of the document before the meeting, and besides, Pound thought that participants had already agreed on this subject. Turner replied that his staff had completed the draft shortly before the start of this meeting, leaving no time for dissemination. Stark played down the oversight, stating there were only a few minor edits to the earlier draft. The British were displeased, and participants redirected the paper back to the Joint Planning Committee.[84]

Stark introduced two more papers, neither of which had been staffed before the meeting. The Grand Strategy paper caused the greatest commotion between the respective chiefs because Pound thought this was already agreed to on 24 December and was upset that the Americans were revisiting everything previously agreed on. Turner insisted that the Americans had not fully agreed, citing the precise meaning of the term "agreed in principal." The British understood it to mean it was a finished product; the Americans to mean accepted pending further revisions. Pound agreed that certain amendments were pending on air routes, but otherwise the draft was complete. Stark agreed with him, and the paper returned to the Joint Planning Committee for finalization.[85]

The staff paper on North Africa irked the Anglo-American chiefs. None had seen it before the session because US Navy planners had not seen fit to disseminate it. Stark simply brought copies to the conference table and passed them around before his presentation. Arnold and Marshall were as upset as their British counterparts, more so since naval planners had not resolved the size of the expeditionary force. Arnold and Portal concurred that there were too many air units. The two air chiefs were beginning to see the war from a similar perspective. Marshall wanted the paper returned for further study. He warned the group that this would be the first engagement between the American and German forces, and a setback would damage US confidence and morale. In short, the Americans had to win the first battle, and any plan that cut corners on troop levels jeopardized success. All three papers ultimately were returned to the planning committee for rewrite.[86]

The lackluster quality of the American staff work and the inability of the American Army and Navy staffs to coordinate with each other left the British fuming. Dykes commented, "Their secretarial arrangements are just non-existent; they don't understand the drill at all." Dill was so upset by this whole process that at the end of the meeting he sent a formal note of concern to Marshall and Stark, stating that at the meeting on 24 December, "our impression was that the United States Chiefs of Staff were in agreement with the review which we had prepared and circulated on general strategy, subject to certain minor amendments, which were agreed at the meeting, and to the inclusion of a paragraph defining essential air communications." Dill then politely asked, "We think it important that an agreed document on general strategy should be tabled and circulated as soon as possible so that there shall be a firm basis for the planning on which our Joint Staffs are now engaged."[87]

After this inauspicious and acrimonious start, Stark introduced the contentious topic of unity of command. He asked for Pound's opinions. Pound elaborated on Churchill's obsession about a single commander dealing with naval matters and his reluctance to subordinating the autonomy of the British Navy to another service or nation. Marshall agreed that no single individual selected as the supreme commander could possibly possess the specialized expertise of each individual service chief. But the supreme commander was not selected for technical competence but for a record of good judgment. In a unified command superior judgment trumped a brilliant theater commander dependent on cooperation.[88]

Marshall then introduced the proposal on the South West Pacific theater. Eisenhower had designed it as a letter of instruction signed by the supreme commander's government. Representatives from each of the allied coalition powers would countersign the document. The succinct paper clearly defined the supreme commander's duties, responsibilities, and authorities. It listed seven restrictions to protect national sovereignty and allay the concerns of the signatory governments. The supreme commander could not (1) relieve national commanders or their subordinates; (2) alter their tactical organizations; (3) commandeer their supplies, munitions, or resources without the permission of the appropriate commander; (4) interfere with their communications with their respective governments; (5) interfere with subordinate commanders carrying out the instructions of their government to move troops to another theater; (6) assume direct control of any units assigned to him but must exercise control through the government's designated commanders; and finally, (7) he must establish his headquarters so as to exercise balanced control of the entire theater.[89]

Overall Dill approved of Marshall's proposal but was concerned that the numerous restrictions would impede a commander's ability to exercise control of his forces. Dill supported fewer restrictions. Marshall strongly believed that the current system was the least efficient method of allocating scarce resources against Japan. Anything would be an improvement in Marshall's words: "If the Supreme Commander ended up with no more authority than to tell Washington what he wanted, such a situation was better than nothing, and an improvement over the present situation." Earlier that day King's support was decisive in securing navy acceptance of Marshall's recommendation. Now King countered British concerns by stressing that the restrictions were needed to secure the ABDU (Australia, British, Dutch, and United States) government's concurrence. Only such restrictions, King argued, would reassure the signatory governments who were turning over their respective national autonomy to a commander from another service and country.[90]

Dill and Portal admired Marshall's effort. The British staff was likewise impressed. Dykes saw that Marshall "made his points very well—nothing could be worse than the present system! It is a fine bold concept—but who is the man?" Pound expressed no view in public but did say that he realized a decision had to be made quickly. The positive reaction surprised Marshall, especially when the normally reticent Dill hugged and praised him for the concept and his briefing.[91]

In a subsequent aide-mémoire from the British chiefs to Churchill, the British chiefs explained, "it was apparent that the United States

Navy and Army had reached agreement on this question and regarded it as a matter of utmost urgency." Their aide-mémoire recommended that Churchill approve a single unified command in the Far East.[92]

The British chiefs had two other outstanding issues when they met with Churchill that evening. Admiral Pound was aware that British Admiral Geoffrey Layton (Commander in Chief, Eastern Fleet) in Singapore and American Admiral Thomas Hart (Commander in Chief, US Asiatic Fleet) in Manila were not cooperating and that the American Navy was maintaining tight control of its forces. A Supreme Commander in the theater would commit the American forces to an agreed strategy, not one dependent on the personalities of local commanders. Pound's reservations had not completely disappeared, as he still hoped that the Royal Navy could cooperate with rather than be incorporated within a unified command structure. Churchill sought to word the instructions accordingly.[93]

Who would command in the South West Pacific was the larger issue. The Americans recommended Wavell while the British thought it better that an American command the theater based on their clear-eyed appreciation of events in the Pacific. The Japanese were advancing rapidly in a vast theater of operations. The Allies' limited ability to reinforce the defenders guaranteed that whoever was selected would fail. Dill captured their attitude in a note to General Alan Brooke: "It would, I think, be fatal to have a British commander responsible for the disasters that are coming to the Americans, as well as ourselves. . . . Never was a soldier given a more difficult task. . . . It is of first importance that we should not be blamed for the bloody noses that are coming to them."[94]

Churchill begged to differ. He discerned no subterfuge in the Americans' recommending Wavell to command the South West Pacific Area and forcefully told the chiefs that he did not think the Americans were "attempting to shift disaster onto our shoulders." Being Churchill he had his personal subtext. He disliked the idea of handing the defense of Singapore over to an American, and Wavell's appointment would solve this dilemma. Furthermore, a British commander would muffle Australian outbursts about the lack of British support.[95]

Although Churchill took a firm line with Portal, Pound, and Dill on the selection of Wavell, the Americans' choice must have surprised him. Churchill personally had a strained relationship with the reserved, intellectual Wavell and had a rocky relationship with Wavell when he was the Commander in Chief, Middle East. They just rubbed each other wrong. Wavell, although very competent, was too quiet and had treated several of Churchill's meddling military recommendations with little patience and courtesy. In August 1940, when the British evacuated Somaliland, Churchill dispatched a snide cable arguing that the small number of British casualties sustained in the withdrawal was grounds for a board of inquiry. Wavell responded with an equally tactless cable saying "a big butcher's bill was not necessarily evidence of good tactics." Dill told Wavell that "this telegram and especially the last sentence roused Winston to greater anger than he had ever seen him in before." In the first months of 1941 the situation in Cyrenaica deteriorated due to the arrival of German forces to support the faltering Italians. A frustrated Churchill blamed Wavell. "I do not understand his intellect. It may be my own fault, but I always feel as if in the presence of the chairman of a golf club." In June, Churchill had moved Wavell out of the Middle East and sent him to India, and a forced obscurity, contemptuously commenting that Wavell would enjoy "sitting under a pagoda tree." It was, therefore, quite unexpected that six months later the Americans would advocate for Wavell to command the new theater.[96]

Wavell, on notification was also surprised. He described the new assignment as "a pretty tall order. I accepted it of course, merely writing to Jack Dill that I had been handed not just a baby but quadruplets." To Churchill Wavell simply said, "I will of course, as you know, undertake to the best of my ability any task which you consider can further war effort."[97]

That evening Churchill drafted two telegrams to the Lord Privy Seal, Clement Attlee. The first, sent the following morning, informed Attlee about unified command. "Last night President urged upon me appointment of a single officer to command Army, Navy and Air Force of Britain, America, and Dutch, and this morning General

Marshall visited me at my request and pleaded case with great conviction . . . it is certain that a new far-reaching arrangement will have to be made. The man the President has in mind is Wavell. Marshall has evidently gone far into detailed scheme and has draft letter of instructions. So far I have been critical of plan, and while admiring broadmindedness of offer have expressed anxiety about effects on American opinion."[98]

Churchill accepted that events were moving quickly in Washington and the Far East and that he had to decide on unified command. His second cable, presented to Hopkins for review before transmission, informed Attlee that he accepted the American proposal for unity of command.[99]

This was an unprecedented accommodation by Churchill that demonstrated his commitment to the alliance and his desire to build a relationship with Roosevelt. Never before had one British service subordinated itself to another. Although in this case the ABDA Area (American-British-Dutch-Australian) was commanded by a British general, he was astute enough to realize that in the future this would not be the case. If this concept worked, potentially Churchill would have agreed to give up self-autonomy of his land, sea, and air forces to the commander of another nation. As the United States contributed more men and equipment to the alliance, they would want a theater commander of their own choosing. Churchill's acceptance of unity of command would in the long run diminish Britain's influence and position within the alliance vis-à-vis the United States.[100]

Churchill and Roosevelt had maintained an extraordinary pace throughout the Arcadia Conference. Men half their age would have been hard-pressed to keep up with them. Besides the military discussions on the twenty-seventh, they conducted five separate meetings that day and also spent five hours personally authoring what came to be the Declaration of the United Nations. They met in the Red Room of the White House with delegations from China, the Soviet Union, the British Dominions, Chiefs of Missions to South American Republics, and with the Chiefs of Missions of all nations at war with the Axis powers. Churchill and Roosevelt told them of the draft resolution articulating the democratic principles the Allies were fighting to guarantee. All Allied nations would be invited to sign the document to demonstrate their resolve to defeating the Axis powers.[101]

The stress on both was immense. Accomplishments shone—Churchill had secured American support for the Germany First strategy; Roosevelt realized the potential of American industrial mobilization; each tentatively approved the unity of command concept; and allied support was growing for the Declaration of the United Nations. It exacted a toll. Churchill summoned his personal physician, Charles Wilson (Lord Moran), and anxiously explained, "It was hot last night and I got up to open a window. It was very stiff. Had to use considerable force and I noticed all at once that I was short of breath. I had a dull pain over my heart. It went down my left arm. It didn't last very long." Wilson knew the symptoms of a heart attack, but he also knew that there was much more to be accomplished during the next few weeks and kept his worries to himself.[102]

Figure 1. President Roosevelt signing the Lend-Lease Bill (US Army Heritage and Education Center Photograph).

Figure 2. Atlantic Charter Conference, 10–12 August 1941. *Left to Right* (*standing*): General George C. Marshall (*leaning over talking to FDR*), Admiral Ernest J. King, and Admiral Harold R. Stark. *Sitting*: President Franklin D. Roosevelt and Prime Minister Winston Churchill (Naval History and Heritage Command Photograph, NH 67211).

Figure 3. Burning and damaged ships at Pearl Harbor, result of Japanese attack on 7 December 1941. *Left to Right* as shown, USS *West Virginia*, USS *Tennessee*, and USS *Arizona* (Army Heritage and Education Center Photograph).

Figure 4. Secretary of the Navy Frank Knox at his desk in the Navy Department, Washington, DC (Naval History and Heritage Command Photograph, 80-G-399009).

Figure 5. Secretary of War Henry L. Stimson (Army Heritage and Education Center Photograph).

Figure 6. General George C. Marshall, Army Chief of Staff (Army Heritage and Education Center Photograph).

Figure 7. Lieutenant General Henry "Hap" Arnold, chief of the Army Air Forces, at War Department Munitions Building (Army Heritage and Education Center Photograph).

Figure 8. Admiral Harold R. Stark, Chief of Naval Operations Portrait Photograph (Naval History and Heritage Command Photograph, NH 49967).

Figure 9. Admiral Ernest J. King, Commander in Chief, United States Fleet (Naval History and Heritage Command Photograph, 80-G-K-1624).

Figure 10. Secretary of the Navy Frank Knox with Admiral Harold R. Stark (Naval History and Heritage Command Photograph, NH 70490).

Figure 11. General George C. Marshall in conference with Secretary of War Henry L. Stimson, January 1942 (Courtesy of the George C. Marshall Foundation, Lexington, Virginia).

Figure 12. General George C. Marshall and Admiral of the Fleet Sir Dudley Pound, Royal Navy (Courtesy of the George C. Marshall Foundation, Lexington, Virginia).

Figure 13. General George C. Marshall with Field Marshal Sir John Dill, Chief of the British Joint Staff Mission (Courtesy of the George C. Marshall Foundation, Lexington, Virginia).

Figure 14. Air Chief Marshal Sir Charles Portal, Royal Air Force (Imperial War Museum Photograph).

Figure 15. Harry Hopkins confers with General George C. Marshall and Admiral Ernest J. King (Courtesy of the George C. Marshall Foundation, Lexington, Virginia).

Figure 16. Admiral Ernest J. King and General George C. Marshall in discussion (Courtesy of the George C. Marshall Foundation, Lexington, Virginia).

Figure 17. Arcadia Conference, British American Army and Naval Chiefs at informal luncheon, January 1942. *Left to Right*: General George C. Marshall, US Army; Admiral of the Fleet Sir Dudley Pound, Royal Navy; Admiral Harold R. Stark, US Navy; Field Marshal Sir John Dill, British Army; and Admiral Ernest J. King, US Navy (Courtesy of the George C. Marshall Foundation, Lexington, Virginia).

Figure 18. Admiral Harold R. Stark hosts luncheon during Arcadia Conference. *Left to Right*: Admiral of the Fleet Dudley Pound, Royal Navy; Admiral Harold R. Stark, US Navy; Field Marshal John Dill, British Army; Admiral Ernest J. King, US Navy; Air Chief Marshal Sir Charles Portal, Royal Air Force (Naval History and Heritage Command, NH 120087).

Figure 19. James A. Ernst sketch of the Arcadia Conference. *Left side of table*: Rear Admiral Richmond Kelly Turner, US Navy; Major General Thomas Holcomb, US Marine Corps; Rear Admiral John H. Towers, US Navy; Major William T. Sexton, US Army; Rear Admiral Frederick J. Horne, US Navy; Admral Ernest J. King, US Navy; Admiral Harold R. Stark, US Navy; General George C. Marshall, US Army; Lieutenant General Henry H. Arnold, US Army; Brigadier General Leonard T. Gerow, US Army; Lieutenant Colonel Paul Robinett, US Army; Captain John L. McCrea, US Navy. *Right side of table*: Lieutenant General Colville B. Wemyss, British Army; Air Marshal Arthur T. Harris, Royal Air Force; Air Chief Marshal Sir Charles Portal, Royal Air Force; Field Marshal Sir John Dill, British Army; Admiral of the Fleet Sir Dudley Pound, Royal Navy; Brigadier Vivian Dykes, British Army; Admiral Charles Little, Royal Navy (Courtesy of the George C. Marshall Foundation, Lexington, Virginia).

Figure 20. Admiral Richmond Kelly Turner, US Navy (Naval History and Heritage Command, 38-MCN-537–1).

Figure 21. British Staff Mission in Washington, DC. *Left to Right*: Commander R. D. Coleridge, Royal Navy; Rear Admiral W. R. Patterson, Royal Navy; Brigadier Vivian Dykes, British Army (Courtesy of the George C. Marshall Foundation, Lexington, Virginia).

Figure 22. General Dwight D. Eisenhower, US Army (Army Heritage and Education Center Photograph).

Figure 23. Major General Joseph Stilwell, US Army (Army Heritage and Education Center Photograph).

Figure 24. Lieutenant General Hugh Drum, US Army (Army Heritage and Education Center Photograph).

Figure 25. Joint Chiefs of Staff at a luncheon meeting, circa 1943. Present are (*from left to right*): General Henry H. Arnold, Commanding General US Army Air Forces; Admiral William D. Leahy, Chief of Staff to the Commander in Chief; Admiral Ernest J. King, Chief of Naval Operations and Commander in Chief, US Fleet; and General George C. Marshall, Chief of Staff, US Army (Naval History and Heritage Command, 80-G-K-14010).

Figure 26. Meeting of Combined Chiefs of Staff. *Left to right*: Admiral Ernest J. King, US Navy; General George C. Marshall, US Army; Lieutenant General Henry Arnold, US Army Air Force; Brigadier General John R. Deane, US Army; Brigadier V. Dykes, British Army; Brigadier General Albert C. Wedemeyer, US Army; Admiral Dudley Pound, Royal Navy; General Alan Brooke, British Army; Air Marshal Charles Portal, Royal Air Force; and Field Marshal Sir John Dill, British Army, later in 1942 (Courtesy of the George C. Marshall Foundation, Lexington, Virginia).

4

Unity of Command and the Chiefs Coalesce

28 December

Roosevelt's situation report on 28 December raised more questions than it answered. He could not get a clear picture of the fighting in the Philippines. His military update simply stated that there was "no report of any change on the general situation." He seemed to get better information from the press, which continued to describe concentrated air attacks and heavy casualties in Manila. British reporting was no better that morning. In Malaya, the British continued to be pushed back, and the military acknowledged that reports at the front were confusing. In Libya, the British attacked the German defenses at Agedabia and suffered heavy tank losses that they could ill afford. Attacks over the next two days proved costly and futile as stubborn German resistance forced the British to withdraw. Crusader's end marked the end of British momentum in Libya. As Brooke and the Chiefs of Staff Committee in London had anticipated three days earlier, the situation in North Africa did not favor operation Gymnast.[1]

The British and American Chiefs of Staff did not meet on Sunday, 28 December. This was the first break in meetings for the chiefs in Washington. Staff planners, however, enjoyed no such respite because the Joint Planning Committee had not kept pace with the chiefs' vociferous demands for more and more information. The overworked planners reviewed their assignments in a contentious atmosphere that interfered with the committee's productivity. The British were still smarting over Turner's and the Americans' handling of the previous day's session, which ended with three separate papers being returned to the planners for revision. Pound remonstrated to the Americans about reviewing formerly approved papers at the chiefs' meeting the previous day. Brigadier Dykes was especially perturbed that the Americans had issued papers to the chiefs as final drafts before the British planners even had a chance to review them.[2]

In a letter to the chief of the Imperial General Staff in London, Dill poured out British frustrations with the American staff system's slipshod operating fashion. "There are no regular meetings of their Chiefs of Staff, and if they do meet there is no secretariat to record their proceedings. They have no joint planners and executive planning staff.... Then there is the great difficulty of getting stuff over to the President. He just sees the Chiefs at odd times, and again there is no record. . . . At present this country has not—repeat not—the slightest conception of what war means, and their armed forces are more unready than it is possible to imagine." Dill's biting conclusion summed up the problem: "The whole organization belongs in the days of George Washington who was made Commander-in-Chief of all the Forces and just did it. To-day the President is Commander-in-Chief of all the Forces, but it is not so easy to just do it."[3]

Only after four days of meetings did the planners do what they should have done initially; they prepared a draft agenda and set priorities for their work. Regardless, the joint discussions were soon interrupted when the British planners were summoned to a meeting with their chiefs. The British chiefs did not want to discuss the situation in Libya or Malaya. Instead, the most pressing issue that morning was unity of command in the Far East. As soon as they learned that Churchill had approved Marshall's recommendation the British chiefs tasked their planners to review the proposed directive and recommend improvements. Their draft described a supreme commander reporting to an unspecified "appropriate joint body." The British chiefs wanted to know to whom and how the supreme commander reported.[4]

As this was happening, Roosevelt gathered the American chiefs, Hopkins, Stimson, and Knox, to the White House. The president sought an update from his military advisors on the now three-week-old war effort. According to the latest intelligence, which was very ambiguous, American forces in the Philippines were still under strong Japanese pressure, and Manila, despite being declared an open city, suffered four air raids and heavy civilian casualties.[5]

MacArthur's sketchy reports frustrated the president, who demanded specifics on Japanese and American losses. He was hungry for more detailed information. Embarrassed, Marshall confessed that he did not know additional details and was reluctant to pester MacArthur about it in the middle of a battle. Marshall was also unclear about the timetable for the American withdrawal on Luzon, although it was his conviction that MacArthur had slowed the Japanese advance and at present was withdrawing more deliberately than originally anticipated. Put differently, Marshall and Roosevelt were both at the mercy of awaiting MacArthur's next cable, which might or might not clarify matters.[6]

Roosevelt desperately wanted to help. The indiscriminate bombing of Manila and the consequent loss of innocent lives deeply disturbed him. He wondered if the army air force could provide air support to MacArthur. Unfortunately, all the heavy bombers had evacuated Luzon, leaving MacArthur mainly with light observation planes. He was buoyed by Arnold's assurance that eighteen B-17s would depart for the Islands the next day.[7]

Roosevelt was also mulling over sending a military mission in China to assist Chiang Kai-shek to plan and coordinate operations. He believed that the presence of a senior US military advisor would enhance Chiang's prestige and encourage the Chinese to take the offensive against the occupying Japanese forces. A Chinese attack would tie down Japanese forces, thus denying their use elsewhere in the Pacific. Marshall too thought it a good idea.[8]

The president then informed the gathering that Churchill had agreed in principle to unity of command in the Far East, had prepared a cable to send to London requesting Privy Council approval, and had graciously asked the Americans to review it before transmission.

The prime minister's cable endorsed unity of command in the South West Pacific even though the theater's boundaries were not yet fixed, but were generally considered to include Malaya, Burma, the Philippines, and Australia. Wavell would be the supreme commander and relocate his headquarters from Singapore to Surabaya, Dutch East Indies. However, Churchill remained leery of a unified command. His carefully worded cable placed the British and Dutch naval forces under an American admiral's command with the caveat that the British naval commander would be "directed to conform with the plans and policies of the supreme commander."[9]

Roosevelt requested an opinion on the draft from Marshall, who immediately saw the loophole in the language that implied the British Navy was cooperating with, not under the command of, the supreme commander. Marshall strongly urged it be rewritten to read that the British Navy "will operate under the direction of the supreme commander," to insure there was no misunderstanding about the authority of a single commander. Roosevelt directed that Marshall, King, and Hopkins redraft the telegram to that effect. King's selection again indicated the president's growing trust in the admiral as his principal naval advisor. The three quickly altered the wording to read, "That the American, British, Dutch and Australian naval forces in theater should be placed under the command of an American Admiral." This revision united the four allied navies under one admiral who reported to General Wavell.[10]

Churchill's cable also declared that: "The British will assume responsibility for the security of the Atlantic Ocean in the existing close collaboration with the United States naval forces there assigned." This was clearly an attempt by the prime minister to gain a concession for acquiescing to unity of command in the Far East. He had gotten a British commander in the Far East and now wanted to divide the global war into spheres of interest, one of his original goals. Such a policy would allow Britain to continue to dictate strategy in the war against Germany bolstered by unlimited access to American resources. But Churchill and Roosevelt had not discussed any quid pro quo that would allow the British to run the war in the Atlantic in exchange for their acquiescence that the Americans would run the war in the Pacific. Furthermore, the American side had made no such commitments in exchange for British acceptance of the unity of command principle. Churchill simply overreached, hoping to maintain central control of the war against Germany and to preserve the Empire. Marshall, King, and Hopkins unanimously agreed to strike the sentence.[11]

Roosevelt then showed the revisions to Churchill, who was waiting in a nearby room. The prime minister quickly accepted, a major concession because it not only deleted his proviso for dividing the war into spheres of interest but also established a precedent that might in the future require the sacrifice of British autonomy over their air, sea, and land forces to another nation. Considering that the Royal Navy had never allowed itself to be placed under command of another British service, much less a commander from another country, it signaled the depth of his commitment to an Anglo-American alliance.[12]

One matter remained unresolved. Who would Wavell as supreme commander report to? According to Churchill's ambiguous cable, "He would receive his orders from the appropriate joint body, who will be responsible to me as Minister of Defense and to the President of the United States, who is also Commander-in-Chief of all United States Forces." Churchill had directed his chiefs to study who or what constituted the "appropriate joint body" and recommend its composition and organization as an agenda item for tomorrow's chiefs' meeting.[13]

With Marshall and King absent revising the draft cable, Roosevelt expressed his unhappiness with the navy's performance in the opening weeks of the war. Stimson described it as "spanking" naval officers about their lack of initiative in the Pacific. He complained about Admiral Hart's lack of cooperation with the Dutch and Hart's insistence that his orders precluded him from participating in joint action with them. Roosevelt was irked by his South West Pacific naval commander's attitude at the moment he was working to establish unity of command in the theater.[14]

The president next turned on Stark about the navy's failure to reinforce Wake Island. Breaking a week-long silence, Roosevelt now wanted the rationale for turning the reinforcing task force around and returning it to Pearl Harbor. He remarked that recent naval operations had "used a lot of oil and had accomplished nothing."[15]

Roosevelt wanted a victory in the Pacific and implored the navy to take the initiative. After all, the Japanese navy was scattered all over the vast ocean, and that dispersion opened the way for the US Navy to exploit local superiority and attack overextended and outnumbered Japanese fleet units. He insisted the navy could conduct minor offensives against the Japanese under advantageous conditions.[16]

Implicit in the president's remarks was his loss of confidence in Stark. Stimson was certain the rebuke had nothing to do with King, whose energy, decisiveness, and forceful support of unity of command in the Far East had impressed Roosevelt.[17]

When Marshall and King returned to the meeting, Roosevelt shifted the discussion to the Atlantic. He intended to make a public announcement that week about US troops deploying to the British Isles. Could Marshall guarantee that a small contingent of US forces (the number was incidental) be aboard convoys scheduled for departure to England? Even a tiny force could provide an outsized boost for home-front morale in both nations. Marshall promptly replied that it would be done.[18]

Marshall's stock continued to rise with the president, who was impressed by his unity of command arguments and ability to sway opponents to his position. But what about North Africa? An opposed landing near Casablanca worried Roosevelt, who was far more skeptical than Churchill about French willingness to invite the Allies into French Morocco. Marshall reassured the president that planners were carefully scrutinizing the North Africa campaign and agreed that armed resistance was a distinct possibility, endangering the operation. The general forcefully reiterated that the US Army had to win its first battle against the Germans because a defeat would devastate American home-front morale.[19]

This sort of frank appraisal and measured response had, in the early days of the conference, also earned Marshall the respect of the British chiefs. Dill wrote to Brooke: "Marshall improves greatly on further acquaintance. His difficulties are immense, but he is straight, clear headed and undoubtedly dominates the conferences on the American side."[20]

Churchill had been at the White House for almost a week when he decided to go to Canada for a few days to address the Canadian House of Commons as a way to thank Canadians publicly for their sacrifices and loyal support that provided troops, material, food, and funding for the Empire's war effort. (His departure gave Roosevelt a much-needed respite from constant late night sessions with the prime minister.)[21]

Before departing, Churchill again met with Roosevelt and Hull over the unresolved question of French occupation of the Saint Pierre and Miquelon islands. The British and Anglo-Canadians were content that the Free French had seized the islands and shut down its wireless station, but Hull, determined to preserve good relations with the Vichy government, insisted the occupiers withdraw immediately from the islands. Churchill objected, and during a spirited give-and-take told Hull that he would not jeopardize his relationship with the Free French by making General Charles de Gaulle (who had refused to accept his government's armistice with Germany, encouraged the nation to resist occupation, and led the government in exile and Free French military forces against the Nazis) withdraw. Roosevelt mediated the argument, but Hull was not placated and the issue festered in the State Department. Although Churchill later dismissed it as a trifling affair that never interfered with the main Arcadia agenda, the subject would remain a distraction by cropping up periodically in the next few days.[22]

Churchill sent a note to De Gaulle advising him of the diplomatic contretemps caused by his unilateral actions. "I pleaded your case strongly to our friends in the United States. You have broken away from agreement about Miquelon and St Pierre and raised a storm which might have been serious had I not been on the spot to speak to the President. Undoubtedly, result of your activities there has been to make things more difficult with United States, and has, in fact, prevented some favorable developments which were occurring."[23]

Churchill left Washington on an overnight train bound for Ottawa. Riding by car from the White House to nearby Union Station, he again complained to Lord Moran about shortness of breath. Both worried that the symptoms indicated another heart attack, but Churchill insisted on maintaining his frenetic pace. On the train to Ottawa, he drafted his speech to the Canadian parliament, reviewed the edited telegram from Marshall, finalized it with a few minor changes, and prepared cables to the prime ministers of New Zealand and Australia informing them of the decision for a unified command in the South West Pacific.[24]

29 December

Roosevelt's situation report on 29 December again did not provide him much insight into conditions on Luzon. He was already frustrated by the lack of information, and that morning's update did not help, stating, "no substantial change in the last twenty-four hours." The president was desperate for information, and the little he gleaned that morning was depressing. The press reported that in Manila the civilian population was cleaning up after the severe bombing by the Japanese. As noted, MacArthur had declared Manila an open city to spare its inhabitants, but the Japanese had bombed it anyway. In Malaya, the news continued to be bad as British attempts to halt the Japanese along the Perak River had failed. The Japanese had forced a crossing and were continuing to drive toward Singapore.[25]

The Joint Planning Committee met early on 29 December in a much improved working environment. Marshall and Stark had obviously discussed the previous day's lack of synchronization with their respective planners and made clear that the planners' ineptitude had caused them great personal embarrassment. During the Joint Planning Committee meeting, the American representatives made a concerted effort to collaborate and coordinate with their counterparts. Even the irascible Turner appeared chastened after two days of American fumbling. "Turner was amenable" Dykes remembered. "The atmosphere was excellent—everyone flat out to cooperate." Planners refined the directive on unity of command in light of Marshall's proposed letter of instruction to General Wavell. The British were impressed by Eisenhower, who authored the draft, and agreed that he "proved himself first-class."[26]

The planners' proposed directive to the ABDA (American-British-Dutch-Australian) commander generated much discussion at the chiefs' afternoon meeting and won grudging admiration from Dykes, who commented, "The final paper does not look too bad at all, though somewhat long and definitive." The major obstacle was the "appropriate joint body" language. Eisenhower originally intended the directive be signed by the supreme commander's home government, that is, the British in the case of South West Pacific. As a consequence Wavell's instruction would originate from the British chiefs. British planners harbored reservations about possible political repercussions if London bore responsibility or blame in case of failure. Better if Washington issued Wavell's orders.[27]

The Australians and the Dutch liaisons in London also had concerns over an "appropriate joint body." Both nations were apprehensive about the Japanese advance into the ABDA Area and demanded input into the decisions that affected strategy and resources in their regions. They naturally insisted that they be represented on the "appropriate joint body" that would decide how their forces would be used. The prime minister's cabinet no sooner received Churchill's cables on unity of command than they too queried him about the composition of this "joint body." The British chiefs counseled Churchill to delay any response until after their afternoon meeting with their American counterparts when they hoped to develop mechanisms for the strategic direction of the war.[28]

At noon Roosevelt met with the Netherlands minister (later ambassador) Alexander Loudon and handed him a copy of Churchill's 28 December cable on unity of command. Loudon in general accepted unity of command in the South West Pacific, even with "joint body" left undefined. The Dutch government, however, later insisted on representation on any "joint body." The president was concerned with responding to the requests for participation by the Dutch, New Zealanders, and Australians. He accepted that each nation providing forces to the coalition wanted a vote on how and where they were used. At the same time he understood that the larger the coordinating body the greater the bureaucratic friction and delays in consultation, which in turn would diminish its efficiency and give the Axis powers time to adjust their operations.[29]

Roosevelt vigorously supported the unity of command concept, but he also wanted to know how his military leaders felt about it. The army had taken the lead on the subject to date, and the president wanted to insure the navy was also fully behind unified command. Since King had been the only navy supporter of the concept, Roosevelt sounded out King over lunch to determine his position and the other admirals' perspectives on the specifics for the organization, especially the "appropriate joint body," which troubled the president. There were no minutes of this lunch meeting, but based on subsequent events, King, caught off guard, recommended a solution to the president's dilemma. King suggested creating a new body, the Southwestern Pacific Council, from the existing military organizations in Washington. This council would be made up of one representative from the American Joint Board, the British Joint Staff Mission, the Dutch military representatives in Washington, and include an Anzac representative. This council would make strategic recommendations to Roosevelt and a British deputy appointed by Churchill. Although this approach created another bureaucratic layer, it satisfied the president's desire to include the Dutch, Australia, and New Zealand in the decision-making process. As important as King's insight was, the significance was Roosevelt now looked to King, and not Stark, for advice on matters of strategic concern to the US Navy.[30]

By instructing King that he expected the admiral to report back from the afternoon meeting with a commitment by both sides to unity of command in the Pacific, Roosevelt in effect designated King his emissary to deliver an ultimatum to the assembled chiefs—endorse unity of command without further debate.[31]

Meanwhile, Stimson and Marshall, unaware of the presidential maneuvering, prepared to argue the case of a joint body at an afternoon meeting with the British chiefs. Stimson gave Marshall full credit. "We have made a good start on it, due largely—almost wholly—to Marshall's initiative and vigor, and we feel that if we could carry this through and get this as an example in the Far East, why, it will save a year of disaster which has attended the Allies in the last war arising out to disunity."[32]

At the president's request, Hopkins met with Stimson and Marshall to ensure all agreed on the outstanding issues before the chiefs' session. Topping their list was the composition and organization of the "appropriate joint body" that the supreme commander in the South West Pacific would be responsible to. Roosevelt and Hopkins sought a theater command based on mutual understanding and cooperation. But obstacles remained, notably Churchill's previous notification to Roosevelt of his cabinet's unease over who the supreme commander would report to. Questions also hovered around the participants. What means existed for other allies like Australia and New Zealand to provide their input to this "joint body"? Relations between Australia and Britain, already deteriorating, were not improved when the British emphasized Germany as the primary threat as Japanese naval and air forces directly threatened Australia's northern shores. Churchill's refusal to release regular Australian troops previously committed by Prime Minister John Curtin to British command in the Middle East convinced many in Australia that Churchill did not take the imminent danger to their homeland seriously. Hopkins and Roosevelt sought to avoid throwing gasoline on the fire by implying that Australia had no say on the use of their national military forces in the South West Pacific. Hopkins wanted to allay Curtin's apprehensions, although how to do so was left unsaid. Marshall, ever attuned to Roosevelt's intentions, expected that Australian and New Zealand liaison officers assigned to Washington could convey Canberra's advice and recommendations to the American chiefs and would discuss their participation separately with the British that afternoon.[33]

China also worried Roosevelt. He regarded China as an essential partner in the Allied war effort and was loath to offend Chiang Kai-shek by excluding China from the unified supreme command for British, Dutch, American, and Australian forces in the South West Pacific theater. The president proposed to explain to Chiang the reasoning behind a unified command and its geographic boundaries. Any explanation of the division of zones of command in East Asia, however, was complicated by the strategic importance of Burma, a British colony and the British buffer zone for the defense of India, the Empire's paramount colony. But the Burma Road, running through northern Burma into southern China, was the major outside logistic lifeline to Chiang's regime. Resolving these strategic, political, and logistical complexities was exacerbated by British and Chinese personalities.[34]

On 22 December, the day Churchill and his chiefs arrived in Washington, Wavell met with Chiang Kai-shek in Chungking. Neither man impressed the other. Wavell said Chiang "was not a particularly impressive figure at first sight: he speaks no English, but makes clucking noises like a friendly hen when greeting one." The Chinese attitude that the meeting was solely about Chinese needs further frustrated Wavell. Chiang believed that "China had carried the whole weight of the war for five years or so and now it was up to the Americans to finish business and be quick about it." Wavell, not empathetic to China's situation, was solely concerned with the defense of Burma and came to ask China to redeploy the airmen of the American Volunteer Group, known as the Flying Tigers, to help him defend the important port of Rangoon. Realizing that this port supplied both Burma and China via the Burma Road, Chiang eventually agreed. He also offered to provide two Chinese armies as well as to defend the area if the British supplied them and demarcated a clear Chinese area of operations. Wavell tactlessly rejected this offer. Wavell worried that the undersupplied Chinese, with a reputation for acquisitiveness, would live off the land (as they did in China) and strip Burma like a swarm of locusts. Politically, Wavell was reluctant to invite a large Chinese force into Burma given China's anti-imperialist proclivity and territorial ambitions in Burma. Furthermore, Wavell anticipated Indian reinforcements and failed to grasp that the Japanese were poised to invade Burma. Wavell later admitted his mistake in dismissing Chiang's offer by agreeing to accept only a single Chinese division. The brusque rejection stung Chiang, who considered China a major military power and himself a world leader entitled to a seat at Allied councils. The generalissimo would not be happy with Wavell's selection as the commander in the South West Pacific.[35]

Nor would the Americans be happy with slights directed at Chiang. To avoid further friction because of the Chinese, Churchill cabled Wavell, "I must enlighten you upon the American view. China bulks as large in the minds of many of them as Great Britain. . . . The American Chiefs of Staff insisted on Burma being in your command for the sole reason that they considered your giving your left hand to China and the opening of the Burma Road indispensable to world victory. . . . If I can epitomize in one word the lesson I learned in the USA, it was 'China.'"[36]

Roosevelt thought a similar command of united powers in China would appeal to Chiang's ego. Stimson and Hopkins suggested a new China theater might also include Thailand and Indochina. The larger the area, they reasoned, the more important Chiang would feel and more highly regarded by the Allies. The Chinese generalissimo would naturally be the supreme commander, and an American, British, and Dutch joint planning staff would assist Chiang, who would command any Allied forces in his theater. Subsequently, Marshall prepared a brief memo for the president to send to Chiang and coordinated it with the Chiefs of Staff later the same day.[37]

Beaverbrook's insights on production goals for 1942 during their 26 December meeting had so impressed Roosevelt that he asked Vice President Wallace to preside at a special session that afternoon at the capitol to allow the British minister of supply to address influential American industrialists. In effect it gave Beaverbrook a platform to exhort US manufacturers to think big and expand wartime production goals, a public exposition of his previous confidential remarks to the president. Churchill wanted Beaverbrook to convince the Americans to increase their production of military arms and equipment and to assist in their distribution. He expected that Beaverbrook could influence events to guarantee the flow of more war materiel to Britain.[38]

Beaverbrook had successfully shaken the British aircraft industry out of its peacetime doldrums and as minister of aircraft production had worked wonders during the Battle of Britain by dramatically increasing the production of warplanes. He was, though, a notoriously difficult personality who made many lasting enemies while refitting the aircraft industry. He had worked the labor force long hours, seven days a week and alienated the Ministry of Labour in Britain. As one observer noted, "Beaverbrook's ruthless, cut-throat, steam-roller approach to every problem made him feared as well as respected." He enjoyed Churchill's utmost confidence and protection while he ran roughshod over anyone who opposed him.[39]

But even Churchill could not rectify Beaverbrook's notoriously unorthodox managerial abilities. Beaverbrook's capricious and erratic personality plus an aversion to detailed planning offset his boundless energy. When he did not get his way he petulantly offered to resign, something he did six times as minister of aircraft production. Churchill always brought him back. A contemporary remarked that Churchill's "faith in Beaverbrook is lamentable. The latter thinks only of the sensational and dramatic: for instance, he did produce a lot of tanks but only at the expense of their own spare-parts, and the result was that most of our tanks in Libya went out of action." But the sensational and the dramatic were what appealed to Churchill, who told a cabinet member that "Max is a magician—positively a magician." To which the minister replied, "You're quite right Prime Minister. I was always taught when I was young that magic is nine-tenths illusion."[40]

Churchill admitted that Beaverbrook was troublesome and "just did not begin to understand how to get on with the military." Likewise, the military had a mixed view of him. The Royal Air Force, which benefited most from his efforts, admired him, but the army resented his prioritizing the nation's limited resources into aircraft at the expense of tank and artillery production. On the American stage he became a polished diplomat, objectively and dispassionately identifying the challenges and potential production shortfalls to industrial mobilization. While his audience sometimes found his remarks painful, the Americans universally praised Beaverbrook's honesty and willingness to help. According to Vice President Wallace, "He was a power house with regard to what could be done and what had to be done. From a practical point of view I would remember him as having much more of an influence on Don Nelson [director of priorities in the United States Office of Production Management] and myself than Churchill. Some people did not like the Beaver but he stands out in my mind more than anyone else at this particular moment."[41]

As seen earlier, Beaverbrook did have an excellent grasp on the industrial potential of the United States. If the Americans shortchanged that potential and did not increase their 1942 production goals, then the United States and the Allies would be in grave danger. He relied on the same three weapons systems he discussed earlier with Roosevelt—tanks, antiaircraft guns, and antitank guns—to make his point. As of 1 October, he observed, the United States had about 630 tanks and Great Britain had more than 5,000. Admittedly, some of the disparity resulted from American Lend-Lease generosity, but even so Axis's industrial production far outstripped these numbers. Hitler's Russian campaign deployed 30,000 tanks! These were the production figure that the Allies had to match to win the war. US industrial mobilization was virtually starting from scratch in military production and neither included a reserve to replace battlefield losses nor spare parts to fix mechanical failures. True, estimated American tank production for 1942 was 30,000 vehicles, remarkable enough given the conversion from a peacetime economy, but still too low. Beaverbrook thought America could, and should, produce 45,000 tanks during 1942.[42]

Beaverbrook shifted to antitank gun requirements in 1942. Again using the 1 October 1941 baseline, he pointed out Britain had three times as many antitank guns as the United States. In 1942, Britain needed 15,000 antitank guns, most of which they hoped would be produced by the Americans. The Soviet Union and China also needed antitank guns. The current American plan was to produce a paltry 7,000 antitank guns in 1942. Canada alone would produce half that number. With its far larger industrial capacity, he insisted that the United States could easily produce fifteen times as many tanks, antitank, and antiaircraft guns as Canada. A more realistic goal for antitank production in 1942 was 36,000 guns.[43]

Beaverbrook's Canadian figures relied more on guesswork than substantive analysis, but they made his point to Hopkins that while the United States had raised its production sights "immensely," they were still "not nearly high enough." Victory depended on more tanks and aircraft. He used France as an example and said it fell because the Allies lacked tanks and planes. He told Hopkins directly that "America cannot stand on the programmes of 1942."[44]

Late that afternoon the chiefs met for the fifth time. Turner updated conferees on the progress of the Joint Planning Committee's work. One report in final draft assigned priority to Iceland and Northern Ireland for potential employment of American and British troops in the Atlantic area. The planners next listed in order of importance potential areas to occupy worldwide, assuming the respective governments would request Allied forces, and recommended a division of labor among Allies. Subject to the agreement and invitation of national governments, American troops would occupy the Curaçao and Aruba islands, French West Africa, and northeast Brazil. The British would occupy the Azores the Canary Islands and Diego Suarez in Madagascar. Anglo-American troops would occupy French North Africa. Due to the shipping shortage, the requirements for the French North Africa operation would delay all the other Atlantic deployments for at least three months. The chiefs approved the draft while recognizing that Churchill would not like it.[45]

Participants postponed discussions related to Allied strategy, Northwest Africa, and support for the South West Pacific theater to move to the understood purpose of the meeting, defining the "appropriate joint body" to direct the new command in Asia. Pound related that Churchill had notified his cabinet of his approval of unity of command in the South West Pacific, but had deferred responding to London's questions about the structure and composition of the headquarters, pending the chiefs' discussion. Pound emphasized the need to determine the nature of this organization as soon as possible.[46]

This became one of the bedrock discussions of the war. It laid the foundation for the centralized headquarters arrangements that would run the Allies' global war effort. Somewhat surprisingly, the usually reticent Pound proposed an organizational structure. The British position envisaged the organization's primary role was to decide the distribution of resources and determine necessary policy changes and revisions to the supreme commanders' guidance. As Pound explained it, unity of command would allow a theater supreme commander to coordinate limited resources and quickly respond to urgent requirements. Conversely, a new headquarters, expanded to include Dutch, Australian, and New Zealand representatives, would be a cumbersome, unwieldy, and slow decision-making because all members would have to consult their home governments before acting. Time lost in consultation would undercut rapid response and defeat the purpose of a unified command.[47]

Pound emphasized a bilateral structure where the current Anglo-American chiefs should direct the supreme commander in the South West Pacific. Pound outlined the process: The supreme commander would cable his requests to the Chiefs of Staff in both capitals. The British chiefs from London would notify the British Mission in Washington of their opinions. The American chiefs would then meet with the British Mission representatives in Washington to prepare recommendations for the president and prime minister's decision. The British government would coordinate with the Dutch, Australian, and New Zealand government representatives in London thereby ensuring that these other allies had a voice in strategic deliberations affecting their nations. Upon agreement, Washington would dispatch orders to the supreme commander. Innovative in design and elegant in simplicity, Pound's recommendation maintained the core British desire that Washington and not London issue directives to this new command, that is, Washington would control the war against Japan. Central control of the war against Germany was a subject for another day, indicating that the notion of spheres of influence still had life.[48]

Even before the chiefs discussed Pound's proposal, King interjected an alternative. He revealed that over lunch with the president he had discussed the "appropriate joint body." None of the attendees was more surprised than the US Navy's representatives since King had not bothered to tell this to anyone, not even his own service. Out of the blue he recommended a new Southwestern Pacific Council as a military body made up of one representative from the American Joint Board, the British Joint Staff Mission, the Dutch military liaison in Washington, and a single representative for Australia and

New Zealand (Anzac). This new council would recommend actions to the president and a Churchill-appointed deputy in Washington. This recommendation made no sense to Marshall, who feared that the British and American participants were widely divided on the nature of the "appropriate joint body." In a stalling tactic to maintain momentum on the unity of command concept, he recommended that decision be deferred on this topic.[49]

Following Roosevelt's instructions to obtain an immediate resolution, King dismissed any delay, arguing that a command apparatus was essential for unity of command, and the sooner the Allies agreed on it the sooner the South West Pacific Area would become operational. Given King's insistence, Marshall said he would accept Pound's proposal because it was streamlined and easier to implement. He did not want another council, committee, or layer of command interposed between the theater commander and higher decision makers because that would only inhibit expeditious decisions. He likewise opposed any organization that cut the chiefs out of the decision-making process. King accepted Marshall's rationale and agreed to support Pound's concept; Stark then concurred and the chiefs added their endorsement. Stark forwarded the recommendation to the president for his approval and the British Chiefs of Staff cabled Churchill in Ottawa and the War Cabinet in London for approval.[50]

Marshall then introduced the sensitive subject of Chiang Kai-shek. Roosevelt wanted to notify Chiang in advance of the new South West Pacific Command before Chiang learned about it in the newspaper. Chiang was already upset with Wavell over his rejection of Chinese troops to defend Burma and was further angered over another misunderstanding that recently occurred when Wavell commandeered Lend-Lease equipment earmarked for China. No matter Wavell's belief that any aid to China was wasted, he still had to keep the vital port of Rangoon open not only to resupply Chiang but also to sustain his own forces. To do so, he unilaterally seized Lend-Lease ammunition and material scheduled for China to defend Rangoon. The generalissimo was naturally upset and sent a formal written protest to Roosevelt denouncing Wavell's arbitrary action. Roosevelt understandably did not want to ruffle the generalissimo's feathers any further and worked with Hopkins and Stimson on a cable to sooth Chiang's bruised ego.[51]

Roosevelt insisted that China be treated as an equal Allied partner in the war against Japan, beyond cosmetic gestures, and insisted that notifying Chiang about the impending new command was an important means of reassuring the generalissimo that the Allied powers valued his military expertise and China's contributions to the war effort. Participants quickly approved the draft with minor comments, although the chiefs believed that imperial sensitivities about Burma argued against its inclusion in a Chinese theater and decided not to mention Burma's disposition in the cable approving the South West Pacific Command. The meeting adjourned.[52]

That evening Churchill and Roosevelt independently reviewed the chiefs' recommendations for the headquarters controlling the South West Pacific commander. Churchill approved Pound's proposal, but Roosevelt personally rewrote the proposal to emphasize King's plan of a separate committee that included representatives from New Zealand, Australia, and the Netherlands, while incorporating certain of the chiefs' concepts.[53]

Roosevelt wanted a new special body for "consultation and advisory purposes" made up of three American, three British, one Australian, one Dutch, and one New Zealand representatives. He foresaw the supreme commander cabling his proposals to the committee in Washington. The committee in turn would coordinate with London and amalgamate its recommendations or suggestions and submit an agreed-on proposal to the president and prime minister for a decision. If the two leaders agreed, the Washington committee would relay their decision and guidance to the supreme commander. The prime minister could consult with the Dutch, Australian, or New Zealand representatives, as necessary. The president's rewrite was consistent with his earlier discussion with King, at least judging from King's proposal at the fifth chiefs' meeting.[54]

Roosevelt's radical revision aimed to deflect fallout among the Allies over the "appropriate joint body" statement in the unity of command proposal. Hopkins related: "The suggestion of an 'appropriate joint body' has kicked up a hell of a row. . . . It now develops that everybody and his grandmother wants to be on the joint body." Roosevelt's attempt to placate the Allies by giving them a voice on a committee left the chiefs from both Britain and the United States unhappy because it was unwieldy and would only create another bureaucratic layer, which, not incidentally, would limit their access and authority. The chiefs were not finished with the matter.[55]

30 December

Roosevelt's situation report on 30 December finally provided some specificity on the fighting on Luzon. The Japanese had bombed the American fortress of Corregidor at the entrance of Manila Bay. Sixty planes had attacked and four had been shot down. This was the type of detailed information Roosevelt desired. Elsewhere on Luzon, the fighting was heavy but the tactical situation was unchanged. MacArthur and the American and Filipino forces were putting up a credible defense. However, in Malaya the news was different. After crossing the Perak River, the Japanese had quickly captured the town of Ipoh. The British retreat continued and they had yet to find a defensive position to halt the Japanese.[56]

The British chiefs in Washington met that morning to review Roosevelt's proposed organization for the "appropriate joint body" and rejected it immediately. Without mincing words, they declared it "would not be a workable scheme," merely another administrative layer suffocating the decision-making process and lacking the broader perspective that the chiefs' advocated. As a consequence, the first topic of the chiefs sixth conference that afternoon was the president's redraft of command relations in the South West Pacific Area. The British took comfort that the American chiefs were also dissatisfied with the proposal, and both sides sought to find common ground. They unanimously opposed a new organization to deal with the South West Pacific theater now referred to as ABDA (American-British-Dutch-Australian) and agreed that only the American chiefs and their British counterparts, via their representatives in Washington, could appreciate the big picture and weigh ABDA's needs against those of other theaters. London already had mechanisms in place to consult with the Australian, Dutch, and New Zealand governments, and it was wasteful duplication to conduct consultations in Washington and London and would only confuse and delay decisions. Although Australian, Dutch, and New Zealand representatives in Washington might be informed of ongoing developments, if required, the chiefs insisted that official consultation with these other allies occur only in London.[57]

The chiefs also agreed that the supreme commander should cable Washington and London simultaneously; the former for decision, the latter for advice. Churchill approved, but the chiefs understood that Roosevelt's support was critical. They presented a two-part memorandum to the president. Part one was the American chiefs' covering note that synopsized their reasons for opposing a separate Washington Committee and supporting the previously recommended structure. Part two was a revised draft on the direction of the war in the ABDA Area that incorporated a few of Roosevelt's minor suggestions but retained the major tenets of the original proposal. The chiefs were adamant and unanimous that there was no need for a new organization because the most efficient decision-making structure for ABDA already existed with the American Chiefs of Staff and the representatives of the British Chiefs of Staff in Washington. Only this one body was capable of assessing requirements and allocating resources throughout all theaters.[58]

ABDA also dominated the afternoon's conversation. The chiefs refined the ABDA commander's guidance to achieve a definitive outline of his area of responsibility, delineated as including Burma, Malaya, the Dutch East Indies, and the Philippines. The basic strategic guidance was to execute a strategic defensive in the ABDA theater. As reinforcements later became available, the allies would mount limited and eventually large-scale offensive operations against Japan. The Chiefs of Staff assigned the ABDA commander four missions: (1) hold the Malaya barrier as the central defensive feature in the theater; (2) hold Burma and Australia as supporting positions; (3) reestablish communications with the Dutch East Indies and Luzon, Philippines; and (4) maintain communications throughout the area. They agreed on the strategic concept, distribution of forces, and the limitations placed on the supreme commander and then moved on to debate the boundaries of the new ABDA Area. Stark started the boundary discussions by recommending that Indochina and Thailand be excluded from the ABDA command. He said these would be included in a China command under Chiang. The British also had a boundary change for the new ABDA command. Pound and Dill would include Burma, arguing that it had recently been moved from the British Far Eastern Command to the India Command owing to its vital strategic importance to the defense of India. Although they believed the Americans overestimated China's military potential, the British recognized the importance of keeping China's large army in the war against Japan. They were reluctant to include Burma in the new ABDA command, but if the Allies excluded it Chiang might claim Burma for his theater, which the British believed would be even worse because it might fatally endanger India. Both sides quickly accepted these boundary changes.[59]

The American chiefs wanted a directive that required the ABDA governments to designate a deputy commander and a combined naval forces commander. The British chiefs concurred and with these additions and the boundary change the document went to the president and prime minister for final approval. As this session ended, Turner told Dykes that the Americans would send troops to Northern Ireland soon and that planners would meet the next day to formulate a deployment timetable.[60]

Meanwhile, Roosevelt and Stimson assuaged Chiang's bruised pride. Stimson met with the Chinese foreign minister, T. V. Soong, to emphasize US disapproval of Britain's diverting Lend-Lease material intended for China. Stimson related that he had just rejected a British request to cancel a consignment of supplies to China and turn them over to Wavell. He urged Soong to tell Chiang of America's admiration and support for the Chinese leader.[61]

Roosevelt personally notified Chiang through the American embassy in Chungking about his reaction to the British diversion of China's Lend-Lease equipment. "The action taken was contrary to the policy of the Government of the United States which is directed toward furnishing all possible aid to China." He assured Chiang that it would not happen again and praised Chiang for his "statesmanship and unselfish attitude" during the unfortunate affair.[62]

Churchill meantime was juggling multiple issues while in Ottawa. He responded to questions from his war cabinet and the dominions on unity of command, establishment of the ABDA command, and the issue of the "appropriate joint body." He acted as intermediary between the Free French and Secretary Hull over the former's occupation of Saint Pierre and Miquelon islands and addressed recommended changes to the Joint Declaration of the United Nations. During his press conference at Government House in Ottawa a reporter asked, "Do you think Singapore can hold on?" He quickly replied, "I sure do." The Canadian press was also interested if Churchill had received any "peace feelers" from the Axis powers. He replied: "We have had none at all, but then I really think they must be hard pressed for materials of all kinds, and would not want to waste the paper and ink."[63]

Churchill's whirlwind schedule continued with attendance at various parades, meetings, and receptions. He somehow fit in an afternoon address to the Canadian House of Commons with more than two thousand dignitaries in attendance. The prime minister again delivered a tour de force performance, praising the wartime contributions of the Canadian people. "We are most grateful for all you have done in common cause. . . . The contribution of Canada to the Imperial war effort in troops, in ships, in aircraft, in food, and in finance has been magnificent." He told his rapt audience of the forthcoming Joint Declaration of the United Nations. "We have been concerting the united pacts and resolves of more than thirty States and nations to fight on in unity together and fidelity to one another."[64]

Churchill played to the French population of Canada as he denounced the Vichy regime in the harshest terms. "They lay prostrate at the foot of the conqueror. They fawned upon him [Hitler]. What have they got out of it? The fragment of France that is left to them is just as powerless, just as hungry as, and even more miserable, because more divided, than the occupied regions." He praised De Gaulle and the Free French, who "have continued to fight on the side of the allies. They have been condemned to death by the men of Vichy, but their names will be held and are being held in increasing respect by nine Frenchmen out of ten." His concluding remarks brought the house down when he regaled his audience with his warning to France in 1940 that if they surrendered the British would fight on. The French generals retorted, "'in three weeks England will have her neck wrung like a chicken.' Some Chicken: some neck."[65]

Churchill's speech had its desired effect, impressing Canadians, who appreciated his support for the Free French seizure of the wireless station on Saint Pierre and condemnation of the Vichy regime. Cordell Hull's reaction differed. The US secretary of state was disappointed and offended. Hull was still smarting over the Free French occupation of the Saint Pierre and Miquelon islands and had hoped that Churchill would publicly condemn the invasion. Churchill was far too astute a politician to denounce something that was so popular in Canada. Hull continued to sulk about Churchill's lack of support.[66]

31 December

Roosevelt's situation report on 31 December continued the litany of bad news in the Far East. In the Philippines, the Japanese pressure on MacArthur's troops continued. The American and Filipino forces continued their rearguard action and conducted their planned withdrawals toward Bataan. Japanese air attacks again struck Manila, which was still holding out. In Malaya, the Japanese ground advance seemed unstoppable, and Japanese warplanes bombed Singapore.[67]

That morning the American and British chiefs met separately with their respective staffs. For the Americans, the imminent fall of Manila was a major concern. Secretary of War Stimson, who had strong ties to the Philippines, was heartbroken over the destruction and death wrought by the Japanese. In the face of unrelenting Japanese pressure, MacArthur's withdrawal to Bataan and Corregidor seemed to be going well, but Stimson was less certain about Filipino morale. An old friend and close personal colleague, Joaquín Elizalde, the current resident commissioner to the Philippines, visited Stimson that morning. Japanese troops had seized Elizalde's estates, and he had no idea if his family was even alive. He did not come for personal reasons, but to ask Stimson to rescue President Quezon, then on Corregidor, and bring him to the United States. Elizalde believed that Quezon in America could become a rallying point for the Filipino people to resist the Japanese invaders. Stimson agreed wholeheartedly and cabled MacArthur for his thoughts.[68]

Meanwhile, British planners reviewed the US plan to deploy American troops to Northern Ireland. Colonel Frank S. Ross, the chief of the Port and Water Section of the War Department General Staff, explained to the British the timeline of the deployment. Ross was a transportation officer and the army's expert on rail and sea movements. (He would later serve as Eisenhower's chief of transportation in the European theater as a major general.) The initial US Army contingent was already en route by rail from its Louisiana training ground to the port of New York for shipment to Northern Ireland. Ross's knowledge and enthusiasm impressed Dykes and the British, but the shoddy American staff work and still ineffective staff coordination again disappointed the British side. It became apparent during Ross's presentation that the US Army's War Plans Division knew nothing of the move and was surprised and embarrassed by the G-4, Supply and Transportation section's failure to coordinate with them. At least the British were pleased that the move was going smoothly and arrangements were in place for the quick deployment to Northern Ireland and Iceland.[69]

Roosevelt and Admiral King lunched again that day in anticipation of the formal meeting of the British and American Chiefs of Staff. The president expressed concerns over the size of the "appropriate joint body" because he did not want to offend the China, Australia, New Zealand, nor the Dutch by excluding them. King reassured the president: "It was obvious," King later remarked, "that with so many participants in the war, decisions could not be made by a show of hands. Nothing could be accomplished by such means. As the United States and Great Britain were financing the war and doing most of the fighting, they should therefore run the war, make the final decisions, and control the military machine. This is a hard-boiled method bound to cause friction and unhappiness among the smaller nations who thought they should have a voice in military decisions, but it is the only way to function effectively." Roosevelt accepted this explanation and approved the chiefs' proposal for the organization of the "appropriate joint body."[70]

That afternoon the chiefs held their seventh conference. Stark opened the session and requested permission to withdraw 4,500 US Marines then stationed in Iceland for use in the Pacific theater. Dill was very supportive and agreed to notify London as soon as Stark gave him the draft plan. The conferees next agreed on Anglo-American strategy, essentially as the British originally had presented it on 24 December. The only change by the Americans was to the list of air routes that had to be secured by the Allies to maintain lines of communication between the United States and Britain. Air Marshall Harris was instructed to coordinate with General Arnold on the amendments and after careful review submit the paper to the president and prime minister for final approval. The chiefs then examined the Joint Planning Committee's stopgap measures for the South West Pacific, pending the activation of a unified command system. They concurred with planners' proposals and issued the region's Anglo-American theater commanders' interim guidance, pending the establishment of a single supreme commander in the ABDA Area.[71]

The chiefs tasked the Joint Planning Committee with assessing the relative importance and interrelationship among four imminent troop movements: relief of British troops in Iceland, deployment of four American divisions to Northern Ireland, movement of American air force units to England, and the relief of British troops in Curacao and Aruba. They concurrently would analyze three potential projects: (1) the joint American-British occupation of French North Africa; (2) US occupation of French West Africa and Cape Verde Islands, and Northeast Brazil; and (3) British occupation of the Azores, Canaries and Madeira, and Diego Suarez.[72]

The Northwest Africa question slowed the chiefs' progress. A visibly frustrated Turner asked them to reconsider Northwest Africa planning because shipping was still in short supply. Whether or not the French would agree to Allied landings in Northwest Africa was also an open question. Casablanca on Morocco's Atlantic coast was the entryway to French North Africa, but its small port with limited facilities restricted the Allies' ability to disembark large numbers of troops there. In the event the Vichy French opposed a landing, Casablanca's port was inadequate to sustain the invading forces. Turner pronounced the operation unworkable. Pound, Portal, and Dill had to realize, as Brooke and the Chiefs of Staff Committee in London did, that the plan was not advisable. But it was a pet Churchill project and his military delegation loyally continued to press for its study. At an impasse, the chiefs agreed to defer further discussion on North Africa. The British chiefs realized this would not satisfy the prime minister and did not relish another disagreement with him.[73]

During the session, Robinett again found Stark's leadership unimpressive. "Admiral Stark talked a great deal, the British little and General Marshall not at all." Admiral King arrived late from his luncheon with the president, but still observed Stark's typical long-winded rambling and simply cut him off. Robinett commented that "he [King] was quite rude to Admiral Stark and showed his impatience more openly than at any previous meeting. It is increasingly clear that Admiral Stark is on his way out."[74]

The British planners and secretariat similarly regarded King as a "dominating personality." Jacob observed, "He [King] quite overshadows Admiral Stark, many of whose functions he has taken over. At our meetings with the US Chiefs of Staff, Stark, with the title of Chief of Naval Operations, took the Chair. But he would not go a yard without being sure of King's backing. Admiral 'Betty' Stark was christened 'Tugboat Annie' by Dumbie [Dykes], and that about hit him off. He is a little man, with a perky face, and looks as if he should be Captain of Showboat."[75]

King got right to the point: Roosevelt had accepted their revisions for "an appropriate joint body," thereby eliminating any additional bureaucratic layer between the chiefs and the supreme commander. He further thought Roosevelt was receptive to their guidance for the ABDA supreme commander and wanted the chiefs to prepare a public announcement on the unified command arrangements in

ABDA for his consideration. King's pronouncement broke the logjam blocking the adoption of unified command.[76]

After seven meetings spread over eight days, it is fair to say that the chiefs were coalescing as professional colleagues intent on identifying common beneficial ground. True, there still were pitfalls that required constant attention and compromise to overcome. Yet they had agreed on a blueprint for a wartime strategy and an organization to supervise an entirely new concept for a unified theater command in the South West Pacific. They further assigned agreed-on priority for deployments in the Atlantic, and arrangements were underway to move troops to Iceland and Northern Ireland. Neither side got everything it wanted, but both got major concessions.

Compromises, of course, could not completely satisfy everyone. Back in London the chief of the Imperial General Staff, General Brooke, grew increasingly annoyed. His inability to influence the proceedings in Washington frustrated him. ABDA's creation was especially galling because it made no strategic sense to him. Brooke, not privy to the lengthy discussions in Washington, regarded it unwise to separate Burma from its natural supply base in India and assign it to ABDA's newly established headquarters in Java, two thousand miles distant. "The whole scheme [was] wild and half-baked, and only catering for one area of action, namely the Western Pacific, one enemy Japan, and no central control. . . . Cabinet was forced to accept P.M.'s new scheme owing to the fact that it was almost a *fait accompli*."[77]

The united front that the British chiefs constantly presented to the Americans belied the lack of unity by Brooke and the Combined Chiefs of Staff Committee in London, who denounced the proceedings. For their part, British representatives in Washington resented the Monday morning quarterbacking from Brooke and the staff in London. Dykes complained that London pressed them hard to exclude Burma from the ABDA at a time when the British chiefs in Washington (unlike Brooke in London) knew firsthand that Roosevelt's unyielding support of Chiang left them little alternative but to include Burma.[78]

Stimson learned from Chinese Foreign Minister Soong that Roosevelt's cable had gone a long way in mollifying Chiang, who wanted Roosevelt to know that he was still willing to send Chinese troops to Burma and place them under a foreign commander. Soong did not, however, press Chiang's offer or make an issue of Burma. Stimson resurrected the idea of assigning a senior American military advisor to China to advise Chiang. Besides adding gravitas to the newly established China theater, Stimson expected that Chiang would see the officer as a symbol of American recognition of China's dignity. Flattery worked. Soong quickly accepted Stimson's offer.[79]

Afterward, Stimson met with Marshall and recommended sending Lieutenant General Hugh Drum, a very senior officer, to serve as Chiang's advisor. Drum had a distinguished combat record in World War I and was currently serving as the commander of the Eastern Defense Command. He had been a general officer for twenty years. He was smart, ambitious, and a shameless self-promoter. As Marshall's rival for the position of Army Chief of Staff in 1939, Drum had alienated Roosevelt with his unabashed campaign to gain the appointment. (Roosevelt was so irate over this campaigning for the Chief of Staff position that he told the press, "Drum, Drum, I wish he would stop beating his own drum.") Marshall, who had served in China, knew that Drum was unfamiliar with the region and asked Stimson for time to consider who would be the best candidate for this urgent and politically sensitive assignment.[80]

In the midst of all this discussion of grand strategy and personalities, Roosevelt and Churchill still found time to coordinate for a Joint Declaration of the United Nations. The two leaders had spent several days personally revising a document amenable to twenty-six national signatories. Revisions were inevitable. The Soviet ambassador to the United States, for example, reported that Stalin opposed the words "freedom of religion." Roosevelt countered that freedom of religion could also mean freedom from religion. Stalin accepted this loose interpretation, and the phrase remained.[81]

The Soviet premier approved "against those members of the Tripartite Pact and its adherents with which such government is at war," but expressed the reservation that Japan might interpret this as a

Soviet declaration of war on Japan, something Stalin was in no position to do. Roosevelt parsed the words "with which such government is at war" to mean actually engaged in war, which calmed Stalin's concern.[82]

Stalin was not the only one with issues on the wording of the Joint Declaration. Many nations offered word changes. Roosevelt and Churchill also received recommendations from their respective governments. During the last days of December, Roosevelt's views on the declaration grew more rigid than Churchill's as he proved less willing to compromise and assumed more of a role as senior partner.

Churchill displayed extraordinary forbearance throughout the conference. Although his unstated agenda envisaged guiding Roosevelt on wartime strategy, maintaining control of the direction of the war against Germany from London, and preserving the British Empire, in the end he displayed great flexibility. Churchill continually sacrificed and compromised for the sake of an Anglo-American alliance. His concessions in the negotiations on the Joint Declaration were significant. A long-time harsh opponent of the Indian nationalist independence movement, Churchill balked at allowing Indian representatives sign the Arcadia Declaration until after the war. Roosevelt saw Indian troops fighting the Germans, Italians, and Japanese in every major theater and insisted that they be signatories. Churchill ultimately acquiesced. When Attlee and the War Cabinet asked to have the words "social security" included as an allied goal, Roosevelt objected, fearing a fight with the conservatives in Congress. Churchill pigeon-holed Attlee's requests. When Roosevelt insisted that the United States be the first to sign the declaration and the United Kingdom second, Churchill concurred and further agreed when Roosevelt insisted that China be the fourth signatory. Churchill came to Washington to conclude an Anglo-American strategic alliance without which the march to victory would be longer, bloodier, and ultimately leave Britain broken by the tremendous burden. With that motivation, he willingly sacrificed personal desires for the greater goal.[83]

5

Conference Interlude

1 January 1942

During the opening week of the New Year, Allied defeats continued in the Philippines, Malaya, and North Africa. The Japanese juggernaut overrunning Southwest Asia seemed unstoppable, and Churchill's dreams of a decisive victory in Tripolitania were turning into nightmares. Battlefield reverses naturally siphoned some of the chiefs' attention from the conference but, as fate would have it, no formal meetings between the American and British chiefs were scheduled between 1 and 9 January.

Nonetheless, Anglo-American planners continued to refine the myriad details involved in transporting and garrisoning thousands of US troops to Iceland and Northern Ireland. The Joint Planning Committee used the meeting hiatus to research options for Gymnast and consult with the chiefs regarding the assumptions and objectives for the proposed North Africa landing. Churchill had repeatedly voiced his disappointment with their efforts to date, and planners were likewise frustrated by the prime minister's and his civilian advisors' refusal to acknowledge that resources were unavailable to move forces to Northern Ireland, Iceland, and North Africa and simultaneously reinforce the Far East. At least now the Joint Planning Committee had some breathing room to match resources against objectives in a more realistic fashion that could promise success.[1]

Included in the Joint Planning Committee's large and growing backlog of sundry taskings and requests from Roosevelt and Churchill were an examination of the Victory Program and the synchronization of war material production with grand strategy as finalized on 31 December. In the Pacific, more work remained to establish the ABDA command, support China and Australia, and defend the various island bases lying between Hawaii and Australia. The Joint Planning Committee tackled all these issues and many more during the next nine days.[2]

Despite the enormous pressures of tight deadlines and sometimes-outlandish requests, Anglo-American planners established a legacy of unequaled productivity and unrivaled quality regardless of national prerogatives and cultural biases. Of all the dedicated staff officers, none were more anonymous than the planners. As one historian noted, those "overtired workhorses" imbued with "amazing energy" drafted and redrafted hundreds of papers, "produced often at a moment's notice and at late hours, in which their contribution is often unrecognized."[3]

The British planners were all handpicked by the chiefs. They worked harmoniously, being familiar with an integrated staff system, and always displayed a united front to their American counterparts. They were an especially talented group. The Royal Air Force planner was Air Commodore William F. Dickson, later Air Marshal of the Royal Air Force, Chief of the Air Staff, and the first Chief of the Defence Staff. Captain Charles L. Lambe, the navy planner, went on to become Admiral of the Fleet and First Sea Lord. The army planner was Vivian Dykes, a brilliant staff officer who worked exceedingly well with the Americans. Field Marshall Dill had handpicked Dykes to remain as the first secretary of the Combined Chiefs of Staff in Washington. Unfortunately Dykes perished in an airplane crash in 1943 following the Casablanca Conference.

The absence of coordination and integration of plans between US Army and Navy planners frustrated the British throughout the conference. Since 1923 the Chiefs of Staff Committee provided British planners with twenty years of experience to refine and integrate the three service staffs into a cohesive infrastructure that relied on well-tried procedures for reviewing problems and developing a consensus.

The Americans' disjointed approach vexed them because the US Army and Navy planners at Arcadia were not a united, cohesive, and synchronized joint staff. Arcadia succeeded because the respective American staffs were filled with immensely talented officers capable of overcoming a corporate lack of organization. Although anonymous at the time, before the war was over many would become household names. As individuals the American planners were every bit the equal of their British counterparts.[4]

One army planner, then Brigadier General Dwight D. Eisenhower, rose to five stars to become the Supreme Allied Commander of the Allied Expeditionary Force in Europe. Four more became four-star generals. Brigadier General Leonard T. Gerow, the lead army planner, would command a corps and army in Europe. Brigadier General Joseph W. Stilwell commanded US forces in the China-Burma-India theater. Brigadier General Thomas T. Handy went on to command of the postwar US Army European Command, and Lieutenant Colonel Albert C. Wedemeyer would lead US forces in China. Colonel Harold L. George, the air force planner, was ultimately promoted to lieutenant general and commanded the Air Transport Command that airlifted personnel and equipment worldwide throughout the war. The navy planners were equally talented. Rear Admiral Richmond Kelly Turner, the lead navy planner, went on to four stars and commanded several Amphibious Force Commands in major assaults in the Pacific throughout the war. Captain Forrest P. Sherman, another navy planner, went on to four stars and later served as the chief of Naval Operations. Captain Harry W. Hill went on to three stars and commanded an amphibious task force at Luzon and was the first commandant of the National War College. Captain Bertram J. Rodgers also went on to three stars and commanded amphibious groups during the invasions of Iwo Jima and Okinawa.

But that lay in an unknown future. The present seemed consumed by the unrestrained Japanese advance. On New Year's Day, MacArthur retreated toward Bataan and Corregidor and successfully linked his northern Luzon force with his southern Luzon force to deny the Japanese the chance to defeat the divided commands in detail. His decision forced him to leave Manila undefended. American and Filipino (Am-Fil) forces previously had destroyed anything of military value in the city. Moreover, fortifications guarding the entrance to Manila Harbor remained and prevented the Japanese Navy from using its port facilities. Rather than ending the campaign, the capture of Manila proved an ephemeral propaganda coup for Tokyo. The most vicious fighting shifted to the Bataan Peninsula. Japanese ground forces simultaneously advanced rapidly in Malaya, disrupting British attempts to establish a solid defensive line. Air raids on Singapore and the British defenses increased. Stimson's diary entry succinctly captured the grim mood. "This New Year's was not a holiday."[5]

Still the Allies looked to the future. For several days President Roosevelt, Vice President Wallace, and Lord Beaverbrook discussed the future production goals of tanks, planes, and guns during the next two years. Stimson judged current weapons production wanting. His morning staff meeting only added to his frustration when he learned of shortages in antiaircraft guns and ammunition. As disappointing as that was, what really irked him was the amount of US-manufactured military equipment sent to other Allied nations. Most American-made tanks, planes, and guns went to Britain and Russia with some finding their way to China. Stimson's task was to equip the expanding United States Army, and he resented constantly begging the president for US-produced material for American forces. The morning's downbeat reports from the Philippines coupled with his desire to get aid added to Stimson's angst.[6]

Churchill marked his return from Ottawa by attending a religious service with Roosevelt and a small party at Christ Church, in nearby Alexandria, Virginia. After the services, the party made the ten-mile drive to Mount Vernon where Churchill laid a memorial wreath at Washington's tomb and toured the home of America's first president. The two leaders then returned to the White House where they met with the Soviet ambassador to the United States, Maxim Litvinov, to finalize the draft of the joint "Declaration by United Nations." Churchill pushed hard for a minute wording change from "governments" to "governments and authorities" to allow the Free French to sign the declaration. Hull, still miffed with the Free French over their occupation of Saint Pierre and Miquelon, offered tepid support for the last-minute modification, but Roosevelt, ever the peacekeeper, overruled his secretary of state and approved the addition.[7]

Litvinov, however, did not. Stalin had approved "governments" and the Soviet ambassador was unwilling to agree on any change without the Soviet premier's concurrence. Returning the document to Moscow would be time consuming, and Roosevelt and Churchill wanted no delay. The British prime minister insisted Litvinov agree, but the ambassador would not budge. Churchill's temper flared as he told Litvinov that he was not much of an ambassador if he could not change a single word. Unmoved by the outburst, Litvinov answered only to Stalin and rejected any modification. Consequently, the Free French representatives initially did not sign the Declaration by United Nations.[8]

That evening Roosevelt and Churchill met with the American and British Chiefs of Staff to discuss the ABDA command. Churchill read Wavell's cable proposing that he delay assuming command until he could organize his headquarters. Wavell also resurrected ABDA's boundary issue and echoed Brooke and the military advisors in London by advocating Burma's exclusion from ABDA. Roosevelt wanted a boundary acceptable to China, and that meant including Burma. He sought to mollify Chiang not to offend him, because the president's deep-seated conviction that China's continued resistance to the Japanese invasion was essential to the Allied war effort. As he told his son Elliott, "If China goes under, how many divisions of Japanese troops do you think will be freed—to do what? Take Australia, take India. . . . Move straight on to the Middle East."[9] Although histrionic, the remark did reveal the president's forebodings should China collapse.

Churchill disagreed about China's importance. He found the "extraordinary significance in American minds, even at the top, strangely out of proportion." He shared with Roosevelt his feeling that "American opinion overestimated the contribution which China could make to a general war." Roosevelt reacted strongly, reminding the prime minister that there were "five hundred million people in China. What would happen if this enormous population developed in the same way as Japan had done in the last century and got hold of modern weapons?" Roosevelt's arguments did not sway Churchill, but he was savvy enough to acquiesce to the president's opinion.[10]

A lengthy discussion ensued about where to assign Burma. London adamantly opposed assigning it to the ABDA Area. Other options were: place it under the British Indian Command, under Chiang in the China Theater, assign it to the ABDA, or create an independent command. The chiefs ruled out option one for reasons of command and control, and option two, assigning it Chiang, was absolutely unacceptable to the British. Option four would result in three separate commands in Asia, which was, if nothing else, a logistics impossibility. By the process of elimination, the only workable solution was to assign it to the ABDA Area. Churchill and his chiefs in Washington accepted the decision as the least of all evils. The prime minister and the president then approved this course and directed the British staff to notify Wavell of their decision.[11]

East Asia presented another concern for Churchill. London recommended that Australia and New Zealand be geographically incorporated into the ABDA theater. Churchill rejected this because he recognized that national sensitivities would make this expansion extremely difficult if not impossible. Noninclusion, however, left a vacuum in the area between Australia, New Zealand, and the ABDA zone, and Churchill nominated the US Navy to fill it. King initially balked at this. The US Navy was already stretched thin by battle losses and commitments, so Australia and New Zealand should use their own national forces to defend this region. In a rare display of equanimity, Admiral King relented and circumvented the impasse by indicating his willingness to study this question. Marshall then gave the Anglo-American leaders some good news by announcing that before mid-January, the United States would send 14,000 troops to Northern Ireland and 6,000 to Iceland. Staff planners at the conference and throughout the US Army and Navy had overcome all shipping and logistical problems. Both heads of state were ecstatic and told Marshall to proceed at once. The meeting adjourned on that high note.[12]

A few hours later, Roosevelt, Churchill, Litvinov, and Soong met in the president's study and with minimum fanfare signed the Declaration by United Nations. Roosevelt signed first and then complained that he should have signed as commander in chief. Churchill was next and Roosevelt teased him that he should have signed as prime minister of "Great Britain and Ireland." Not to be outdone, Churchill quickly added "Ireland" to his title. Litvinov's signature was followed by Soong's. Churchill then dramatically announced, "Four fifths of the human race were represented on the document." Twenty-two other Allied nations would sign the document over the next two days.[13]

Churchill and Roosevelt agreed on the declaration's importance to the war effort. The document offered a ringing statement of Allied solidarity and framed the war effort in terms of democratic principles. The Allies were fighting to "defend life, liberty, independence, and religious freedom, and to preserve human rights and justice in their own lands as well as others." It promised that each nation would dedicate its full economic and military resources to the war effort. Here was a clear message to the Axis powers that all twenty-six nations were united in the struggle. There would be no separately concluded peace or armistice arrangements until the utter defeat of the Axis. Conversely, an Axis victory entailed defeating all the Allied nations. As Churchill put it, "The Declaration by itself could not win battles, but it set forth who we were and what we were fighting for."[14] Any euphoria was short-lived.

2 January

Stimson arrived at his office early to read the "somber and blue" news from the Philippines. MacArthur's latest cable notified the secretary of Manila's fall. It was especially depressing for Stimson, a former governor-general of the Philippines. He loved the city—for almost half a century the jewel of American power and prestige in Asia—and had many friends there. The Japanese now occupied Manila, and the fate of his associates was unknown.[15]

MacArthur's cables on 1 and 2 January also sobered the secretary. On New Year's Day, MacArthur stressed the isolation of his forces in the Philippines but opposed Stimson's recommendation to evacuate

Philippine Commonwealth President Manuel Quezon, believing that Quezon's departure would cause Filipino morale to collapse. Since the overwhelming number of his troops was Filipino, only 7,000 were American, that would mean disaster. (He did not mention the 12,000 Philippine Scouts who were part of the American Army.) With a characteristic Olympian pronouncement, MacArthur warned, "In view of the Filipinos' effort, the United States must move strongly to their support or withdraw in shame from the Orient."[16]

The same day MacArthur submitted his Far East strategy to Marshall and Stimson. MacArthur insisted that the Philippines were the key to saving Singapore, Australia, and India, not vice versa, as Churchill would have it. It followed that MacArthur should have control of all American and British resources throughout the region. He envisaged a joint air, sea, and land advance via the Dutch East Indies toward Mindanao to relieve his embattled forces. Although it was understandable that MacArthur wanted to save his command, his proposed strategy was as fantastic as Churchill's North African one. Both ignored the absence of personnel, equipment, and logistic support that rendered such grandiose schemes impossible. Still, something had to be done because barring resupply and reinforcements MacArthur only had enough food and ammunition to hold out for three months. Stimson and Marshall discussed both cables, and Stimson sent copies to the president. Marshall and Stimson agonized over the fate of the troops in the Philippines and felt powerless. At most they could try to find a means for the navy to get some relief to the beleaguered troops on Bataan. Marshall also sent a message to MacArthur, expressing his sympathy and informing the Philippine commander that Washington was doing everything possible to assist him. Marshall candidly informed MacArthur of Arcadia's priorities: the strategic focus in the Far East was not the Philippines, but instead on holding the Malay barrier and protecting Australia and Borneo.[17]

Marshall, Eisenhower, and Stimson met that morning with General Hugh Drum to describe Drum's role in the new China theater as the principal military advisor to Chiang Kai-shek. Stimson updated Drum on the tensions between Wavell and Chiang, suggested possible ways to minimize such differences, and informed him of Chiang's recent offer to place two Chinese armies under American control. In a blatant appeal to Drum's ego, the secretary expressed his confidence that a dynamic field commander like Drum would surely lead the Chinese to victory.[18]

Simple seniority accounted for Drum's selection. Marshall found Drum's imperious attitude, self-promotion, and inflated opinion of his military importance off-putting. But Drum was a general and Marshall needed somewhere to assign him. He had discussed Drum's qualifications the previous day with Stilwell, a trusted advisor and old China hand, having been stationed there and conversant with the language. Stilwell knew Chiang personally and he thought Drum was a perfect fit, but for the wrong reasons. "The Generalissimo is a stuffed shirt; let's send him the biggest stuffed shirt we have. . . . Drum will be ponderous and take time through interpreters; he will decide slowly and insist on his dignity; [send] Drum by all means." Stilwell's verdict expressed orthodox army thinking that China was a backwater command of no strategic importance. China remained a problem as the ABDA was activated.[19]

The 2 January "Directive for the Supreme Commander in the ABDA Area" officially notified Wavell to assume command effective that day. He was to take physical charge over the ABDA theater as soon as possible and to notify the Chiefs of Staff of the earliest date that might occur. Churchill and Roosevelt revised the directive's strategic concept before sending it. They sought to dispel a common perception that the Allies had created the command solely for defensive purposes. Better the public believes that ABDA command was seizing the initiative from Japan. They directed Wavell to "maintain as many key positions as possible, but to take the offensive at the earliest opportunity and ultimately conduct an all-out offensive against Japan."[20] Wishful thinking and illusion again outpaced a realistic strategy.

Numerous last-minute rewrites and editing frustrated planners working on the ABDA. They were exhausted by the constantly shifting demands for new or revised studies under tight deadlines to support this position or that. An exasperated Eisenhower, a principal architect of the original concept, wrote in his diary, "Unity of Command in ABDA area seems assured. Good start, but what an effort. Talk, Talk, Talk."[21] The talking continued on matters great and small.

Shortly before noon, Churchill and Roosevelt met briefly with Hull on the Saint Pierre and Miquelon issue. It was an inauspicious time for Hull to press Churchill to endorse a State Department communiqué supporting Vichy France's position regarding the islands. Churchill was still smarting because the Free French were unable to sign the Declaration by United Nations. The prime minister conveniently overlooked the Soviet's role and took out his anger on Hull's negative attitude. Hull did not help matters by expressing his displeasure over Churchill's Ottawa speech. As they argued back and forth Roosevelt intervened, ending the discussion in a draw, not a consensus.[22]

At noon Churchill and Roosevelt met with their shipping advisors, with Lord Beaverbrook and Admiral Emory S. Land also present. Admiral Land as the chairman of the US Maritime Commission was responsible for the construction of all ships for the United States Merchant Marine. Per usual Churchill continued to demand more US merchant ships. Beaverbrook backed his prime minister by insisting that more American shipping was available and that the United States just needed to do a better job of organizing it. Although he had proved insightful in assessing the potential for production of military equipment in the United States, he had absolutely no idea of the current state of American merchant shipping. However, this did not stop him from giving his opinion. Beaverbrook was a master of generalizations about shipping but always seemed to lack specifics (because he had none). If pressed he relied on his gut feeling that the Americans had more ships and bulldozed those daring to disagree. He made few American converts as he displayed the same imperious attitude that had offended his contemporaries in Britain. As a friend noted, Beaverbrook "did as he liked, when he liked" and got away with it because Churchill protected him. Earlier that morning General Brehon Somervell (the Army Service Forces Commander) complained to the British planners about Beaverbrook's domineering attitude and constant badgering for more ships. The British Army planners, who had suffered a similar fate from Beaverbrook, sympathized.[23]

The president had always paid close attention to maritime resources. Land described Roosevelt as "the most ship-minded gentleman I have ever heard of or known with Naval ships number one and merchant ships number two." When Churchill pressed for more ships, Roosevelt told him that the United States had reached the "bottom of the barrel." Churchill misjudged the president, who really knew the details of his maritime fleet and was telling him the bottom line. There were no more ships at this time. Churchill, still believing that the United States possessed unlimited resources for Britain to draw on, tartly replied that America should "scrape the barrel." This attitude may have worked well with his own military advisors, but Churchill's petulance seemed to Roosevelt a strange way to obtain much-needed resources. Despite the rude and ungracious response, Roosevelt took the high road and directed Land to provide the British with more ships at American expense.[24] How to accomplish this questionable feat was left to Land.

Roosevelt understood Land's frustration with the prime minister. The United States simply did not have the number of merchant ships that Churchill and Beaverbrook believed. In 1941, the United States had only produced 1.1 million deadweight tons of merchant shipping. The British, Allies, and neutrals were losing an average of about 360,000 tons every month of 1941. The president appreciated that the United States had to dramatically increase production of troop transport and cargo ships in 1942 and 1943. This session helped him clarify his thinking on the goals for maritime production in 1942 and 1943. He already had the vice president looking at expanding production of planes, tanks, and guns. Now it was time for shipping. In a memo to Land the next day, Roosevelt outlined his ambitious agenda by setting a goal of eight million deadweight tons of merchant ships in 1942. He expected that to rise to ten million tons during 1943. The president was also preparing to gain overwhelming congressional approval for his production goals when he delivered his State of the Union address on 6 January.[25]

3 January

One of the few constants was that Joint Planning Committee discussions remained emotional and contentious, now over the defense of the island bases lying between Hawaii and Australia, in particular, Fiji and New Caledonia. These way stations were essential for control of the sea line of communication for convoys carrying troops and supplies from the United States to Australia. The British insisted the US Navy take responsibility for the defense of these far-flung islands. Its Pacific Fleet, depleted by combat losses, left the American Navy loath to take on any additional missions. Admiral Turner adamantly argued that the agreed principles of ABC-1 stated that the security of the various islands was the responsibility of the nation who had strategic responsibility for the area. This meant that New Zealand should protect Fiji and Australia defend New Caledonia.[26]

Dykes found himself caught in the middle. The British Navy was too overstretched to help, prewar commitments notwithstanding. Both Australia and New Zealand had small navies and lacked the resources to accomplish such a demanding mission. Turner at first refused to budge, forcing Dykes to ask Australia and New Zealand if they could scrape up the forces to protect the islands. After more heated discussion, Turner reluctantly relented. The United States would, if necessary, augment the base defenses with men and equipment but would have to divert these resources from the reinforcements earmarked for the ABDA Area to do it.[27]

This disagreement lasted several days and soured relations within the Joint Planning Committee. New Zealand, after discussion, agreed to provide troops to defend Fiji. Australia, however, heavily committed to fighting alongside the British in North Africa and in Malaya had no troops to spare for New Caledonia. The Canberra government doubted that London fully appreciated Australia's security concerns. Planners' tempers flared as emotional national priorities overrode coldly objective staff plans. The British considered American assets as a pool available for them to tap any time and for any amount they thought necessary. They also resented American reluctance to protect British dominions given the abundance of resources and personnel available in the United States. According to Dykes, "The Yanks are very sticky about sending anything at all to our territories. They are quite shamelessly pressing the small Dominions who are in the forefront to strip themselves of all home defense troops, while they themselves with a population hundreds of times bigger sit cowering on their west coast."[28]

Planners on the American side were just as frustrated with the British. Two weeks of working together in close quarters had worn the relationship thin. Eisenhower, who later developed a reputation for model interactions with the British, was especially upset. His Far East Desk at the War Department was the army voice calling for aid and assistance to the Philippines. He had served in the islands under MacArthur and knew many of the officers fighting and dying on Luzon. The incessant British demands for more and more resources for their dominions galled Eisenhower. "The conversations with the British grow wearisome. They're difficult to talk to, apparently afraid someone is trying to tell them what to do and how to do it. Their practice of war is dilatory."[29]

Such attitudes were probably more attributable to the frenetic planning schedule than to deep-rooted animosity and never seemed to reach the level of the Chiefs of Staff. The American and British chiefs tried to approach issues from their counterpart's perspective. Although Admiral King would gain a reputation for prickliness, this trait was not in evidence at Arcadia. King, for example, brokered a compromise of the matter of New Caledonia. Although Turner tried to force the British to assume responsibility for New Caledonia, King instead directed the navy staff to study the issue. He also rejected planners' recommendations to divert troops from ABDA to garrison New Caledonia. King realized that the Americans were building a major airfield on the island, whose mines supplied nickel to the United States. He made the others and his own service aware that the loss of New Caledonia, which was only nine hundred miles from Australia, would dramatically extend the transit time for convoys steaming from the United States to the ABDA theater. In brief, New Caledonia was quite valuable to the Allies. The chiefs eventually compromised. New Caledonia became an Australian responsibility, but American forces would temporarily defend it until resolution of the ABDA crisis.[30]

ABDA was not the only crisis. Stimson spent most of the day with the army staff reviewing the North Africa plans. The War Department staff report highlighted the advantages and disadvantages of such an operation. The five advantages were: first, it seized the initiative from the Germans and prevented them from moving into Northern or Western Africa. This, in turn, would protect the Allies' sea lanes in the South Atlantic and the air ferry route across Africa; second, it would provide partial control of the western Mediterranean and the sea route to the Near East; third, it would prevent raw materials from the area from reaching Germany; fourth, it would provide airfields to launch bombers against Italy and Germany; fifth, it would have a profound morale boost for the allies.[31]

These advantages were offset by five disadvantages: first, armed French opposition would doom any landing; second, the Germans might capitalize on their shorter lines of communication to rapidly reinforce the area; third, to secure this area would require a large commitment of troops in a location peripheral for Germany's ultimate defeat; fourth, naval vessels to support the operation would have to be diverted from convoys and the defense of the British Isles; fifth, Allied and neutral morale would suffer if the operation failed.[32]

The secretary discussed these pros and cons, and the North Africa operation, with Marshall, Arnold, and Gerow. Stimson and his advisors found the British planning assumptions of French reactions overly optimistic and agreed with the War Department staffers that the operation would fail if the French opposed the landing. The participants worried that the British were willing to accept excessive risk while minimizing the potential German response. Stimson understood the vital importance attached to the United States winning its first major battle against the Germans. After the drumbeat of failures in the Pacific, American morale needed a victory. Stimson, Marshall, and Arnold could not risk failure. Afterward, Stimson laid out their concerns on North Africa for the president to preempt Churchill's eloquent appeals that might convince the president to make a precipitous decision without all the facts. Roosevelt promised to discuss Gymnast the next day with Churchill and all the Chiefs of Staff present.[33]

That evening Roosevelt, Churchill, and their advisors reconvened on the subject of war production and maritime shipbuilding. Roosevelt sought realistic production goals for 1942 and 1943 on aircraft, tanks, antiaircraft guns and antitank guns to announce three days hence during his State of the Union address. His goal was to gain congressional endorsement of his detailed plan for armament construction over the next two years. The consensus was that during 1942 the United States would build 45,000 airplanes, 45,000 tanks, 20,000 antiaircraft guns, and 14,900 antitank guns, all dramatic increases over previously announced goals. In 1943, he proposed 100,000 airplanes, 75,000 tanks, and 35,000 antiaircraft guns. He would use these figures to promote a budget that ensured America was the Arsenal of Democracy. An ecstatic Churchill cabled London: "Max [Beaverbrook] has been magnificent. . . . Hope you will be pleased with immense resultant increase in programme."[34]

4 January

The Japanese advance in the Philippines rolled on, despite an American delaying action that had disrupted Tokyo's timetable. Bataan and Corregidor remained in Am-Fil hands, rendering the best harbor in Southeast Asia unusable by the Japanese. MacArthur's tactics bought time to strengthen the defenses on the Bataan Peninsula where Am-Fil units now concentrated.[35]

On the Malay Peninsula, the Japanese advance surged along the east and west coasts. Unrelenting Japanese pressure kept the British off balance and unable to establish strong defensive positions. Japanese troops resorted to a series of amphibious landings combined with headlong frontal assaults that scattered British units, leaving their defenses exposed to flanking attacks. By 4 January, the British tried to consolidate a line along the Slim River about 275 miles northwest of Singapore.[36]

Arcadia's participants equated the military situations in the Philippines and Malaya. The Americans accepted that barring reinforcements the Philippines were doomed. But they were confident that MacArthur could hold out for months on the mountainous and jungled Bataan Peninsula. The British, especially Churchill, believed the same applied to Malaya and, even as Japanese units moved steadily down both coasts, insisted that Singapore could hold out until US war potential was brought to bear against Japan.[37]

At the previous day's Joint Planning Committee meeting, the Americans presented a copy of their proposed Victory Program to the British, who were naturally interested in the availability of American resources. Once again, the American Army and Navy failed to coordinate. The Victory Program was actually two plans—one for the army and army air force and one for the navy. Lieutenant Colonel Albert Wedemeyer, a principal author of the plan, explained army and army air force requirements. It projected an army expanding to eight million men, a figure that staggered the British. They were also gratified to see that the army program made allowances to meet British equipment needs. The navy plan, however, ignored every British recommendation and requirement. Irate British planners spent most of the day devising a rejoinder to the US Navy.[38]

The expansion and organization of the army air forces concerned the president and Hopkins, who invited Arnold to the White House that afternoon. Three separate meetings resulted, the first with Hopkins, the second with Roosevelt, and the third with Churchill. In an effort to help Arnold, Hopkins asked the air force general for an update on the expansion program to include any problems. Arnold reassured him that everything was on track for the air arm to expand to one million men with 115 fighter or bomber groups by year's end. Army leaders had synchronized ground and air requirements with available manpower and equipment and were finalizing the results for the president's approval.[39]

Arnold also informed Hopkins that he was deploying 800 heavy bombers to England by December and was prepared to station two aviation pursuit groups each in England, Northern Ireland, and North Africa, respectively. As for Asia, Arnold was dispatching two Heavy Bombardment Groups (80 planes), four Pursuit Groups (320 planes), two medium Bombardment Groups (114 planes), and one

Dive Bomber Group (52 planes) to the Philippines, the Dutch East Indies, and Australia. Their arrival within the next few months combined with British aerial reinforcements he hoped would enable the allies to regain local air superiority against the Japanese.[40]

Arnold next met with Roosevelt at 1430 to discuss the same issues. Roosevelt brought up his worries about potential obstacles to the army air force expansion. He also inquired about US support to the British, in particular the aircraft intended for England, Ireland, and North Africa and was gratified by Arnold's reassurances that he intended to hold nothing back from Portal. Roosevelt expressed satisfaction on the warming relationship between the two air leaders. While at the White House, Arnold spent about twenty minutes with Churchill, whose questions were similar to those of Hopkins and Roosevelt. The relationship between the two air chiefs especially interested Churchill, who worried that the two might not be getting along. Arnold assured him this was not the case.[41]

The Arcadia Conference had opened with a tense exchange between Arnold and Portal over Portal's demands for air support for Singapore. At the first session of the American and British chiefs on 24 December, Stark's insistence that American airmen would operate the US air groups had upset Portal. Arnold mollified the British airman with reassurances that this did not apply to Lend-Lease aircraft. The British had pilots but needed aircraft from the United States. They reasoned that the RAF should enjoy priority in aircraft allocation because they were already fighting the Axis powers. Before 7 December, British aircraft requirements did have priority over the needs of the army air force. With the United States in the war, not only had priority in favorable apportionment for Britain ended but also the demands of the expanding American air forces left fewer aircraft available for transfer to the Allies. Churchill assumed that as Portal and Arnold spent more time together and exchanged ideas they could settle on a reasonable and mutually beneficial aircraft distribution plan.[42]

In midafternoon, Stimson met with Arnold, Marshall, Stark, Gerow, and Turner in his War Department office to align their thoughts on Gymnast for a later discussion with Roosevelt, Churchill, and the

British chiefs at the White House. Gymnast's planning assumptions had too many "ifs" for the Americans—if the French invited the Allies into North Africa, if the landing was unopposed, and if the Germans did not counterattack immediately, the mission was sound. Turner voiced skepticism about the logistical problems posed by the operation. According to Stimson, "Turner, as usual, was the devil's advocate in stressing all the obstacles possible but he was also a master of all the facts and was the one whom the possibilities of shipping and making landings largely rested."[43]

Late that afternoon Roosevelt and Churchill met with their military advisors. Stimson's phone call the previous day had resonated with Roosevelt's concerns on Gymnast, and he asked the secretary to review planning efforts to date. Stimson accordingly remarked that the Northern Ireland Operation (now codenamed Magnet) had a scheduled embarkation date and the troops were ready to ship. Had the British completed the arrangements in Northern Ireland to accommodate the arrival of the Americans? Dill and Churchill assured him that all was ready. Arnold answered the president's question about air support to Magnet, stating that two Pursuit Groups, 160 planes, would be stationed in Northern Ireland. Roosevelt then asked Portal how many planes that would enable the British to withdraw from Northern Ireland. None, Portal replied, because there were no planes there to withdraw.[44]

Stimson moved to the Gymnast operation. Churchill pedantically mentioned that Gymnast referred only to the British operation in North Africa. Supergymnast was the code name for the Anglo-American combined operation. Stimson duly noted this distinction and reviewed Supergymnast's planning assumptions, the "ifs." He reiterated the US belief that success hinged on two geopolitical considerations: first, the French would invite the Allies to land, and second, Spain would delay any German response to the invasion via the Iberian Peninsula. An unchallenged landing was, in Roosevelt's words, in the "lap of the gods." The president did expect a powerful German response because the Spanish government would offer little opposition on the Iberian Peninsula. All agreed that the Spanish would not delay the Germans long enough for the Allies to occupy

North Africa. Turner then outlined the Supergymnast schedule, including the number of ships, detailed troop manifests, convoy turnaround times, port unloading procedures, and air cover during the operation. The admiral displayed his usual mastery of essential data and specifics. Based on available shipping resources using the limited port facilities, he concluded that it would take four months to off-load the transports.[45]

Such snail-like progress astonished and disappointed Roosevelt and Churchill, who refused to believe the timetable. The plan as described was just too slow. Irritated that facts did not support his expectations, Churchill irascibly inquired why the Allies needed four months to get ashore in North Africa when the Japanese had landed on Luzon in one day. Turner explained that the Allies had only one small port to unload their forces, and unloading was possible only during daylight hours under Allied air cover. Each convoy needed two weeks to discharge its troops and cargoes. Furthermore, air support mandated stationing aircraft carriers offshore for extended periods, and that in turn rendered them vulnerable to German and Italian submarine attacks. As conceived, the plan was dangerous.[46]

During this conversation the British chiefs were silent. Despite the fact that ten days earlier General Brooke recognized that the North Africa operation was fraught with danger and should not be undertaken, they said nothing. Colonel John E. Hull, an American Army planner who went on to four stars and became the army's vice chief of staff, later observed that the British chiefs sometimes would not argue when the Americans had strong reasons for not doing something and simply fell back on the attitude "the Prime Minister wants this done and we must support him." Hull felt that Churchill did not listen and "considered his judgement superior to that of even his chiefs of staff."[47]

Perhaps, but the same day Churchill informed General Hastings Ismay, "some months delay might be accepted." Churchill acknowledged that the British advance had slowed due to the "stubborn resistance of the enemy in Cyrenaica." He conceded that Rommel had escaped destruction and received reinforcements through Tripoli while the British had difficulties resupplying their own troops.

Regardless of Churchill's candid admissions to the British Chiefs of Staff in London, he continued to press the Americans for an immediate North Africa operation.[48]

A four-month unloading operation spelled disaster. It afforded the Germans ample time to mount counterattacks by air, land, and sea against an exposed and understrength Allied force. They could certainly react in that scenario. Churchill and Roosevelt directed the staffs to reevaluate the plan, yet again, to expedite the landing. The only positive note was the decision that despite the shortage of shipping, the Magnet operation should proceed immediately.[49]

5 January

Three long weeks of contentious discussions and travel had taken their toll on sixty-seven-year-old Winston Churchill. He still hoped to accomplish more in Washington, but Churchill's doctor thought he needed a break. Edward Stettinius, an American friend, offered him the use of a beach bungalow at Pompano north of Miami. His secretary, Colonel Jacob, also noted that Churchill "felt his continued presence in the White House might be irksome and liable to cause suspicion in the minds of the officials of the Services and the members of the Cabinet, who might think he was trying to establish too intimate a connection with the President." So he decided a brief separation and rest would be useful. Churchill departed the White House for five days in the warm Florida sunshine.[50]

This trip to Florida was not all fun. Churchill stayed in daily contact with Roosevelt. He also arranged for a daily courier to fly down from Washington with telegrams and important papers for him to review. He worked on a myriad of topics while in Florida, including: the details of Wavell's new command in the Far East; the need to provide naval and air support to the deteriorating situation in the Middle East; the strategic bombing offensive against Germany; providing reassurance to Australia and New Zealand of British support; providing more resources for Singapore; and the constitutional discussions in India. He also took the time to review the papers he wrote on the *Duke of York* before the conference and provided Roosevelt on 23 December. He updated them based on the discussions and decisions at Arcadia. The Americans agreed with the "Germany First" strategy and had supported his broad blueprint for general strategy. He was optimistic about Supergymnast in 1942 and hoped for "large offensive operations" in Europe in 1943. He planned to share these revised papers with Roosevelt, the British Cabinet, and the Chiefs of Staff Committee in London.[51]

Churchill's departure allowed the British chiefs more free time to spend with their American counterparts as both sides got to know and measure each other. Arnold and Portal went to Florida, which allowed the two air chiefs to discuss their views on air power candidly and exchange ideas free of outside interference or interruption. The trip south enabled Portal to see firsthand the training and potential of the expanding army air force. Arnold later fondly recalled, "We had a wonderful time fishing and loafing." Social pleasantries aside, the two hammered out a compromise for the distribution of American aircraft between the two nations that would be finalized on their return to Washington.[52]

Roosevelt arranged for Marshall to accompany the prime minister on his plane ride south to Pompano, Florida, and then immediately return by train to Washington. The two used the flight to get to know each other. Marshall's handling of the unity of command issue had impressed Churchill, who realized that Roosevelt trusted and relied on his Army chief's judgment. It was important for Churchill to have Marshall's support not only for Magnet and Supergymnast but also for other strategic decisions that lay in the future.[53]

Stimson agreed that the prime minister looked tired and needed a rest, but he was unhappy that Churchill took Marshall with him. Marshall too was "very busy, very much overworked, and should not have been taken from his work." Stimson regarded the trip as a waste of time, while Roosevelt saw the potential in Churchill talking to Marshall and developing a rapport. The secretary needed Marshall urgently because of the War Plans Division's blunt assessment of the Philippines. The straightforward analysis recommended against any relief operations for the islands because dispatching reinforcements would be "an entirely unjustifiable diversion of forces from the principal theater—the Atlantic." This War Plans Division study concluded that MacArthur could hold out for another three months on Bataan. After that the Philippines, which they saw as "the key to the Far East position of the Associated Powers," would fall in a decisive Allied defeat. The loss of the Dutch East Indies and Singapore would follow defeat in the Philippines, threatening the sea lines of communication to Australia and isolating China.[54]

Stimson refused to give up hope. He pronounced the study too "gloomy" and forbid its distribution throughout the army staff. Marshall's absence complicated Stimson's position because it deprived the secretary of his most trusted subordinate's advice.[55]

6 January

Marshall arrived by train at Washington's Union Station at 0200. and was at his desk a few hours later, much to Secretary Stimson's relief. That morning Stimson and Eisenhower met General Drum, the second time Stimson conferred with Drum about the China mission. As Stimson described the new China theater and Drum's role vis-à-vis Chiang Kai-shek, the general barely concealed his disappointment. With his inflated self-importance Drum had fancied himself a serious rival to Marshall for the Chief of Staff position, and he now expected Stimson to appoint him commander of American forces in Europe. Instead, he got China, a backwater command. Stimson mistakenly felt that he had done a good job of convincing Drum of China's strategic importance, although he left Drum's exact responsibilities vague.[56]

The day's most notable event was the president's State of the Union address to Congress at noon. Roosevelt explained to the Congress and via radio to the American people that the purpose of the Arcadia Conference and the Declaration by United Nations was "the consolidation of the United Nations' total war effort against our common enemies." He emphasized that "plans have been laid here and in other capitols for coordinated and cooperative action by all the United Nations—military and economic action," and proudly enumerated Arcadia's recent accomplishments. "Already we have established a unified command of land, sea, and air forces in the southwestern theater of war. There will be a continuation of conferences and consultations among military staffs, so that the plans and operations of each will fit into a general strategy designed to crush the enemy. We shall not fight isolated wars—each nation going its own way. These twenty-six nations are united—not in spirit and determination alone, but in the broad conduct of the war in all phases."[57]

The president then laid out his ambitious goals for manufacturing and transporting America's "weapons of war." They were impressive and bold, announcing the figures previously arrived at during numerous Arcadia deliberations. The enormous productivity, he told the American people, would show the Japanese and Nazis "what they had accomplished in the attack on Pearl Harbor." Roosevelt concluded with a call for complete victory. "No compromise can end this conflict. There never has been—there never can be—successful compromise between good and evil. Only total victory can reward the champions of tolerance, and decency, and freedom, and faith."[58]

7, 8, 9 January

After the State of the Union address, Roosevelt departed for a much-needed rest at his home in Hyde Park, New York. Churchill was still in Florida and several chiefs were out of town. Stimson also left the capital on 7 January for a short vacation to recuperate from the previous two weeks. There was, however, no such respite for the overworked planning staffs. They returned to their cramped offices and set to work always looking over their shoulders at the deteriorating situations in North Africa and the Pacific.[59]

By 7 January, a month after Pearl Harbor, the Am-Fil forces had withdrawn to their final defensive positions on Bataan, where they repulsed Japanese probing attacks. Now isolated, Bataan was under siege, and how long the well-constructed defenses could hold out was a matter of conjecture—the War Plans Division concluded a few months, the secretary of war hoped for a longer campaign. News from the Middle East likewise was discouraging. The British offensive had run into Rommel's main defenses at El Agheila, a vital port on the Gulf of Sirte between Cyrenaica and Tripolitania that kept open the German and Italian sea lane of communication. The strongpoint was bordered by the sea, and its land approaches passed through salt marshes, sand, and broken ground that precluded slashing armor maneuvers. On 5 January a large Axis convoy reached Tripoli carrying tanks and armored vehicles that gave Rommel numerical superiority over his British opponents. As Rommel's situation dramatically improved, the overextended British felt the impact of Churchill's earlier decisions to divert forces to the Far East. Unable to sustain the advance, Operation Crusader ground to a halt. Rommel was poised to take the offensive.[60]

The British Army chief, General Brooke, realized that the delays in capturing Cyrenaica and the diversion of reinforcements to the Far East had fatally disrupted the timetable for capturing Tripoli. He acknowledged that the Germans would continue to reinforce Rommel from Italy and that the British chances for Acrobat (the attack on Tripoli) were slipping away. As for Supergymnast, Brooke came to the American view that without French cooperation the Allied landings were not possible.[61]

In Malaya, the situation was far worse. On 7 January, a Japanese surprise, hard-hitting attack, spearheaded by tanks, shattered British defenses along the Slim River and mauled the Eleventh Indian Division. The Japanese quickly pushed on toward Kuala Lumpur, the British administrative base on the Malayan Peninsula.[62]

The British chiefs and Churchill failed to grasp the gravity of what was happening in Malaya or to appreciate the implications of the speed and audacity of the Japanese advance. Singapore's naval base was never intended to repulse a ground attack, and neglect of ground defenses on the Malaya Peninsula left open a backdoor overland route to the "fortress." Yet reading the daily British assessments of the withdrawal, one was left with the impression that Singapore would somehow hold despite the previous twenty years of half-hearted improvements that left the naval base without a fleet and without proper ground defenses.

Wavell, as ABDA commander, arrived in Singapore to see for himself what was happening. He immediately traveled to the front lines and reached Kuala Lumpur shortly after the Slim River disaster, which opened the way to Singapore. He could not have come at a more critical moment. With the Japanese halfway to Singapore, the

British commanders he spoke to seemed befuddled by the tactical situation. Without reserves to mount a counterattack, Wavell could only retreat, and on 9 January he ordered a strategic withdrawal to Muar River in the Johore Province, the last natural obstacle to delay the Japanese before reaching Singapore Island. This defensive line was a mere one hundred miles northwest of Singapore.[63]

The same day Wavell cabled his observations to the British Chiefs of Staff. His comments shocked them. The Ninth and Eleventh Indian Divisions both were near collapse. British forces were still retreating. The Japanese were relentlessly advancing. The prime minister and the British chiefs had no idea of the disaster unfolding in Malaya. Like a drowning man grasping for a life jacket, Churchill clung to the belief that "Fortress Singapore" could hold for six months. Now the senior commander in the new theater was dispelling those illusions. With characteristic understatement, the British planners described Wavell's cable as "very gloomy."[64]

As the British faced crises worlds apart, the Joint Planning Committee analyzed three topics—Supergymnast, the Victory Program, and China. Supergymnast remained contentious because of its unsupportable planning assumptions, including but not limited to lack of air cover, lack of shipping, inadequate port facilities, and the German submarine threat. Major General Stillwell, an army planner, summarized the operation: "All against . . . all agree that means are meagre, transportation uncertain, the complications numerous, the main facts unknown, the consequences serious." The British planners, despite their desire to please Churchill, had no answers either.[65]

As for the Victory Program, British planners continued to complain that Turner had not incorporated the British requirements into the navy section of the plan. Dykes approached William Donovan, a well-connected Washington, DC, lawyer soon to head the Office of Strategic Services, to complain about Turner. Donovan promised to talk to Secretary Knox about Turner's attitude. However, at the Joint Planning Committee meeting, on 8 January, the British planners had a chance to raise the Turner matter and chose not to. They believed that too much time would be taken up with this contentious topic and would shortchange the time available to resolve other major and more time-sensitive issues. Word of the meeting with Donovan likely reached Turner (possibly through Knox), because the admiral offered to create a special American-British Joint Committee to review and make recommendations on the Victory Program. The British agreed, content that an acrimonious and potentially time-consuming problem had been informally resolved.[66]

On 9 January, Eisenhower informed the Joint Planning Committee about the need for immediate aid to China. Washington was concerned that the loss of Hong Kong and Manila would weaken Chiang's resolve to continue fighting. Eisenhower sought British approval for the United States to send a senior army officer to stiffen Chiang's resolve and with appropriate authority to secure funds and reinforcements for the China theater. British staff planners were receptive, although still advocating that the best way to help China was to support Burma (and therefore India). Eisenhower, frustrated by the British attitude on China, confided to his diary, "Becoming increasingly evident that something must be done in China. War effort lagging there, and China shows signs of being willing to quit. Apparently, the British don't take this seriously. They should."[67]

The day's major staff issue involved who to send to China. Despite all Stimson's efforts, Drum proved obdurate. The previous day Drum handed Marshall a paper that outlined his vision for his role in China, which was totally inconsistent with Stimson's and Marshall's goals. Drum proposed a large buildup of American army and air forces to conduct major field operations from India through Burma into China. Naturally, Drum would command this China-Burma-India theater. Marshall curtly dissected this paper and told Drum that his role was to assist Chiang and keep China in the war. No massive influx of American ground and air forces would occur. Drum vigorously disagreed and the two exchanged harsh words when both lost their tempers. Marshall was unwilling to smooth Drum's ruffled ego. If Drum was not willing to go where the army needed him, then Marshall had no qualms about eliminating him as a candidate for the command. A disappointed Stimson accepted Marshall's verdict. Eisenhower remarked, "He [Drum] seemingly cannot understand that we've got to do the best we can with what we've got."[68]

Roosevelt returned to Washington on 9 January to find another ABDA problem. The Dutch representatives were irritated that they did not have a seat on the Washington council that provided direction to ABDA (Dutch input originated through the British chiefs in London). Then, without prior notification, came the official public announcement of Wavell as ABDA's supreme commander. Roosevelt tried to pacify the Dutch with promises of military aid and instructed Marshall to arrange for a small number of tanks, depth charges, and some ammunition to the Dutch East Indies. The president felt "it is very important in our relations with the Dutch that they fully understand that we are going to do everything we can for them." Marshall immediately dispatched fifty tanks.[69]

Churchill was already looking beyond Arcadia for a means to sustain collaboration between the American and British Chiefs of Staff. A mutually beneficial relationship had developed, and Churchill wanted to nourish the partnership. But how could the allies institutionalize a command structure to provide strategic guidance along the lines of the single theater commander model? Dill and Pound recommended defining key terms to avoid future confusion.[70]

The term "Joint" would henceforth identify "inter-service collaboration" within a single nation. "Combined" connoted collaboration between two or more nations. Accordingly, the organization for strategic coordination between the American and British Service Chiefs would be known as the Combined Chiefs of Staff. That for coordinating strategic guidance among the American Army, Navy and Air Force chiefs would be known as the Joint Chiefs of Staff.[71]

The British also proposed that a British Mission remain in Washington to represent the interests of the British Minister of Defense and the British Chiefs of Staff and to coordinate with the American Chiefs on a daily basis. A senior officer would represent each British service. Lieutenant General Colville Wemyss represented General Alan Brooke, the British Army chief; Admiral Sir Charles Little represented Admiral Pound and the Royal Navy; and Air Marshal Arthur Harris represented Air Marshal Portal and the Royal Air Force. Field Marshal Sir John Dill, who had a good working and personal relationship with Marshall specifically and the American leaders in general, took charge of the British Mission as the "representative of the Minister of Defence (Churchill concurrently held the portfolio)." This ranked Dill above the Combined Chiefs of Staff and permitted him to "have contacts with such authorities on the highest level as may be arranged between the President and Prime Minister." Churchill expected to capitalize on Dill's friendly connections with the American leaders.[72]

The British also recommended the creation of a Combined Intelligence Committee in Washington for intelligence sharing purposes and offered to provide intelligence experts from the Joint Intelligence Committee in London. To link resources with strategy, they proposed a Combined Allocation Committee to assist the Combined Chiefs of Staff in the "distribution of the available weapons of war." Finally, concerned with limited but vital shipping assets, the British recommended establishment of a Movements Committee to advise the chiefs on the best way to regulate the shipment of personnel and equipment for optimum results. The British chiefs submitted a finalized draft of proposals for post-Arcadia collaboration and sent it to the Americans for review, in expectation of approval at the eighth meeting of the Combined Chiefs set for 10 January.[73]

Staff officers from both nations plunged into a new round of activity on the evening of 9 January. Over the next five days the American and British chiefs would meet five times to resolve Supergymnast planning; assistance to China; reinforcements for the Far East; supplies for Russia; boundary adjustments for ABDA; post-Arcadia collaboration; and new agencies for cooperation on raw materials, intelligence, shipping, and assignment of munitions. A relationship would either be solidified and an organization developed for the direction of the war, or the effort would founder on petty disagreements and nationalistic prerogatives.

6

Final Discussions

10 January 1942

The American and British chiefs anticipated daily meetings for the rest of the conference because they had numerous issues to cover in the short time remaining. British concerns centered on their plans for strategic collaboration and the allocation of munitions and shipping resources. The Americans expected to finalize the details for the ABDA command, settle the China theater question, and deploy troops to Ireland and Iceland. All the chiefs—American and British—sought a final agreement on Supergymnast's timeline. Competing priorities and differing national perspectives were manageable, but the enemy was not. During the next few days continued Japanese military successes in the Far East and the stiffened German defense in North Africa disrupted the conference agenda.

Fighting had diminished in the Philippines on 10 January as the Japanese contented themselves with minor probes of the Filipino-American defenses on Bataan while regrouping in preparation for a massive coordinated assault. The situation in Malaya and in the Middle East continued to deteriorate. Heavy fighting near Kuala Lumpur resulted in another British withdrawal and the loss of a key British airfield nearby. Lacking sufficient Allied air support, the British reported that Japanese air forces owned the skies. In the Middle East, British Eighth Army ran headlong into the German's formidable defenses near El Agheila.[1]

Wavell, the ABDA commander, returned to Singapore after personally observing conditions on Malaya and grimly assessed the gravity of the situation. To date, the Japanese ground campaign in Malaya had operated along tenuous supply lines. The Slim River debacle had exposed the vulnerable British rear areas to marauding Japanese troops. In their haste to withdraw to Kuala Lumpur, British forces abandoned a large supply depot containing supplies and equipment to support two brigades for one month plus numerous personnel carriers and trucks. This windfall of food, ammunition, and equipment, coupled with the capture of nearby airfields, dramatically improved the Japanese logistical situation and allowed them to increase the pace of their advance on Singapore.[2]

Wavell, however, was an experienced combat leader who grasped that the critical situation was not necessarily hopeless even though Japanese control of the sea lines of communication and local air superiority threatened Allied reinforcements from India. True, Wavell's forces on Malaya had suffered serious losses, but he might be able to salvage the campaign by concentrating his troops for a stand in Jahor Province to buy time until reinforcements could arrive to rescue Singapore.[3]

In Washington, the British and American staffs separately prepared for the eighth formal meeting of the Combined Chiefs of Staff. The US staff sought to address increased U-boat activity in the Atlantic and its threat to planned future deployments of American troops to Iceland, Ireland, and North Africa. During the conference, the German Navy had shifted its operational area of activity closer to the continental United States, thereby extending the danger zone for ships transiting the Atlantic. Their latest strategy would eventually claim fifty-eight American, Allied, and neutral ships during January between the US East Coast and the British Isles. Even in early January it was clear that shipping losses were mounting. Lieutenant Colonel Robinett, the army's secretary at the conference, expressed American apprehension. "The submarine threat in the Atlantic is becoming more serious. Our big situation map of the world is becoming well dotted with the tabs showing reported submarines."[4]

Before the end of the month this threat would become more critical. Since the summer of 1941, British cryptanalysts had been deciphering German U-boat Enigma-enciphered message traffic to track the movement of enemy submarines. At the time submarines, surface ships, and administrative headquarters used common Enigma encrypting machines. In late January 1942, however, the U-boats adopted their own unique Enigma machine that differed from the rest of the German Navy. This change temporarily deprived the Allies of access to submarine movements just as the Americans began to ship men and material in the Atlantic and the Germans were expanding the size of their U-boat fleet as well as moving long-range submarines to American home waters. This was a recipe for disaster over the next six months.[5]

Despite the growing U-boat threat, Churchill demanded the Iceland and Ireland convoys be expedited while simultaneously executing Supergymnast. At a 4 January meeting with the chiefs, Churchill urged that the large ocean liners, *Queen Mary*, *Queen Elizabeth*, *Aquitania*, and *Normandie*—previously converted to troop transports—be pressed into service to transport the reinforcements. These behemoths were fast and each could carry more than ten thousand men, if necessary. But putting so many troops aboard a single ship ran great risks because their lifeboat capacity was just three thousand. The loss of so many lives should a U-boat sink one of the liners was a planner's nightmare. Besides the human disaster, such a catastrophe would devastate American home-front morale. Admiral Pound had earlier articulated the concern that "the price is frightful if the ship would be sunk."[6]

As for Asia, the British chiefs somewhat surprisingly did not focus on Wavell's cable or the dire tactical situation in Malaya, perhaps conceding the prime minister's steadfast position that the fortress would hold. Instead, that morning, they and their planners limited their discussion to the American proposal on Drum's mission to China. Who would be responsible for the supply route between Chungking and Rangoon? Marshall had recommended that the United States assume sole responsibility for the Burma Road and the appointment of an American officer to command the air and ground forces assigned to it. The British disagreed because they did not want British troops in

Burma completely dependent on an American-controlled logistical lifeline. They proposed amendments that delineated responsibilities between Wavell and ABDA and the American commander in China, which they intended to offer at the Combined Chiefs of Staff afternoon meeting.[7]

The British wanted a rapid decision to smooth the way for Wavell to formally assume command of ABDA before the Australians and Dutch raised more objections about the new command. (On 1 January, Wavell had deferred taking command until he could organize a headquarters and assess the situation.) For more than a week, the Australians and Dutch had presented formal written requests for changes to the consultation process for the ABDA theater. Although both had advisory input to the British chiefs in London, they wanted formal participation on the Combined Chiefs of Staff in Washington. The Dutch feared that without a direct presence the Anglo-Americans might subordinate Dutch interests in the Dutch East Indies, their most important colonial possession, to the needs of other allies. The Australians wanted a greater say in developing the strategy for their own defense against the seemingly unstoppable Japanese southward advance. The British, however, wanted to restrict important Allied decision-making solely to two nations—themselves and the United States. They believed that multinational consultation would be slow and laborious and give other nations the perception that they had an equal voice in deliberations. For these reasons the British chiefs wanted the Burma Road question settled and, following the afternoon session with their American counterparts, expedited resolution by dispatching instructions establishing the ABDA theater. This fait accompli negated any attempt to block the command's establishment by the other allies and left them little choice but to do as they were directed.[8]

The eighth formal session of the Combined Chiefs of Staff convened in midafternoon, and, as if following a perverse cycle, again turned into an administrative disaster. The British chiefs expected to finalize their objectives enunciated in their staff paper, "Post-Arcadia Collaboration." They had provided the American chiefs with a draft two days earlier and expected that it would be the day's primary agenda item. They were surprised and disappointed to learn that the US Navy secretariat had failed to distribute copies of this document to planners and leaders. The resulting confusion over the agenda forced postponement of any discussion on the subject.[9]

The British secretariat was incensed. Brigadier Dykes, the army planner slated to assume responsibilities as secretary for the British Mission after the conference, was especially irate and thought the entire meeting between the chiefs was a disappointment. "Little good work [was] done." After the session Dykes met with the respective heads of the US Army and Navy secretariats. "Tried to get their secretarial organization sorted after the meeting, but it really is a hopeless task"; he described both secretaries as "plain stupid."[10]

The secretariats' latest blunder embarrassed the American side and in fact would continue to do so in the coming months. Admiral King clearly recognized the weakness of his secretariat, but he could not remedy it overnight. King complained after the war that the inept secretariat was responsible for the sketchy record keeping of US Joint Chiefs. "The British Chiefs on the other hand," he wrote, "were assisted by two or three secretaries who had been trained in that kind of work for several years." With discussion of the Post Arcadia Collaboration postponed, the disjointed meeting continued. Per usual, Admiral Stark sat in the head seat, but he again failed to articulate a direction for the meeting. One British observer noted, "Old Stark produced one item after another out of a hat—in none of which were our men prepared."[11]

Without an agreed agenda, the Combined Chiefs returned to a discussion of shipping and timelines for Supergymnast. Pound explained that the British had independently studied the factors that affected the timing of the operation. He neither addressed planning assumptions nor specifics on the availability of shipping, troops, or equipment. Pound, in line with Churchill's desires, stated that if 7 January (three days earlier) was selected as the date planning commenced then the first convoy could begin loading on 4 February. In other words, if the Americans endorsed the earlier British position a convoy could land troops in Algiers and Casablanca as early as 3 March. Furthermore, Pound disregarded previous American analysis and confidently predicted that 29,000 men could be unloaded in two weeks at Casablanca.[12]

The Americans, chagrined by the secretariats' inferior performance, sat silently. Then Marshall, taken aback by the unilateral British assertion, questioned Pound about British capability to undertake both Algiers and Casablanca landings. Pound insisted they could. Rather than challenge Pound openly, Marshall remarked that he would reexamine shipping availability for additional convoys to support the troops landed in the first wave. He mentioned diplomatically that the American side would have to confirm whether or not they could implement the official planning date (which the British had not coordinated with them) for the operation. The British mistakenly construed American reticence as consent.[13]

Stilwell, tasked with much of the planning for Supergymnast, was not nearly as politic as Marshall. He was already frustrated by the repeated British unwillingness to face the complicated realities involved in Supergymnast and fumed about the overly casual British analysis. He thought Churchill had "completely hypnotized" Roosevelt. As far as Stilwell was concerned the Allies were getting into, "a rat hole that is under the guns, sure of punishment and hard to supply." The entire operation was a "crazy gamble . . . the whole goddamned thing is cockeyed. We should clean the Pacific first and then face east." Instead, he had to reevaluate Pound's proposals, whose flimsy analytical backing infuriated the mercurial Stilwell.[14]

The chiefs then addressed the Dutch attitude toward the ABDA command. The Dutch had still not approved the Anglo-American allies' insistence that Wavell assumes command immediately. Netherlands' representatives resented Wavell's arbitrary selection as the supreme commander and were further upset by their failure to gain membership on the Combined Chiefs of Staff, which was providing strategic direction to the ABDA theater where they had major interests. They protested to Roosevelt over their inadequate representation in London, putting the Americans in the middle of an inter-Allied dispute and none too happy that the Dutch were complaining to them about the British. Marshall had previously offered to "smooth down" the ruffled Dutch feathers with promises of additional equipment and munitions, and Admiral Pound conveyed his appreciation for American loyalty and patience in this matter. He added that the British chiefs would direct Wavell to establish his headquarters in Batavia, NEI (Netherlands East-Indies, present-day Jakarta) that very day. This was another move to convince the Dutch that the new command would protect the NEI colonies.[15]

The question of direct participation on the Combined Chiefs of Staff for coordination of the ABDA theater was not confined to the Netherlands government. Australia and New Zealand were also openly dissatisfied with the proposed arrangement. Australian prime minister John Curtin vociferously protested the Anglo-Americans making unilateral strategic decisions because his was one of the most threatened ABDA allies. It was natural that these other allies were suspicious of American and British motives and resented their deliberate exclusion from the decision-making process since they had the most to lose. The chiefs acknowledged that Australian, Dutch, and New Zealand requirements might necessitate possible future amendments to ABDA's command structure. Regardless of Marshall's promises of more equipment and the chiefs' vague assurances that they would consider changes, these other allies continued to insist on direct participation.[16]

For the Dutch, Australian, and New Zealand governments the problem extended beyond representation on the Combined Chiefs of Staff. Their overriding concern revolved around competing national interests determining the strategic direction and resource allocation in the theater. The British believed the primary focus of the command should be the defense of Singapore, Burma, and the Malay Peninsula. The Dutch sought to preserve their colonial possessions in the East Indies. Australia and New Zealand wanted more resources against the imminent Japanese threat to their respective homelands. The United States was intent on preserving the sea lines of communication from the Malay Barrier to the Southwest Pacific. In theory ABDA's supreme commander would somehow have to balance these diverse and often contradictory war aims.[17]

Establishing the headquarters in Batavia and selecting a Dutch officer, Lieutenant General Hein ter Poorten, as the ground commander was another gesture that failed to appease the Dutch government, which continued to criticize the ABDA command. As late as 28 January, Roosevelt met with the chiefs and the British Mission at the White House to explain that the Dutch government was still in "an angry frame of mind" over the lack of consultation during the selection of the ABDA commander. He cited several messages from Australian and the Netherlands governments that Churchill had forwarded to him that requested direct input to the staff in Washington, rather than London. Roosevelt sympathized with these other allies' situations but recognized that increasing the number of participants on the Combined Chiefs of Staff might create bureaucratic and administrative paralysis. The Dutch government in London, for example, was notoriously slow and ponderous and would retard, not complement, the Washington staff. Roosevelt ultimately compromised by directing the Washington staff to consult with these additional allies on military matters rather than incorporating them into the decision-making body. But the Anglo-Americans quickly exercised their arbitrary power.[18]

Admiral Pound notified the chiefs, as directed, that Wavell would establish ABDA headquarters in Batavia. Without waiting for approval from Australia and the Dutch governments, the chiefs cabled General George Brett and Admiral Thomas Hart to report to General Wavell, in Batavia, and assume duties as Deputy Supreme Commander and Commander Combined Naval Forces ABDA respectively. This slight was exactly what upset the other allies and made them all the more anxious to have a seat at the decision-making table.[19]

China was the next topic on the session's agenda. The American chiefs had earlier discussed their memorandum on immediate assistance to China with the British chiefs, who agreed that aid to China was important. Pound told the group that the British were in general agreement with the American proposal but requested several revisions consistent with the spirit of unity of command. Marshall made the first change. After his confrontational meeting with Drum, Marshall withdrew Drum's name from consideration and inserted the designation "the United States Representative," meaning that the US military advisor to Chiang had yet to be identified. The British concurred without comment and approved the appointment of an American general officer to serve as Roosevelt's representative to Chiang and command US forces in China.[20]

The British then addressed their concerns about logistic control for the Burma Road. A brief discussion quickly reached a compromise that authorized the United States representative to the generalissimo to supervise all military aid to China and responsibility for the supervision of the Burma Road. He would exercise control of the Burma Road in China and the British would do likewise for the Burma portion of the road. The American representative, however, had the leverage to require the British military and civilian authorities to make directed improvements along the route. In exchange the United States would provide all technical assistance and equipment for road improvements and the rehabilitation of the port of Rangoon. This interim solution calmed British fears of outside encroachment on their Burma colony. The meeting then adjourned, leaving the British disappointed and the Americans chagrined over the Post Arcadia Collaboration fiasco.[21]

11 January 1942

Mixed reports from the Asian battlefields were delivered on 11 January. American-Filipino units had repulsed a determined Japanese attack on the Bataan defenses and inflicted heavy casualties on the enemy. The situation in Malaya was less clear. Reports of heavy fighting around Kuala Lumpur reached Washington that morning, by which time the Japanese already had occupied the city and captured the valuable British supply depots. This latest reverse and Wavell's straightforward assessment of its consequences disrupted the agenda for the afternoon Combined Chiefs of Staff (CCS) meeting.[22]

As yet unaware of the drastic turn of events, the British chiefs did not accord priority to Malaya and the Far East. Instead, they revised Churchill's draft synopsis of conference discussions to date. The prime minister had returned from Florida the prior evening and had sent a copy of his revised papers on the Atlantic Front, the Pacific Front, and the Campaign of 1943 to Dill, Pound, and Portal for their review. He remained highly optimistic on his North Africa operation.

After their edits were incorporated, he intended to give Roosevelt a copy as well as send one to the Defence Committee in London to keep them apprised of his perceptions and progress. An account destined for such high-level recipients demanded accuracy, clarity, and brevity, a demanding editorial task. During the long and laborious session, participants meticulously vetted each paragraph aloud followed by discussion. Following their point-by-point review, the British chiefs went to the White House to discuss their comments on the draft paper with the prime minister.[23]

Churchill's assessment of future operations contained no new insights. The proposed rapid expansion of the American military astounded him, especially the US Army Air Forces, which he considered could strike the German homeland during 1942. While the concomitant growth of the US Army was impressive, shipping shortages limited the number of American troops available to engage the enemy in 1942. (This is an interesting point given Churchill's adamancy that no shortage of shipping interfered with Supergymnast.) Projected US production of munitions and shipping dazzled Churchill, although he believed the full effect of America's wartime industrial mobilizations would not be brought to bear until 1943. Rommel's stubborn defense and reinforcements to his Afrika Korps may have ended plans to capture Tripoli, but Churchill urged the study of Supergymnast to continue. Magnet could be executed immediately. As for the Far East, he displayed no awareness of the seriousness of the situation in Malaya and insisted that Fortress Singapore could hold on for months.[24]

The American chiefs were meeting simultaneously in Admiral Stark's office to review several British proposals. General Marshall arrived late, after the meeting had started, and was very agitated by the British proposal on the Post Arcadia Collaboration. The British envisaged Field Marshall Dill serving as the personal representative of the British minister of defense (Churchill), with "contacts with such authorities on the highest level as may be arranged between the President and Prime Minister." Dill would interact with the president and the secretaries, bypassing the American chiefs, who would deal solely with representatives of their British military counterparts.

This would create a military layer between the heads of state and the Chiefs of Staff, enabling Dill to circumvent the American chiefs on strategic and resource distribution issues. Marshall found this anathema, but not because of Dill.[25]

Marshall stressed to the group his utmost respect for Dill, telling them that while Dill was "the best possible type person to deal with" the British concept of the "personal representative" role, which originated with Churchill, was unacceptable and it actually had even embarrassed Dill. Put simply, Churchill could not be allowed a direct conduit to the president that enabled him to discuss strategy without the knowledge or input of the American chiefs. Admirals Stark and King agreed with Marshall's assessment.[26]

US Army and Navy planners had also put a great deal of thought and effort into studying the proposal during the previous twenty-four hours. Admiral Turner's scathing criticism of the Post Arcadia Collaboration, which he sent to General Gerow, declared, "British officials would be given half the total authority for matters now solely under US control." Turner's premise was that combining the American and British staffs would create a cumbersome organization. He was further convinced that the British would have a hard time making rapid decisions if the Joint Mission had to constantly cable London for advice. He recommended rejecting the proposal and maintaining separate military missions in London and Washington. In so doing he ignored the advantage of concentrating key decision-making agencies in Washington.[27]

Turner sought to maintain the status quo. The American military system had autonomous War and Navy Departments that independently reported to the president, who exercised centralized command and control. Roosevelt's informal style in dealing with army and navy leaders valued familiarity and personal discussion to reach consensus on decisions. There was no corporate body for high command, leaving the United States without an institutional organization for interservice collaboration comparable to the British Chiefs of Staff Committee. Rather, power was vested in individuals, Roosevelt as commander in chief and his principal military advisors, the Army Chief of Staff and Chief of Naval Operations. Below the level of the president, interservice coordination was haphazard. "Officers then serving in the Army and the Navy were often deeply suspicious of one another, inclined by temperament, tradition, and culture to remain separate and jealously guard their turf."[28]

Interservice collaboration, such as it was, resided with the Joint Board, which at this time was made up of the army chief of staff, deputy chief of staff, the chief of the War Plans Division, chief of naval operations, assistant chief of naval operations, and director of the naval War Plans Division. In 1939, Roosevelt instructed the board to report directly to him, bypassing the service secretaries. Still, the Joint Board remained solely an advisory body to the military services and through them to the president, never achieving a command and control function equivalent to that of the British Chiefs of Staff Committee.[29]

The British recommendation to institutionalize the Combined Chiefs of Staff created a dilemma for the Americans. As mentioned, they lacked an organization that corresponded with the British Chiefs of Staff Committee. The US Army Air Force, unlike its Royal Air Force counterpart, was not a separate service. The creation of a Joint Chiefs of Staff similar to the British Chiefs of Staff Committee represented a momentous undertaking, more so during wartime. As Admiral Stark put it, "it is not too strong to state that in some spots there is dynamite." Thus the Americans had carefully subjected the issue to several days of study, despite British prodding to make a quick decision.[30]

Marshall raised another concern during the meeting in Stark's office. The morning situation report from the Far East convinced him to speed up reinforcements to the theater. Such a move would, of course, disrupt the scheduled movement of US troops to Iceland and Ireland. He conceded Churchill's displeasure at such a development but argued its necessity and proposed to discuss the issue at their late afternoon meeting with the British chiefs.[31]

Stark's office session again highlighted coordination problems plaguing the American Army and Navy. Interservice cooperation was a larger issue than collaboration with the British. Major General Joseph Stilwell, the lead planner on Supergymnast, addressed the group. Unused to sitting in on discussions at this "rarified atmosphere," he found himself surprised by the wide diversity of opinion between the services over reinforcing the ABDA. All recognized the importance of rapidly getting men and material to the Pacific to stem the Japanese advance. Stilwell, however, was unprepared for the interservice animosity. Marshall asked the navy, "Can you hold Hawaii?" King, extremely sensitive about this topic since Pearl Harbor, testily replied, "Can the Army do it?" Marshall replied, "If the Army says it can hold it, will the Navy say so?" King, whose animosity toward the army bubbled just below the surface, responded, "Yes," in a lukewarm fashion. Stilwell was stunned; he had expected a vigorous, confident response from the navy. He said, "Imagine. Doubt about Hawaii." To be fair to King, the navy seemed to get a new requirement daily that spread its ships and sailors across the Atlantic and Pacific. Defend Hawaii; protect the US West Coast; convoy troop transports and merchantmen to Ireland, Iceland, and simultaneously to Australia, and New Caledonia on the other side of the globe; and the list went on and on. The navy was understrength and overcommitted. A great deal of difficult planning was needed to revamp the shipping schedules to reinforce the ABDA. Stilwell's army bias rendered him immune to the navy's problems. It was illustrative that the two services' parochial prejudices and resentment over Pearl Harbor still hindered cooperation. An organization that systematized collaboration, the sharing of information, and unified planning was certainly needed.[32]

Stilwell, a noted Anglophobe, did sympathize with the navy's complaints about the incessant British demands, "all agreed on being disgusted with the British hogging of all the material: quite willing to divide ours with us, but never any mention of putting theirs in the pot." The navy was "aghast" at the requirements for Magnet and wondered aloud where all the shipping would come from. Marshall heard similar complaints by the army planners, "everybody shrieking for more men, more guns, more planes, more everything. Our small supply melts as soon as it accumulates." Nonetheless, the American chiefs kept their own counsel and did not let planners' complaints influence relations with their British counterparts.[33]

At the ninth meeting of the Combined Chiefs of Staff the British side was disappointed that the Americans again deferred discussion on the Post Arcadia Collaboration. Admiral Pound instead read a cable from General Wavell, reporting the opening of his headquarters on Java and meeting with General Brett, Admiral Hart, and the Dutch commander. Wavell, who had just departed Singapore, offered a grim picture of the tactical situation in the ABDA Area. This cable, coupled with another from Wavell that Dill had shared previously, impressed the Americans with the precariousness of the situation. For his part, Dykes thought it was a mistake for Dill to have shared such a "gloomy" telegram because he felt that the Americans were "badly rattled by the Malaya news."[34]

Dykes's worries seemed justified when the Americans unexpectedly pushed for speeding up reinforcements to Asia and the Pacific, something the British neither prepared for nor anticipated. Stark, playing off the meeting with the American chiefs, recommended a new priority in shipping men and equipment from the United States that gave highest precedence to the ABDA for the next few weeks. He would accomplish this by reducing the shipment of troops to Iceland and Ireland and increasing the flow of men and material to the Pacific. Marshall interjected that the United States had the troops and equipment to do both but limited shipping meant enforcing strict priorities. If the Combined Chiefs agreed to accelerate the flow of reinforcements to the ABDA Area then they would have to reduce the flow to Ireland, Iceland, and North Africa. At the operational level this would interfere with Supergymnast, and the British could live with that. Viewed strategically, did the US proposal suggest that Japan, not Germany, was their highest priority? This the British could not abide, especially because the British were more sanguine about the situation in the Far East than their American counterparts.[35]

Anticipating pushback from Churchill, Dill recommended that the planners review the shipping resources to recommend possible changes to the deployments to Iceland and Ireland. The Americans were curious about why the British were not as concerned as they were over the situation in the Far East. If anything, operations in Malaya were going worse than in the Philippines. Stark asked Dill if Singapore was in immediate danger. Dill answered, "If the projected reinforcements arrived, there seemed no reason why Singapore should not hold out indefinitely."[36]

Portal defended the current schedule for shipment of troops and equipment to Iceland and Ireland. He pointed out that the timetable for the Atlantic forged a chain of interrelated movements that he was loath to break. Portal echoed Beaverbrook and Churchill by asking if more shipping resources might be found. The consistent British refusal to accept that the United States had a finite supply of transports wore on American patience. A compromise tasked shipping experts "to make proposals for providing shipping from the United States and British resources to carry to the ABDA Area the urgent reinforcements of men and matériel which the United States Army wishes to send in the immediate future; and to show at what cost to other commitments this shipping can be found."[37]

British reluctance to agree to a rapid diversion of forces comported with Churchill's views on the importance of Magnet and Supergymnast. Without the prime minister's agreement, however, the British chiefs could not act. They understood the strategic necessity. In London, Brooke and the Chiefs of Staff Committee recognized that the "situation in Malaya [is] getting more and more critical daily. Only hope reinforcements are not intercepted." Even though they agreed with the Americans, the British chiefs at the conference were compelled out of loyalty to press Churchill's desires. This loyalty, however, sent mixed messages to their American counterparts. The British chiefs had just said that Singapore could hold if reinforcements arrived in time. Yet when the Americans offered to send reinforcements to ABDA immediately, the British demurred. It seemed to the frustrated Americans that their ally was saying one thing but meaning quite another.[38]

Joint planners took some consolation when the chiefs accepted two of their papers—"Establishment of US Forces in Northern Ireland" and "Defense of Island Bases between Hawaii and Australia." The former detailed the troops to be deployed to Ireland, their mission, command and control, strategic direction and table of organization and equipment. The latter identified the air and sea lines of communication from the United States and finalized responsibility for Fiji and New Caledonia by compromising to resolve contentions. The final wording gave each side a measure of accountability. "That the defense of New Caledonia should, in principle, be accepted as an Australian responsibility, but that the United States should, as a temporary measure, furnish forces for the defense of the Island immediately after meeting the emergency in the ABDA Area." Admiral Pound next introduced Wavell's request to include Port Darwin, Australia, in the ABDA Area because the northern Australian port was a critical supply base for the ABDA operations and control of the Timor Sea. Admiral Stark agreed and on that note, the meeting ended.[39]

Upon his early return from Hyde Park, the president met with Marshall to discuss the Post Arcadia Collaboration paper. The president, exhibiting his growing confidence in Marshall's insight and judgment, wanted the general's views on Post Arcadia and recalled him before the chiefs' session ended. Marshall explained his objections to the president for two hours. He stressed the American chiefs' unanimous opinion that placing Dill between the president and the Combined Chiefs of Staff was unacceptable. If the Combined Chiefs were the principal military advisors to the political leaders, then why create a layer of bureaucracy between them and the president? If approved as Churchill had proposed, the British would enjoy access to the American president on matters of strategy and resources that the US chiefs had neither discussed nor evaluated.[40]

Marshall correctly intuited Churchill's intentions in proposing Dill's position. As Colonel Jacob pointed out, Churchill, "never liked the idea that when problems were to be discussed there must be present a triumvirate of the three services. He wanted to see Dill dealing directly with Marshall and King. At the same time he wanted to be able to use him as his representative with Hopkins or the President." In brief, Churchill sought to unilaterally influence US strategy and have the ability to distribute American resources. The prime minister sadly underestimated Marshall's standing with the president.[41]

After the presidential meeting, Marshall informed Stimson, who was supposedly still on vacation. Stimson supported Marshall's and the other chiefs' objections. The secretary of war was still seething over Churchill's 24 December end run to divert resources intended for the Philippines to Singapore, which thereafter colored his view of the prime minister. He now saw Churchill again "taking advantage of the President's well-known shortcomings in ordinary administrative methods and are striving to take advantage of his readiness to accept shortcuts and back door information which has not passed through his regular constitutional advisors."[42]

Later that evening Churchill and Roosevelt discussed Secretary of State Hull's pet peeve, the occupation of the islands of Saint Pierre and Miquelon. Roosevelt thought that cordial US relations with Vichy—he had sent a close friend and confidant, Admiral William Leahy, to serve as ambassador to Vichy—might secure the much sought after French invitation to the Allies to enter their North African colonies for the Supergymnast operation. He asked Churchill to encourage De Gaulle to withdraw the Free French troops from the islands. Regardless of Churchill's disgust with Vichy, Roosevelt emphasized that Vichy's goodwill would be a great boost for Supergymnast.[43]

Churchill did agree that on his return to London he would urge De Gaulle to accept a compromise: the islands were French and would remain so; the American and Canadian governments would supervise the wireless stations; the islands would be neutralized and de-militarized; the current (Free French) administrator and all troops would be withdrawn; and the American and Canadian governments would provide economic support to the island's inhabitants. That closed the book on a minor, but extremely vexing, matter.[44]

12 January 1942

Military activity in the Philippines was again scarce 12 January as the Japanese continued to methodically move troops on Luzon toward the Bataan defenses. The press announced the loss of Kuala Lumpur and that British forces were rapidly withdrawing toward Johore. In the Dutch East Indies, the Japanese invaded Tarakan (a rich oil center on northeast Borneo) and Minahasa (the northern tip of Celebes Island).[45]

The British chiefs and Churchill spent most of the morning mulling over the diversion of American troops and resources from the Atlantic to the Pacific. The Americans were clearly disturbed with Wavell's grim assessment on Malaya and wanted to do something immediately to help. Added to British discomfort was American reluctance to discuss Post Arcadia Collaboration arrangements.[46]

Churchill notified his chiefs that he was preparing a plan to allocate finished war materials because "some arrangement would be required to ensure the adequate allocations were given to the British by the American services." The British chiefs originally thought that the Combined Chiefs of Staff would oversee allocations, but Churchill offered a separate and independent committee headed by two civilians, one British and the other American. Unlike the prime minister, the British military chiefs immediately recognized that their American counterparts would violently object to such an arrangement.[47]

Churchill's idea grew out of a paper written by Major General Gordon N. Macready, the assistant chief of the Imperial General Staff, who had accompanied Churchill to the conference. Macready's report was initially a response to a Dutch request for large stocks of material and military equipment sent simultaneously from both the Americans and British without supporting justification. Macready concluded from this that the Allies needed a system to allocate war equipment based on operational requirements and to ensure an ally could not play the British and Americans off against each other. To avoid duplication of effort, he recommended that the British and Americans divide the United Nations into two groups of allied nations, or "protégés." The British group would include the Free French, all Empire nations (including India), Belgium, Poland, Czechoslovakia, Norway, Greece, Yugoslavia, Dutch East Indies, Egypt, and Turkey. The United States group would include China, Latin America, and Iceland. Both the US and Britain would share responsibility for Russia. Each would be responsible for reviewing requirements and arranging distribution of equipment according to operational needs for their respective "protégés."[48]

Two joint allocation committees, one in Washington and one in

London, would manage distribution requests. They were not, however, equal. An official US Army history explained that Macready "proposed a combined allocation committee in Washington to make bulk allocations to the British and their protégés out of American production, but a War Office, purely British, allocation committee in London to divide up these bulk allocations, as well as British production, among the Empire countries and the British protégés." While Churchill discussed allocation committees with his chiefs that morning, this paper circulated throughout the American Army and Navy staffs, creating suspicions that the British intended to hijack the distribution system. This attitude dampened the atmosphere of cooperation developed so far during the conference.[49]

Senior US civilian leaders rejected Macready's scheme. Hopkins asked Edward Stettinius, the administrator of the Lend-Lease office, to conduct a legal review of the proposal. Stettinius concluded, "Russia, China, and the Dutch East Indies and other allies cannot be treated as stepchildren protégés if we want to win this war sooner rather than later. They, together with the US and the UK, should sit at the table as a full member of the family." Macready's proposal would reduce the United States to allocating its own war production only after reviewing the requirements of all the allies. The report was blunt: "It is important not only to the United States, but to winning the war for all of us, that all of the allies—Russia, China, and all the others, as well as the UK—feel they are getting a just and fair share of *our* production by *our* good grace, rather than by the good grace of the UK." The British, it appeared, had not abandoned their initial demands to control the distribution of US industrial mobilization. It seemed as if the conference was back to day one.[50]

As this latest storm cloud formed, American planners were frantically working on a new deployment schedule for the Far East and the Atlantic to present to the Combined Chiefs of Staff that afternoon. The number of deployments kept increasing while the timelines kept decreasing. The pressure on the planners was palpable. Eisenhower, who headed the Pacific planning group, described the issue succinctly in his diary, "Ships! Ships! All we need is ships! Also ammunition, anti-aircraft guns, tanks, airplanes, what a headache!"[51]

As planners put together the new timetables, Marshall updated Stimson on conference proceedings. Stimson expressed interest in Marshall's plans to rapidly reinforce the Far East and the Post Arcadia Collaboration. He agreed with the general that a rapid reinforcement of ABDA might halt the Japanese advance and save the Dutch East Indies. But Stimson cautioned Marshall that Churchill's focus remained on the Atlantic and that Marshall had to balance the two theaters. This, Stimson believed, was possible if the navy could find the ships.[52]

Stimson then met with Hopkins at the White House to solicit Hopkins's support for the ABDA reinforcement. After the 24 December contretemps over reinforcements for Singapore, Stimson was determined to keep Hopkins apprised of his thinking. Hopkins agreed with Stimson on the plans to rearrange deployment priorities to help the ABDA before it was too late. As for Post Arcadia Collaboration, Stimson and Hopkins supported Marshall's position regarding Dill. The secretary of war "strongly opposed" Churchill's proposal to create a military layer of bureaucracy above the Combined Chiefs of Staff and did not want Churchill to have a means of bypassing the chiefs on strategic and resource allocation issues. Stimson also wanted Hopkins to ensure that the president did not make another off-the-cuff agreement with Churchill.[53]

The tenth formal meeting of the Combined Chiefs started at 1600 hours with Marshall outlining a plan to expedite the flow of reinforcements to the Pacific. American and British shipping specialists had worked well into the previous night identifying all ships available for this changed mission. By using the great prewar ocean liners such as the *Queen Mary* and the largest American transports, *Wakefield*, *West Point*, and *Mount Vernon*, Marshall could send 21,800 men from New York to Asia on 20 January, including 10,000 men slated for New Caledonia and the remainder as support for aerial squadrons. This reduced the deployment to Iceland from 8,000 to 2,500 troops and that to Northern Ireland from 16,000 to 4,000.[54]

The British were surprised because they had not anticipated the Americans using the *Queen Mary* to carry troops from New York to the United Kingdom and then pick up British troops to move to Asia.

Nor had they expected the three large military transports. Marshall accepted the calculated risk posed by German to U-boats but gambled that the liner's top speed of 29 knots would enable them to outrun the slower U-boats and accomplish the simultaneous rapid deployments to Northern Ireland, Iceland, and the Far East.[55]

Marshall's approach impressed the British chiefs and they seemed receptive. Stark outlined the pros and cons, but clearly if participants accepted the plan, it would rapidly strengthen the Allies' Far East position. It would only delay the complete relief of British forces in Northern Ireland by one month while the immediate deployment of 4,000 US troops would accomplish the political purpose of showing the flag. Its glaring disadvantage was the requirement to cut Lend-Lease aid to the Soviet Union by 30 percent for four months to compensate for the lack of shipping. One theater's feast became another theater's famine. The chiefs accepted the urgency of the situation in Asia and pledged cooperation and support, unanimously agreeing to refer it for decision to the president and prime minister that evening. Dill worried that cutting supplies to the USSR was a sensitive political topic between the two heads of state, so the military leaders should expect a tough grilling when they met their political leaders at the White House later that evening.[56]

Roosevelt opened the evening session by broaching the subject of Supergymnast. Much to the chiefs relief, Churchill's response was moderate and realistic. The prime minister reported that Rommel's stiffer than expected defenses and German reinforcements had delayed plans to capture Tripoli. In fact, the day before Churchill had recognized that his plan to clear Tripoli was finished and cabled Auchinleck: "I am sure you and your armies did all in human power, but we must face facts as they are." However, he still did not give up on Supergymnast. He simply acknowledged that the Allies now had more additional time to plan Supergymnast. Roosevelt concurred and interjected that this would also give the Allies more time to negotiate with the Vichy French. The decision augured well for the chiefs' plan to reinforce the Far East.[57]

Next, Marshall explained the military dimension of troop deployments. Almost 22,000 US troops could depart the United States on

20 January and reach the ABDA by mid-February. Twenty additional cargo ships would also sail eastward carrying hundreds of pursuit aircraft and bombers as well as more than 200 tons of cargo and four million gallons of gasoline. He did not mince words about the ramifications of the decision. These changes, said Marshall, would delay shipping troops to Iceland and Northern Ireland, and the rearranged convoy schedules would add to the congestion at the already overcrowded port of New York. Shipping was in such short supply that the United States would have to borrow three ships from the British and recall two American vessels currently in South America just to meet the revised timetable. The changes would also require a 30 percent reduction in aid to the Soviet Union over the next four months.[58]

Roosevelt did not blink at this most sensitive political issue and still supported Marshall's plan. He appreciated both the effort made to shift priorities to meet the Japanese threat in the Pacific and accepted its consequences. Churchill ominously observed that the reduction of Lend-Lease supplies would greatly upset Stalin. The Soviets, fighting for their very existence, were pushing the enemy back, but that could all change when Germany launched its spring offensive in Russia. Because the Soviets needed everything they could get from America militarily and politically, Churchill opposed cutting support to the Soviet Union for the sake of the Grand Alliance.[59]

Were the chiefs in agreement on the reduction, he asked? They were. The British and American Chiefs closed ranks and supported the concept, a significant move knowing Churchill's predilections. Hopkins supported the chiefs, noting that the issue with Moscow really came down to seven cargo ships. With seven additional merchantmen, aid to the USSR need not be interrupted. Surely, he pleaded, among 1,200 merchant ships, seven more could be found somewhere. Stark asked Churchill which had priority—the Soviet Union or the Far East. Both replied Churchill, but he admitted either was more important than Northern Ireland and Iceland reinforcement.[60]

Roosevelt shared Churchill's concerns over cutting Russian supplies, leaving open the possibility of last-minute changes. Marshall, however, needed a decision because the Magnet convoy was scheduled to depart in three days and the adjusted priorities would affect its sailing. Hopkins interceded to ask Churchill if reduced aid to the USSR was the only reason he opposed the plan. The prime minister replied that was correct. Hopkins then recommended approving immediate deployments to Asia while he identified the required seven additional cargo ships. That settled, both heads of state agreed to reinforce the Pacific.[61]

As the meeting wound down, Churchill again broached the subject of North Africa. Despite his earlier comments that changing battlefield conditions had forced a postponement of Gymnast, he now voiced concern over the effects of the new deployment schedule on Gymnast and Supergymnast. What was the earliest date either operation could be conducted? Would the necessary troops be available? Was the original landing date at Algiers or Casablanca on 1 March now in doubt? What was the new date? King estimated that loading could not begin before mid-April, dictating a landing in mid-May. An unhappy Churchill directed the chiefs to again relook the question. He still believed the Americans could produce the necessary ships to launch Supergymnast.[62]

That evening Churchill hosted a dinner party at the British embassy. Conversation drifted into a discussion of strategic plans. Knox and Beaverbrook thought the diversion of forces to the Far East foolish. Churchill disagreed, claiming that the support to the Far East was "absolutely necessary," especially since it did not seriously interfere with planned operations in other theaters. Then Churchill, with Knox's backing, called for the immediate execution of Supergymnast. William Donovan, the information coordinator, chimed in his support. Stimson was "disgusted" with Knox's undercutting the American military advisors and incensed by Knox's temerity in criticizing a presidential decision at a cocktail party.[63]

The fractious dinner, likely due to the stress of constant meetings with grave implications, next saw Hull and Churchill take the floor. Hull, seemingly tone-deaf to the arguments swirling around him, took the opportunity to tell Churchill that Great Britain should forsake preferential tariffs within its Empire to ensure the passage of Lend-Lease appropriation bills then before Congress. Hull's timing was dreadful because Churchill had discussed the issue with the president the previous day. They reached no agreement, but Roosevelt promised to forestall State Department pressure while Churchill indicated his unwillingness to entertain this matter until his return to London. Unsurprisingly, the prime minister harshly dismissed Hull out of hand and gave the American a very public "official bludgeoning."[64]

13 January 1942

Japanese probes continued against the Bataan defenses. On Malaya, the British withdrawal toward Johore continued. Japanese aircraft were routinely bombing Singapore, where Wavell had again returned to assess the fighting, an indication of the ABDA commander's belief that the best way to defend the Dutch East Indies was to defend Malaya and Singapore. British reinforcements arrived in Singapore, and in the Dutch East Indies the Japanese operations near Tarakan continued unabated.[65]

Wavell's trip to the front that day involved a dangerous eighty-mile trek to Malaya Command's advance headquarters in Johore Province, transiting bad roads and constantly dodging Japanese patrols. He met with the Australian commander, Major General Gordon Bennett, to get a firsthand sense of the battle conditions. The situation was growing desperate, a point Wavell made when he cabled the Chiefs of Staff his thoughts on the difficulty in holding Singapore.[66]

That morning the British chiefs met with their staff to prepare for a late afternoon meeting with their American counterparts to discuss the Post Arcadia Collaboration paper as the principal agenda item. The British chiefs were well aware that the Americans found their motives suspect. The previous afternoon Gerow sought out Dykes in an effort to fathom British intentions. Gerow cited the ABC-1 agreement on American British collaboration from January to March 1941, and Dykes reassured him that the British were merely trying to augment the system in light of the creation of ABDA.[67]

The March 1941 US Joint Letter of Transmittal after the ABC-1 talks stated that both nations would "collaborate continuously, always with an eye to an assurance that the arrangement would not allow the British to gain an inordinate voice in the affairs of the US armed forces." Yet US interservice collaboration remained rudimentary as the Americans had still not yet developed a mechanism similar to the British Chiefs of Staff Committee to direct the war effort. Lacking an organization for interservice collaboration, much less coalition warfare, it was difficult to imagine how the Allies would formulate and execute strategy and operations. The British wanted an institution for formal collaboration while the Americans were content with an informal arrangement. Regardless of the ABC-1 discussions, the Americans had shown little interest in a British proposal to establish a combined collaborative organization.[68]

What had instead emerged from ABC-1 was the exchange of military missions, a British mission in Washington made up of three officers, a flag officer of the Royal Navy, an army general, and a Royal Air Force officer, supported by a secretariat and four staffs—joint planning, army, navy, and air force. The US mission in London consisted of an army general and navy flag officer, supported by a secretariat and three separate staffs—an army, navy, and planning. During wartime, the missions would represent their respective governments and collaborate with their service counterparts on strategy. Improving this cumbersome staff structure became the topic at the 13 January morning meeting of the British chiefs.[69]

At this session, General Macready "expounded his scheme for [munitions] allocation from US and UK pools by military committees in Washington and London." Macready's protégé plan had come too late for inclusion in the Post Arcadia paper, accounting for his oral remarks. The British chiefs listened quietly to Macready's thoughts on munitions allocations and pools, but at this juncture, after waiting four days for a discussion, they were unwilling to add new concepts to the recommendations of the Post Arcadia Collaboration proposal that might upset the Americans. Rather, the Post Arcadia plan emphasized the importance of synchronizing strategy and production. It proposed that the Combined Planning Staffs monitor the production programs and advise the chiefs of discrepancies. Macready's plan viewed the allocation committees as entities separate from the Combined Chiefs but did not address the process for coordinating strategy and finished military equipment.[70]

The American chiefs had also carefully reviewed the Post Arcadia Collaboration paper, relying on the ABC-1 arrangements as their benchmark for strategic collaboration. Turner stressed the utility of continuing to operate through the developed military missions in each capitol, but the US chiefs accepted that changes were necessary. They had moved beyond a simple discussion of developing staff missions and saw the utility of building on the structure created for ABDA. They understood the benefits of moving from a system with two separate and independent organizations, with advisors from other nations, into a coherent, integrated, collaborative machine. Strong opinions remained on how best to achieve that goal.[71]

The American and British chiefs convened for their eleventh session at 1600. All carried a copy of the Post Arcadia Collaboration memo. Pound argued for American concurrence with the British proposal for continuing collaboration for the strategic conduct of the war. Collaborative arrangements for the ABDA theater were excellent and could serve as the model in other theaters as well. He underscored the utility of the combined (adopting the term in the paper for collaboration of two or more nations) planning committee and advocated a combined intelligence committee as well. Pound endorsed the need for distributing war materials based on strategic requirements determined by the Combined Chiefs of Staff and reiterated Macready's recommendation that the British and Americans adopt protégé groups for the purposes of weapons and material distribution.[72]

The chiefs then reviewed Post Arcadia Collaboration line by line. They quickly agreed to adopt the paper's definitions for joint and combined organizations. Stark then identified the Americans' main contention in the document. He politely expressed the American chiefs' great admiration for Field Marshal Dill but regretfully could not accept a British representative in a position of authority above the Combined Chiefs of Staff. Pound said he would have to refer the matter to Churchill for decision. The Americans quickly agreed. Having already gained the support of Roosevelt, Hopkins, and Stimson before the meeting, the US chiefs were confident of the outcome.[73]

The Americans did accept in principle the British proposal to coordinate intelligence sharing. Like so many other wartime arrangements, the American interservice intelligence coordination was still subject to friction and rivalry that detracted from overall efficiency. More time was needed to work on US Army and Navy intelligence sharing before the US chiefs could agree on specifics to work with the British. This became a job for the Combined Planning Committee.[74]

Next, attention turned to priorities and allocations. The Americans accepted that "the Combined Chiefs of Staff should settle the broad programme of requirements based on strategic policy," meaning that war material (tanks, planes, and guns) would be distributed in support of strategic goals. As yet, however, the United States had no system to determine requirements for munitions and equipment, allocate these resources, or establish shipping priorities. Able to agree on the overarching principle, they were consequently unprepared to accept specific details. Clearly disappointed, Pound offered an amendment that "finished war equipment shall be allocated in accordance with strategical needs." The British, perhaps as a result of their difficult experience with Beaverbrook as Minister of Aircraft Production, had privately agreed before the meeting to add a draft minute, "that appropriate bodies should be set up under authority of the Combined Chiefs of Staff in Washington, and of a corresponding body in London, for the purpose of giving effect to this principle."[75]

The addition implied that there would be two Combined Chiefs of Staff, one in London and one in Washington. This idea comported with Churchill's expectations of dividing the conflict into spheres with the United States directing the war against Japan and the British the war against Germany. Marshall vigorously protested that "there could be no question of having any duplication of the Combined Chiefs of Staff organization in Washington and in London. There could be only one Combined Chiefs of Staff who would give broad direction on the allocation of material." Marshall found parallel allocation committees in Washington and London acceptable, provided they reported to a single Combined Chiefs of Staff. As for the organization of the allocating committees, that was a decision for senior civilian leaders.[76]

The US chiefs were not about to agree to any arrangement that allowed others to decide how to distribute American-produced material. That was a political decision to be made on the basis of strategy and available resources. The British chiefs understood the importance of subordinating resources to strategy and broke ranks with the prime minister and Beaverbrook by asking the Americans for a written commitment subordinating allocation committees to the Combined Chiefs of Staff. Their subsequent draft note clarified their position for the political leaders, especially Churchill. "We, the Combined US-British Chiefs of Staff are agreed in principle that finished war equipment shall be allocated in accordance with strategic needs. We accordingly submit that an appropriate body should be set up under authority of the Combined Chiefs of Staff."[77]

Pound then addressed the thorny issue of control of shipping resources. The American side again opposed any statement beyond, "The Combined Chiefs of Staff would settle the broad issues of priority of overseas movements." Marshall appreciated that strategic shipping requirements had to balance military necessity with domestic exports and imports. No single organization currently existed in the United States government to control all facets of US shipping, but Marshall was loath to agree to anything beyond a general principle until the respective political leaders developed a system for allocating and prioritizing shipping. As had become glaringly apparent throughout the conference, the Americans' lack of a joint organization comparable to the British Chiefs of Staff Committee placed them at a great disadvantage. Without joint agencies to collaborate on intelligence sharing, supply distribution, munitions allocation, and shipping, the US chiefs could hardly agree on detailed combined collaboration. General principles were fine, but specifics would have to wait.[78]

Still, the day's discussions were fruitful. Each side had candidly addressed complex and sensitive issues involving operational, logistical, and organizational considerations. They had agreed in principle on the general organization and concept for the Combined

Chiefs of Staff with its ramifications for national sovereignty. The American side's numerous edits needed to be incorporated into a final, agreed-on document. Since the British had taken the lead on the initial draft, the Americans would update the revised paper and have it ready for final approval the next day.[79]

Before adjourning, the chiefs briefly examined two Joint Planning Committee papers. The first was on "Movements and Projects in the Atlantic Theater—First Half of 1942," which analyzed the importance and interrelationship of military movements and operations in the Atlantic that supported the agreed-on Grand Strategy. The second, Supergymnast, was deferred to the next day as participants felt that the lengthy discussion of Post Arcadia matters precluded sufficient time for a thorough assessment of the paper.[80]

As the Americans rewrote the Post Arcadia Collaboration, the British chiefs prepared for an evening session with Churchill. They were apprehensive about the prime minister's reaction to the American stand on Dill's role since, after all, it was Churchill's idea. Roosevelt likely coached the prime minister on how important this issue was to the US chiefs because Churchill took everything in stride, much to the British chiefs' surprise. His performance mystified Colonel Jacob. "I do not know what took place behind the scenes then. We came away still not knowing what Dill's functions were to be. The question was not settled until a fortnight later when the Prime Minister at last signed Dill's two-part directive. Part one appointed Dill the head of the Military Mission. Part two, which was a confidential annex, invested him as the Prime Minister's personal representative."[81]

These instructions, when issued after the conference was over, put Dill in an awkward position. The first part, which was public, was in complete accord with the agreement of 13 January at the Arcadia Conference. Dill, as head of the British Joint Mission, received instructions from the Chiefs of Staff Committee in London. He was then tasked to represent these views to the Combined Chiefs of Staff in Washington. The second part, which was confidential and not released to the American chiefs, was not. Churchill directed Dill: "you will in your contacts with the President of the US, Mr. Hopkins and others represent me in my capacity as Minister of Defence. You will from time to time receive from me such guidance as may be necessary to enable you to represent my views; and you are authorized to correspond direct with me as you see fit." If Churchill hoped this confidential annex would allow him to circumvent the American chiefs, he was disappointed. Dill was scrupulously honest and found a unique solution to his dilemma. While Churchill kept his military advisors informed of his correspondence with the president, Roosevelt did not do the same with his own Chiefs of Staff. Dill used his position to keep the American chiefs informed of decisions by sharing the messages between the president and prime minister with them.[82]

That evening Churchill displayed greater interest in munitions allocation than in Dill's role. Lord Beaverbrook, the British minister of supply, did not believe that the allocation agencies should be responsible to and under the authority of the Combined Chiefs of Staff, as recommended by the Chiefs of Staff. Under the British system the Ministry of Supply was responsible for the procurement and distribution of all raw materials, excluding the British military services, from the resource allocation process. Beaverbrook recommended a similar system for the United States, headed by Hopkins and reporting directly to the president. Both national committees would in turn report to a combined organization under Hopkins's leadership. This combined allocation committee would be independent of but equivalent to the Combined Chiefs of Staff and take responsibility for distributing military equipment. Beaverbrook's suggestion went further than Macready's proposal to put American production in a common pool by cutting the Combined Chiefs out of the distribution process and separating grand strategy from war material production and allocation. Roosevelt had reservations with Beaverbrook's approach, but the idea of an organization devoted to munitions allocation intrigued him.[83]

Churchill and Beaverbrook drafted a proposal that evening for a Munitions Assignment Board having two components. Beaverbrook would head the London office and Hopkins the Washington one. This board would report directly to the president and prime minister, enjoy broad powers, and be independent of the Combined Chiefs. Pooling of resources in this fashion clearly was advantageous to the British because they could tap into the vast US industrial and resource base and distribute its holdings as they saw fit. Churchill hoped to get Roosevelt's approval before departing Washington the next day.[84]

The same evening Stimson met with General Drum, who had requested the meeting to present his views on the China mission. Drum, unable to grasp that Marshall and Stimson shared a common view of the China mission, persisted in promoting himself. Drum asserted the role he was being offered was not "big enough for his capabilities." His arrogance deeply offended Stimson, who was further annoyed by Drum wasting his time. He bluntly criticized Drum's self-serving attitude and told the general that he had personally designed Drum's role for the important mission to China that enjoyed the full support of Marshall and the War Department general staff. Instead, Drum's self-seeking display left him no choice but to select another general officer for the assignment.[85]

The same day, Portal and Arnold finally agreed on the distribution of US-produced aircraft, an issue under discussion since 22 December. Roosevelt wanted to help the British, but he also wanted Arnold to expand the USAAF to 115 combat groups. Churchill wanted planes for the Royal Air Force, but he also wanted additional American air combat groups in Europe. Put differently, the British needed planes immediately and the Americans needed planes for air force expansion. Might the resulting competition for aircraft, Churchill worried, damage the Anglo-American relationship established to date? Portal and Arnold rose above their personal national outlooks, took a wider strategic view, and eventually compromised. They agreed to a monthly allocation of US-produced planes for the Royal Air Force in 1942, amounting to almost 25 percent of the anticipated total US airplane production for the year. (The totals were 589 heavy bombers, 1,744 medium bombers, 2,745 light bombers, 4,050 pursuit planes, 402 observation planes, and 852 transports. This was a grand total of 10,382 airplanes for the year.) Some Americans regarded the schedule as too inflexible given the vagaries of aircraft, so a caveat was included in the agreement to account for periodic adjustments as required by fluctuations to production calculations, attrition rates, or future deployments of units to combat areas. This proved prescient in the months ahead.[86]

14 January 1942

On Arcadia's final day the war news from Asia and the Pacific was dreadfully repetitive. Japanese attacks continued against the Bataan perimeter. In Malaya, the British grim withdrawal continued as did Japanese air raids against Singapore. Japanese troops had reached the outskirts of the Johore defenses. In the Dutch East Indies, Japan's combined might defeated Dutch forces and seized the oil rich region around Tarakan.[87]

That day, just as Churchill was preparing to depart Washington, he received a cable from Wavell from his new ABDA headquarters in Batavia. "Battle for Singapore will be a close run thing, and we shall need luck in getting in convoys safely and up to time." Still the prime minister remained optimistic. The *Mount Vernon* with nine thousand British troops arrived in Singapore. Churchill confidently informed the Australian prime minister of its safe arrival. Shortly before leaving Washington Churchill queried Wavell, "What are the defenses and obstructions on the landward side? Are you sure you can dominate with Fortress cannon any attempt to plant siege batteries?"[88]

Churchill was still in denial about Malaya's situation. He had never seen Singapore yet insisted the island "fortress" was "a completely encircled strong place" capable of defending itself against attacks from any direction and able to withstand a prolonged siege. He failed to appreciate that unless Wavell's Johore defenses broke the Japanese, Singapore would be in extreme danger. His cable to Wavell the following day exposed his misunderstanding of the situation. "What would happen in event of your being forced to withdraw into the island? It has always seemed to me," the prime minister asserted, "that the vital need is to prolong defence of the island to the last possible minute, but, of course, I hope it will not come to this." The prime minister's hopes to reorganize and strengthen Singapore's defenses fell apart because the Japanese moved much more rapidly than the British anticipated. Wavell realized that Churchill was misinformed about Singapore's impregnability and responded, "Until quite recently all plans based on repulsing seaborne attacks on Island and holding land attack in Johore or further north, and little or nothing was done to construct defenses on north side of island to prevent crossing Johore straits." In other words Singapore was fatally vulnerable on its north side and the current Johore fighting critical to its defense.[89]

Three days later Wavell cabled Churchill an even blunter assessment: "I must warn you however that I doubt whether island can be held for long once Johore is lost. Fortress guns sited for use against ships and have mostly ammunition for that purpose only, many can only fire seaward. Part of the garrison has already been sent into Johore and many of troops remaining are of doubtful value. I am sorry to give you depressing picture but I do not want you to have false picture of island fortress. Singapore defences were constructed entirely to meet seaward attacks. I still hope Johore may be held until next convoy arrives."[90]

Churchill was shocked. He insisted that he had no idea of Singapore' precariousness: "It never occurred to me for a moment, nor Sir John Dill, with whom I discussed the matter on the outward voyage, that the gorge of the fortress of Singapore, with its splendid moat half a mile to a mile wide, was not entirely fortified against an attack from the northward. What is the use of having an island for a fortress if it is not to be made into a citadel? To construct a line of detached works with searchlights and cross-fire combined with immense wiring and construction of the swamp areas, and to provide the proper ammunition to enable the fortress guns to dominate enemy batteries planted in Johore, was an elementary peace-time provision which it is incredible did not exist in a fortress which has been twenty years in the making."[91]

Churchill was being disingenuous, because as early as May 1941 Dill had warned him of the precarious state of the Singapore defenses. Dill argued that Singapore needed reinforcement despite limited resources. "It has been an accepted principle of our strategy that in the last resort the security of Singapore comes before that of Egypt. Yet the defenses of Singapore are still considerably below standard."

Churchill, confident in the impregnability of "Fortress Singapore," replied, "I do not take that view, nor do I think the alternative is likely to present itself." In August 1941 he said, "I feel confident that Japan will lie quiet for a while." Later, when the subject resurfaced he insisted that simply dispatching a "K.G.B. [King George V] battleship might indeed be a decisive deterrent." After the war he admitted that he took the risk too lightly because he was focused on the German threat.[92]

As Malaya teetered on disaster, American attention focused on the Philippines. Philippine President Quezon had cabled Roosevelt an emotional plea for support. "We decided to fight by your side and we have done the best we could. . . . But how long are we going to be left alone? . . . I want to know, because I have a responsibility to my countrymen. . . . I want to decide in my own mind whether there is justification for allowing all these men to be killed when for the final outcome of the war the shedding of their blood may be wholly unnecessary." Roosevelt asked Knox and Stimson to draft a response. Knox had already prepared a very pessimistic answer, but conscious of the president's commitment, sought Stimson's advice. The best Stimson could do was to draft a more positive, yet honest, reply for Roosevelt to send to Quezon.[93]

By this time much of the British staff was packing for its departure that evening for home. The Combined Chiefs and their principal staff assistants met in the early afternoon for a brief discussion followed by lunch in the Board Room of the Federal Reserve Building. The amiable gathering began with cocktails followed by a simple meal. Stark hosted and the press was invited to take pictures. The final opportunity during the conference to publicize the newly established cooperation and unity between the military leaders of both nations was not to be squandered.[94]

The Combined Chief's twelfth and final session convened in midafternoon. Three important topics were considered: the move of United States reinforcements to the Far East, Supergymnast, and Post Arcadia Collaboration. Marshall's plan to rapidly reinforce the Far East and still conduct the Northern Ireland and Iceland deployments, albeit with some delays, impressed the British. Their supply expert, Brigadier Vernon M. Napier, reviewed the availability of the large ocean liners *Queen Mary*, *Queen Elizabeth*, and the *Aquitania* for the plan. Napier determined that the *Queen Mary* would not be available in January to take troops from New York to Northern Ireland as briefed, but that the British would make three other transports available to compensate for its absence. The three large ocean liners would be available in February to move troops to the Pacific. Napier informed the chiefs that he coordinated this modification with the Americans and General Somervell had accepted the arrangement. Participants promptly approved the revised shipping schedule.[95]

Supergymnast as usual provided the day's drama. The chiefs reviewed a US planner's critique of the Joint Planning Committee's Supergymnast report. This was a follow-up to the meeting at the White House on 12 January when Churchill had questioned the impact on the North Africa operation of reinforcing the Far East, specifically how reinforcing Asia affected the timeline for the North Africa operation. What was the earliest date this operation could be executed?[96]

By this time, the Americans had exhausted ways to say that the shipping was not available to do everything Churchill wanted all at once. The length of the Supergymnast delay depended on the time it took for the ships to return from Australia to ports on the East Coast of the United States. They estimated that passenger ships would be available between 10–20 April and cargo ships from 15–25 May. Using these dates for the return of the Far East convoy, the earliest possible date for Supergymnast D-1 was 25 May, and even that was optimistic because it did not consider unpredictable factors such as shipping losses, additional requirements arising from enemy actions, or increased demands for Lend-Lease equipment.[97]

The British were not pleased. Even after two weeks of talks and agreements on the CCS to broker resources, they continued to act as if they had the prerogative to draw arbitrarily on the apparently limitless resources of the United States. Portal, who often acted as a spokesman during the more contentious deliberations, questioned whether the Americans had considered all their assets. Could they make any further sacrifice? How about outfitting merchantmen currently engaged in carrying imported goods and raw materials to the United States? Somervell explained, yet again, that the American side had reviewed and scheduled all the US shipping resources. They had committed every available US passenger and cargo ship. A brief discussion ended with an agreement to discuss the matter with the president and prime minister that evening.[98]

The chiefs' collegiality put the best face on a serious disagreement. The British felt the Americans "have no view of the whole shipping picture. They don't understand at all that to get ships for operations you have to cut into trade and imports." The British chiefs insisted that the Americans could squeeze out more ships if they tried harder and remained reluctant to go to Churchill and tell him that a lack of shipping would delay Supergymnast.[99]

The Americans were thoroughly frustrated with their counterparts. Supergymnast started with Churchill's belief that British military success in Libya presented an opportunity to deliver a knockout blow to Germans in North Africa. But just two nights ago he admitted that crushing the German troops was no longer possible. Stilwell, one of the lead planners on Supergymnast, summed up the American feeling that they were wasting their time chasing Churchill's whims about "making a plan that we can prove won't work."[100]

The final topic was Post Arcadia Collaboration. Participants reviewed the Americans' revisions line by line. The latest draft outlined the responsibilities of the Combined Chiefs of Staff as: (1) planning for the strategic direction of the war; (2) providing general guidance on the distribution of military equipment (this would be done based on strategic requirements through the appropriate organizations in Washington and London, which report to the Combined Chiefs of Staff); and (3) establishing priorities for shipping men and material overseas.[101]

The British official military history identified an important if unwritten function of this new Combined Chiefs of Staff. "They provided a meeting place between two different chains of professional responsibility; an indispensable link between the British system and the American. It was a neat solution to a vexatious problem, which introduces itself into all attempts to achieve unity of command in time of war."[102]

The draft established a combined planning staff and a combined secretariat. It also named members from the American and Britain delegations to serve on these bodies and identified the heads of the British Joint Staff Mission as General Colville Wemyss (Army), Admiral Charles Little (Navy), and Air Marshall Arthur Harris (Air Force). Although Dill was staying on as the overall head of mission, his name did not appear, pending a precise definition of his role. The Combined Chiefs in Washington would meet weekly or more frequently if the situation warranted. There were no specifics regarding the combined intelligence committee, combined allocations committee, or combined movements committee. These and other ancillary organizations required further review by the combined planners. Such ambiguity was consistent with the current fledgling state of the US military's collaborative mechanisms.[103]

Over lunch and the meeting that followed Dill again impressed the Americans with his bearing and professionalism. He displayed no resentment over the Americans' sharp criticism of his projected role as originally described in the Post Arcadia Collaboration paper. For their part, the American side respected Dill's forbearance, sympathizing because the general had never sought the dominant position that Churchill wanted. More than any other British participant, Dill had earned their respect through "his keen understanding and breadth of view." In short, the Americans admired him.[104]

While the chiefs met in conference, Stimson addressed which general officer would represent American interests in China. Earlier that morning, Eisenhower had proposed three candidates, all suggested by Marshall. Stimson questioned their qualifications. Then Drum, finally realizing that his arrogance had alienated the secretary of war, expressed his willingness to do anything the secretary directed. The offer surprised Stimson, who asked for Marshall's advice. Marshall was blunt. He had already dropped Drum as a serious candidate and regarded his belated apology as "additional evidence of Drum's unfitness," prepared "to protect himself against criticism for having virtually declined to go." Late that afternoon a remorseful Drum visited Stimson's office, admitting his mistake and pleading that he would go wherever the secretary sent him. Stimson found the performance unbecoming of a senior officer and concluded that Drum was indeed an unsuitable candidate.[105]

That evening Stimson asked Stilwell, the army's lead planner on Supergymnast, for an off-the-record account of the latest chiefs' session. Marshall had suggested to Stilwell that he might also use the meeting to update the secretary on the China question. Stilwell, an old China hand, impressed the secretary as "quick-witted and alert-minded." Stilwell displayed a mastery of Supergymnast's details and echoed Stimson's concerns on the riskiness of the whole operation. Regardless of his outspoken opposition to Supergymnast, Stilwell, unlike Drum, did not dismiss the assignment out of hand. He and his planners worked diligently, dutifully followed directions, and prepared a thoroughly researched and written critique for Stimson. On the heels of Drum's self-centered arrogance it must have been a refreshing change for Stimson.[106]

What also impressed Stimson was Stilwell's knowledge of China. He spoke the language and had served as a US military observer for two years with the Chinese army in 1937–39. "In half an hour," Stimson recalled, "he gave me a better first hand picture of the valor of the Chinese armies than I had ever received before. Of this valor, he had a very high opinion." It was apparent why Marshall rated him so highly. Despite his reputation as a difficult personality, Stilwell carried an infectious enthusiasm for China and Stimson knew he had found his general. "I went to bed with a rather relieved feeling that I had discovered a man who will be very useful to us in the problems that are coming." Stilwell had traded one problem (Supergymnast) for another (China).[107]

As the Stimson-Drum drama played out, Marshall met privately with Hopkins and Roosevelt to explore the establishment of a Munitions Assignment Board. Churchill had again used his access to the American president to press his views on this topic. Roosevelt was, of course, willing to listen to Churchill's proposals, but he had learned from previous experience not to make concessions to the prime minister in private that might come back to embarrass him in public. In advance of his evening meeting with Churchill, Roosevelt sought Marshall's opinion of a statement that he, Churchill, and Beaverbrook had crafted. It described a Munitions Assignment Board, "a Supreme Command in supplies as well as in strategy." The board would have two coequal entities, one in London and one in Washington, chaired by Beaverbrook and Hopkins, respectively. They would report to Churchill and Roosevelt, making the board equal to but independent of the Combined Chiefs of Staff. It incorporated Beaverbrook's numerous ideas for pooling resources and creating an agency to allocate munitions. In other words, it was another British attempt to circumvent the Combined Chiefs of Staff and funnel resources to operations that the chiefs had not vetted.[108]

The Munitions Assignment Board was a political and diplomatic issue. Distribution of supplies among allies naturally carried enormous financial implications exacerbated by national interests and preferences. The British, for example, wanted pooled resources although the Americans repeatedly made clear that they did not intend to relinquish control of US-made equipment. Marshall addressed the draft strictly from a military perspective and told Roosevelt that unless the Munitions Assignment Board was subordinate to the Combined Chiefs of Staff, it was a recipe for disaster. He had "no objection whatever to having parallel Allocation Committees in Washington and London dealing with the allocation of American and British war material respectively," but "that there could be no question of having any duplication of the Combined Chiefs of Staff organization in Washington and in London." In brief, the London Allocating Committee had to be subordinate to the Combined Chiefs of Staff in Washington.[109]

Marshall's opposition rested on two considerations. First, he did not want an independent civilian body capable of interfering with military plans by refusing to allocate resources. Second, more subtly, "he feared that a civilian director would be inclined to grant the British a degree of control over American military activities that they could not get from the Combined Chiefs of Staff." Indeed, Churchill's proposal was so risky that he told Roosevelt that, if implemented, "he could not continue to assume the responsibilities as Chief of Staff," because "neither he nor any other Chief of Staff could plan military operations and carry them through if some other authority, over which he had no control, could refuse to allocate the materiel required for such operations." Hopkins agreed with the compelling argument and threw his weight behind Marshall. It made no sense, Hopkins told Roosevelt, to create a system where the military could not control the distribution of weapons. To back up his words, Hopkins told the president he would not serve on the board as Beaverbrook and Churchill proposed it.[110]

At this point, Churchill and the other of his military advisors joined the three Americans for the final and the most acrimonious Arcadia Conference meeting. The recorded minutes of this meeting failed to convey the pent-up strain and emotional special pleading of the embarrassing session. Churchill believed that Roosevelt agreed on the creation of the Munitions Assignment Board that would give the British direct access to US-produced military equipment and had already promised Beaverbrook the chair of the London board. He did not account for Marshall's influence on the president.[111]

Roosevelt announced Anglo-American collaboration on three boards: a Raw Materials Board to supervise the allocation of natural resources, oil, coal, iron, and such, with representatives from all twenty-six nations that signed the Declaration by the United Nations; an Anglo-American Combined Shipping Adjustment Board would coordinate pooled shipping resources between the two nations; and the Munitions Assignment Board. The first two boards elicited little discussion but the third was hotly debated. Marshall had convinced Roosevelt that the Munitions Assignment Board as drafted was a bad idea, but there was not enough time before the meeting for the president to inform Churchill of his decision. As a consequence, Roosevelt's opposition to the Munitions Assignment Board blindsided Beaverbrook and the prime minister, who had anticipated swift approval of their recommendation.[112]

Instead, this Roosevelt-announced board would have two committees, one operating in London and the other in Washington, headed by civilian chairmen and subordinate to the Combined Chiefs of

Staff. Unprepared in a public forum, Churchill and Beaverbrook vainly tried to push their proposal for a board that was independent of and equal to the Combined Chiefs. Marshall would have none of it. He informed the prime minister that was not his understanding of the matter. Rather, "the Munitions Allocation Committee and its civilian chairman would be a subcommittee of the Joint [*sic*], Combined Chiefs of Staff Committee and should deal purely with munitions."[113]

Churchill emotionally argued that the civilian allocation committees could also discuss issues with the Chiefs of Staff Committees in London and Washington, implying again that there were two Combined Chiefs of Staff. Brooke, in London, supported this dual or mirror Combined Chiefs of Staff concept, stating, "I could see no reason why at this stage, with American forces totally unprepared to play a major part, we should agree to central control in Washington." He feared that with a single Combined Chiefs of Staff the British would lose the ability to control the direction of the war and with it their global position vis-à-vis the Americans. Marshall pounced, insisting that there would be no duplicate Chiefs of Staff Committee in London because the system would be an unworkable bureaucratic nightmare. The single Combined Chiefs of Staff would be in Washington, which, after all, was the goal of the Post Arcadia Collaboration agreement. King concurred, and Marshall then emphatically pointed out that strategy and material were interwoven, and with resources, scarce material considerations at present were dominating strategic ones. To reset the proper balance, he concluded that the organization developing strategy had to control munitions distribution to ensure that plans matched available production and vice versa. The civilian heads could always appeal disagreements with the Combined Chiefs of Staff to Roosevelt or Churchill.[114]

Churchill appeared more and more frustrated. He had been stymied on Dill as a separate conduit to the president; his plan for two Combined Chiefs of Staff, which would allow Britain to control strategy against Germany, was thwarted; and now his plan to control resource distribution was blocked. He expediently recommended withholding any announcement about the Munitions Assignment Board until the new concept completed a one-month trial period.

Roosevelt proposed an announcement that the two nations were pooling their resources and exchanging information on material production but without any specifics on the board. In response, Churchill demanded that the Allies constitute the board immediately and the trial period commence because the British needed the equipment now. Forrest Pogue noted that throughout the conference, Churchill had irritated the US side with his assumption that he could draw on US "manpower and weapons as if these had been swept into a common pool for campaigns tailored to suit the interests and convenience of Great Britain" and his condescending attitude that whatever he demanded "was simply good strategic sense and that failure of the Americans to agree showed inexperience, immaturity, and bad manners." Churchill may have lacked tact but his need was real. Lend-Lease was the lifeline for the British economy and Britain's defense, and future operations depended on a share of the increased American production. He pushed hard because he was desperate, and some Americans resented his self-assertiveness while others accepted it. But Churchill's unilateral plan to establish the Munitions Assignment Board independent of the military cut too close to the bone. Marshall curtly informed the prime minister that US military expansion would require greater quantities of US-manufactured equipment than had been the case before Pearl Harbor, implying that Washington would decide where and to whom it would distribute American-produced war stocks. Roosevelt closed on a conciliatory note, declaring, "We will call it a preliminary agreement and try it out that way."[115]

Churchill and Beaverbrook were angry, believing that Roosevelt had double-crossed them. Beaverbrook fumed about his much-diminished role in distributing war equipment. Far from being an equal of the Combined Chiefs of Staff, he was a subordinate. Charles Wilson, Churchill's doctor and confidant, wrote, "The Americans have got their way and the war will be run from Washington, but they will not be wise to push us so unceremoniously in the future. Our people are very unhappy about the decision."[116]

Churchill's irritation went beyond the rejection of his Munitions Assignment Board. His disappointment was another stark reminder that he had failed to achieve an unstated aim for the conference. Charles Wilson said that Churchill's goal at Arcadia was "to show the President how to run the war." The prime minister expected his strategic opinions to dominate the alliance, and the president would simply acquiesce to his superior military expertise. Wilson acknowledged that Churchill realized, "It has not worked out quite like that." Throughout the conference Roosevelt, a superb politician, had frustrated Churchill and advanced US goals.[117]

The final discussion subject appropriately enough was Supergymnast. Dill broke the news to Churchill that despite Herculean efforts no additional shipping was available and the operation would have to be postponed until May. Churchill, who had bullied his chiefs and their planning staffs for three weeks, finally accepted this reality, cushioned somewhat by the unfavorable tactical situation in Libya. The curtain closed on Arcadia at 1830.[118]

Later Roosevelt hosted Churchill and Hopkins at an intimate dinner where they reviewed the conference's accomplishments. Despite flashes of acrimony, overall, the collaboration between the respective militaries was fruitful. Churchill and Roosevelt accentuated the positive and put disagreements to the side. Churchill accepted, perhaps resentfully, that he had pushed the Americans too far. He did not get all he wanted but on aggregate obtained much of what he did. The United States confirmed the Germany First strategy and approved the general design for Churchill's Grand Strategy with little adjustment. The Americans had also agreed to send troops to Iceland, Ireland, and the Far East. Disagreement led to compromise and experiment. Churchill was willing to give the ABDA and unity of command an opportunity and accepted the Munitions Assignment Board on a one-month trial period. Both leaders agreed to collaborate with the (single) Combined Chiefs of Staff regarding strategic matters. When dinner ended, Roosevelt accompanied Churchill to Union Station, where the prime minister boarded a special train to Norfolk and later flew to Britain via Bermuda. The coming months would render judgment on the solid foundation for the Anglo-American alliance laid at Arcadia.[119]

EPILOGUE

Arcadia's Aftermath

The Emergence of the Combined Chiefs of Staff

The Arcadia Conference ended just over one month after the United States entered the war, a period of unremitting Anglo-American defeats. Indeed, for the next several months the strategic military situation in Asia and North Africa continued to deteriorate. US decisions to send more troops and equipment to the Pacific than Europe in the first six months of 1942 appeared to violate the "Germany First" agreement, and critics place much blame for this diversion on the Arcadia Conference.

Churchill was worn out from his efforts at Arcadia but proud of his accomplishments and anticipated a warm welcome home from the press and public. Approaching London on 17 January, he told Charles Wilson, "I have done a good job of work with the President. We got on together. I think we shall soon see dividends. I am sure, Charles, the House will be pleased with what I have to tell them." It was not. Vituperative articles in the morning papers criticizing his wartime leadership shocked Churchill. The press and political opponents excoriated him over the continual strategic setbacks and perceived military ineptitude in North Africa, blaming Churchill's dual roles as prime minister and minister of defense for the debacles. He wearily told Wilson, "There seems to be plenty of snarling."[1]

On 27 January, Churchill directly confronted his critics in the House of Commons requesting a vote of confidence to buttress himself against potential waves of recriminations over his conduct of the war in the Far East. Critics also lambasted him for the reversal of fortune in the Middle East, in part because he had promised so much and delivered so little. Churchill's exaggerations before Arcadia had inflated public expectations of victory in North Africa. He had, after all, predicted the recapture of Cyrenaica, seizure of Benghazi's airfields, and the destruction of Rommel's army. Now, with the British in headlong retreat, he had to eat his words, although he carefully distanced himself from the earlier predictions by reassuring his audience that "I make it a rule never to try and prophesy beforehand how battles will turn out." He likewise downplayed the disaster unfolding in the Pacific, expressing his belief that the beleaguered Dominion forces would fight "to the last inch." But press criticism of his handling of the war was gaining momentum.[2]

The prime minister needed good news to cheer his allies and silence his critics in Commons. He turned to the Arcadia Conference where he had developed a close personal relationship with President Roosevelt, who promised to see the war through, whatever the cost. He took credit for the formation of a "league of 26 United Nations" whose goal was the "destruction of Hitlerism" and underlined his efforts to secure American support, for Britain had already paid dividends. (The first American army units had arrived in Northern Ireland two days earlier.) More was on the way—American fighter and bomber units were coming in greater numbers to defend Britain and to carry out a strategic bombing offensive against Germany. At Arcadia he had arranged with President Roosevelt to establish a Combined Chiefs of Staff to "focus a united view" of the war and enable the allies to work together to defeat the Axis powers. Ending on a high note, he singled out his role in convincing the Americans at Arcadia to create "a vast common pool of weapons and munitions, of raw materials and of shipping." Left unsaid was Churchill's and his military advisors' realization at Arcadia that the war could not be won without American support. It came with a high price—the inevitable recognition that the United States was the senior leader of the wartime alliance.[3]

After three days of debate Churchill won his vote of confidence

464 to 1. His appeals to the triumphs at Arcadia helped turn the tide in his favor. He was also lucky. Even as clerks tallied the vote, Benghazi fell and the Japanese advanced to within eighteen miles of Singapore.[4]

When Wavell officially took command of the ABDA on 15 January, it was already a doomed enterprise. It was impossible to expect that Wavell could fix years of allied omissions and neglect in a matter of days. ABDA's lines of communication were too vulnerable, its intratheater distances too great, and its existing infrastructure too primitive. Allied navies lacked the warships to contest the Japanese control of sea lanes and simultaneously protect the Atlantic convoys. Distances alone ruled out effective air cover. It was a creaky command, with different command channels, different languages, and different communications systems. Wavell later described a command that "worked harmoniously but without success. Time was insufficient for it have any serious influence on events."[5]

On 21 February, Wavell sent an "eyes-only" cable to Churchill requesting permission to disband the command, "I am afraid that the defense of the ABDA area has broken down and that defense of Java cannot now last long. . . . I see little further usefulness for these headquarters. . . . I have failed you and President here where better men might perhaps have succeeded in altering time factor in our favor." Churchill's response was generous, even magnanimous. "I hope you realize how highly I and all your friends here as well as the President and the Combined Chiefs of Staffs in Washington rate your admirable conduct of ABDA operations in the teeth of adverse fortune and overwhelming odds."[6]

Marshall's conviction that a supreme commander for ABDA would "solve nine-tenths of our troubles" was similarly upbeat. Unified command to Marshall was the means to overcome issues of command and control of personnel and resources in Southwest Asia as well as short-circuit the constant bickering over resources for the Pacific that threatened to disrupt the Arcadia Conference. Others disagreed. General Brooke, who was not at the conference, seemed to revel in ABDA's misery. On 22 February he wrote, "It is now quite clear that we can at last dissolve the ABDA organization and run the war on a rational basis!" Brooke believed that the dissolution of the ABDA also spelled the end of the "appropriate joint body" that gave direction to the theater command. An early opponent of the Combined Chiefs of Staff, he fervently hoped that it too would dissolve along with the ABDA and, "We shall now run the war with two main spheres of interest the Americans running the Pacific up to Asia, including Australia and New Zealand, and a British one running the opposite way round the globe, including Middle East, Burma, India and the Indian Ocean." In this he was disappointed. The Combined Chiefs of Staff was a much more resilient organization than Brooke initially realized. The demise of the ABDA did not affect the new Combined Chiefs of Staff.[7]

Indeed, ABDA never surmounted the conflicting strategic interests of the Americans, British, Dutch, and Australian allies nor their diverse political goals. Rather than encourage unity of effort, ABDA seemed to ignite unending diplomatic and military disputes among the allies. Nevertheless, the allies saw the utility and the potential advantages that this concept provided. In this case it was created too late. In the future the British and Americans would strive to learn from the mistakes of ABDA. Marshall, thereafter, staunchly supported the concept of creating a supreme commander in a theater, to control the air, land, and sea assets of multiple countries and used the ABDA experience to translate the concept into reality.

The American chiefs proved much more realistic in their assessment of the operational situation in the Pacific than did their British counterparts. Singapore surrendered on 15 February 1942, quickly followed by Japanese victories throughout the Dutch East Indies and in Burma. Despite the continued Japanese advances on Malaya throughout the conference, the fall of Singapore shocked the British and devastated Churchill. W. Averell Harriman, the president's special envoy in London for Lend-Lease, confided to Roosevelt, "Although the British are keeping a stiff upper lip, the surrender of their troops at Singapore has shattered confidence to the core—even in themselves but more particularly in their leaders. . . . Unfortunately, Singapore shook the Prime Minister himself to such an extent that he has not been able to stand up in this adversity with his old vigor." The Philippines finally surrendered on 9 April having held out for four months without reinforcements as the US chiefs had previously estimated.[8]

The opening months of 1942 were unkind to the British. Military defeat was not confined to the Pacific. Churchill's high hopes that Arcadia would uncritically endorse his North Africa operation were dashed one week after the conference, when Rommel on 21 January launched his counterattack, catching the British completely by surprise. Within a week the Germans had pushed the Eighth Army back two hundred miles and were only forty miles from the strategic port of Tobruk. Churchill demanded an immediate counteroffensive, but he had weakened the Eighth Army by incrementally stripping it of planes and troops to reinforce Singapore. Told by British commanders that an attack was impossible before June, Churchill was frustrated and embarrassed at home and abroad. More than the suspension of his pet Supergymnast operation in May, he realized that his overconfidence might cause Roosevelt and Stalin to question his credibility.[9]

Churchill's British critics used the fall of Singapore and the continued bad news in North Africa to do just that and demand he resign his portfolio as minister of defense. (He refused, but on 19 February was forced to reorganize his cabinet.) Churchill's larger concern was American opinion. Throughout the Arcadia meetings, he had emphasized to Roosevelt and the American military leaders the British Army's prowess in North Africa and had promised future stunning victories, including "the total destruction" of the enemy forces in Libya before the end of the year and the British capture of Tripoli. Now the cold light of defeat spotlighted his overblown claims, which he feared would damage his credibility with Roosevelt.[10]

Singapore made matters worse. Churchill's initial memo to the president at the start of Arcadia had asserted that Singapore could withstand "an attack for at least six months." As late as 7 February 1942, a confident Churchill cabled Roosevelt that Singapore could hold out for another six months. A week later Singapore surrendered.[11]

The catastrophe on Singapore Island drained Churchill. Harriman remarked on the prime minister's loss of "vigor." Throughout Arcadia, Churchill had patronized the Americans over the imminent fall of the

Philippines. Now the tables were turned. The Americans continued to fight the Japanese in the Philippines while the British surrendered on Singapore, casting doubt, as Churchill put it, on "the whole reputation of our country and our race." The disgrace of 100,000 troops surrendering on Singapore Island "left a scar on his mind." Several months later Churchill gloomily confided to his physician, "I cannot get over Singapore."[12]

Although Churchill struggled under military defeats and heavy domestic political pressure, Roosevelt never wavered in his support, sending him encouraging and supportive messages throughout January and February to buoy the prime minister's spirits. Immediately after Singapore's surrender, Roosevelt cabled Churchill to express his sympathy, support, and commitment that regardless of the serious defeats the Allies would hit back at their enemies. He never questioned Churchill's credibility.[13]

Critics also alleged that while the Americans agreed to the "Europe First" strategy that dictated that "only the minimum of force necessary for the safeguarding of vital interests in other theaters should be diverted from operations against Germany" during the first six months of 1942, the United States sent the bulk of their troops and equipment to the Pacific. It is true that the Americans reinforced the Pacific, but they simultaneously deployed troops to Ireland and Iceland as promised. Rommel's victories in early 1942 spelled the end for Gymnast or Supergymnast, negating the troop requirements for North Africa. It became apparent during the conference that contrary to British beliefs the Americans had a serious shortage of available shipping. To worsen matters, German U-boats were sinking ships faster than the United States could build them.[14]

It is well known that the ineptitude of the American secretariat to plan agendas, take accurate notes, and disseminate papers marred the conference, and it is a commonplace that the British staffs outperformed their American counterparts during the war. This interpretation overlooks the high-quality staff work that American planners produced. The talent of the army and navy planners was unequaled. Eisenhower, Gerow, Stilwell, and Turner would become household names during the war. Thrust into war by a surprise attack, the army and navy planners had to overcome long-standing service parochialism, personal animosity, and rivalry to cooperate. Among the numerous high-quality studies they prepared during Arcadia, standouts include: priorities for United States and United Kingdom overseas expeditions in the Atlantic; Supergymnast planning; supporting measures for the Southwest Pacific Area and Far East pending establishment of a unified command; the directive and instructions for the supreme commander of the ABDA; movements in the Atlantic in the first half of 1942; establishing forces in Northern Ireland; defense of bases between Hawaii and Australia; immediate assistance to China; and a review of the British grand strategy proposals.

These papers underwent numerous iterations, but the fact remains that during the conference's three-week life span the American planners worked with their British counterparts to develop the immediate military measures to stem the Japanese advance and support the strategic blueprint. They did a worthy job of planning the allocation of scarce resources to support the "Germany First" strategy. As the conference progressed American planners asserted themselves with increasing success. Marshall later acknowledged that before the conference the American chiefs focused myopically on the short-term missions, such as resupplying the Philippines and other beleaguered garrisons in the Pacific. He grasped that the British approach forced the Americans to take a holistic view of a global, not just American war effort. And of course during the first months of 1942 Axis military successes necessitated modifications to the conference's operational plans. But the plans themselves were well-researched and contained sufficient flexibility to enable modifications as needed.[15]

The British arrived with concerns about the American rearmament program. They left impressed. Roosevelt's Victory Program, announced on 6 January, articulated staggering numbers. The production goals for 1942 and 1943 astonished Churchill and his military advisors. The huge numbers were not plucked from thin air but were the product of diligent and thorough American staff work. Churchill and Beaverbrook came to Arcadia prepared to requisition US war production for British goals. They were disappointed on that score, but American military potential and the Victory Plan's integration of the British requirements answered most of their needs.[16]

A major conference accomplishment was the creation of Anglo-American "machinery for implementing" strategy and allocating resources. This was one of Churchill's objectives as outlined in his goals for Arcadia, but the final "machinery" emerged in a way he never imagined. The structure for the Combined Chiefs of Staff (CCS) grew from Marshall's vision of a unified command in the Far East, ABDA. The US Army Chief of Staff was unwilling to send resources piecemeal to individual commanders scattered across different areas of the vast Pacific to stem the tide of the Japanese advance. He wanted a unified theater command to enable a single commander to decide on resource distribution within his theater. This concept required a centralized organization to coordinate strategy and appropriate resources to the respective theaters. During Arcadia, Pound, Dill, and Portal grasped the future utility of a unified command. Pound wanted a permanent organization, arguing that "arrangements for collaboration on the operational side proposed in the paper would be suitable not only for ABDA, but for all other operational matters as well."[17]

On 23 January, the Combined Chiefs of Staff met for the first time in the Federal Reserve Building in Washington. It began as Arcadia had ended, with the British irritated by the lack of American organization and the American prepared agenda. After the second CCS meeting, an exasperated Dykes, now the British secretary, wrote, "I wish they would get their secretariat set up." By the third CSS meeting held on 3 February, the new American secretary, Brigadier General Walter Bedell Smith, finally got the secretariat organized.[18] He and Dykes worked well together and forged the Combined Chiefs into an effective team. The two secretaries set agendas, preserved the minutes, and improved the quality of discussions.[19]

But there were dissenters, notably General Brooke in London, who opposed both the creation of the ABDA and CCS. Upon their return to London, Brooke angrily told Pound and Portal that they had "sold the birthright for a plate of porridge." He rightly feared that a centralized command post in Washington would shift the locus of power to the Americans, leaving the British to coordinate decisions via their Washington mission.[20]

Before their fourth meeting, on 10 February 1942, the planners proposed the creation of a Combined Intelligence Committee and a Combined Military Transportation Committee to the secretariat. Dykes and Smith placed it on the agenda, and the participants quickly approved charters for both committees at the meeting. Implementing the charters, however, again revealed the mutual suspicion that characterized both camps. Smith and Dykes arranged for the British secretariat, planners, and intelligence committees to collocate these organizations with their American counterparts to ease of coordination.[21]

US interservice rivalry almost unhinged these arrangements. The navy, reluctant to share information with the army, was even more reticent and distrustful of the British. Admiral Turner personally and vehemently opposed the CCS, believing "since the British do not understand the fundamental policies and strategic necessities of the US, it would be expected that US interests would be subordinated to the interests of the British Commonwealth."[22]

Turner's attitude manifested itself when he refused to collocate his planning committee with the British in order to keep them under his control and separate from the British and Combined Staff. The British were irate. Dykes feared that the fledgling CCS would implode because if the navy did not cooperate "the whole concept will fall down." He directed his anger at Turner's high-handed attitude, labeling him "a stubborn swine" who ran roughshod over the planning committee and "at present runs them like a circus of his own." The British appealed to Marshall to get the planners collocated, which he did. Unfortunately, mutual mistrust lingered during the CCS's early days and was a recurring problem.[23]

After Arcadia, King assumed the role as preeminent spokesman for the navy. Stark sat on CSS's meetings until 10 March and then departed for London to head the US Navy mission. While the British had more respect for King, Stark was a more cooperative and diplomatic personality. Admiral Andrew Cunningham, who would replace Pound as First Sea Lord, remarked, "What King does not understand is that his subordinates all take their tune from him, and it is the absence of cooperation and wish to cooperate on his part which spreads itself throughout the whole American Navy." Anglophobia within the US Navy senior officer ranks did not extend to the same degree into the US Army, which developed a strong working rapport with the British. Smith later confided to General Ismay, "the fact is that the Army has been more sympathetic and cooperative to the CCS set-up than has the Navy, as you well know, and your soldiers speak our language and can play closer to the Operations Division of the War Department."[24]

In the early months of 1942, the British too bore responsibility for disrupting the CCS's growth and development. The Chiefs of Staff Committee in London was slow to respond to requests for information from, and decisions for, the British Mission in Washington. This bureaucratic delaying tactic irritated the Americans and British Mission. Dykes cabled London, "If we have to do the idiot boy every time, the US COS will tend more and more to take control and you will always be a day behind. I realize the period of gestation in Whitehall is usually much longer than here where the US COS short-circuit the civilian departments entirely. But it is very hard to stall when we do not know at all how the matter is being processed at home."[25]

Field Marshall Dill became the glue that held the CCS together. More than anyone else, Dill cultivated the emerging very special relationship between the American and British chiefs. If, as George Bernard Shaw said, "England and America are two countries separated by the same language," then Dill interpreted for both sides. He translated the British point of view to the Americans without condescending to or alienating them. He also explained to the British that their incessant demands for resources were testing the limits of US patience. He worked ceaselessly to overcome the potential mistrust between the American and British chiefs, sharing information from Churchill with the Americans to give them a broader perspective on the prime minister's private discussions with the American president. He provided the context for British requirements for the Americans and likewise a window on American thinking for the British. Dill was the rare honest broker who sought to credit both perspectives.[26]

Dill's integrity made the CCS work as an organization. Trusted by both sides, he developed an extremely close relationship with Marshall, who valued Dill's insights, judgment, and perspective on British intentions. He lunched with Marshall before the weekly CCS meeting to resolve contentious issues informally before the formal discussions. Dill also managed to maintain a good rapport with Admiral King, despite the admiral's deep-seated mistrust of the British. Dill still had a "sneaking regard" for him. He accepted King's bombastic personality in public forums because in "off the record" conversations he found King to be "understanding and helpful." For his part, King liked Dill, and although he excoriated most of his contemporaries, King praised Dill. "Sir John Dill was a strength member of the US-UK relations; he was entirely unselfish and would never 'use' his special relationship to the Prime Minister."[27]

The British likewise trusted Dill. Brooke disliked the Americans but reposed great faith in Dill, who eased tensions with General Marshall. "I do not know what I should have done without him [Dill]. He knew Marshall so well that he was able to explain to me the workings of his brain. And as both Marshall and I trusted him implicitly he was the most excellent intermediary, and repeatedly brought us together again when we were at loggerheads."[28]

Dill also devoted his efforts to improve the poor relationship between the American Army and Navy and continually had to cope with the services' notorious lack of coordination and cooperation. They were bitter rivals for resources and equipment. Service parochialism and jealousy, so evident at Arcadia, had continued in the new CCS. Interservice dissension naturally hampered holistic planning, leaving Dill routinely explaining to London the repercussions of this rivalry on CCS deliberations. Dill explained to Brooke that "the two US Staffs are as yet unable to reconcile their views and since they do not like to wash their dirty linen in our presence, they naturally do not relish trying to put down united strategy in black and white."[29]

Ismay later remarked that Dill also ended up brokering solutions to disagreements between the American Army and Navy because both services trusted Dill and were willing to discuss problems with him that they refused to talk about with each other. According to

Ismay, "US Navy and Army people didn't always get along. Dill used to say his chief purpose was to serve as a meeting place for the US naval and military personnel."[30]

Despite these growing pains, in time the organization that Marshall conceived for unified theater command and the "appropriate joint body" to provide its direction proved its worth. In March 1942, the Combined Chiefs developed an understanding to control military operations in support of the broad strategy agreed on at Arcadia. The world was divided into three major theaters of operation that coincided with the interests of the Allies. The United States assumed responsibility for developing and executing strategy in the Pacific, and the British did the same for the Middle East and Indian Ocean. The Atlantic and European theaters became the shared responsibility between the two. In each theater, the Combined Chiefs of Staff had broad authority to recommend to Roosevelt and Churchill the requirements for implementing strategic decisions and prepare directives for the distribution of weapons and equipment in support of the strategy. They also prioritized movement of troops to the theater. Roosevelt strongly favored this arrangement, telling Churchill, "I wish you would think this over. It appeals to me because of the simplification it offers under existing operational difficulties. Incidentally I am inclined to think that the Australians, New Zealanders, Dutch and Chinese would rather welcome it." Churchill concurred.[31]

Brooke, an early critic, gradually changed his tune on the Combined Chiefs of Staff. "I had little faith in this organization at the time, I think mainly due to the fact that it had been set up in Washington with the USA as the predominant partner whilst they had . . . not much knowledge in running of a war and certainly little experience. My views altered completely as time went on and I grew to have the greatest faith in the Combined Chiefs of Staff organization as the most efficient that had ever been evolved for coordinating and correlating the war strategy and effort of two allies."[32]

Admiral Cunningham was more candid than Brooke when describing the CCS's utility and importance. The combined system designed at Arcadia gave Britain "the constitutional right to discuss her needs on equal terms, instead of receiving gratefully such crumbs as may be left from the rich man's table." Churchill initially believed that the confirmation of the Germany First decision was Arcadia's signal decision. As early as 6 February 1942, he told Roosevelt that the new CCS "was functioning smoothly and well. I even think we may plume ourselves a little having brought it all into action so soon." The passage of time only increased his admiration. In the postwar era, he reflected, "It may well be thought by future historians that the most valuable and lasting result of our First Washington Conference—'Arcadia,' as it was codenamed—was the setting up of the now famous 'Combined Chiefs of Staff Committee.'"[33]

While the importance of the CCS cannot be overstated, the Arcadia Conference was also instrumental in the creation of the American Joint Chiefs of Staff (JCS), which formulated US strategy during World War II and continues as the nerve center of the American military to this day. Created in in January 1942, the JCS forced a major shift in coordination and cooperation between the army and navy. Feuding, petty jealousy, and interservice rivalry did not vanish overnight (or forever), but the new organization forced the American military services to integrate planning, intelligence, and resource requirements. Some contend that this was accomplished as much to present a united front to the British as it was to defeat the Axis.

The Joint Chiefs of Staff met for the first time on 9 February 1942. There were four members—Admirals Stark and King and Generals Marshall and Arnold. Key questions involved who should be JCS's members and the new organization's relationship to the Joint Board. The navy endorsed the status quo and continuance of the Joint Board. King recommended the same members sit on both agencies. Marshall dismissed that notion as redundant, arguing, "there was little use in continuing the Joint Board" if the membership was the same. Marshall's logic dominated, and during the next few months the JCS absorbed the role of functions of the Joint Board.[34]

King had a solid rationale for proposing the continuance of the Joint Board. Roosevelt never officially authorized the Joint Chiefs of Staff. King and Marshall sent him a charter establishing the organization, but the president never signed it. King was very uncomfortable with this hazy legal status, believing that a formal charter was needed to circumscribe the Joint Chiefs of Staff's authority and keep it from infringing on the navy's autonomy. Merging the Joint Chiefs of Staff with the Joint Board he believed could derive the legal authorization of the existing organization. Marshall on the other hand was more concerned that the Joint Board might impose restrictions on the authority of the service chiefs. He sought to avoid the legal limitations to the new Joint Chiefs of Staff.[35]

Determining the final composition of the JCS was more complicated. At the first meeting the army and navy each had two representatives. In early March, Admiral Stark, as mentioned, was reassigned to London and Admiral King elevated to Chief of Naval Operations and concurrently commander in chief of the US Fleet. This left the JCS with only three members, two army and one navy. Navy leaders found this imbalance intolerable because it left their service in danger of being consistently outvoted. This was not just interservice paranoia because service rivalry was on full display during the first JCS meetings. At the fourth meeting (three days before Stark departed), army and navy members took opposite sides on almost every topic. Navy Anglophobes did not want to share the current disposition of US forces with the British. Army members saw no point in denying the information to America's major ally. The navy insisted that the British "had lost all interest in the Pacific area," the navy's main focus. The army disagreed and defended the British strategy. The two services, ignoring the agreements at Arcadia, argued about where to deploy troops—England, Australia, and the Middle East. Marshall, a Europe first advocate, closed the contentious meeting by reminding participants that "we should never lose sight of the eventual necessity of fighting Germans in Germany."[36]

Stark's departure highlighted the membership problem. Marshall empathized with King's concerns of being potentially outvoted two to one along service lines. "I therefore thought it would be wise if we had a chairman and one from the Navy, if one could be found that I thought was entirely impersonal and a man of good judgment." A bigger issue was access to the president. Army and navy papers sent to the White House were delayed and in some cases even lost before Roosevelt could review them. Marshall advocated for someone to act as a liaison from the JCS to the president to expedite presidential decisions and to serve as a spokesman on important issues. To accomplish this, Marshall recommended to President Roosevelt that he select Admiral Leahy as the chief of staff to the commander in chief. This would rebalance the JCS with two members from each service. Marshall expected that Leahy's long-standing relationship with the president would facilitate JCS access to the White House. Leahy had known the president since 1913 and was a much-respected close confidant. He had preceded Stark as Chief of Naval Operations and at present was the US ambassador to Vichy France. Although King did not feel the position was necessary, Roosevelt overruled him and appointed Leahy. Leahy's impartiality smoothed over the worst of the interservice tensions, and his unrivaled daily access to the Oval Office provided a vital link between the JCS and president that expedited decision-making.[37]

The Joint Chiefs of Staff was created to mirror the British on the Combined Chiefs of Staff. It had no charter that delineated its duties and responsibilities. This was by design. Roosevelt believed that a charter would "impair the flexibility of operations." The president preferred an informal relationship with his military advisors and was more comfortable getting recommendations from individual service chiefs than from formal meetings with the entire group. Roosevelt regarded the Joint Chiefs of Staff as his principal military advisors on war plans, strategy, munitions, mobilization, and deployments. The services reached a modus operandi where the army took the lead in planning for the Atlantic and Europe, while the navy took on that role in the Pacific.[38]

The JCS evolved gradually, and as the Joint Chiefs of Staff historian, Steven Rearden, noted, once they "found that working together produced better results than working separately," they overcame the worst features of interservice competition and jealousy. By war's end, it was the premier corporate advisory and planning organization at the center of every major strategic military-related decision. The JCS's accomplishments so impressed President Harry Truman that he told Leahy, "Why, Admiral, if the South had had a staff organization like that, the confederates would have won the Civil War. Lee would not have had Johnson, Beauregard, Longstreet, and other generals running around on the loose."[39]

Following the Arcadia Conference Harry Hopkins was hospitalized for exhaustion, which delayed the first meeting of the Munitions Assignment Board until 27 January. During this interval London constantly bombarded Dill and Dykes demanding to know when the board would meet. Illustrative of British emphasis on the board's importance was their decision to send the senior flag representatives of the three services—General Colville Wemyss (Army), Admiral Charles Little (Navy), and Air Marshall Arthur Harris (Air Force) to participate. At the session, Dykes observed, "Hopkins looked very ill indeed, but all went quite well." Hopkins's style of leadership style allowed the board to accomplish Marshall's goal of synchronizing munitions' allocation and military strategy. At the next meeting of the board, Dykes related that "Hopkins runs a meeting very well in his quiet way."[40]

The third CCS meeting quickly approved the Munitions Assignment Board's charter on 3 February 1942. The agency functioned as a dual organization with branches in London and Washington, granting each nation priority on its domestic production of munitions and equipment. As discussed at Arcadia, the British requirements for US-manufactured war equipment far exceeded reciprocal American requests of British-made equipment. As a consequence, the Washington Munitions Assignment Board assumed precedence over the London organization. Hopkins evenhandedly supervised the board, despite initial friction over the Allies' demands for priority on still-limited American equipment. Soaring war production as industrial mobilization gained traction relieved these tensions because there was enough to go around.[41]

In Britain, Churchill tried to assuage Beaverbrook's bruised feelings over the Munitions Assignment Board after Arcadia. The prime minister authorized the consolidation of the Ministries of Supply and Aircraft Production into a single organization—the Ministry of War Production. On 4 February, Beaverbrook was appointed as the head of the new organization. Churchill believed this new role would fit Beaverbrook's talents and ambition. His time in this position proved short-lived. Churchill's ministers found Beaverbrook's leadership style grating and opposed the consolidation. After just three weeks, he resigned from his post and had no further involvement in munitions production and distribution.[42]

The official British and American military histories of the war are dismissive of the Arcadia Conference. A US Army account described it: "as a whole [it] was rather inconclusive except as a sound beginning of continuous, systematic British-American military planning in Washington." British official historians likewise deprecated the conference, dismissing the American side as unprepared and unsophisticated. The American Chiefs of Staff "were reluctant to discuss strategy, except in the most general terms" and their thinking on the subject was "undefined and ambiguous." While neither of these assessments is entirely accurate, they have become the popular interpretation of Arcadia.[43]

Postmortem criticisms of Arcadia highlight the final step in the grand strategy, the European ground offensive, arguing that the chiefs' failure to set a timeline or a location for the return to the continent led to subsequent contentious Anglo-American conferences and discussions about where and when they would return. It seems unreasonable to expect that just three weeks after Pearl Harbor Anglo-American strategists could establish specifics for an invasion of Europe. Facing an uncertain future late in December 1941, their only option was to endorse generalizations. Latent US military power existed on paper, but could the nation convert that potential into a massive expansion of its military and industrial might? Grand strategy was a loose blueprint for the way ahead, and it was the best that planners could accomplish given the time and circumstances. Adjustments were inevitable as the American military expanded and industrial mobilization took hold, and as new weapons came on line. The hard fact was that as the war progressed, the industrial and manpower reserves of the United States manifested themselves and increased America's global influence. The longer the war lasted, the more America dominated the alliance. This was not fully appreciated at the time and helps to explain why Arcadia's accomplishments are overlooked and misunderstood.

The Arcadia Conference lacked the drama of later wartime conferences. But at Arcadia the American and British chiefs met for the first time since the United States had entered the war and gauged each other to assess the talents and abilities of their counterparts. Personalities mattered. Face-to-face relationships that were essential to cultivate trust between the Anglo-American chiefs occurred during these three weeks. Regardless of the disagreements and compromises, of British arrogance and American incompetence, both left impressed by the other and their staffs. Brigadier General Handy, an army war planner at Arcadia who went on to four stars, openly admired the British planners. "The British were very good at planning. They had a lot of techniques. I used to go with [General] Gerow and [Admiral] Kelly Turner from the Navy to meet with the British planners. These planners were just smarter than hell."[44]

The American chiefs were similarly impressed by their counterparts. One observer recalled that the Americans saw the British chiefs as "their top military people and they were good or they wouldn't have been there. . . . So when they expressed an opinion or had a view on some operation or some line of action, you paid a hell of a lot of attention to it. You might not accept it, but you'd certainly give it very serious consideration."[45]

Air Marshal Portal's intelligence and strategic sense impressed the Americans, who, as the conference progressed, realized that Portal was Churchill's cat's-paw. Portal's speaking ability and clear concise presentations resonated with his American audience. He came across as honest and unbiased with a ready sense of humor that saw him through in tough discussions with the Americans who left convinced that he had tried to see their point of view. Rather than resenting Portal's barbed questions, they grew to admire his candor and insights. Handy thought Portal the "ablest" of the chiefs. Marshall agreed that Portal's calm demeanor and ready grasp of the most complex issues made him "the best mind of the lot."[46]

The British had similar high regard for Portal. A senior British officer said, "Peter Portal was the leading spirit in the British COS. [He] seemed to be of a different breed. Thoroughly competent in his own sphere, also knowledgeable on any topic. Always approachable." He was constantly the first British chief to grasp new ideas and concepts.[47]

Pound also impressed the Americans. His quiet demeanor and military bearing stamped him as a gentleman of the old school. At sixty-four he was the oldest of the British chiefs and had led the British Navy since July 1939. Throughout the conference, concern over the growing U-boat threat in the Atlantic left Pound overworked, tired, and ill. In less than two years he would die of a brain tumor.[48]

The British formed definite opinions of their American counterparts. Admiral King was quiet and helpful and supported Marshall on key topics throughout the sessions. He did not display the domineering personality that he would exhibit during later conferences. Portal described him as "gruff and the most nationalistic [of the American Chiefs]—but very helpful once he agreed."[49]

The British appreciated Arnold's intelligence and organizational talents, particularly his designs to expand the army air forces. Portal found Arnold quiet during the conference except on issues related to air power and aircraft production. Arnold's reticence was probably due to his deference to Marshall, who was his superior in the army. He developed a very close relationship with Portal, who thought him a "Grand Fellow." Portal thought Arnold was a "wonderful cooperator" and a "great helper" who in the beginning of the war assisted "the Royal Air Force to get the aircraft we so badly needed from America. And another thing I remember very clearly—is his intense keenness to benefit from our experience.... He was absolutely without preconceived ideas—he appeared to have only one object, which was to get the right answer to all of his problems." Together the two hammered out an agreement on aircraft allocation to Great Britain for 1942.[50]

General Marshall dominated the conference. Previously an unknown quantity to the British, Churchill overlooked Marshall's ability and influence with President Roosevelt. Dill was the only senior British officer who recognized Marshall's talents before the conference because they had worked together since the August 1941 Atlantic Conference in Newfoundland, Canada. During Arcadia the British came to admire and respect Marshall. Portal termed Marshall "the great brain of the American chiefs." Another observer regarded Marshall as the only participant with an original idea. Marshall was the driving force behind the unity of command concept, which in turn led to the creation of the CCS and the JCS. Portal rightly concluded that Marshall was "the big man in the American delegation."[51]

Arcadia, however, was not problem free. General Handy put his finger on the key learning point for the Americans, who eventually realized that the British military leaders did not always express their own opinions. Instead, they would faithfully present Churchill's initiatives, which they did not necessarily support. Handy felt that this left the US chiefs unsure if the recommendations from their British counterparts were based on their "considered military opinion" or if they had been "pushed into it by the Prime Minister. So, we didn't know whether it was the best British military opinion or whether it was Mr. Churchill's." This procedure exasperated the Americans, especially as they sought to establish realistic priorities while Churchill impractically demanded the simultaneous execution of Gymnast, Magnet, and support to Singapore.[52]

The British prime minister arrived for Arcadia from a war-weary nation and was determined to get as much as he could, as fast as he could, from the Americans. This was his responsibility as the British leader. He was his nation's advocate and did not care whose toes he stepped on. But his incessant demands appeared to regard all American-produced military equipment as his personal stockpile to draw on as he saw fit. It grated American planners who had their own war to fight.

On three separate occasions Churchill pushed the British chiefs to propose actions contrary to US interests and beyond American capabilities. Naturally, the Americans took umbrage, and the fragile relationship of the budding alliance was threatened. Churchill's insistence on diverting reinforcements from the Philippines to Singapore was neither militarily sound nor, as presented, an ideal way to build trust and confidence. Portal recalled that Churchill was eager to "attack somewhere—Singapore. . . . He continually came up with some outlandish place . . . he wanted to attack. When we demurred he would say he wished he could get someone who would fight."

Churchill discovered, however, that he could not browbeat Marshall, who to Churchill's chagrin enjoyed Roosevelt's backing.[53]

The Americans saw Churchill's attempt to insert Dill as an intermediary between the CCS and the political heads of state as a blatant attempt to manipulate strategy and divert resources by bypassing the American chiefs. The British chiefs did not agree with Churchill's ploy, which only embarrassed Dill, who was caught in the middle. The US chiefs' strong and unanimous rejection of Churchill's scheme, supported by the president, forced the British chiefs to discuss the matter with their prime minister. Churchill ignored their advice and inserted a confidential annex to Dill's instructions authorizing him to act as his personal representative. The prime minister's well-known bulldog determination sought to wear down the Americans and promote British leadership of the coalition. Roosevelt, who preferred personal relationships, liked Dill and arranged a compromise. Dill would have formal status as a British representative to the Combined Chiefs of Staff and an informal status as the representative of the British Defence Minister (Churchill). Dill presciently realized that this could break the trust of the partnership and made a point to always keep the Americans informed of his actions.[54]

When this failed Churchill again pushed for parallel or coequal Combined Chiefs of Staff in London and Washington. This setup would allow him to maintain more control over the direction of the war against Germany. This redundant system made no sense and would have confused coordination between the two staffs. Marshall again frustrated the prime minister by logically explaining the disadvantages of this organization to the president. Roosevelt again backed Marshall, and Churchill acquiesced.

Churchill also pushed a personal agenda to control the distribution of war equipment and wanted to create a Munitions Assignment Board that he could control. The British chiefs understood that this could potentially undercut the agreed-on strategy by diverting resources to other locations. When discussing the issue they broke ranks with Churchill and insisted on a draft minute for the president and prime minister signed by all the chiefs that required that war material be allocated according to strategic needs. They further stipulated that this be done under CCS's supervision. Churchill tried to arrange the board's role without informing the American chiefs. Marshall again stymied him by making a passionate case for subordinating the board to the Combined Chiefs and offering to resign if his recommendation was unacceptable. Roosevelt supported his general even if it embarrassed the prime minister.

Churchill had a reputation for persuasiveness. Eisenhower compared him to a sunlamp that once turned on could be hard to resist. The prime minister was both eloquent and overwhelming, and the Americans were always concerned that Churchill's charm would convince Roosevelt to make a snap decision or commitment before consulting with his advisors. After Arcadia, the American Joint Chiefs remained wary of Churchill's influence and motivations for the duration of the war.[55]

Nonetheless, the Arcadia Conference left a solid foundation for the Anglo-American alliance. Conducted in secrecy, it has never received its proper recognition. The senior military leaders of both nations made a concerted effort to overcome disagreements and national agendas. In the end, they compromised, settled on solutions, and realized that nothing would help the Japanese and Germans more than the Allies fighting among themselves.[56]

A final and important accomplishment of the conference was the relationship and mutual admiration that developed between Roosevelt and Churchill. Though they had met before, Arcadia cemented their partnership. Three weeks of close contact enabled them to view the strengths and weaknesses of each other. They met formally and informally daily. They discussed a wide range of topics. Both sides came away impressed with the others' intellect, integrity, and willingness to persevere until the Axis powers were finally defeated. Together they crafted an agreement among twenty-six nations that defined the war in democratic principles, pledged all the national resources to defeat the Axis, and promised not to make a separate peace. When the conference opened the Anglo-American civilian and military leaders were strangers. When it ended, friends had forged an alliance that would win World War II.[57]

NOTES

Introduction

1. J. M. A. Gwyer and J. R. M. Butler, *Grand Strategy*, vol. 3, *June 1941–August 1942* (London: Her Majesty's Stationery Office, 1964), 352.

2. Ray Cline, *Washington Command Post: The Operations Division* (Washington, DC: US Government Printing Office, 1951), 89.

3. Brooke Diary, 9 February 1942, in *War Diaries, 1939–1945: Field Marshal Alanbrooke*, ed. Alex Danchev and Daniel Todman (Berkeley: University of California Press, 2001), 228.

4. Brooke Diary, 11 December 1941, in Danchev and Todman, *War Diaries*, 210.

5. Mark Stoler, *Allies and Adversaries: The Joint Chiefs of Staff, the Grand Alliance, and US Strategy in World War II* (Chapel Hill: University of North Carolina Press, 2000), 68.

6. Louis Morton, "Germany First: The Basic Concept of Allied Strategy in World War II," in *Command Decisions*, ed. Kent Roberts Greenfield (Washington, DC: US Government Printing Office, 1960), 11.

7. "Post ARCADIA Collaboration Paper," January 14, 1942, in the Proceedings of the American-British Joint Chiefs of Staff Conferences Held in Washington, DC, on Twelve Occasions Between December 24, 1941 and January 14, 1942, Joint Staff Historical Archives, Pentagon (hereafter cited as Joint Chiefs of Staff files); Frederick Aandahl, William M. Franklin, and William Slany, eds., *Foreign Relations of the United States, the Conferences at Washington, 1941–1942, and Casablanca, 1943* (Washington, DC: US Government Printing Office, 1958), "Memorandum by American and British Chiefs of Staff," 14 January 1942, "Post-Arcadia Collaboration," Document 121, https://history.state.gov/historicaldocuments/frus1941-43 (hereafter cited as FRUS); Lieutenant Colonel Paul M. Robinett Diary, January 14, 1942, Box 20, George C. Marshall Papers, George C. Marshall Foundation Research Library and Archives, Lexington, Virginia (hereafter cited as Marshall Papers, Marshall Library); Winston Churchill, *The Grand Alliance* (Boston: Houghton Mifflin, 1950), 686.

8. Lieutenant Colonel Paul M. Robinett Diary, 14 January 1942, Box 20, Marshall Papers, Marshall Library; D. K. R. Crosswell, *Beetle: The Life of General Walter Bedell Smith* (Lexington: University Press of Kentucky, 2010), 238–39.

9. Lieutenant Colonel Paul M. Robinett Diary, 14 January 1942, Box 20, Marshall Papers, Marshall Library; Crosswell, *Beetle*, 239.

10. "American-British Grand Strategy Paper, 31 December 1941," in the Proceedings of the American-British Joint Chiefs of Staff Conferences Held in Washington, DC, on Twelve Occasions Between December 24, 1941 and January 14, 1942, Joint Chiefs of Staff files; "Memorandum by the United States and British Chiefs of Staff," 31 December 1941, "American-British Grand Strategy," Document 115, in FRUS.

11. Lieutenant Paul M. Robinett Diary, 14 January 1942, Box 20, Marshall Papers, Marshall Library; Crosswell, *Beetle*, 239.

12. Crosswell, *Beetle*, 239.

13. Crosswell, *Beetle*, 239.

Chapter 1

1. Louis Morton, "The Japanese Decision for War," United States Naval Institute Proceedings, vol. 80, no. 12, whole no. 622 (December 1954): 1326, copy in the Center of Military History, Historical Research Collection, Geographical Files, Japan 016, Japan's Decision for War.

2. Morton, "Japanese Decision for War," 1328; Edward Drea, "Japan's Diplomatic and Military Strategy between the Two World Wars," in *Asian Shadows: The Hidden History of World War Two in the Pacific*, ed. Arthur Herman (Washington, DC: Hudson Institute, April 2017), 64–65; Brian Farrell, *The Defence and Fall of Singapore* (Singapore: Monsoon Books, 2017), 161.

3. "A Pearl Harbor Fact Sheet," prepared by the National World War II Museum, New Orleans, LA, www.nationalworldwar2museum.org.

4. Morton, "Japanese Decision for War," 1328; Henry L. Stimson Diary, 7 December 1941, Reel Seven, Volume 36, George C. Marshall Papers, George C. Marshall Library, Lexington, Virginia (hereafter cited as Marshall Papers, Marshall Library), original in Yale University Library, New Haven, Connecticut; Robert Sherwood, *Roosevelt and Hopkins: An Intimate History* (New York: Harper and Brothers, 1948), 431; James MacGregor Burns, *Roosevelt: The Soldier of Freedom* (New York: Harcourt Brace Jovanovich, 1970), 38.

5. Sherwood, *Roosevelt and Hopkins*, 431.

6. Sherwood, *Roosevelt and Hopkins*, 433.

7. Tom Connally and Alfred Steinberg, *My Name Is Tom Connally* (New York: Thomas Y. Crowell, 1954), 249.

8. Connally and Steinberg, *My Name Is Tom Connally*, 249.

9. Marshall was referring to the Battle of Kythera Straits, where on 29 May 1941, during the Battle for Crete, the German Air Force alone sank two British cruisers and four destroyers.

10. Quotation from George C. Marshall to Secretary Henry Stimson, October 1941, in RG 165 Records of the War Department and General and Special Staffs, War Plans Division General Correspondence, 1920–1942, 4402–71, Box 233, National Archives at College Park, MD; Burns, *Roosevelt: The Soldier of Freedom*, 39.

11. Stimson Diary, 7 and 9 December 1941, Reel Seven, Volume 36, Marshall Papers, Marshall Library.

12. Winston Churchill, *The Grand Alliance* (Boston: Houghton Mifflin, 1950), 605.

13. Franklin Roosevelt Address to the Joint Session of Congress, 8 December 1941, Library of Congress, Washington, DC, https://www.loc.gov/static/programs/national-recording-preservation-board/documents/FDR_War_essay.pdf.

14. Churchill, *Grand Alliance*, 606.

15. Stimson Diary, 8 December 1941, Reel Seven, Volume 36, Marshall Papers, Marshall Library.

16. British Information Services, "American Aid to Britain," February 1955, General Historical Research Collection, Geographical files, Great Britain file 123, US Army Center of Military History, Fort McNair, DC; quotation from Secretary of War Stimson to President Roosevelt, 19 February 1942, Franklin Delano Roosevelt Library, Presidential Secretary Files, Confidential Files, Franklin Delano Roosevelt Library and Museum, Hyde Park, New York, http://www.fdrlibrary.marist.edu/archives/collections/franklin/ (hereafter cited as Franklin Delano Roosevelt Library); Stimson Diary, 8 December 1941, Reel Seven, Volume 36, Marshall Papers, Marshall Library.

17. Stimson Diary, 8 December 1941, Reel Seven, Volume 36, Marshall Papers, Marshall Library; Phone Conversation (Transcript) COL Vanaman to COL Olds 8 December 1941, Henry Arnold Papers, Reel 222, Library of Congress, Washington, DC (hereafter cited as Library of Congress).

18. Churchill, *Grand Alliance*, 558; Cable Harriman to Hopkins, 11 December 1941, W. Averell Harriman Papers, Box 161, Library of Congress.

19. Sherwood, *Roosevelt and Hopkins*, 440; quotation from J. M. A. Gwyer and J. R. M. Butler, *Grand Strategy*, vol. 3, *June 1941–August 1942* (London: Her Majesty's Stationery Office, 1964), 321.

20. Cable Harriman to Hopkins, 11 December 1941, W. Averell Harriman Papers, Box 161, Library of Congress.

21. Cable Hopkins to Harriman, 11 December 1941, Harriman Papers, Box 161, Library of Congress.

22. Cable Hopkins to Harriman, 11 December 1941, Harriman Papers, Box 161, Library of Congress.

23. Lord Moran Diary entry 20 December 1941, in Lord Charles Wilson Moran, *Churchill: Taken from the Diaries of Lord Moran; The Struggle for Survival, 1945–1960* (Boston: Houghton Mifflin, 1966), 11.

24. Correlli Barnett, *The Audit of War: The Illusion of Great Britain as a Great Nation* (London: Faber and Faber, 1986), 144–45.

25. Winston Churchill to Sir Kingsley Wood, 20 March 1941, in Martin Gilbert, *The Churchill War Papers: The Ever-Widening War*, vol. 4, *1941* (New York: W. W. Norton, 2000), 372; Warren Kimball, *Churchill and Roosevelt: The Complete Correspondence*, vol. 1, *Alliance Emerging, October 1933–November 1942* (Princeton, NJ: Princeton University Press, 1984), 137.

26. Winston Churchill to Lord Halifax, May 1943, in Martin Gilbert, *Churchill: Road to Victory, 1941–1945* (Hillsdale, MI: Hillsdale College Press, 1986), 410.

27. Gwyer and Butler, *Grand Strategy*, 318.

28. Prime Minister Letter to the King, 8 December 1941, cited in Gwyer and Butler, *Grand Strategy*, 315; Winston Churchill to King George VI, 8 December 1941, in Gilbert, *Churchill War Papers*, 1585.

29. Quotation from Frederick Aandahl, William M. Franklin, and William Slany, eds., *Foreign Relations of the United States, the Conferences at Washington, 1941–1942, and Casablanca, 1943* (Washington, DC: US Government Printing Office, 1958); Pre-Conference Papers, Document 3, Telegram Prime Minister Churchill to President Roosevelt, 9 December 1941, https://history.state.gov/historicaldocuments/frus1941-43 (hereafter cited as FRUS); Churchill, *Grand Alliance*, 609 (note: the State Department historian could not find a copy of this telegram and used Churchill's book as the source of the telegram). Winston S. Churchill to Franklin D. Roosevelt, 9 December 1941, in Gilbert, *Churchill War Papers*, 1592.

30. Quotation from *Foreign Relations of the United States, the Conferences at Washington, 1941–1942, and Casablanca, 1943*, Pre-Conference Papers, Document 6, Telegram Prime Minister Churchill to President Roosevelt, 10 December 1941 (FRUS); Churchill, *Grand Alliance*, 609 (note: the State Department historian could not find a copy of the telegram from Roosevelt to Churchill, 9 December 1941, and used Churchill's book as the source of the telegram). Winston S. Churchill to Franklin D. Roosevelt, 10 December 1941, in Gilbert, *Churchill War Papers*, 1595.

31. Churchill, *Grand Alliance*, 610; Cable R-73x Roosevelt to Churchill, 10 December 1941, in Kimball, *Churchill and Roosevelt*, 286.

32. Forrest Pogue, *George C. Marshall: Ordeal and Hope, 1939–1942* (New York: Viking Press, 1967), 261.

33. Robinett Diary, 9 December 1941, Box 20, Marshall Papers, Marshall Library; Wesley Craven and James Cate, *The Army Air Forces in World War II*, vol. 1, *Plans and Early Operations: January 1939–August 1942* (Chicago: University of Chicago Press, 1948), 279.

34. Craven and Cate, *Army Air Forces in World War II*, 278–79.

35. Pogue, *Ordeal and Hope*, 263.

36. Robinett Diary, 10 December 1941, Box 20, Marshall Papers, Marshall

Library; Stimson Diary, 10 December 1941, Reel Seven, Volume 36, Marshall Papers, Marshall Library.

37. Stimson Diary, 10 December 1941, Reel Seven, Volume 36, Marshall Papers, Marshall Library.

38. Samuel Eliot Morison, *The Two-Ocean War: A Short History of the United States Navy in the Second World War* (Boston: Little, Brown, 1963), 73. Ernest King, Random Notes, Box 35, Admiral Ernest King Papers, Library of Congress.

39. Morison, *Two-Ocean War*, 75.

40. Stimson Diary, 14 December 1941, Reel Seven, Volume 36, Marshall Papers, Marshall Library.

41. Louis Morton, *The Fall of the Philippines* (Washington, DC: US Army Center of Military History, 1985), 61–64; the definitive account of the US Navy's interwar planning is Edward Miller, *War Plan Orange: The US Strategy to Defeat Japan, 1897–1945* (Annapolis, MD: Naval Institute Press, 1991).

42. Stimson Diary, 14 December 1941, Reel Seven, Volume 36, Marshall Papers, Marshall Library.

43. Stimson Diary, 14 December 1941, Reel Seven, Volume 36, Marshall Papers, Marshall Library.

44. Stimson Diary, 15 December 1941, Reel Seven, Volume 36, Marshall Papers, Marshall Library.

45. Gordon Prange, *At Dawn We Slept: The Untold Story of Pearl Harbor* (New York: Penguin Books, 1982), 588.

46. Prange, *At Dawn We Slept*, 589.

47. Prange, *At Dawn We Slept*, 589.

48. Prange, *At Dawn We Slept*, 593–95.

49. Admiral King Random Notes, Admiral Ernest King Papers, Box 35, Library of Congress.

50. Robinett Diary, 15 December 1941, Box 20, Marshall Papers, Marshall Library.

51. Robinett Diary, 17 December 1941, Box 20, Marshall Papers, Marshall Library; Stimson Diary, 17 December 1941, Reel Seven, Volume 36, Marshall Papers, Marshall Library.

52. Lieutenant General Ian Jacob Diary, 12 and 13 December 1941, in Charles Richardson, *From Churchill's Secret Circle to the BBC: The Biography of Lieutenant General Sir Ian Jacob* (London: Brassey's, 1991), 84–85; Ian Jacob Diary, 12 December 1941, in Gilbert, *Churchill War Papers*, 1621.

53. Arthur Bryant, *The Turn of the Tide, 1939–1942* (New York: Doubleday, 1957), 246–47; Forrest Pogue notes on manuscript written by General Frederick Morgan, in a six-week period between the end of SHAEF and his taking over United Nations Relief and Rehabilitation Administration (UNRRA) in Germany, Forrest Pogue files, US Army War College Library, Army Heritage and Education Center, Carlisle, PA (hereafter cited as Morgan Manuscript).

54. Quotation from Pogue notes on Morgan Manuscript, US Army War College Library, Army Heritage and Education Center, Carlisle, PA; Alex Danchev, *Very Special Relationship: Field Marshal Sir John Dill and the Anglo-American Alliance, 1941–1944* (London: Brassey's Defence Publishers, 1986), 123–24.

55. Colville Diary, 28 September 1941, in John Colville, *The Fringes of Power: 10 Downing Street Diaries, 1939–1955* (New York: W. W. Norton, 1985), 443; Larry I. Bland, Sharon Ritenour Stevens, and Clarence E. Wunderlin Jr., eds., *The Papers of George Catlett Marshall* (Lexington, VA: George C. Marshall Foundation, 1981). Electronic version based on *The Papers of George Catlett Marshall*, vol. 2, "We Cannot Delay," July 1, 1939–December 6, 1941 (Baltimore: Johns Hopkins University Press, 1986), 689; Alex Danchev, "Dill," in *Churchill's Generals*, ed. John Keegan (London: Weidenfeld and Nicholson, 1991), 57.

56. First quotation from Forrest Pogue interview with Air Chief Marshal Sir Charles Portal, 7 February 1947, and the second quotation from Forrest Pogue notes on the General Frederick Morgan manuscript, written in the six-week period between the end of SHAEF and his taking over UNRRA in Germany, both in the Pogue Files, US Army War College Library, Army Heritage and Education Center; third quotation from Danchev, "Dill," in Keegan, *Churchill's Generals*, 52.

57. First quotation from Bryant, *Turn of the Tide*, 227. Second quotation from Danchev, "Dill," in Keegan, *Churchill's Generals*, 57.

58. Brooke Diary entries, 25 December 1941–12 January 1942, in Alex Danchev and Daniel Todman, *War Diaries, 1939–1945: Field Marshal Lord Alanbrooke* (Berkeley: University of California Press, 2001), 214–19.

59. Jacob Diary, 12 December 1941, Richardson, *Churchill's Inner Circle*, 84.

60. Brian Farrell, *The Defence and Fall of Singapore* (Singapore: Monsoon Books, 2017), 22.

61. Gwyer and Butler, *Grand Strategy*, 318–19.

62. William Manchester, *The Last Lion: Winston Spencer Churchill, Defender of the Realm, 1940–1965* (New York: Little Brown, 2012), 464.

63. Brief on ABC Agreements (Washington, January–March 1941), Ernest King Papers, Box 20, Library of Congress.

64. British United States Staff Conversations, 25 March 1941, Records of the War Department General and Special Staffs, Record Group 165, War Plans Division General Correspondence, 1920–1941, Box 233, National Archives and Records Administration, College Park, MD.

65. H. P. Willmott, *Empires in the Balance: Japanese and Allied Pacific Strategies to April 1942* (Annapolis, MD: Naval Institute Press, 1989), 99–100.

66. Willmott, *Empires in the Balance*, 121.

67. British United States Staff Conversations, "The Far East—Appreciation By The United Kingdom Delegation," 11 February 1941, Records of the War Department General and Special Staffs, Record Group 165, War Plans Division

General Correspondence, 1920–1941, Box 233, National Archives and Records Administration, College Park, MD; Farrell, *Defence and Fall of Singapore*, 81.

68. War and Navy Departments, 13 February 1941, "Minutes of joint meetings of Army and Navy sections, United States Staff Committee, held in Navy Department Building. February 13, 1941," Records of the War Department General and Special Staffs, Record Group 165, Correspondence Related to the Location and Leasing of Atlantic Bases in British Possessions, Allied Military Conferences of World War II, and Plans for Strategic Direction of Operations of Military Forces in Theaters of Operation, 1940–1945, Box 21, National Archives and Records Administration, College Park, MD.

69. British United States Staff Conversations, "The Far East—Appreciation By The United Kingdom Delegation," 11 February 1941, Records of the War Department General and Special Staffs, Record Group 165, War Plans Division General Correspondence, 1920–1941, Box 233, National Archives and Records Administration, College Park, MD.

70. British United States Staff Conversations, "Declaration By The United States Staff Committee," 19 February 1941, Records of the War Department General and Special Staffs, Record Group 165, War Plans Division General Correspondence, 1920–1941, Box 233, National Archives and Records Administration, College Park, MD.

71. Rear Admiral Roger Bellair to Major General Stanley Embick, 19 February 1941, and British United States Conversations, "Notes by the United Kingdom Delegation," 19 February 1941, in Records of the War Department General and Special Staffs, Record Group 165, Correspondence Related to the Location and Leasing of Atlantic Bases in British Possessions, Allied Military Conferences of World War II, and Plans for Strategic Direction of Operations of Military Forces in Theaters of Operation, 1940–1945, Box 21, National Archives and Records Administration, College Park, MD.

72. British United States Staff Conversations, 25 March 1941, Records of the War Department General and Special Staffs, Record Group 165, War Plans Division General Correspondence, 1920–1941, Box 233, National Archives and Records Administration, College Park, MD; Mark Stoler, *Allies and Adversaries: The Joint Chiefs of Staff, the Grand Alliance, and US Strategy in World War II* (Chapel Hill: University of North Carolina Press, 2000), 38; quotation in Winston S. Churchill to A. V. Alexander and Admiral Pound, 17 February 1941, in Gilbert, *Churchill War Papers*, 235.

73. Churchill, *Grand Alliance*, 435.

74. Churchill, *Grand Alliance* (quotation from p. 440) and p. 446; quotation also in Winston S. Churchill Narrative of Events, 11 August 1941, in Gilbert, *Churchill War Papers*, 1046.

75. "General Strategy, Review by the British Chiefs of Staff," 11–12 August 1941, Records of the War Department General and Special Staffs, Record Group 165,

War Plans Division General Correspondence, 1920–1941, WPD 4402–64, Box 230, National Archives and Records Administration, College Park, MD.

76. "General Strategy, Review by the British Chiefs of Staff," 11–12 August 1941, Records of the War Department General and Special Staffs, Record Group 165, War Plans Division General Correspondence, 1920–1941, WPD 4402–64, Box 230, National Archives and Records Administration, College Park, MD.

77. First quotation from "General Strategy, Review by the British Chiefs of Staff," 11–12 August 1941, Records of the War Department General and Special Staffs, Record Group 165, War Plans Division General Correspondence, 1920–1941, WPD 4402–64, Box 230, National Archives and Records Administration, College Park, MD; second quotation from Gwyer and Butler, *Grand Strategy*, 319.

78. "General Strategy, Review by the British Chiefs of Staff," 11–12 August 1941, Records of the War Department General and Special Staffs, Record Group 165, War Plans Division General Correspondence, 1920–1941, WPD 4402–64, Box 230, National Archives and Records Administration, College Park, MD.

79. Vernon Davis, *The History of the Joint Chiefs of Staff: Organizational Development*, vol. 1, *Origin of the Joint and Combined Chiefs of Staff* (Historical Division Joint Secretariat Joint Chiefs of Staff, 1972), Record Group 218, US Joint Chiefs of Staff, Office of the Director of the Joint Chiefs of Staff/Joint Secretariat Historical Division, Entry UD 104, History of the Joint Chiefs of Staff in World War II: Organizational Development (vols. 1 and 2), Container 1, National Archives and Records Administration, College Park, MD, p. 137.

80. First two quotations from Martin Gilbert, *Winston Churchill: Road to Victory, 1941–1945*, vol. 7 (Hillsdale, MI: Hillsdale College Press, 1986), 9; third quotation in Harriman notes on board *Duke of York*, 20 December 1941, W. Averell Harriman Papers, Box 161, Library of Congress.

81. Telegram Prime Minister Churchill to President Roosevelt, 18 December 1941, *Foreign Relations of the United States, the Conferences at Washington, 1941–1942, and Casablanca, 1943*, Pre-Conference Papers, Document 24, in FRUS.

82. Lord Moran Diary entry, 1 January 1942, in Lord Moran, *Churchill*, 21; Crosswell, *Beetle*, 231; Louis Morton, *Strategy and Command: The First Two Years* (Washington, DC: US Government Printing Office, 1962), 158; David Bercuson and Holger Herwig, *One Christmas in Washington* (New York: Overlook Press, 2005), 268.

83. Churchill, *Grand Alliance*, 576–77.

84. Franklin Roosevelt to Lord Halifax, 14 December 1941, Franklin Delano Roosevelt Library, Presidential Secretary Files, Safe Files, Box 2, Franklin Delano Roosevelt Library; Vernon Davis, *History of the Joint Chiefs of Staff: Organizational Development*, vol. 1, *Origin of the Joint and Combined Chiefs of Staff* (Historical Division Joint Secretariat Joint Chiefs of Staff, 1972), Record Group 218, US Joint Chiefs of Staff, Office of the Director of the Joint Chiefs of Staff/Joint Secretariat Historical Division, Entry UD 104, History of the

Joint Chiefs of Staff in World War II: Organizational Development (vols. 1 and 2), Container 1, National Archives and Records Administration, College Park, MD, p. 149.

85. Quotation from Message from Colonel Brink, 21 December 1941, in Records of the War Department General and Special Staffs, Record Group 165, Correspondence Related to the Location and Leasing of Atlantic Bases in British Possessions, Allied Military Conferences of World War II, and Plans for Strategic Direction of Operations of Military Forces in Theaters of Operation, 1940–1945, Box 22, National Archives and Records Administration, College Park, MD; Grace Hayes, *The History of the Joint Chiefs of Staff in World War II: The War against Japan* (Annapolis, MD: Naval Institute Press, 1982), 45.

86. Manchester, *Last Lion*, 464.

87. General Arnold Notes on Conference in the White House, 21 December 1941, General Henry Arnold Papers, Reel 205, Library of Congress.

88. "Tentative US Views on Subjects of British Memorandum, Dec.18," dated 21 December 1941, in Records of the War Department General and Special Staffs, Record Group 165, Correspondence Related to the Location and Leasing of Atlantic Bases in British Possessions, Allied Military Conferences of World War II, and Plans for Strategic Direction of Operations of Military Forces in Theaters of Operation, 1940–1945, Box 22, National Archives and Records Administration, College Park, MD; Charles Kirkpatrick, *An Unknown Future and a Doubtful Present: Writing the Victory Plan of 1941* (Washington, DC: US Army Center of Military History, 2013), 1.

89. General Arnold Notes on Conference in the White House, 21 December 1941, General Henry Arnold Papers, Reel 205, Library of Congress; Stimson Diary, 21 December 1941, Reel Seven, Volume 36, Marshall Papers, Marshall Library.

Chapter 2

1. Stimson Diary, 22 December 1941, Reel Seven, Volume 36, Marshall Papers, George C. Marshall Foundation Research Library and Archives, Lexington, Virginia (hereafter cited as Marshall Papers, Marshall Library). Original in Yale University Library, New Haven, Connecticut; Ronald Spector, *Eagle against the Sun: The American War with Japan* (New York: Vintage Books, 1985), 127.

2. Samuel Eliot Morison, *The Battle of the Atlantic: September 1939–May 1943* (Boston: Little, Brown, 1947), 41.

3. Morison, *Battle of the Atlantic*, 115; quotation from Ernest King and Walter Muir Whitehall, *Fleet Admiral King: A Naval Record* (London: Eyre and Spottiswoode, 1953), 204; Forrest Pogue, *George C. Marshall: Ordeal and Hope, 1939–1942* (New York: Viking Press, 1966), 22.

4. John McCrea, *Captain McCrea's War: The World War II Memoirs of Franklin D. Roosevelt's Naval Aide and USS* Iowa*'s First Commanding Officer*, ed. Julia C. Tobey (New York: Skyhorse Publishing, 2016), 178.

5. Stimson Diary, 22 December 1941, Reel Seven, Volume 36, Marshall Papers, Marshall Library; Mary Williams, *The US Army in World War II: Chronology, 1941–1945* (Washington, DC: US Government Printing Office, 1989), 7.

6. Samuel Eliot Morison, *The Two-Ocean War: A Short History of the United States Navy in the Second World War* (Boston: Little, Brown, 1963), 138; Spector, *Eagle against the Sun*, 103–4.

7. Stimson Diary, 22 December 1941, Reel Seven, Volume 36, Marshall Papers, Marshall Library; "Notes on a Conference with the British Mission," 20 December 1941, Record Group 165, Correspondence Relating to the Location and Leasing of Atlantic Bases in British Possessions, Allied Military Correspondences of World War II, and Plans for Strategic Direction of Operations of Military Forces in Theaters of Operation, 1940–1945, Entry 422, Box 22, National Archives and Records Administration, College Park, MD.

8. "Notes on a Conference with the British Mission," 20 December 1941, Record Group 165, Correspondence Relating to the Location and Leasing of Atlantic Bases in British Possessions, Allied Military Correspondences of World War II, and Plans for Strategic Direction of Operations of Military Forces in Theaters of Operation, 1940–1945, Entry 422, Box 22, National Archives and Records Administration, College Park, MD; "Record of Staff Conference Held on 19 December 1941 at 12:30 P.M.," War Cabinet and Chiefs of Staff Committee, Records of the Proceedings at the Washington War Conference, December 1941–January 1942 in CAB-99/17 Records of the Cabinet, War Cabinet and Cabinet: Commonwealth International Conferences; Minutes and Papers, "Arcadia" Record of Proceedings at Washington Conference 1941–1942, the National Archives, Kew, Richmond, Surrey, TW94DU, www.nationalarchives.gov.uk (hereafter cited as CAB-99/17 British Archives).

9. Charles Richardson, *From Churchill's Secret Circle to the BBC: The Biography of Sir Ian Jacob* (London: Brassey's, 1991), 88; Martin Gilbert, *The Churchill War Papers: The Ever Widening War*, vol. 4, *1941* (New York: W. W. Norton, 2000), 1667.

10. Richardson, *From Churchill's Secret Circle to the BBC*, 88; Dykes Diary, 22 December 1941, in Alex Danchev, *Establishing the Anglo-American Alliance* (London: Brassey's, 1991), 76.

11. Richardson, *From Churchill's Secret Circle to the BBC*, 9, 28, and quotation on p. 45.

12. Richardson, *From Churchill's Secret Circle to the BBC*, 28 and 188.

13. The losses to the British fleet and the subsequent effect on Axis reinforcements to the region, coupled with Churchill's diversion of forces from Libya to the Far East after Pearl Harbor, had yet to affect Crusader.

14. Winston Churchill, *The Grand Alliance* (Boston: Houghton Mifflin, 1950), 664; quotation from Memorandum By The Prime Minister (Aboard the H.M.S. "Duke of York"), dated 16 December 1941, in Frederick Aandahl, William Franklin, and William Slany, eds., *Foreign Relations of the United States, the Conferences at Washington, 1941–1942, and Casablanca, 1943* (Wash-

ington, DC: US Government Printing Office, 1958), Pre-Conference Papers, Document 23, https://history.state.gov/historicaldocuments/frus1941–43/comp1 (hereafter cited as FRUS). Although dated 16 December 1941, Churchill did not give this to President Roosevelt until 23 December 1941.

15. Winston S. Churchill to Clementine Churchill, 21 December 1941, in Gilbert, *Churchill War Papers*, 1664.

16. "Roosevelt-Churchill Meeting, evening," 22 December 1941, Document 44, in FRUS.

17. Robert Murphy, *A Diplomat among Warriors* (New York: Doubleday, 1964), 82; "Roosevelt-Churchill Meeting, evening," 22 December 1941, Document 44, in FRUS; Churchill, *Grand Alliance*, 665.

18. "Roosevelt-Churchill Meeting, evening," 22 December 1941, Document 44, inFRUS; Churchill, *Grand Alliance*, 665; quotations from Robert Sherwood, *Roosevelt and Hopkins: An Intimate History* (New York: Harper and Brothers, 1948), 9.

19. Henry Arnold, *Global Mission* (New York: Harper and Brothers, 1949), 276; J. M. A. Gwyer and J. R. M. Butler, *Grand Strategy*, vol. 3, *June 1941—August 1942* (London: Her Majesty's Stationery Office, 1964), 393; Denis Richards, *Portal of Hungerford: The Life of Marshal of the Royal Air Force Viscount Portal of Hungerford KG, GCB, OM, DSM, MC* (London: Heinemann, 1977), 250.

20. Forrest Pogue interview with Marshal of the Royal Air Force Portal on 7 February 1947, and Pogue notes on Morgan Manuscript written between end of SHAEF and his start as head of UNRRA in Germany, in Pogue interviews, US Army War College Library, in the US Army Heritage and Education Center, Carlisle Barracks, PA; Robert McHenry, ed., *Webster's American Military Biographies* (New York: Dover, 1978), 14.

21. Arnold, *Global Missions*, 276; quotation from "Notes by General Arnold, Arnold-Portal Meeting," 22 December 1941, Document 45, in FRUS; "Conference With Air Marshal Portal," 22 December 1941, Henry Arnold Papers, Reel 205, Library of Congress, Washington, DC.

22. General Wemyss to General Marshall, 2 January 1942, cited in Grace Hayes, *The History of the Joint Chiefs of Staff in World War II: The War against Japan* (Annapolis, MD: Naval Institute Press, 1982), 743.

23. Quotation from Arnold, *Global Missions*, 276–77; "Notes by General Arnold, Arnold-Portal Meeting," 22 December 1941, Document 45, in FRUS; "Conference with Air Marshal Portal," 22 December 1941, Henry Arnold Papers, Reel 205, Library of Congress.

24. Richards, *Portal of Hungerford*, 250.

25. Arnold, *Global Missions*, 277; "Notes by General Arnold, Arnold-Portal Meeting," 22 December 1941, Document 45, in FRUS; "Conference With Air Marshal Portal," 22 December 1941, Henry Arnold Papers, Reel 205, Library of Congress; Gwyer and Butler, *Grand Strategy*, 392.

26. "Notes by General Arnold, Arnold-Portal Meeting," 22 December 1941,

Document 45, Fin RUS; "Conference With Air Marshal Portal," 22 December 1941, Henry Arnold Papers, Reel 205, Library of Congress.

27. Stimson Diary, 23 December 1941, Reel Seven, Volume 36, Marshall Papers, Marshall Library; Williams, *US Army in World War II: Chronology*, 8.

28. Stimson Diary, 23 December 1941, Reel Seven, Volume 36, Marshall Papers, Marshall Library; Dykes Diary 23 December 1941, in Danchev, *Establishing the Anglo-American Alliance*, 76.

29. "Roosevelt Churchill meeting, forenoon," 23 December 1941, Document 46, in FRUS; quotation from "Oral Message From President Roosevelt to General Weygand," 23 December 1941, pp. 234–36, in FRUS.

30. "Memorandum by Prime Minister Churchill (Aboard the 'Duke of York,' December 16–29, 1941)," Document 23, handed to President Roosevelt on 23 December 1941, in FRUS.

31. "Memorandum by Prime Minister Churchill (Aboard the 'Duke of York,' December 16–29, 1941)," Document 23, handed to President Roosevelt on 23 December 1941, in FRUS.

32. Correlli Barnett, *The Desert Generals* (New York: Viking Press, 1961), 123.

33. General Sir Alan Brooke Diary, 24 December 1941, in Gilbert, *Churchill War Papers*, 1680.

34. "Memorandum by Prime Minister Churchill (Aboard the 'Duke of York,' December 16–29, 1941)," Document 23, handed to President Roosevelt on 23 December 1941, in FRUS.

35. Martin Gilbert, *Winston S. Churchill: Road to Victory* (Hillsdale, MI: Hillsdale College Press, 1986), 7: 13.

36. "Memorandum by Prime Minister Churchill (Aboard the 'Duke of York,' December 16–29, 1941)," Document 23, handed to President Roosevelt on 23 December 1941, in FRUS.

37. Forrest Pogue interview with Marshal of the Royal Air Force Portal on 7 February 1947, Pogue Interviews, US Army Military History Institute, US Army Heritage and Education Center, Carlisle Barracks, PA.

38. Churchill, *Grand Alliance*, 667.

39. Spector, *Eagle against the Sun*, 104–6.

40. "Meeting of Roosevelt and Churchill with their military advisors," 4:45 p.m., in FRUS; "Notes of Meeting At The White House With the President and British Prime Minister Presiding (23 December 1941)," Memorandum by the Chief of Staff, United States Army (Marshall), Document 47, in FRUS; Jacob Diary, 23 December 1941, cited in Richardson, *From Churchill's Secret Circle*, 88–89.

41. Grace Hayes interview with Admiral Stark on 17 June 1949, cited in Hayes, *Joint Chiefs of Staff and War with Japan*, 38 and 743.

42. "Notes of Meeting At The White House With the President and British Prime Minister Presiding," 23 December 1941, Memorandum by the Chief of

Staff, United States Army (Marshall), Document 47, in FRUS; Memorandum by Lieutenant General Arnold on Conference in the White House Tuesday Afternoon, 4:45 P.M. December 23, 1941, Document 48, in FRUS; James MacGregor Burns, *Roosevelt: The Soldier of Freedom* (New York: Harcourt Brace Jovanovich, 1970), 180.

43. "Notes of Meeting At The White House With the President and British Prime Minister Presiding," 23 December 1941, Memorandum by the Chief of Staff, United States Army (Marshall), Document 47, in FRUS; Memorandum by Lieutenant General Arnold on Conference in the White House Tuesday Afternoon, 4:45 P.M., December 23, 1941, Document 48, in FRUS; Stimson Diary, 23 December 1941, Reel Seven, Volume 36, Marshall Papers, Marshall Library.

44. "Notes of Meeting At The White House With the President and British Prime Minister Presiding" 23 December 1941, Memorandum by the Chief of Staff, United States Army (Marshall), Document 47, in FRUS; Memorandum by Lieutenant General Arnold on Conference in the White House Tuesday Afternoon, 4:45 P.M., December 23, 1941, Document 48, in FRUS.

45. "Notes of Meeting At The White House With the President and British Prime Minister Presiding," 23 December 1941, Memorandum by the Chief of Staff, United States Army (Marshall), Document 47, in FRUS.

46. "Notes of Meeting At The White House With the President and British Prime Minister Presiding," 23 December 1941, Memorandum by the Chief of Staff, United States Army (Marshall), Document 47, in FRUS; quotation from Memorandum by Lieutenant General Arnold on Conference in the White House Tuesday Afternoon, 4:45 P.M. December 23, 1941, Document 48, in FRUS.

47. Gwyer and Butler, *Grand Strategy*, 355.

48. First quotation from Stimson Diary, 23 December 1941, Reel Seven, Volume 36, Marshall Papers, Marshall Library; second quotation from Memorandum by Lieutenant General Arnold on Conference in the White House Tuesday Afternoon, 4:45 P.M. December 23, 1941, Document 48, in FRUS; "Notes of Meeting At The White House With the President and British Prime Minister Presiding," 23 December 1941, Memorandum by the Chief of Staff, United States Army (Marshall), Document 47, in FRUS.

49. Memorandum by Lieutenant General Arnold on Conference in the White House Tuesday Afternoon, 4:45 P.M. December 23, 1941, Document 48, in FRUS.

50. Memorandum by Lieutenant General Arnold on Conference in the White House Tuesday Afternoon, 4:45 P.M. December 23, 1941, Document 48, in FRUS; "Notes of Meeting At The White House With the President and British Prime Minister Presiding," 23 December 1941, Memorandum by the Chief of Staff, United States Army (Marshall), Document 47, in FRUS.

51. Stimson Diary, 23 December 1941, Reel Seven, Volume 36, Marshall Papers, Marshall Library; quotation from Dykes Diary, 23 December 1941, cited in Danchev, *Establishing the Anglo-American Alliance*, 77.

52. Paul Robinett Diary, 23 and 24 December 1941, Box 20, Marshall Papers, Marshall Library. Quotation in Robinett Diary of 23 December 1941, Box 20, Marshall Papers, Marshall Library.

53. Rick Atkinson, *An Army at Dawn: The War in North Africa, 1942–1943* (New York: Henry Holt, 2002), 222.

54. Paul Robinett Diary, 23 and 24 December 1941, Box 20, Marshall Papers, Marshall Library.

55. First quotation from General Thomas T. Handy interview by Lieutenant Colonel Edward M. Knoff Jr., p. 41, Senior Officer Debriefing Program, US Army Military Research Collection, US Army Military History Institute, US Army Heritage and Education Center, Carlisle, PA; Andrew Roberts, *Masters and Commanders: How Four Titans Won the War in the West, 1941–1945* (New York: Harper Perennial, 2009), 71; second quotation from Thomas Buell, *Master of Seapower: A Biography of Fleet Admiral Ernest J. King* (Boston: Little, Brown, 1980), 163; third quotation from Robinett Diary, 24 December 1941, Box 20, Marshall Papers, Marshall Library.

56. Jacob Diary, 24 December 1941, in Richardson, *From Churchill's Secret Circle*, 89.

57. Proceedings of the American British Joint Chiefs of Staff Conferences, Held in Washington, DC, On Twelve Occasions Between December 24, 1941 and January 14, 1942, "Minutes from the Chiefs of Staff Conference, Federal Reserve Building, Washington, DC, 1030 A.M., December 24, 1941," in Joint Staff Historical Archives, Pentagon (hereafter cited as Joint Chiefs of Staff files); quotation from "Meeting of the United States and British Chiefs of Staff, 1030 a.m., 24 December 1941," Document 52, in FRUS.

58. "Probable Maximum Scale Attacks on West Coast of North America," 24 December 1941, in Proceedings of the American British Joint Chiefs of Staff Conferences, Held in Washington, DC, On Twelve Occasions Between December 24, 1941 and January 14, 1942, annex to "Minutes from the Chiefs of Staff Conference, Federal Reserve Building, Washington, DC, 1030 A.M., December 24, 1941," in Joint Chiefs of Staff files.

59. Jacob Diary, 24 December 1941, in Richards, *From Churchill's Secret Circle*, 90.

60. Proceedings of the American British Joint Chiefs of Staff Conferences, Held in Washington, DC, On Twelve Occasions Between December 24, 1941 and January 14, 1942, "Minutes from the Chiefs of Staff Conference, Federal Reserve Building, Washington, DC, 1030 A.M., December 24, 1941," in Joint Chiefs of Staff files; "Meeting of the United States and British Chiefs of Staff, 10:30 a.m., 24 December 1941," Document 52, in FRUS.

61. Proceedings of the American British Joint Chiefs of Staff Conferences,

Held in Washington, DC, On Twelve Occasions Between December 24, 1941 and January 14, 1942, "Minutes from the Chiefs of Staff Conference, Federal Reserve Building, Washington, DC, 1030 A.M., December 24, 1941," in Joint Chiefs of Staff files; "Meeting of the United States and British Chiefs of Staff, 10:30 a.m., 24 December 1941," Document 52, in FRUS.

62. Proceedings of the American British Joint Chiefs of Staff Conferences, Held in Washington, DC, On Twelve Occasions Between December 24, 1941 and January 14, 1942, "Minutes from the Chiefs of Staff Conference, Federal Reserve Building, Washington, DC, 1030 A.M., December 24, 1941," in Joint Chiefs of Staff files; "Meeting of the United States and British Chiefs of Staff, 10:30 a.m., 24 December 1941," Document 52, in FRUS.

63. Proceedings of the American British Joint Chiefs of Staff Conferences, Held in Washington, DC, On Twelve Occasions Between December 24, 1941 and January 14, 1942, "Minutes from the Chiefs of Staff Conference, Federal Reserve Building, Washington, DC, 1030 A.M., December 24, 1941," in Joint Chiefs of Staff files; "Meeting of the United States and British Chiefs of Staff, 10:30 a.m., 24 December 1941," Document 52, in FRUS.

64. Proceedings of the American British Joint Chiefs of Staff Conferences, Held in Washington, DC, On Twelve Occasions Between December 24, 1941 and January 14, 1942, "Minutes from the Chiefs of Staff Conference, Federal Reserve Building, Washington, DC, 1030 A.M., December 24, 1941," in Joint Chiefs of Staff files; "Meeting of the United States and British Chiefs of Staff, 10:30 a.m., 24 December 1941," Document 52, in FRUS.

65. Proceedings of the American British Joint Chiefs of Staff Conferences, Held in Washington, DC, On Twelve Occasions Between December 24, 1941 and January 14, 1942, "Minutes from the Chiefs of Staff Conference, Federal Reserve Building, Washington, DC, 1030 A.M., December 24, 1941," in Joint Chiefs of Staff files; "Meeting of the United States and British Chiefs of Staff, 10:30 a.m., 24 December 1941," Document 52, in FRUS.

66. Proceedings of the American British Joint Chiefs of Staff Conferences, Held in Washington, DC, On Twelve Occasions Between December 24, 1941 and January 14, 1942, "Minutes from the Chiefs of Staff Conference, Federal Reserve Building, Washington, DC, 1030 A.M., December 24, 1941," in Joint Chiefs of Staff files; "Meeting of the United States and British Chiefs of Staff, 10:30 a.m., 24 December 1941," Document 52, in FRUS; Robinett Diary, 24 December 1941, Box 20, Marshall Papers, Marshall Library.

67. Proceedings of the American British Joint Chiefs of Staff Conferences, Held in Washington, DC, On Twelve Occasions Between December 24, 1941 and January 14, 1942, "Minutes from the Chiefs of Staff Conference, Federal Reserve Building, Washington, DC, 1030 A.M., December 24, 1941," in Joint Chiefs of Staff files; "Meeting of the United States and British Chiefs of Staff, 10:30 a.m., 24 December 1941," Document 52, in FRUS.

68. Pogue, *George C. Marshall: Ordeal and Hope*, 265.

69. Quotation from Annex 1 to ABC-4 JCCSs-1, Washington War Conference, "American and British Strategy: Memorandum By the British Chiefs of Staff, Revised by US Chiefs of Staff (W.W.-1.)," in Proceedings of the American British Joint Chiefs of Staff Conferences, Held in Washington, DC, On Twelve Occasions Between December 24, 1941 and January 14, 1942, "Minutes from the Chiefs of Staff Conference, Federal Reserve Building, Washington, DC, 10:30 A.M., December 24, 1941," in Joint Chiefs of Staff files; Louis Morton, "Germany First," in *Command Decisions*, ed. Kent Roberts Greenfield (Washington, DC: Office of the Chief of Military History, Department of the Army, 1960), 11.

70. Annex 1 to ABC-4 JCCSs-1, Washington War Conference, "American and British Strategy: Memorandum By the British Chiefs of Staff, Revised by US Chiefs of Staff (W.W.-1.)," in Proceedings of the American British Joint Chiefs of Staff Conferences, Held in Washington, DC, On Twelve Occasions Between December 24, 1941 and January 14, 1942, "Minutes from the Chiefs of Staff Conference, Federal Reserve Building, Washington, DC, 10:30 A.M., December 24, 1941," in Joint Chiefs of Staff files.

71. By 1942 this was reduced to 23 million tons.

72. Annex 1 to ABC-4 JCCSs-1, Washington War Conference, "American and British Strategy: Memorandum By the British Chiefs of Staff, Revised by US Chiefs of Staff (W.W.-1.)," in Proceedings of the American British Joint Chiefs of Staff Conferences, Held in Washington, DC, On Twelve Occasions Between December 24, 1941 and January 14, 1942, "Minutes from the Chiefs of Staff Conference, Federal Reserve Building, Washington, DC, 10:30 A.M., December 24, 1941," in Joint Chiefs of Staff files; quotation from Samuel Eliot Morison, *The Battle of the Atlantic: September 1939–May 1943* (Boston: Little, Brown, 1947), 127–28; "Statistics Relating to the War Effort of the United Kingdom" (London: His Majesty's Stationery Office, 1944), 19–20, in Geographical files Great Britain, 123 Reciprocal aid #1, Historical Research Collection, US Army Center of Military History.

73. Annex 1 to ABC-4 JCCSs-1, Washington War Conference, "American and British Strategy: Memorandum By the British Chiefs of Staff, Revised by US Chiefs of Staff (W.W.-1.)," in Proceedings of the American British Joint Chiefs of Staff Conferences, Held in Washington, DC, On Twelve Occasions Between December 24, 1941 and January 14, 1942, "Minutes from the Chiefs of Staff Conference, Federal Reserve Building, Washington, DC, 10:30 A.M., December 24, 1941," in Joint Chiefs of Staff files.

74. Annex 1 to ABC-4 JCCSs-1, Washington War Conference, "American and British Strategy: Memorandum By the British Chiefs of Staff, Revised by US Chiefs of Staff (W.W.-1.)," in Proceedings of the American British Joint Chiefs of Staff Conferences, Held in Washington, DC, On Twelve Occasions Between December 24, 1941 and January 14, 1942, "Minutes from the Chiefs

of Staff Conference, Federal Reserve Building, Washington, DC, 10:30 A.M., December 24, 1941," in Joint Chiefs of Staff files.

75. Annex 1 to ABC-4 JCCSs-1, Washington War Conference, "American and British Strategy: Memorandum By the British Chiefs of Staff, Revised by US Chiefs of Staff (W.W.-1.)," in Proceedings of the American British Joint Chiefs of Staff Conferences, Held in Washington, DC, On Twelve Occasions Between December 24, 1941 and January 14, 1942, "Minutes from the Chiefs of Staff Conference, Federal Reserve Building, Washington, DC, 10:30 A.M., December 24, 1941," in Joint Chiefs of Staff files.

76. Annex 1 to ABC-4 JCCSs-1, Washington War Conference, "American and British Strategy: Memorandum By the British Chiefs of Staff, Revised by US Chiefs of Staff (W.W.-1.)," in Proceedings of the American British Joint Chiefs of Staff Conferences, Held in Washington, DC, On Twelve Occasions Between December 24, 1941 and January 14, 1942, "Minutes from the Chiefs of Staff Conference, Federal Reserve Building, Washington, DC, 10:30 A.M., December 24, 1941," in Joint Chiefs of Staff files.

77. J. M. A. Gwyer and J. R. M. Butler, *Grand Strategy*, vol. 3, *June 1941–August 1942* (London: Her Majesty's Stationery Office, 1964), 357.

78. Quotation in Gwyer and Butler, *Grand Strategy*, 360; Mark Stoler, *George C. Marshall: Soldier Statesman of the American Century* (Boston: Twayne Publishers, 1989), 93–94; H. P. Willmott, *Empires in the Balance: Japanese and Allied Pacific Strategies to April 1942* (Annapolis, MD: Naval Institute Press, 1982), 257.

79. Stimson Diary, 24 December 1941, Reel Seven, Volume 36, Marshall Papers, Marshall Library; Stephen Ambrose, *Eisenhower: Soldier, General of the Army, President-Elect, 1890–1952* (New York: Simon and Schuster, 1983), 137.

80. Dykes Diary, 24 December 1941, in Danchev, *Establishing the Anglo-American Alliance*, 77; D. Crosswell, *Beetle: The Life of Walter Bedell Smith* (Lexington: University Press of Kentucky, 2010), 272.

81. George C. Dyer, *The Amphibians Came to Conquer: The Story of Admiral Richmond Kelly Turner* (Washington, DC: US Government Printing Office, 1972), xix–xx, http://www.ibiblio.org/hyperwar/USN/ACTC/index.html#prologue.

82. Danchev, *Establishing the Anglo-American Alliance*, 77–85; Robert McHenry, ed., *Webster's American Military Biographies* (New York: Dover Publications, 1978), 140.

83. I. C. B. Dear and M. R. D. Foot, eds., *The Oxford Companion to World War II* (Oxford: Oxford University Press, 1995), 974; Churchill, *Grand Alliance*, 666.

84. Remarks by Winston Churchill at the Christmas Tree Lighting Ceremony, 1630 Hours, 24 December 1941, Franklin D. Roosevelt Master Speech File, Box 64 File 1406, Franklin D. Roosevelt Library and Museum, Hyde Park, New York, http://www.fdrlibrary.marist.edu/archives/collections/franklin/index.php?p=collections/findingaid&id=582; Gilbert, *Winston Churchill:*

Road to Victory, 27; Winston S. Churchill: BBC Broadcast, 24 December 1941, in Gilbert, *Churchill War Papers*, 1679.

85. Quotation from Churchill, *Grand Alliance*, 669; "The Secretary of the British Chiefs of Staff (Hollis) to the Secretary, War Department General Staff (Smith)," 24 December 1941, in FRUS, 267–68.

86. Willmott, *Empires in the Balance*, 218–19 and 237.

87. First quotation from Gilbert, *Winston Churchill: Road to Victory*, 26; second quotation from Alex Danchev, *Very Special Relationship: Field Marshall Sir John Dill and the Anglo-American Alliance* (London: Brassey's Defence Publishers, 1986), 39; Franklin Roosevelt Calendar, 24 December 1941, in the Franklin D. Roosevelt Day by Day, a project of the Pare Lorentz Center at the FDR Presidential Library, http://www.fdrlibrary.marist.edu/daybyday/daylog/december-24th-1941/.

Chapter 3

1. "Situation Report, December 25, 1941," Franklin Delano Roosevelt, Papers as President: Map Room Papers, 1941–1945, Military Files, Box 38, #41, Roosevelt Presidential Library and Museum, http://www.fdrlibrary.marist.edu/archives/collections/franklin/ (hereafter cited as Franklin Delano Roosevelt Library); Stimson Diary, 25 December 1941, Reel Seven, Volume 36, Marshall Papers, George C. Marshall Foundation Research Library and Archives (hereafter cited as Marshall Papers, Marshall Library).

2. Winston S. Churchill to Clementine Churchill, 21 December 1941, in Martin Gilbert, *The Churchill War Papers: The Ever-Widening War*, vol. 3, *1941* (New York: W. W. Norton, 2000), 1663.

3. "Situation Report, December 25, 1941," Franklin Delano Roosevelt, Papers as President: Map Room Papers, 1941–1945, Military Files, Box 38, #41, Roosevelt Presidential Library and Museum, http://www.fdrlibrary.marist.edu/archives/collections/franklin/, Franklin Delano Roosevelt Library; Correlli Barnett, *The Desert Generals* (New York: Viking Press, 1961), 123; Winston S. Churchill to General Auchinleck, 25 December 1941, in Gilbert, *Churchill War Papers*, 1681.

4. Dykes Diary, 25 December 1941, in Alex Danchev, *Establishing the Anglo-American Alliance* (London: Brassey's, 1991), 77.

5. Stimson Diary, 25 December 1941, Reel Seven, Volume 36, Marshall Papers, Marshall Library.

6. Stimson Diary, 25 December 1941, Reel Seven, Volume 36, Marshall Papers, Marshall Library.

7. Charles Wilson, *Churchill: Taken from the Diaries of Lord Moran* (Boston: Houghton Mifflin, 1966), 14; quotation from Winston S. Churchill Recollection in Gilbert, *Churchill War Papers*, 1683.

8. Forrest C. Pogue, *George C. Marshall: Ordeal and Hope, 1939–1942* (New York: Viking Press, 1967), 274.

9. Stimson Diary, 25 December 1941, Reel Seven, Volume 36, Marshall Papers, Marshall Library.

10. Stimson Diary, 25 December 1941, Reel Seven, Volume 36, Marshall Papers, Marshall Library.

11. Paul M. Robinett Diary, 25 December 1941, Box 20, Marshall Papers, Marshall Library)

12. Code Cablegram Received at the War Department at 06:55, June 17, 1941, from Colonel Fellers, Records of the War Department General and Special Staffs, Record Group 165, War Plans Division General Correspondence, 1920–1941, Box 231, #4402–84, National Archives and Records Administration, College Park, MD.

13. Telegram No. 1421, to Department of State from Cairo, 18 September 1941, in Records of the War Department General and Special Staffs, Record Group 165, War Plans Division General Correspondence, 1920–1941, Box 231, #4402–84, National Archives and Records Administration, College Park, MD.

14. Major Fellers Review of the Command Situation of the Middle East, 5 October 1941, Part 1, Records of the War Department General and Special Staffs, Record Group 165, War Plans Division General Correspondence, 1920–1941, Box 231, #4402–84, National Archives and Records Administration, College Park, MD.

15. Personal Letter from Major General George Brett to General Marshall, Cairo, 21 September 1941, result of direct observations, Records of the War Department General and Special Staffs, Record Group 165, War Plans Division General Correspondence, 1920–1941, Box 231, #4402–84, National Archives and Records Administration, College Park, MD.

16. Major Fellers Review of the Command Situation of the Middle East, 5 October 1941, Part 3, Records of the War Department General and Special Staffs, Record Group 165, War Plans Division General Correspondence, 1920–1941, Box 231, #4402–84, National Archives and Records Administration, College Park, MD.

17. Memorandum Admiral Stark to General Marshall 8 October 1941 and Recommendation General Gerow (WPD) to General Marshall, 8 October 1941, in Records of the War Department General and Special Staffs, Record Group 165, War Plans Division General Correspondence, 1920–1941, Box 231, #4402–84, National Archives and Records Administration, College Park, MD.

18. Quotation from "Report on the Inter-Allied Conference, Singapore, December 18th and 20th, 1941," From Lieutenant Colonel Brink to Chief of Staff, dated 25 December 1941, Record Group 218, US Joint Chiefs of Staff, Central Decimal file 1942–1945, Box 32, National Archives and Records Administration, College Park, MD; Pogue, *Ordeal and Hope*, 275.

19. Quotation from "Report on the Inter-Allied Conference, Singapore, December 18th and 20th, 1941," From Lieutenant Colonel Brink to Chief of Staff, dated 25 December 1941, Record Group 218, US Joint Chiefs of Staff,

Central Decimal file 1942–1945, Box 32, National Archives and Records Administration, College Park, MD.

20. Proceedings of the American British Joint Chiefs of Staff Conferences, Held in Washington, DC, On Twelve Occasions Between December 24, 1941 and January 14, 1942, "Minutes of the Chiefs of Staff Conference, Federal Reserve Building, Washington, DC, 4 P.M., December 25, 1941," Joint Staff Historical Archives, Pentagon (hereafter cited as Joint Chiefs of Staff files); "Meeting of the United States and British Chiefs of Staff, 4 p.m., 25 December 1941," Document 54, in Frederick Aandahl, William Franklin, and William Slany, eds., *Foreign Relations of the United States, the Conferences at Washington, 1941–1942, and Casablanca, 1943* (Washington, DC: US Government Printing Office, 1958), https://history.state.gov/historicaldocuments/frus1941-43/comp1 (hereafter cited as FRUS).

21. The others being the USS *West Point* and the USS *Wakefield.*

22. Proceedings of the American British Joint Chiefs of Staff Conferences, Held in Washington, DC, On Twelve Occasions Between December 24, 1941 and January 14, 1942, "Minutes of the Chiefs of Staff Conference, Federal Reserve Building, Washington, DC, 4 P.M., December 25, 1941," Joint Chiefs of Staff files; "Meeting of the United States and British Chiefs of Staff, 4 p.m., 25 December 1941," Document 54, in FRUS; Samuel Eliot Morison, *The Battle of the Atlantic: September 1939–May 1943* (Boston: Little, Brown, 1947), 110.

23. Proceedings of the American British Joint Chiefs of Staff Conferences, Held in Washington, DC, On Twelve Occasions Between December 24, 1941 and January 14, 1942, "Minutes from the Chiefs of Staff Conference, Federal Reserve Building, Washington, DC, 4 P.M., December 25, 1941," Joint Chiefs of Staff files; "Meeting of the United States and British Chiefs of Staff, 4 p.m., 25 December 1941," Document 54, in FRUS.

24. Proceedings of the American British Joint Chiefs of Staff Conferences, Held in Washington, DC, On Twelve Occasions Between December 24, 1941 and January 14, 1942, "Minutes from the Chiefs of Staff Conference, Federal Reserve Building, Washington, DC, 4 P.M., December 25, 1941," Joint Chiefs of Staff files ; "Meeting of the United States and British Chiefs of Staff, 4 p.m., 25 December 1941," Document 54, in FRUS; Wesley Craven and James Cate, *The Army Air Forces in World War II*, vol. 1, *Plans and Early Operations* (Chicago: University of Chicago Press, 1948), 230.

25. "Proceedings of the American British Joint Chiefs of Staff Conferences, Held in Washington, DC, On Twelve Occasions Between December 24, 1941 and January 14, 1942, "Minutes from the Chiefs of Staff Conference, Federal Reserve Building, Washington, DC, 4 P.M., December 25, 1941," Joint Chiefs of Staff files; "Meeting of the United States and British Chiefs of Staff, 4 p.m., 25 December 1941," Document 54, in FRUS.

26. Brigadier General Dwight Eisenhower, "Notes Taken at Joint Conference of Chiefs of Staff on Afternoon, December 25," dated 28 December 1941,

in Records of the War Department General and Special Staffs, Record Group 165, War Plans Division General Correspondence, 1920–1941, Box 234, #4402–136, National Archives and Records Administration, College Park, MD.

27. Pogue, *Ordeal and Hope*, 264 and quotation from p. 271.

28. Robinett Diary, 25 December 1941, Box 20, Marshall Papers, Marshall Library; Brigadier General Dwight Eisenhower, "Notes Taken at Joint Conference of Chiefs of Staff on Afternoon, December 25," dated 28 December 1941, in Records of the War Department General and Special Staffs, Record Group 165, War Plans Division General Correspondence, 1920–1941, Box 234, #4402–136, National Archives and Records Administration, College Park, MD.

29. Proceedings of the American British Joint Chiefs of Staff Conferences, Held in Washington, DC, On Twelve Occasions Between December 24, 1941 and January 14, 1942, "Minutes of the Chiefs of Staff Conference, Federal Reserve Building, Washington, DC, 4 P.M., December 25, 1941," Joint Chiefs of Staff files; quotation from "Meeting of the United States and British Chiefs of Staff, 4 p.m., 25 December 1941," Document 54, in FRUS.

30. Brigadier General Dwight Eisenhower, "Notes Taken at Joint Conference of Chiefs of Staff on Afternoon, December 25," dated 28 December 1941, in Records of the War Department General and Special Staffs, Record Group 165, War Plans Division General Correspondence, 1920–1941, Box 234, #4402–136, National Archives and Records Administration, College Park, MD; Mark Stoler, *George C. Marshall: Soldier Statesman of the American Century* (Boston: Twayne Publishers, 1989), 91; Robinett Diary, 25 December 1941, Box 20, Marshall Papers, Marshall Library.

31. Robinett Diary, 25 December 1941, Box 20, Marshall Papers, Marshall Library; Minutes of the Chiefs of Staff Conference, Federal Reserve Building, Washington, DC, 4 P.M., December 25, 1941, Joint Chiefs of Staff files; "Meeting of the United States and British Chiefs of Staff, 4 p.m., 25 December 1941," Document 54, in FRUS.

32. Pogue, *Ordeal and Hope*, 276–77; Proceedings of the American British Joint Chiefs of Staff Conferences, Held in Washington, DC, On Twelve Occasions Between December 24, 1941 and January 14, 1942, "Minutes of the Chiefs of Staff Conference, Federal Reserve Building, Washington, DC, 4 P.M., December 25, 1941," Joint Chiefs of Staff files; "Meeting of the United States and British Chiefs of Staff, 4 p.m., 25 December 1941," Document 54, in FRUS.

33. Robinett Diary, 25 December 1941, Box 20, Marshall Papers, Marshall Library.

34. Robinett Diary, 25 December 1941, Box 20, Marshall Papers, Marshall Library.

35. Quotation from Brigadier General Dwight Eisenhower, "Notes Taken at Joint Conference of Chiefs of Staff on Afternoon, December 25," dated 28 December 1941, in Records of the War Department General and Special Staffs,

Record Group 165, War Plans Division General Correspondence, 1920–1941, Box 234, #4402–136, National Archives and Records Administration, College Park, MD; Pogue, *Ordeal and Hope*, 277.

36. Stimson Diary, 25 December 1941, Reel Seven, Volume 36, Marshall Papers, Marshall Library.

37. Stimson Diary, 25 December 1941, Reel Seven, Volume 36, Marshall Papers, Marshall Library.

38. Quotations from Dykes Diary, 25 December 1941, in Danchev, *Establishing the Anglo-American Alliance*, 78; "Chiefs of Staff Directive to the Joint Planning Committee on The Southwest Pacific Area," 25 December 1941, in Records of the War Department General and Special Staffs, Record Group 165, Office of the Director of Plans and Operations, 337, Arcadia, Box 263, National Archives and Records Administration, College Park, MD.

39. Dan Majors, "Christmas 1941: With World at War, Churchill joins FDR for Washington Yule," Pittsburgh *Post-Gazette*, Sunday, December 25, 2011, http://www.post-gazette.com/local/region/2011/12/25/Christmas-1941-With-world-at-war-Churchill-joins-FDR-for-Washington-Yule/stories/201112250236; Meredith Hindley, "Christmas at the White House with Winston Churchill," *Humanities* 37, no. 4 (Fall 2016), https://www.neh.gov/humanities/2016/fall/feature/christmas-the-white-house-winston-churchill; General Garrison Norton's recollections to Martin Gilbert, in Gilbert, *Churchill War Papers*, 1684.

40. Franklin Roosevelt Daily Activities, 25 December 1941, http://www.fdr library.marist.edu/daybyday/daylog/december-25th-1941.

41. "Situation Report, December 26, 1941," Franklin Delano Roosevelt, Papers as President: Map Room Papers, 1941–1945, Military Files, Box 38, #41, Roosevelt Presidential Library and Museum, http://www.fdrlibrary .marist.edu/archives/collections/franklin/ (hereafter cited as Franklin Delano Roosevelt Library); Stimson Diary, 26 December 1941, Reel Seven, Volume 36, Marshall Papers, Marshall Library.

42. Stimson Diary, 26 December 1941, Reel Seven, Volume 36, Marshall Papers, Marshall Library.

43. First quotation from Stimson Diary, 26 December 1941, Reel Seven, Volume 36, Marshall Papers, Marshall Library; Ian Beckett, "Wavell," in *Churchill's Generals*, ed. John Keegan (New York: Quill, William Morrow, 1991), 85; second quotation from Maurice Matloff and Edwin Snell, *Strategic Planning for Coalition Warfare: 1941–1942* (Washington, DC: Center of Military History United States Army, 1999), 124.

44. Winston Churchill, "Address to the Joint Session of US Congress," 26 December 1941, in www.nationalchurchillmuseum.org/churchill-address-to-congress.html; Winston S. Churchill Speech, 26 December 1941, in Gilbert, *Churchill War Papers*, 1685–90.

45. Winston S. Churchill, "Address to Joint Session of US Congress," 26 December 1941, in Gilbert, *Churchill War Papers*, 1685–90.

46. Quotation from Robinett Diary, 26 December 1941, Box 20, Marshall Papers, Marshall Library; Minutes of the Chiefs of Staff Conference, Federal Reserve Building, Washington, DC, 3 P.M., December 26, 1941, Joint Chiefs of Staff files; "Meeting of the United States and British Chiefs of Staff, 3 p.m., 26 December 1941," Document 56, in FRUS.

47. Robinett Diary, 26 December 1941, Box 20, Marshall Papers, Marshall Library.

48. First quotation from Samuel Eliot Morison, *The Two-Ocean War: A Short History of the United States Navy in the Second World War* (Boston: Little, Brown, 1963), 71; second quotation from Charles Richardson, *From Churchill's Secret Circle to the BBC: The Biography of Lieutenant General Ian Jacob* (London: Brassey's, 1991), 97; Dykes Diary, 26 December 1941 in Danchev, *Establishing the Anglo-American Alliance*, 78.

49. Robinett Diary, 20 November 1941, Box 20, Marshall Papers, Marshall Library.

50. Proceedings of the American British Joint Chiefs of Staff Conferences, Held in Washington, DC, On Twelve Occasions Between December 24, 1941 and January 14, 1942, "Minutes of the Chiefs of Staff Conference, Federal Reserve Building, Washington, DC, 3 P.M., December 26, 1941," Joint Chiefs of Staff files; "Meeting of the United States and British Chiefs of Staff, 3 p.m., 26 December 1941," Document 56, in FRUS.

51. Proceedings of the American British Joint Chiefs of Staff Conferences, Held in Washington, DC, On Twelve Occasions Between December 24, 1941 and January 14, 1942, "Minutes of the Chiefs of Staff Conference, Federal Reserve Building, Washington, DC, 3 P.M., December 26, 1941," Joint Chiefs of Staff files; "Meeting of the United States and British Chiefs of Staff, 3 p.m., 26 December 1941," Document 56, in FRUS; Matloff and Snell, *Strategic Planning for Coalition Warfare*, 108.

52. Proceedings of the American British Joint Chiefs of Staff Conferences, Held in Washington, DC, On Twelve Occasions Between December 24, 1941 and January 14, 1942, "Minutes of the Chiefs of Staff Conference, Federal Reserve Building, Washington, DC, 3 P.M., December 26, 1941," Joint Chiefs of Staff files; "Meeting of the United States and British Chiefs of Staff, 3 p.m., 26 December 1941," Document 56, in FRUS; Matloff and Snell, *Strategic Planning for Coalition Warfare*, 108.

53. Matloff and Snell, *Strategic Planning for Coalition Warfare*, 105–6.

54. Stimson Diary, 26 December 1941, Reel Seven, Volume 36, Marshall Papers, Marshall Library.

55. "Meeting of Roosevelt and Churchill with their military advisors, 4:30 p.m., 26 December 1941," Minutes by Major Sexton, Document 58, in FRUS.

56. "Meeting of Roosevelt and Churchill with their military advisors, 4:30 p.m., 26 December 1941," Minutes by Major Sexton, Document 58, in FRUS.

57. First quotation from Alex Danchev, "Dill," in Keegan, *Churchill's Gen-*

erals, 59; second quotation from "Meeting of Roosevelt and Churchill with their military advisors, 4:30 p.m., 26 December 1941," Minutes by Major Sexton, Document 58, in FRUS.

58. "Meeting of Roosevelt and Churchill with their military advisors, 4:30 p.m., 26 December 1941," Minutes by Major Sexton, Document 58, in FRUS.

59. General Sir Alan Brooke Diary, 25 December 1941, in Gilbert, *Churchill War Papers*, 1684.

60. Brooke Diary entry and postscript, 25 December 1941, in Alex Danchev and Daniel Todman, eds., *War Diaries, 1939–1945: Field Marshal Lord Alanbrooke* (Berkeley: University of California Press, 2001), 214.

61. "Meeting of Roosevelt and Churchill with their military advisors, 4:30 p.m., 26 December 1941," Minutes by Major Sexton, Document 58, in FRUS.

62. "Meeting of Roosevelt and Churchill with their military advisors, 4:30 p.m., 26 December 1941," Minutes by Major Sexton, Document 58, in FRUS.

63. "Meeting of Roosevelt and Churchill with their military advisors, 4:30 p.m., 26 December 1941," Minutes by Major Sexton, Document 58, in FRUS; also Notes by Brigadier General Gerow from the "Meeting of Roosevelt and Churchill with their military advisors, 430 p.m.," 26 December 1941, Document 59, in FRUS.

64. "Meeting of Roosevelt and Churchill with their military advisors, 4:30 p.m., 26 December 1941," Minutes by Major Sexton, Document 58, in FRUS; also Notes by Brigadier General Gerow from the "Meeting of Roosevelt and Churchill with their military advisors, 4:30 p.m.," 26 December 1941, Document 59, in FRUS.

65. "Roosevelt-Beaverbrook meeting, 3:30 p.m., 26 December 1941," Document 57, and "The British Minister of Supply [Beaverbrook] to President Roosevelt, 27 December 1941," Document 188, in FRUS; Gwyer and Butler, *Grand Strategy*, 389; "Munitions and Supply Matters, Memorandum by Lord Beaverbrook to Prime Minister and Chiefs of Staff, Annex V, 21 December 1941, in War Cabinet and Chiefs of Staff Committee, Records of the Proceedings at the Washington War Conference, December 1941–January 1942, in CAB-99/17 Records of the Cabinet, War Cabinet and Cabinet: Commonwealth International Conferences: Minutes and Papers, "Arcadia" Record of Proceedings at Washington Conference 1941–1942, the National Archives, Kew, Richmond, Surrey, TW94DU, www.nationalarchives.gov.uk (hereafter cited as CAB-99/17 British Archives).

66. "Roosevelt-Beaverbrook meeting, 3:30 p.m., 26 December 1941," Document 57, and "The British Minister of Supply (Beaverbrook) to President Roosevelt, 27 December 1941," Document 188, in FRUS.

67. "Roosevelt-Beaverbrook meeting, 3:30 p.m., 26 December 1941," Document 57, and "The British Minister of Supply (Beaverbrook) to President Roosevelt, 27 December 1941," Document 188, in FRUS.

68. "Record of Staff Conference held at the White House, on Friday, 26

December 1941, at 7 P.M., in CAB-99/17, British Archives; Gwyer and Butler, *Grand Strategy*, 369; Martin Gilbert, *Winston S. Churchill: Road to Victory, 1941–1945*, vol. 7 (Hillsdale, MI: Hillsdale College Press, 1986), 30.

69. "Roosevelt-Churchill Dinner meeting, evening 26 December 1941," Document 62, in FRUS; J. M. A. Gwyer and J. R. M. Butler, *Grand Strategy*, vol. 3, *June 1941–August 1942* (London: Her Majesty's Stationery Office, 1964), 368–69; Vernon Davis, *The History of the Joint Chiefs of Staff: Organizational Development*, vol. 1, *Origin of the Joint and Combined Chiefs of Staff* (Historical Division Joint Secretariat Joint Chiefs of Staff, 1972), Record Group 218, US Joint Chiefs of Staff, Office of the Director of the Joint Chiefs of Staff/Joint Secretariat Historical Division, Entry UD 104, History of the Joint Chiefs of Staff in World War II: Organizational Development (vols. 1 and 2), Container 1, National Archives and Records Administration, College Park, MD, 163.

70. "Roosevelt-Churchill Dinner meeting, evening 26 December 1941," Document 62, in FRUS; Gwyer and Butler, *Grand Strategy*, 368–69; quotation from Robert Sherwood, *Roosevelt and Hopkins: An Intimate History* (New York: Harper and Brothers, 1948), 457; Keegan, *Churchill's Generals*, 4.

71. "Churchill-Marshall meeting, forenoon, 27 December 1941," Document 63, in FRUS; Pogue, *Ordeal and Hope*, 279.

72. Mark Stoler, *George C. Marshall: Soldier Statesman of the American Century* (Boston: Twayne Publishers, 1989), ix–x.

73. Stoler, *George C. Marshall: Soldier Statesman*, 65.

74. Stoler, *George C. Marshall: Soldier Statesman*, 66.

75. Pogue, *Ordeal and Hope*, 280.

76. Pogue, *Ordeal and Hope*, 280.

77. First quotation from "Meeting of Roosevelt with certain military advisors, 10 a.m." 27 December 1941, Document 64, in FRUS; second quotation from Lord Moran, *Churchill: Taken from the Diaries of Lord Moran* (Boston: Houghton Mifflin, 1966), 22.

78. "Meeting of Roosevelt with certain military advisors, 10 a.m." 27 December 1941, Document 64, in FRUS.

79. "Meeting of Roosevelt with certain military advisors, 10 a.m." 27 December 1941, Document 64, in FRUS.

80. "Meeting of Roosevelt with certain military advisors, 10 a.m." 27 December 1941, Document 64, in FRUS.

81. "Meeting of Roosevelt with certain military advisors, 10 a.m." 27 December 1941, Document 64, in FRUS.

82. Robinett Diary, 27 December 1941, Box 20, Marshall Papers, Marshall Library.

83. Admiral Ernest King to Colonel C. Donnelly, 12 January 1949, Ernest King Papers, Box 35, Library of Congress.

84. Proceedings of the American British Joint Chiefs of Staff Conferences, Held in Washington, DC, On Twelve Occasions Between December 24, 1941

and January 14, 1942, "Minutes of the Chiefs of Staff Conference, Federal Reserve Building, Washington, DC, 3 P.M., 27 December 1941," Joint Chiefs of Staff files; "Meeting of the United States and British Chiefs of Staff, 3 p.m., 27 December 1941," Document 67, in FRUS; Robinett Diary, 27 December 1941, Box 20, Marshall Papers, Marshall Library.

85. Proceedings of the American British Joint Chiefs of Staff Conferences, Held in Washington, DC, On Twelve Occasions Between December 24, 1941 and January 14, 1942, "Minutes of the Chiefs of Staff Conference, Federal Reserve Building, Washington, DC, 3 P.M., 27 December 1941," Joint Chiefs of Staff files; "Meeting of the United States and British Chiefs of Staff, 3 p.m., 27 December 1941," Document 67, in FRUS.

86. Proceedings of the American British Joint Chiefs of Staff Conferences, Held in Washington, DC, On Twelve Occasions Between December 24, 1941 and January 14, 1942, "Minutes of the Chiefs of Staff Conference, Federal Reserve Building, Washington, DC, 3 P.M., 27 December 1941," Joint Chiefs of Staff files; "Meeting of the United States and British Chiefs of Staff, 3 p.m., 27 December 1941," Document 67, in FRUS.

87. Second quotation from John Dill to General George C. Marshall, 27 December 1941, in Records of the War Department General and Special Staffs, Record Group 165, War Plans Division General Correspondence, 1920–1941, Box 234, #4402–136, National Archives and Records Administration, College Park, MD; first quotation from Dykes Diary, 27 December 1941, in Danchev, *Establishing the Anglo-American Alliance*, 79.

88. Proceedings of the American British Joint Chiefs of Staff Conferences, Held in Washington, DC, On Twelve Occasions Between December 24, 1941 and January 14, 1942, "Minutes of the Chiefs of Staff Conference, Federal Reserve Building, Washington, DC, 3 P.M., 27 December 1941," Joint Chiefs of Staff files; "Meeting of the United States and British Chiefs of Staff, 3 p.m., 27 December 1941," Document 67, in FRUS.

89. "Memorandum by the United States Chief of Staff," 27 December 1941, Document 151, in FRUS.

90. Quotation from "Meeting of the United States and British Chiefs of Staff, 3 p.m., 27 December 1941," Document 67, in FRUS; Robinett Diary 27 December 1941, Box 20, Marshall Papers, Marshall Library; H. P. Willmott, *Empires in the Balance: Japanese and Allied Pacific Strategies to April 1942* (Annapolis, MD: Naval Institute Press, 2008), 259.

91. Robinett Diary, 27 December 1941, Box 20, Marshall Papers, Marshall Library; quotation from Dykes Diary, 27 December 1941, in Danchev, *Establishing the Anglo-American Alliance*, 79; Pogue, *Ordeal and Hope*, 279.

92. "Chiefs of Staff Committee, Unity of Command in the Far East, Aide Memoire, 27 December 1941, Enclosure to Staff Conference Held at the White House, on Saturday, 27 December 1941, at 10 P.M., in CAB 99/17, British Ar-

chives; Vernon Davis, *The History of the Joint Chiefs of Staff: Organizational Development*, vol. 1, *Origin of the Joint And Combined Chiefs of Staff* (Historical Division Joint Secretariat Joint Chiefs of Staff, 1972), Record Group 218, US Joint Chiefs of Staff, Office of the Director of the Joint Chiefs of Staff/Joint Secretariat Historical Division, Entry UD 104, History of the Joint Chiefs of Staff in World War II: Organizational Development (vols. 1 and 2), Container 1, National Archives and Records Administration, College Park, MD, 154.

93. Davis, *History of the Joint Chiefs of Staff*, 155; Gwyer and Butler, *Grand Strategy*, 369.

94. Quotation from Dill to Brooke, 28 December 1941, in Arthur Bryant, *The Turn of the Tide: A History of the War Years Based on the Diaries of Field-Marshal Lord Alanbrooke, Chief of the Imperial General Staff* (New York: Doubleday, 1957), 235; Staff Conference Held at the White House, on Saturday, 27 December 1941, at 10 P.M., in CAB 99/17, British Archives; Gwyer and Butler, *Grand Strategy*, 370.

95. Gwyer and Butler, *Grand Strategy*, 370.

96. Ronald Lewin, *The Chief: Field Marshal Lord Wavell, Commander-in-Chief and Viceroy, 1939–1945* (New York: Farrar, Straus, Giroux, 1980), 25–26 and 140.

97. John Connell and Michael Roberts, *Wavell: Supreme Commander* (London: Collins, 1969), 71.

98. Winston S. Churchill to Clement Attlee, 27 December 1941, in Gilbert, *Churchill War Papers*, 1696; Churchill, *Grand Alliance*, 674.

99. "Draft Telegram by Prime Minister Churchill at Washington to the British Privy Seal (Attlee)," December 28, 1941," Document 152, in FRUS.

100. Andrew Roberts, *Masters and Commanders: How Four Titans Won the War in the West, 1941–1945* (New York: HarperCollins, 2009), 67; David Bercuson and Holger Herwig, *One Christmas in Washington* (New York: Overlook Press, 2005), 266.

101. "Meetings of Roosevelt and Churchill with chiefs of various diplomatic missions," 27 December 1941, Document 68, in FRUS.

102. Lord Moran, *Churchill*, 17.

Chapter 4

1. "Situation Report, 28–30 December 1941," in Franklin Delano Roosevelt, Papers as President: Map Room Papers, 1941–1945, Military Files, Box 38, #41, Franklin Delano Roosevelt Library and Museum, Hyde Park, NY, http://www.fdrlibrary.marist.edu/archives/collections/franklin/ (hereafter cited as Franklin Delano Roosevelt Library); Mary Williams, *The US Army in World War II: Chronology, 1941–1945* (Washington, DC: US Army Center of Military History, 1989), 9–10; Brooke Diary, 25 December 1941, in Alex Danchev and Daniel Todman, *War Diaries, 1939–1945: Field Marshal Lord Alanbrooke* (Berkeley: University of California Press, 2001), 214.

2. Dykes Diary, 27 and 28 December 1941, in Alex Danchev, *Establishing the Anglo-American Alliance: The Second World War Diaries of Brigadier Vivian Dykes* (London: Brassey's, 1990), 79–80.

3. Dill to Brooke, 3 January 1942, cited in Arthur Bryant, *The Turn of the Tide: A History of the War Years Based on the Diaries of Field Marshal Lord Alanbrooke, Chief of the Imperial General Staff* (Garden City, NY: Doubleday, 1957), 234.

4. Dykes Diary, 28 December 1942, in Danchev, *Establishing the Anglo-American Alliance*, 80; Vernon Davis, *The History of the Joint Chiefs of Staff: Organizational Development*, vol. 1, *Origin of the Joint and Combined Chiefs of Staff* (Historical Division Joint Secretariat Joint Chiefs of Staff, 1972), Record Group 218, US Joint Chiefs of Staff, Office of the Director of the Joint Chiefs of Staff/Joint Secretariat Historical Division, Entry UD 104, History of the Joint Chiefs of Staff in World War II: Organizational Development (vols. 1 and 2), Container 1, National Archives and Records Administration, College Park, MD, p. 156.

5. "Meeting of Roosevelt with his military advisors, 1145 a.m.," Notes by Major Sexton, 28 December 1941, document 73, in Frederick Aandahl, William Franklin, and William Slany, eds., *Foreign Relations of the United States, the Conferences at Washington, 1941–1942, and Casablanca, 1943* (Washington, DC: US Government Printing Office, 1958), https://history.state.gov/historical-documents/frus1941-43/comp1 (hereafter cited as FRUS); "Situation Report, 28 December 1941," in Franklin Delano Roosevelt, Papers as President: Map Room Papers, 1941–1945, Military Files, Box 38, #41, Franklin Delano Roosevelt Library.

6. "Meeting of Roosevelt with his military advisors, 11:45 a.m.," Notes by Major Sexton, 28 December 1941, Document 73, in FRUS.

7. "Meeting of Roosevelt with his military advisors, 11:45 a.m.," Notes by Major Sexton, 28 December 1941, Document 73, in FRUS.

8. "Meeting of Roosevelt with his military advisors, 11:45 a.m.," Notes by Major Sexton, 28 December 1941, Document 73, in FRUS.

9. Quotation from "Meeting of Roosevelt with his military advisors, 11:45 a.m.," Notes by Major Sexton, 28 December 1941, document 73, and Draft Telegram by Prime Minister at Washington to British Lord Privy Seal, December 28, 1941, 277–79, in FRUS; Stimson Diary, 28 December 1941, Reel Seven, Volume 36, George C. Marshall Foundation Research Library and Archives, Lexington, VA (original in the Yale University Library, New Haven, Connecticut) (hereafter cited as Marshall Papers, Marshall Library).

10. "Meeting of Roosevelt with his military advisors, 11:45 a.m.," Notes by Major Sexton, 28 December 1941, Document 73, in FRUS; quotation from Draft Telegram by Prime Minister at Washington to British Lord Privy Seal, December 28, 1941, 277–79, in FRUS.

11. Draft Telegram by Prime Minister at Washington to British Lord Privy Seal, December 28, 1941, 277–79, in FRUS.

12. Stimson Diary, 28 December 1941, Reel Seven, Volume 36, Marshall Papers, Marshall Library.

13. Quotation from Draft Telegram by Prime Minister at Washington to British Lord Privy Seal, December 28, 1941, 277–79, in FRUS; Winston S. Churchill to John Curtain, Peter Fraser, and Field Marshal Smuts, 28 December 1941, in Martin Gilbert, *The Churchill War Papers: The Ever-Widening War*, vol. 3, *1941* (New York: W. W. Norton, 2000), 1703; Davis, *Origin of Joint and Combined Chiefs of Staff*, Record Group 218, US Joint Chiefs of Staff, Office of the Director of the Joint Chiefs of Staff/Joint Secretariat Historical Division, Entry UD 104, History of the Joint Chiefs of Staff in World War II: Organizational Development (vols. 1 and 2), Container 1, National Archives and Records Administration, College Park, MD, 156.

14. Stimson Diary, 28 December 1941, Reel Seven, Volume 36, Marshall Papers, Marshall Library; "Meeting of Roosevelt with his military advisors, 11:45 a.m.," Notes by Major Sexton, 28 December 1941, document 73, in FRUS.

15. "Meeting of Roosevelt with his military advisors, 11:45 a.m.," Notes by Major Sexton, 28 December 1941, document 73, in FRUS.

16. "Meeting of Roosevelt with his military advisors, 11:45 a.m.," Notes by Major Sexton, 28 December 1941, Document 73, in FRUS.

17. Stimson Diary, 28 December 1941, Reel Seven, Volume 36, Marshall Papers, Marshall Library.

18. "Meeting of Roosevelt with his military advisors, 11:45 a.m.," Notes by Major Sexton, 28 December 1941, document 73, in FRUS.

19. "Meeting of Roosevelt with his military advisors, 11:45 a.m.," Notes by Major Sexton, 28 December 1941, document 73, in FRUS.

20. Alex Danchev, *Very Special Relationship: Field Marshal Sir John Dill and the Anglo-American Alliance, 1941–1944* (London: Brassey's Defence Publishers, 1986), 50.

21. Winston Churchill, *The Grand Alliance* (Boston: Houghton Mifflin, 1950), 678.

22. "Roosevelt-Churchill Hull meeting, afternoon," 28 December 1041, Document 74, in FRUS; Churchill, *Grand Alliance*, 667.

23. Winston S. Churchill to General De Gaulle, 29 December 1941, in Gilbert, *Churchill War Papers*, 1705.

24. Churchill, *Grand Alliance*, 676–77; Lord Moran Diary, 28 December 1941, in Lord Moran, *Churchill: Taken from the Diaries of Lord Moran; The Struggle for Survival, 1940–1965* (Boston: Houghton Mifflin, 1966), 19; "White House Itinerary," 28 December 1941, in Gilbert, *Churchill War Papers*, 1704.

25. "Situation Report, 29 December 1941," in Franklin Delano Roosevelt, Papers as President: Map Room Papers 1941–1945, Military Files, Box 38, #41, Franklin Delano Roosevelt Library.

26. Dykes Diary, 29 December 1941, in Danchev, *Establishing the Anglo-American Alliance*, 80.

27. Quotation from Dykes Diary, 29 December 1941, in Danchev, *Establishing the Anglo-American Alliance*, 80; "Joint Planning Committee Minutes—Fifth Meeting," 29 December 1941, in Records of the War Department and General Staffs, Record Group 165, Office of the Director of Plans and Operations, 337, Arcadia, Box 263, National Archives and Records Administration, College Park, MD.

28. Grace Hayes, *The History of the Joint Chiefs of Staff in World War II: The War against Japan* (Annapolis, MD: Naval Institute Press, 1982), 48; Robert Sherwood, *Roosevelt and Hopkins: An Intimate History* (New York: Harper Brothers, 1948), 469.

29. "Roosevelt-Loudon meeting, 12 noon," 29 December 1941, Document 76, and pp. 306–7, in FRUS; Thomas Buell, *Master of Seapower: A Biography of Fleet Admiral Ernest J. King* (Boston: Little, Brown, 1980), 167.

30. Franklin D. Roosevelt Daily Calendar, 29 December 1941, http://www.fdrlibrary.marist.edu/daybyday/daylog/december-29th-1941/; "Meeting of the United States and British Chiefs of Staff, 4 p.m.," 29 December 1941, Document 80, in FRUS.

31. Buell, *Master of Seapower*, 168.

32. Stimson Diary, 29 December 1941, Reel Seven, Volume 36, Marshall Papers, Marshall Library.

33. Stimson Diary, 29 December 1941, Reel Seven, Volume 36, Marshall Papers, Marshall Library; "Stimson-Hopkins-Marshall meeting, 2:30 p.m.," Notes by Lieutenant Colonel Wyman, 29 December 1941, Document 78, in FRUS.

34. Stimson Diary, 29 December 1941, Reel Seven, Volume 36, Marshall Papers, Marshall Library.

35. H. P. Willmott, *Empires in the Balance: Japanese and Allied Strategies to April 1942* (Annapolis, MD: Naval Institute Press, 1989), 409; Ronald Lewin, *The Chief: Field Marshal Lord Wavell Commander-in-Chief and Viceroy, 1939-1947* (New York: Farrar, Straus, Giroux, 1980), 159; quotations from John Connell and Michael Roberts, *Wavell: Supreme Commander* (London: Collins, 1969), 62.

36. Winston S. Churchill to General Wavell, 23 January 1942, in Martin Gilbert, *Churchill War Documents*, vol. 17, *Testing Times, 1942* (Hillsdale, MI: Hillsdale College Press, 2014), 134.

37. Stimson Diary, 29 December 1941; "Stimson-Hopkins-Marshall meeting, 2:30 p.m.," Notes by Lieutenant Colonel Wyman, 29 December 1941, Document 78, and "Draft Memorandum by the Chief of Staff, United States Army (Marshall), 29 December 1941, Document 155, in FRUS.

38. Memorandum by Mr. Nelson on "Meeting of the United States production leaders with the British Minister of Supply, 2:30 p.m., 29 December 1941," Document 79, in FRUS.

39. Quotation from James Leasor, *War at the Top* (London: Michael Joseph, 1959), 102 and 110–11.

40. First quotation from Harold Nicholson Diary, 14 January 1942, in Gilbert, *Churchill Documents*, 84; second quotation from Richards, *Portal of Hungerford*, 195 and 197.

41. First quotation from John Colville Diary, 3 June 1941, in Gilbert, *Churchill War Papers*, 749; second quotation from Wallace to State Department Historian, 4 May 1963, in footnote to Memorandum by Mr. Nelson on "Meeting of the United States production leaders with the British Minister of Supply, 2:30 p.m., 29 December 1941," Document 79, in FRUS.

42. "Meeting of the United States production leaders with the British Minister of Supply, 2:30 p.m., 29 December 1941," Document 79, in FRUS, and "The British Minister of Supply (Beaverbrook) to President Roosevelt, 29 December 1941," Document 191, in FRUS.

43. "The British Minister of Supply [Beaverbrook] to President Roosevelt, 29 December 1941," Document 191, in FRUS.

44. "The British Minister of Supply [Beaverbrook] to the President's Special Assistant (Hopkins), 29 December 1941," Document 193, in FRUS.

45. Report by the Planning Committee of the United States and British Chiefs of Staff, 29 December 1941, "Priorities for the United States and United Kingdom Overseas Expeditions in the Atlantic," Document 130, in FRUS.

46. Proceedings of the American British Joint Chiefs of Staff Conferences, Held in Washington, DC, On Twelve Occasions Between December 24, 1941 and January 14, 1942, "Minutes from the Chiefs of Staff Conference, Federal Reserve Building, Washington, DC, 4 P.M., December 29, 1941," in Joint Staff Historical Archives, Pentagon (hereafter cited as Joint Chiefs of Staff files); "Meeting of the United States and British Chiefs of Staff, 4 p.m.," 29 December 1941, Document 80, in FRUS.

47. Proceedings of the American British Joint Chiefs of Staff Conferences, Held in Washington, DC, On Twelve Occasions Between December 24, 1941 and January 14, 1942, "Minutes from the Chiefs of Staff Conference, Federal Reserve Building, Washington, DC, 4 P.M., December 29, 1941," in Joint Chiefs of Staff files; "Meeting of the United States and British Chiefs of Staff, 4 p.m.," 29 December 1941, Document 80, in FRUS; Annex 2, "Memorandum by the British Chiefs of Staff on Proposed Method of Handling Matters Concerning the Southwest Pacific Theater," 29 December 1941, p. 282, in FRUS.

48. Annex 2, "Memorandum by the British Chiefs of Staff on Proposed Method of Handling Matters Concerning the Southwest Pacific Theater," 29 December 1941, p. 282, in FRUS.

49. Proceedings of the American British Joint Chiefs of Staff Conferences, Held in Washington, DC, On Twelve Occasions Between December 24, 1941, and January 14, 1942, "Minutes from the Chiefs of Staff Conference, Federal Reserve Building, Washington, DC, 4 P.M., December 29, 1941," in Joint Chiefs of Staff files; "Meeting of the United States and British Chiefs of Staff, 4 p.m.," 29 December 1941, Document 80, in FRUS.

50. Proceedings of the American British Joint Chiefs of Staff Conferences, Held in Washington, DC, On Twelve Occasions Between December 24, 1941, and January 14, 1942, "Minutes from the Chiefs of Staff Conference, Federal Reserve Building, Washington, DC, 4 P.M., December 29, 1941," in Joint Chiefs of Staff files; "Meeting of the United States and British Chiefs of Staff, 4 p.m.," 29 December 1941, Document 80, in FRUS.

51. Proceedings of the American British Joint Chiefs of Staff Conferences, Held in Washington, DC, On Twelve Occasions Between December 24, 1941 and January 14, 1942, "Minutes from the Chiefs of Staff Conference, Federal Reserve Building, Washington, DC, 4 P.M., December 29, 1941," in Joint Chiefs of Staff files; "Meeting of the United States and British Chiefs of Staff, 4 p.m.," 29 December 1941, Document 80, in FRUS; Stimson Diary, 30 December 1941; "Message to American Embassy, Chungking, President Roosevelt to Chiang Kai-Shek, 30 December 1941," Franklin Delano Roosevelt, Papers as President, Presidential Secretary Files, Confidential Files, Lend Lease November–December 1941 in Box 12, Franklin Delano Roosevelt Library.

52. Proceedings of the American British Joint Chiefs of Staff Conferences, Held in Washington, DC, On Twelve Occasions Between December 24, 1941 and January 14, 1942, "Minutes from the Chiefs of Staff Conference, Federal Reserve Building, Washington, DC, 4 P.M., December 29, 1941," in Joint Chiefs of Staff files; "Meeting of the United States and British Chiefs of Staff, 4 p.m.," 29 December 1941, Document 80, in FRUS.

53. Davis, *History of the Joint Chiefs of Staff in World War II, Organizational Development*, vol. 1, *Origin of the Joint and Combined Chiefs of Staff* (Historical Division Joint Secretariat Joint Chiefs of Staff, 1972), Record Group 218, US Joint Chiefs of Staff, Office of the Director of the Joint Chiefs of Staff/Joint Secretariat Historical Division, Entry UD 104, History of the Joint Chiefs of Staff in World War II: Organizational Development (vols. 1 and 2), Container 1, National Archives and Records Administration, College Park, MD, 158–59.

54. "Memorandum Revised by President Roosevelt, on Proposed Method of Handling Matters Concerning The Southwest Pacific Theater," 30 December 1941, Document 159, in FRUS.

55. Sherwood, *Roosevelt and Hopkins*, 469.

56. "Situation Report, 30 December 1941," in Franklin Delano Roosevelt, Papers as President: Map Room Papers 1941–1945, Military Files, Box 38, #41, Franklin Delano Roosevelt Library.

57. Quotation from Davis, *History of the Joint Chiefs of Staff in World War II: Organizational Development, Origin of the Joint and Combined Chiefs of Staff*, vol. 1 (Historical Division Joint Secretariat Joint Chiefs of Staff, 1972), Record Group 218, US Joint Chiefs of Staff, Office of the Director of the Joint Chiefs of Staff/Joint Secretariat Historical Division, Entry UD 104, History of the Joint Chiefs of Staff in World War II: Organizational Development (vols. 1 and 2), Container 1, National Archives and Records Administration, College

Park, MD, 159; Proceedings of the American British Joint Chiefs of Staff Conferences, Held in Washington, DC, On Twelve Occasions Between December 24, 1941 and January 14, 1942, "Minutes from the Chiefs of Staff Conference, Federal Reserve Building, Washington, DC, 3 P.M., December 30, 1941," in Joint Chiefs of Staff files; "Meeting of the United States and British Chiefs of Staff, 3 p.m.," 30 December 1941, Document 82, in FRUS; and Annex 2, Part 1, "Draft Memorandum by the United States Chief of Staff, Memorandum for the President, Higher Direction of War in the ABDA Area," 30 December 1941, p. 287, in FRUS; Gwyer and Butler, *Grand Strategy*, 373.

58. Proceedings of the American British Joint Chiefs of Staff Conferences, Held in Washington, DC, On Twelve Occasions Between December 24, 1941, and January 14, 1942, "Minutes from the Chiefs of Staff Conference, Federal Reserve Building, Washington, DC, 3 P.M., December 30, 1941," in Joint Chiefs of Staff files; "Meeting of the United States and British Chiefs of Staff, 3 p.m.," 30 December 1941, Document 82, and Annex 2, Parts 1 and 2, "Draft Memorandum by the United States Chief of Staff, Memorandum for the President, Higher Direction of War in the ABDA Area," 30 December 1941, pp. 287–88, in FRUS.

59. Report by the United States and British Chiefs of Staff, "Draft Directive to the Supreme Commander in the ABDA Area," 30 December 1941, p. 289, in FRUS; Proceedings of the American British Joint Chiefs of Staff Conferences, Held in Washington, DC, On Twelve Occasions Between December 24, 1941, and January 14, 1942, "Minutes from the Chiefs of Staff Conference, Federal Reserve Building, Washington, DC, 3 P.M., 30 December, 1941," in Joint Chiefs of Staff files; "Meeting of the United States and British Chiefs of Staff, 3 p.m." 30 December 1941, Document 82, in FRUS; J. M. A. Gwyer and J. R. M. Butler, *Grand Strategy* (London: Her Majesty's Stationery Office, 1964), 376–77.

60. Proceedings of the American British Joint Chiefs of Staff Conferences, Held in Washington, DC, On Twelve Occasions Between December 24, 1941, and January 14, 1942, "Minutes from the Chiefs of Staff Conference, Federal Reserve Building, Washington, DC, 3 P.M., December 30, 1941," in Joint Chiefs of Staff files; "Meeting of the United States and British Chiefs of Staff, 3 p.m." 30 December 1941, Document 82, in FRUS; Dykes Diary, 30 and 31 December 1941, in Danchev, *Establishing the Anglo-American Alliance*, 81.

61. Stimson Diary, 30 December 1941, Reel Seven, Volume 36, Marshall Papers, Marshall Library.

62. "Message to American Embassy, Chungking, President Roosevelt to Chiang Kai-Shek, 30 December 1941," Franklin Delano Roosevelt, Papers as President, Presidential Secretary Files, Confidential Files, Lend Lease November–December 1941 in Box 12, Franklin Delano Roosevelt Library.

63. President's Assistant [Hopkins] to the President, 29 December 1941, Document 81, FRUS; Churchill, *Grand Strategy*, 676–78; quotation in Martin

Gilbert, *Winston S. Churchill: Road to Victory, 1941–1945*, vol. 7 (Hillsdale, MI: Hillsdale College Press, 1986), 34.

64. Churchill Address to the Canada House of Commons, 30 December 1941, www.winstonchurchill.org/resources/speeches/1941-1945-war-leader; Winston S. Churchill Speech, 30 December 1941 in Gilbert, *Churchill War Papers*, 1709–16.

65. Winston S. Churchill Speech, 30 December 1941, in Gilbert, *Churchill War Papers*, 1709–16.

66. "Roosevelt-Churchill-Hull meeting, 11:40 a.m.," 2 January 1942, Document 91, in FRUS; *New York Times*, 26 December 1941, "Canadians Support St. Pierre Seizure; Free French Action Pleases the People, Who View Matter as One for Island's Decision," by P. J. Philip, https://www.nytimes.com/1941/12/26/archives/canadians-support-st-pierre-seizure-free-french-action-pleases-the.html.

67. "Situation Report, 31 December 1941," in Franklin Delano Roosevelt, Papers as President: Map Room Papers 1941–1945, Military Files, Box 38, #41, Franklin Delano Roosevelt Library.

68. Stimson Diary, 31 December 1941, Reel Seven, Volume 36, Marshall Papers, Marshall Library.

69. Dykes Diary, 31 December 1941, in Danchev, *Establishing the Anglo-American Alliance*, 81.

70. Buell, *Master of Seapower*, 169.

71. Proceedings of the American British Joint Chiefs of Staff Conferences, Held in Washington, DC, On Twelve Occasions Between December 24, 1941 and January 14, 1942, "Minutes from the Chiefs of Staff Conference, Federal Reserve Building, Washington, DC, 2 P.M., December 31, 1941," in Joint Chiefs of Staff files; "Meeting of the United States and British Chiefs of Staff, 2 p.m., 31 December 1941," Document 83, in FRUS.

72. Proceedings of the American British Joint Chiefs of Staff Conferences, Held in Washington, DC, On Twelve Occasions Between December 24, 1941 and January 14, 1942, "Minutes from the Chiefs of Staff Conference, Federal Reserve Building, Washington, DC, 2 P.M., December 31, 1941," in Joint Chiefs of Staff files; "Meeting of the United States and British Chiefs of Staff, 2 p.m., 31 December 1941," Document 83, in FRUS.

73. Proceedings of the American British Joint Chiefs of Staff Conferences, Held in Washington, DC, On Twelve Occasions Between December 24, 1941 and January 14, 1942, "Minutes from the Chiefs of Staff Conference, Federal Reserve Building, Washington, DC, 2 P.M., December 31, 1941," in Joint Chiefs of Staff files; "Meeting of the United States and British Chiefs of Staff, 2 p.m.," 31 December 1941, Document 83, in FRUS.

74. Robinett Diary, 31 December 1941, Box 20, Marshall Papers, Marshall Library.

75. Jacob Diary, 1 January 1942, in Richardson, *From Churchill's Secret Circle*, 97.

76. Proceedings of the American British Joint Chiefs of Staff Conferences, Held in Washington, DC, On Twelve Occasions Between December 24, 1941 and January 14, 1942, "Minutes from the Chiefs of Staff Conference, Federal Reserve Building, Washington, DC, 2 P.M., December 31, 1941," in Joint Chiefs of Staff files; "Meeting of the United States and British Chiefs of Staff, 2 p.m., 31 December 1941," Document 83, in FRUS.

77. Bryant, *Turn of the Tide*, 236.

78. Dykes Diary, 31 December 1941, in Danchev, *Establishing the Anglo-American Alliance*, 82; Winston S. Churchill to Clement Attlee, 2 January 1942, in Gilbert, *Churchill Documents*, 10.

79. Stimson Diary, 31 December 1941, Reel Seven, Volume 36, Marshall Papers, Marshall Library.

80. Stimson Diary, 31 December 1941, Reel Seven, Volume 36, Marshall Papers, Marshall Library; quotation in Mark Stoler, *George C. Marshall: Soldier-Statesman of the American Century* (Boston: Twayne Publishers, 1989), 66.

81. William Manchester and Paul Reed, *The Last Lion: Winston Spencer Churchill Defender of the Realm, 1940–1945* (New York: Little, Brown, 2012), 460–61.

82. Manchester and Reed, *Last Lion*, 460–61.

83. Manchester and Reed, *Last Lion*, 460–61; Sherwood, *Hopkins and Roosevelt*, 447; James MacGregor Burns, *Roosevelt: Soldier of Freedom, 1940–1945* (New York: Harcourt, Brace, Jovanovich, 1970), 184; Winston S. Churchill to Clement Attlee, 1 January 1942, in Gilbert, *Churchill Documents*, 3.

Chapter 5

1. Dykes Dairy, 1 January 1942, in Alex Danchev, *Establishing the Anglo-American Alliance: The Second World War Diaries of Brigadier Vivian Dykes* (London: Brassey's, 1990), 82.

2. Dykes Dairy, 1 January 1942, in Danchev, *Establishing the Anglo-American Alliance*, 82.

3. Forrest Pogue, *George C. Marshall: Ordeal and Hope, 1939–1942* (New York: Viking Press, 1967), 122.

4. Brian Farrell, *The Defence and Fall of Singapore* (Singapore: Monsoon Press, 2017), 22; Dykes Diary, 2, 4, 6, 8, 10 January 1942, in Danchev, *Establishing the Anglo-American Alliance*, 83–88.

5. "Situation Report, January 1, 1942," Franklin Delano Roosevelt, Papers as President: Map Room Papers, 1941–1945, Military Files, Box 38, #41, Roosevelt Presidential Library and Museum, Hyde Park, NY, http://www.fdrlibrary.marist.edu/archives/collections/franklin/ (hereafter cited as Franklin Delano Roosevelt Library); quotation from Stimson Diary, 1 January 1942, Reel Seven, Volume 37, George C. Marshall Foundation Research Library and

Archives, Lexington, VA (original in the Yale Library, New Haven, CT) (hereafter cited as Marshall Papers, Marshall Library).

6. Stimson Diary, 1 January 1942, Reel Seven, Volume 37, Marshall Papers, Marshall Library.

7. Franklin Delano Roosevelt Stenographers Diary, January 1, 1942, in http://fdrlibrary.marist.edu/daybyday/daylog/january-1st-1942; "Notes by the President's Special Assistant (Hopkins)," Roosevelt-Churchill-Litinov luncheon meeting, January 1, 1942, Document 87, in Frederick Aandahl, William Franklin and William Slany, eds., *Foreign Relations of the United States, the Conferences at Washington, 1941–1942, and Casablanca, 1943* (Washington, DC: US Government Printing Office, 1958), https://history.state.gov/historicaldocuments/frus1941–43/comp1 (hereafter cited as FRUS); Winston S. Churchill to Clement Attlee, 1 January 1942, in Martin Gilbert, *The Churchill Documents*, vol. 7, *1942* (Hillsdale, MI: Hillsdale College Press, 2014), 3.

8. "Notes by the President's Special Assistant (Hopkins)," Roosevelt-Churchill-Litinov luncheon meeting, January 1, 1942, Document 87, in FRUS.

9. "Notes by General Gerow," Meeting of Roosevelt and Churchill with their military advisors, about 6 p.m., 1 January 1942, Document 89, in FRUS; quotation from Robert Dallek, *Franklin D. Roosevelt: A Political Life* (New York: Viking, 2017), 450.

10. Churchill Recollections, 1 January 1942, in Gilbert, *Churchill Documents*, 5.

11. "Notes by General Arnold," Meeting of Roosevelt and Churchill with their military advisors, about 6 p.m., 1 January 1942, Document 88, in FRUS; "Record of Staff Conference held at the White House, on Thursday, 1 January 1942, at 4:30 P.M.," in War Cabinet and Chiefs of Staff Committee, Records of the Proceedings at the Washington War Conference, December 1941–January 1942, in CAB-99/17 Records of the Cabinet, War Cabinet and Cabinet: Commonwealth International Conferences: Minutes and Papers, "Arcadia" Record of Proceedings at Washington Conference, 1941–1942, the National Archives, Kew, Richmond, Surrey, TW94DU, www.nationalarchives.gov.uk (hereafter cited as CAB-99/17 British Archives).

12. "Notes by General Arnold," Meeting of Roosevelt and Churchill with their military advisors, about 6 p.m., 1 January 1942, Document 88, in FRUS; "Notes by General Gerow," Meeting of Roosevelt and Churchill with their military advisors, about 6 p.m., 1 January 1942, Document 89, in FRUS.

13. Quotation from James MacGregor Burns, *Roosevelt: The Soldier of Freedom, 1940–1945* (New York: Harcourt, Brace, Jovanovich, 1970), 185; "Meeting for the signing of the Declaration by the United Nations, 10 p.m., 1 January 1942, Document 90, in FRUS.

14. First quotation from "Declaration by the United Nations, 1 January 1942," Document 228, in FRUS; second quotation from Winston Churchill, *Grand Alliance* (Boston: Houghton Mifflin, 1950), 683; Winston S. Churchill Recollection, 1 January 1942, in Gilbert, *Churchill Documents*, 1.

15. Stimson Diary, 2 January 1942, Reel Seven, Volume 37, Marshall Papers, Marshall Library; Louis Morton, *The Fall of the Philippines* (Washington, DC: US Army Center of Military History, 1985), 234.

16. Morton, *Fall of the Philippines*, 239.

17. Louis Morton, *Strategy and Command: The First Two Years* (Washington, DC: US Army Center of Military History, 1962), 186–87; Stimson Diary, 2 January 1942, Reel Seven, Volume 37, Marshall Papers, Marshall Library.

18. Stimson Diary, 2 January 1942, Reel Seven, Volume 37, Marshall Papers, Marshall Library.

19. Quotation from both Barbara Tuchman, *Stilwell and the American Experience in China, 1911–1945* (New York: Macmillan, 1970), 311–12, and Theodore H. White, ed., *The Stilwell Papers* (New York: DaCapo Press, 1991), 19.

20. Grace Hayes, *The History of the Joint Chiefs of Staff in World War II: The War against Japan* (Annapolis, MD: Naval Institute Press, 1982), 52.

21. Eisenhower Diary, 2 January 1942, in Robert Ferrell, *The Eisenhower Diaries* (New York: Norton, 1981), 40.

22. Roosevelt-Churchill-Hull meeting, 11:40 a.m., 2 January 1942, Document 91, in FRUS.

23. Dykes Diary, 2 January 1942, in Danchev, *Establishing the Anglo-American Alliance*, 83; "Meeting of Roosevelt and Churchill with their advisors on shipping, noon," 2 January 1942, Document 92, in FRUS; quotation in James Leasor, *War at the Top* (London: Michael Joseph, 1959), 102.

24. "Meeting of Roosevelt and Churchill with their advisors on shipping, noon," 2 January 1942, Document 92, in FRUS.

25. "The President to the Chairman of the United States Maritime Commission (Land)," 3 January 1942, Document 198, in FRUS.

26. Dykes Diary, 3 January 1942, in Danchev, *Establishing the Anglo-American Alliance*, 84; Minutes of the Sixth Meeting of the Joint Planning Committee, 3 January 1942, in Records of the War Department General and Special Staffs, Record Group 165, Office of the Director of Plans and Operations, 337, Arcadia, Box 263, National Archives and Records Administration, College Park, MD.

27. Dykes Diary, 3 January 1942, in Danchev, *Establishing the Anglo-American Alliance*, 84; Minutes of the Sixth Meeting of the Joint Planning Committee, 3 January 1942, in Records of the War Department General and Special Staffs, Record Group 165, Office of the Director of Plans and Operations, 337, Arcadia, Box 263, National Archives and Records Administration, College Park, MD.

28. Dykes Diary, 7 January 1942, in Danchev, *Establishing the Anglo-American Alliance*, 86–87.

29. Eisenhower Diary, 5 January 1942, in Ferrell, *Eisenhower Diaries*, 40.

30. Hayes, *History of the Joint Chiefs of Staff in World War II: The War against Japan*, 56; Meeting of the United States and British Chiefs of Staff, 4 p.m., 11

January 1942, Document 100, in FRUS; Winston S. Churchill to John Curtin, 3 January 1942, in Gilbert, *Churchill Documents*, 15–16.

31. Memorandum for General Gerow from Colonel A. B. Kibler, 1 January 1942, in Records of the War Department General and Special Staffs, Record Group 165, Correspondence Related to the Location and Leasing of Atlantic Bases in British Possessions, Allied Military Conferences of World War II, and Plans for Strategic Direction of Operations of Military Forces in Theaters of Operation, 1940–1945, Box 22, National Archives and Records Administration, College Park, MD.

32. Memorandum for General Gerow from Colonel A. B. Kibler, 1 January 1942, in Records of the War Department General and Special Staffs, Record Group 165, Correspondence Related to the Location and Leasing of Atlantic Bases in British Possessions, Allied Military Conferences of World War II, and Plans for Strategic Direction of Operations of Military Forces in Theaters of Operation, 1940–1945, Box 22, National Archives and Records Administration, College Park, MD.

33. Stimson Diary, 3 January 1942, Reel Seven, Volume 37, Marshall Papers, Marshall Library.

34. "Meeting of Roosevelt and Churchill with their advisors on war production, 5 p.m., 3 January 1942," Document 94, in FRUS; Churchill, *Grand Alliance*, 690; quotation in Winston S. Churchill to Clement Attlee, 3 January 1941, in Gilbert, *Churchill Documents*, 31.

35. Mary Williams, *The US Army in World War II: Chronology: 1941–1945* (Washington, DC: US Army Center of Military History, 1989), 12.

36. Williams, *US Army in World War II: Chronology*, 12; Morton, *Strategy and Command: The First Two Years*, 166.

37. Morton, *Fall of the Philippines*, 245.

38. Dykes Diary, 3 and 4 January 1942, in Danchev, *Establishing the Anglo-American Alliance*, 84–85.

39. Memorandum by Lieutenant General Arnold, Arnold Conversations with Hopkins, Roosevelt, and Churchill, 4 January 1942, Document 95, in FRUS.

40. Memorandum by Lieutenant General Arnold, Arnold Conversations with Hopkins, Roosevelt, and Churchill, 4 January 1942, Document 95, in FRUS.

41. Memorandum by Lieutenant General Arnold, Arnold Conversations with Hopkins, Roosevelt, and Churchill, 4 January 1942, Document 95, in FRUS.

42. Memorandum by Lieutenant General Arnold, Arnold Conversations with Hopkins, Roosevelt, and Churchill, 4 January 1942, Document 95, in FRUS; Wesley Craven and James Cate, *The Army Air Forces in World War II*, vol. 1, *Plans and Early Operations* (Chicago: University of Chicago Press, 1948), 248; Franklin Roosevelt to Winston Churchill, 19 May 1942, in Warren Kimball, *Churchill and Roosevelt: The Complete Correspondence*, vol. 1, *Alliance Emerging, October 1933–November 1942* (Princeton, NJ: Princeton University Press, 1984), 487.

43. Stimson Diary, 4 January 1942, Reel Seven, Volume 37, Marshall Papers, Marshall Library.

44. Stimson Diary, 4 January 1942, Reel Seven, Volume 37, Marshall Papers, Marshall Library; "United States Minutes, Meeting of Roosevelt and Churchill with their military advisors, 5:30 p.m.," 4 January 1942, Document 96, in FRUS.

45. Stimson Diary, 4 January 1942, Reel Seven, Volume 37, Marshall Papers, Marshall Library; quotation from "United States Minutes, Meeting of Roosevelt and Churchill with their military advisors, 5:30 p.m.," 4 January 1942, Document 96, in FRUS.

46. "United States Minutes, Meeting of Roosevelt and Churchill with their military advisors, 5:30 p.m.," 4 January 1942, Document 96, in in FRUS.

47. Quotation from Interview of General John Hull by Lieutenant Colonel James Wurman on 5 December 1974, at the US Army War College, in the Senior Officer Oral History Program, US Army Military History Institute, Army Heritage and Education Center, Carlisle Barracks, PA; Brooke Diary, 25 December 1941, in Danchev and Todman, *War Diaries*, 214.

48. Winston S. Churchill to General Hastings Ismay, for the Chiefs of Staff Committee, 4 January 1942, in Gilbert, *Churchill Documents*, 22.

49. United States Minutes, Meeting of Roosevelt and Churchill with their military advisors, 5:30 p.m.," 4 January 1942, Document 96, in FRUS.

50. Churchill, *Grand Alliance*, 691; quotation in Charles Richardson, *From Churchill's Secret Circle to the BBC: The Biography of Lieutenant General Sir Ian Jacob* (London: Brassey's, 1991), 101; Sir Charles Wilson Diary, 5 January 1942, in Gilbert, *Churchill Documents*, 32.

51. Martin Gilbert, *Winston S. Churchill: Road to Victory, 1941–1945* (Hillsdale, MI: Hillsdale College Press, 1986), 37–38; Winston S. Churchill to General Hastings Ismay for the Chiefs of Staff Committee, 4 January 1942, in Gilbert, *Churchill Documents*, 19–29.

52. Henry Arnold, *Global Mission* (New York: Harper and Brothers, 1949), 288.

53. Churchill, *Grand Alliance*, 691.

54. First quotation from Stimson Diary, 5 January 1942, Reel Seven, Volume 37, Marshall Papers, Marshall Library; second quotation from Morton, *Fall of the Philippines*, 240.

55. Stimson Diary, 5 January 1942, Reel Seven, Volume 37, Marshall Papers, Marshall Library.

56. Stimson Diary, 6 January 1942, Reel Seven, Volume 37, Marshall Papers, Marshall Library; Pogue, *Ordeal and Hope*, 357.

57. President Roosevelt State of the Union Address, 6 January 1942, Morgenthau Diaries, 6 January 1942, Volume 482, Roosevelt Presidential Library and Museum, Hyde Park, New York, http://www.fdrlibrary.marist.edu/_resources/images/morg/md0658.pdf.

58. President Roosevelt State of the Union Address, 6 January 1942, Morgenthau Diaries, 6 January 1942, Volume 482, Roosevelt Presidential Library and Museum, Hyde Park, New York, http://www.fdrlibrary.marist.edu/_resources/images/morg/md0658.pdf.

59. Stimson Diary, 7–10 January 1942, Reel Seven, Volume 37, Marshall Papers, Marshall Library.

60. Williams, *US Army in World War II: Chronology*, 12–13; "Situation Report, January 2, 6 and 7, 1942," Franklin Delano Roosevelt, Papers as President: Map Room Papers, 1941–1945, Military Files, Box 38, #41, Franklin Delano Roosevelt Library; Barnett, *Desert Generals*, 122; Vincent J. Esposito, *The West Point Atlas of American Wars*, vol. 2, *1900–1953* (New York: Praeger, 1959), map 75; David Fraser, *Knights Cross: A Life of Field Marshal Erwin Rommel* (New York: Harper Collins, 1993), 299.

61. General Brooke Diary, 9 January 1942, in Alex Danchev and Daniel Todman, eds., *War Diaries, 1939–1945: Field Marshal Lord Alanbrooke* (Berkeley: University of California Press, 2001), 219.

62. Williams, *US Army in World War II: Chronology*, 13.

63. Farrell, *Defence and Fall of Singapore*, 239–40; Victoria Schofield, *Wavell: Soldier and Statesman* (London: John Murray, 2006), 232.

64. Dykes Diary, 9 January 1942, in Danchev, *Establishing the Anglo-American Alliance*, 87.

65. Minutes of the Seventh Meeting of the Joint Planning Committee, 8 January 1942, in Records of the War Department General and Special Staffs, Record Group 165, Office of the Director of Plans and Operations, 337, Arcadia, Box 263, National Archives and Records Administration, College Park, MD; Dykes Diary, 8 January 1942, in Danchev, *Establishing the Anglo-American Alliance*, 87; quotation in Tuchman, *Stilwell and the American Experience in China*, 312; quotation also in White, *Stilwell Papers*, 21.

66. Dykes Diary, 6 January 1942, in Danchev, *Establishing the Anglo-American Alliance*, 86; Minutes of the Seventh Meeting of the Joint Planning Committee, 8 January 1942, in Records of the War Department General and Special Staffs, Record Group 165, Office of the Director of Plans and Operations, 337, Arcadia, Box 263, National Archives and Records Administration, College Park, MD.

67. Minutes of the Eighth Meeting of the Joint Planning Committee, 9 January 1942, in Records of the War Department General and Special Staffs, Record Group 165, Office of the Director of Plans and Operations, 337, Arcadia, Box 263, National Archives and Records Administration, College Park, MD; quotation from Eisenhower Diary, 3 January 1942, in Ferrell, *Eisenhower Papers*, 40.

68. Pogue, *Ordeal and Hope*, 358; Stimson Diary, 8, 9, 10, 11 January (these four days are written as a single diary entry [8,9,10,11]), Reel Seven, Volume

37, Marshall Papers, Marshall Library; quotation from Eisenhower Diary, 9 January 1942, in Ferrell, *Eisenhower Diaries*, 42.

69. Quotation from "Memorandum for General Marshall, 9 January 1942," in Franklin Delano Roosevelt Presidential Secretary Files, Departmental Correspondence, Box 83, Franklin Delano Roosevelt Library; "General Marshall to President, 10 January 1942," Franklin Delano Roosevelt Library, Presidential Secretary Files, Confidential Files, Box 12, Franklin Delano Roosevelt Library.

70. "Record of Staff Conference Held in the Embassy Annex, on 1 January 1942, at 12:30 P.M.," CAB 99/17, British Archives; Vernon Davis, *The History of the Joint Chiefs of Staff: Organizational Development*, vol. 1, *Origin of the Joint and Combined Chiefs of Staff* (Historical Division Joint Secretariat Joint Chiefs of Staff, 1972), Record Group 218, US Joint Chiefs of Staff, Office of the Director of the Joint Chiefs of Staff/Joint Secretariat Historical Division, Entry UD 104, History of the Joint Chiefs of Staff in World War II: Organizational Development (vols. 1 and 2), Container 1, National Archives and Records Administration, College Park, MD, 164.

71. "Memorandum by the British Chiefs of Staff—Post Arcadia Collaboration," 8 January 1942, Document 116, in FRUS.

72. "Memorandum by the British Chiefs of Staff—Post Arcadia Collaboration," 8 January 1942, Document 116, in FRUS.

73. "Memorandum by the British Chiefs of Staff—Post Arcadia Collaboration," 8 January 1942, Document 116, in FRUS.

Chapter 6

1. "Situation Report, January 10, 1942," Franklin Delano Roosevelt, Papers as President: Map Room Papers, 1941–1945, Military Files, Box 38, #41, Roosevelt Presidential Library and Museum, Hyde Park, NY, http://www.fdrlibrary.marist.edu/archives/collections/franklin/ (hereafter cited as Franklin Delano Roosevelt Library).

2. Brian Farrell, *The Defence and Fall of Singapore* (Singapore: Monsoon, 2017), 240.

3. Farrell, *Defence and Fall of Singapore*, 257–58.

4. Samuel Eliot Morison, *The Two-Ocean War: A Short History of the United States Navy in the Second World War* (Boston: Little, Brown, 1963), 111; quotation from the Robinett Diary, 10 January 1942, Box 20, George C. Marshall Foundation Research Library and Archives, Lexington, VA (hereafter cited as Marshall Papers, Marshall Library).

5. Martin Gilbert, *Winston S. Churchill: Road to Victory, 1941–1945* (Hillsdale, MI: Hillsdale College Press, 1986), 68–69.

6. Quotation from Frederick Aandahl, William M. Franklin, and William Slany, eds., *Foreign Relations of the United States, the Conferences at Washington,*

1941–1942, and Casablanca, 1943 (Washington, DC: US Government Printing Office, 1958), "United States Minutes, Meeting of Roosevelt and Churchill with their military advisors, 5:30 p.m.," 4 January 1942, Document 96, https://history.state.gov/historicaldocuments/frus1941-43 (hereafter cited as FRUS); "Voyages to Victory: RMS Queen Mary's War Service," by Eric Niderost, Warfare History Network, 16 January 2017, in http://warfarehistorynetwork.com/daily/wwii/voyages-to-victory-rms-queen-marys-war-service.

7. Dykes Diary, 10 January 1942, in Alex Danchev, *Establishing the Anglo-American Alliance: The Second World War Diaries of Brigadier Vivian Dykes* (London: Brassey's, 1990), 88; J. M. A. Gwyer and J. R. M. Butler, *Grand Strategy*, vol. 3, *June 1941–August 1942* (London: Her Majesty's Stationery Office, 1964), 377.

8. Dykes Diary, 10 January 1942, in Danchev, *Establishing the Anglo-American Alliance*, 88; "The Under Secretary of State (Welles) to the President, January 5, 1942," Document 177, in FRUS; "The Chief of Naval Operations (Stark) to the President's Special Assistant (Hopkins), January 6, 1942," Document 176, in FRUS; "The Ambassador to the United Kingdom (Winant) to the Secretary of State, January 9, 1942," Document 180, in FRUS; Gwyer and Butler, *Grand Strategy*, 373–74; H. P. Willmott, *Empires in the Balance: Japanese and Allied Pacific Strategies to April 1942* (Annapolis, MD: Naval Institute Press, 1989), 267.

9. Dykes Diary, 10 January 1942, in Danchev, *Establishing the Anglo-American Alliance*, 88.

10. Dykes Diary, 10 January 1942, in Danchev, *Establishing the Anglo-American Alliance*, 88.

11. First quotation from "Admiral King to Colonel C. H. Donnelly, Executive Officer Historical Section Joint Chiefs of Staff, 16 May 1949," Admiral Ernest King Papers, Library of Congress, Box 35; second quotation from Dykes Diary, 10 January 1942, in Danchev, *Establishing the Anglo-American Alliance*, 88.

12. Proceedings of the American British Joint Chiefs of Staff Conferences, Held in Washington, DC, On Twelve Occasions Between December 24, 1941, and January 14, 1942, "Minutes from the Chiefs of Staff Conference, Federal Reserve Building, Washington, DC, 3:00 P.M., January 10, 1942," in Joint Staff Historical Archives, Pentagon (hereafter cited as Joint Chiefs of Staff files); "Meeting of the United States and British Chiefs of Staff, 3 p.m., 10 January 1942," Document 99, in FRUS.

13. Proceedings of the American British Joint Chiefs of Staff Conferences, Held in Washington, DC, On Twelve Occasions Between December 24, 1941, and January 14, 1942, "Minutes from the Chiefs of Staff Conference, Federal Reserve Building, Washington, DC, 3:00 P.M., January 10, 1942," in Joint Chiefs of Staff files; "Meeting of the United States and British Chiefs of Staff, 3 p.m., 10 January 1942," Document 99, in FRUS.

14. Quotation from Barbara Tuchman, *Stilwell and the American Experience*

in China, 1911–1945 (New York: Macmillan, 1970), 312; Theodore H. White, ed., *The Stilwell Papers* (New York: DaCapo Press, 1991), 21.

15. Proceedings of the American British Joint Chiefs of Staff Conferences, Held in Washington, DC, On Twelve Occasions Between December 24, 1941, and January 14, 1942, "Minutes from the Chiefs of Staff Conference, Federal Reserve Building, Washington, DC, 3:00 P.M., January 10, 1942," in Joint Chiefs of Staff files; "Meeting of the United States and British Chiefs of Staff, 3 p.m., 10 January 1942," Document 99, in FRUS; Willmott, *Empires in the Balance*, 261.

16. "Memorandum by the British Chiefs of Staff: Procedure for Assumption of Command by General Wavell," 10 January 1942, Document 183, in FRUS; Willmott, *Empires in the Balance*, 261; Winston S. Churchill to John Curtin, 8 January 1942, in Martin Gilbert, *The Churchill Documents*, vol. 17, *Testing Times, 1942* (Hillsdale, MI: Hillsdale College Press, 2014), 45.

17. Louis Morton, *Strategy and Command: The First Two Years* (Washington, DC: US Army Center of Military History, 1985), 172.

18. Winston S. Churchill to Pieter Gerbrandy, 5 January 1942, in Gilbert, *Churchill Documents*, 35; "Conference at the White House, 2:00 P.M., January 28, 1942," General Henry Arnold Papers, Reel 205, Library of Congress.

19. Proceedings of the American British Joint Chiefs of Staff Conferences, Held in Washington, DC, On Twelve Occasions Between December 24, 1941, and January 14, 1942, "Minutes from the Chiefs of Staff Conference, Federal Reserve Building, Washington, DC, 3:00 P.M., January 10, 1942," in Joint Chiefs of Staff files; "Meeting of the United States and British Chiefs of Staff, 3 p.m., 10 January 1942," Document 99, in FRUS.

20. Proceedings of the American British Joint Chiefs of Staff Conferences, Held in Washington, DC, On Twelve Occasions Between December 24, 1941, and January 14, 1942, "Minutes from the Chiefs of Staff Conference, Federal Reserve Building, Washington, DC, 3:00 P.M., January 10, 1942," in Joint Chiefs of Staff files; "Meeting of the United States and British Chiefs of Staff, 3 p.m., 10 January 1942," Document 99, in FRUS.

21. Proceedings of the American British Joint Chiefs of Staff Conferences, Held in Washington, DC, On Twelve Occasions Between December 24, 1941, and January 14, 1942, "Minutes from the Chiefs of Staff Conference, Federal Reserve Building, Washington, DC, 3:00 P.M., January 10, 1942," Annex 3 Immediate Assistance to China, US-ABC-4/9, British WW-10, in Joint Chiefs of Staff files; "Report of the Planning Committee of the United States and British Chiefs of Staff, Immediate Assistance to China, 10 January 1942, Document 184, in FRUS; Gwyer and Butler, *Grand Strategy*, 377.

22. "Situation Report, January 11, 1942," Franklin Delano Roosevelt, Papers as President: Map Room Papers, 1941–1945, Military Files, Box 38, #41, Franklin Delano Roosevelt Library.

23. Dykes Diary, 11 January 1942, in Danchev, *Establishing the Anglo-American*

Alliance, 88; Winston Churchill, *The Grand Alliance* (Boston: Houghton Mifflin, 1950), 700–704.

24. Winston S. Churchill to General Ismay Hastings, for the Chiefs of Staff Committee, 4 January 1942, in Gilbert, *Churchill Documents*, 19–29; Churchill, *Grand Alliance*, 700–704.

25. Robinett Diary, 11 January 1942, Box 20, Marshall Papers, Marshall Library; quotation from "Memorandum from British Chiefs of Staff, Post Arcadia Conference," 8 January 1942, Document 116, in FRUS.

26. Robinette Diary, 11 January 1942, Box 20, Marshall Papers, Marshall Library.

27. Vernon Davis, *The History of the Joint Chiefs of Staff: Organizational Development*, vol. 1, *Origin of the Joint and Combined Chiefs of Staff* (Historical Division Joint Secretariat Joint Chiefs of Staff, 1972), Record Group 218, US Joint Chiefs of Staff, Office of the Director of the Joint Chiefs of Staff/Joint Secretariat Historical Division, Entry UD 104, History of the Joint Chiefs of Staff in World War II: Organizational Development (vols. 1 and 2), Container 1, National Archives and Records Administration, College Park, MD, 166.

28. Steven L. Rearden, *Council of War: A History of the Joint Chiefs of Staff, 1942–1991* (Washington, DC: National Defense University Press, 2012), 2–3.

29. Rearden, *Council of War*, 3–4.

30. Alex Danchev, *Very Special Relationship: Field Marshal Sir John Dill and the Anglo-American Alliance, 1941–1944* (London: Brassey's Defence Publishers, 1986), 12.

31. Robinett Diary, 11 January 1942, Box 20, Marshall Papers, Marshall Library.

32. White, *Stilwell Papers*, 23–24.

33. White, *Stilwell Papers*, 23–24.

34. Quotation in Dykes Diary, 11 January 1942, in Danchev, *Establishing the Anglo-American Alliance*, 88; Proceedings of the American British Joint Chiefs of Staff Conferences, Held in Washington, DC, On Twelve Occasions Between December 24, 1941 and January 14, 1942, "Minutes from the Chiefs of Staff Conference, Federal Reserve Building, Washington, DC, 4:00 P.M., January 11, 1942," in Joint Chiefs of Staff files; "Meeting of the United States and British Chiefs of Staff, 4 p.m., 11 January 1942," Document 100, in FRUS

35. Proceedings of the American British Joint Chiefs of Staff Conferences, Held in Washington, DC, On Twelve Occasions Between December 24, 1941, and January 14, 1942, "Minutes from the Chiefs of Staff Conference, Federal Reserve Building, Washington, DC, 4:00 P.M., January 11, 1942," in Joint Chiefs of Staff files; "Meeting of the United States and British Chiefs of Staff, 4 p.m., 11 January 1942," Document 100, in FRUS.

36. Proceedings of the American British Joint Chiefs of Staff Conferences, Held in Washington, DC, On Twelve Occasions Between December 24, 1941, and January 14, 1942, "Minutes from the Chiefs of Staff Conference, Federal Reserve Building, Washington, DC, 4:00 P.M., January 11, 1942," in Joint

Chiefs of Staff files; "Meeting of the United States and British Chiefs of Staff, 4 p.m., 11 January 1942," Document 100, in FRUS.

37. Proceedings of the American British Joint Chiefs of Staff Conferences, Held in Washington, DC, On Twelve Occasions Between December 24, 1941, and January 14, 1942, "Minutes from the Chiefs of Staff Conference, Federal Reserve Building, Washington, DC, 4:00 P.M., January 11, 1942," in Joint Chiefs of Staff files; "Meeting of the United States and British Chiefs of Staff, 4 p.m., 11 January 1942," Document 100, in FRUS.

38. Brooke Diary, 12 January 1942, in Alex Danchev and Daniel Todman, eds., *War Diaries, 1939–1945: Field Marshal Lord Alanbrooke* (Berkeley: University of California Press, 2001), 219.

39. Proceedings of the American British Joint Chiefs of Staff Conferences, Held in Washington, DC, On Twelve Occasions Between December 24, 1941, and January 14, 1942, "Minutes from the Chiefs of Staff Conference, Federal Reserve Building, Washington, DC, 4:00 P.M., January 11, 1942," in Joint Chiefs of Staff files; "Meeting of the United States and British Chiefs of Staff, 4 p.m., 11 January 1942," Document 100, in FRUS.

40. Stimson Diary, 8, 9, 10, 11 January 1942, Reel Seven, Volume 37, Marshall Papers, Marshall Library.

41. Charles Richardson, *From Churchill's Secret Circle to the BBC: The Biography of Lieutenant General Sir Ian Jacob* (London: Brassey's, 1991), 102.

42. Stimson Diary, 8, 9, 10, 11 January 1942, Reel Seven, Volume 37, Marshall Papers, Marshall Diary.

43. "Roosevelt-Churchill meeting, evening," 11 January 1942, Document 103, in FRUS; Winston S. Churchill to Anthony Eden, 12 January 1942, in Gilbert, *Churchill Documents*, 65.

44. Telegram, "Prime Minister Churchill to the British Secretary of State for Foreign Affairs (Eden)," 12 January 1942, Documents and Supplementary Papers, 399, in FRUS; Winston S. Churchill to Anthony Eden, 12 January 1942, in Gilbert, *Churchill Documents*, 65.

45. "Situation Report, January 12, 1942," Franklin Delano Roosevelt, Papers as President: Map Room Papers, 1941–1945, Military Files, Box 38, #41, Franklin Delano Roosevelt Library.

46. Dykes Diary, 12 January 1942, in Danchev, *Establishing the Anglo-American Alliance*, 89.

47. Vernon Davis, *The History of the Joint Chiefs of Staff: Organizational Development*, vol. 1, *Origin of the Joint And Combined Chiefs of Staff* (Historical Division Joint Secretariat Joint Chiefs of Staff, 1972), Record Group 218, US Joint Chiefs of Staff, Office of the Director of the Joint Chiefs of Staff/Joint Secretariat Historical Division, Entry UD 104, History of the Joint Chiefs of Staff in World War II: Organizational Development (vols. 1 and 2), Container 1, National Archives and Records Administration, College Park, MD, 172.

48. Telegram, "The Secretary of the British Chiefs of Staff [Hollis] to the

President's Special Assistant [Hopkins]," 9 January 1942, attachment "Allocation of Furnished Military Equipment to the Allies, 7 January 1942," Document 203, in FRUS.

49. Richard M. Leighton and Robert W. Coakley, *Global Logistics and Strategy, 1940–1943* (Washington, DC: United States Army Center of Military History, 1995), 250.

50. "The Legal Counsel, Office of Lend Lease Administration [Cox] to the Lend-Lease Administrator [Stettinius], Subject: The Macready Recommendation on the Allocation of Finished Military Equipment to Allies. 12 January 1942," Document 208, in FRUS.

51. Eisenhower Diary, 12 January 1942, in Robert Ferrell, ed., *The Eisenhower Diaries* (New York: W. W. Norton, 1981), 43.

52. Stimson Diary, 12 January 1942, Reel Seven, Volume 37, Marshall Papers, Marshall Library.

53. Stimson Diary, 12 January, 1942, Reel Seven, Volume 37, Marshall Papers, Marshall Library.

54. Proceedings of the American British Joint Chiefs of Staff Conferences, Held in Washington, DC, On Twelve Occasions Between December 24, 1941, and January 14, 1942, "Minutes from the Chiefs of Staff Conference, Federal Reserve Building, Washington, DC, 4:00 P.M., January 12, 1942," in Joint Chiefs of Staff files; "Meeting of the United States and British Chiefs of Staff, 4 p.m., 12 January 1942," Document 104, in FRUS.

55. Proceedings of the American British Joint Chiefs of Staff Conferences, Held in Washington, DC, On Twelve Occasions Between December 24, 1941, and January 14, 1942, "Minutes from the Chiefs of Staff Conference, Federal Reserve Building, Washington, DC, 4:00 P.M., January 12, 1942," in Joint Chiefs of Staff files; "Meeting of the United States and British Chiefs of Staff, 4 p.m., 12 January 1942," Document 104, in FRUS; Answers.com, "Queen Mary Transporting Troops in World War 2?" http://www.answers.com/Q/Queen_Mary_Transporting_troops_in_World_War_2.

56. Proceedings of the American British Joint Chiefs of Staff Conferences, Held in Washington, DC, On Twelve Occasions Between December 24, 1941, and January 14, 1942, "Minutes from the Chiefs of Staff Conference, Federal Reserve Building, Washington, DC, 4:00 P.M., January 12, 1942," in Joint Chiefs of Staff files; "Meeting of the United States and British Chiefs of Staff, 4 p.m., 12 January 1942," Document 104, in FRUS.

57. "Meeting of Roosevelt and Churchill with their military advisors, 5:30 p.m., 12 January 1942, United States Minutes," Document 105, FRUS; quotation from Gilbert, *Winston Churchill: Road to Victory*, 39; Winston S. Churchill to General Claude Auchinleck, 11 January 1942, in Gilbert, *Churchill Documents*, 57.

58. "Meeting of Roosevelt and Churchill with their military advisors, 5:30 p.m., 12 January 1942, United States Minutes," Document 105, in FRUS.

59. "Meeting of Roosevelt and Churchill with their military advisors, 5:30 p.m., 12 January 1942, United States Minutes," Document 105, in FRUS.

60. "Meeting of Roosevelt and Churchill with their military advisors, 5:30 p.m., 12 January 1942, United States Minutes," Document 105, in FRUS.

61. "Meeting of Roosevelt and Churchill with their military advisors, 5:30 p.m., 12 January 1942, United States Minutes," Document 105, in FRUS; *Foreign Relations of the United States, the Conferences at Washington, 1941–1942, and Casablanca, 1943*; "Meeting of Roosevelt and Churchill with their military advisors, 5:30 p.m., 12 January 1942, Lieutenant Arnold Notes," Document 106, in FRUS.

62. "Meeting of Roosevelt and Churchill with their military advisors, 5:30 p.m., 12 January 1942, United States Minutes," Document 105, in FRUS; "Meeting of Roosevelt and Churchill with their military advisors," 5:30 p.m., 12 January 1942, Lieutenant Arnold Notes," Document 106, in FRUS.

63. Stimson Diary, 12 January 1942, Reel Seven, Volume 37, Marshall Papers, Marshall Library.

64. Quotation in "Dinner party at the British Embassy, 8 p.m., 12 January 1942," Document 108, in FRUS; Cordell Hull, *The Memoirs of Cordell Hull*, vol. 2 (New York: Macmillan, 1948), 1152–53; Winston S. Churchill to Lord Halifax, 10 January 1942, in Gilbert, *Churchill Documents*, 53.

65. "Situation Report, January 13, 1942," Franklin Delano Roosevelt, Papers as President: Map Room Papers, 1941–1945, Military Files, Box 38, #41, Franklin Delano Roosevelt Library; Mary Williams, *The US Army in World War II: Chronology, 1941–1945* (Washington, DC: US Army Center of Military History, 1989), 14; Morton, *Strategy and Command: The First Two Years*, 172.

66. Victoria Schofield, *Wavell: Soldier and Statesman* (London: John Murray Press, 2006), 234.

67. Dykes Diary, 12 and 13 January 1942, in Danchev, *Establishing the Anglo-American Alliance*, 89.

68. "ABC-1, Joint Letter of Transmittal, CCS 381, 27 March 1941," cited in Vernon Davis, *The History of the Joint Chiefs of Staff: Organizational Development*, vol. 1, *Origin of the Joint and Combined Chiefs of Staff* (Historical Division Joint Secretariat Joint Chiefs of Staff, 1972), Record Group 218, US Joint Chiefs of Staff, Office of the Director of the Joint Chiefs of Staff/Joint Secretariat Historical Division, Entry UD 104, History of the Joint Chiefs of Staff in World War II: Organizational Development (vols. 1 and 2), Container 1, National Archives and Records Administration, College Park, MD, 119.

69. Arnold was upset that the army air force was not represented on this mission. Vernon Davis, *The History of the Joint Chiefs of Staff: Organizational Development*, vol. 1, *Origin of the Joint And Combined Chiefs of Staff* (Historical Division Joint Secretariat Joint Chiefs of Staff, 1972), Record Group 218, US Joint Chiefs of Staff, Office of the Director of the Joint Chiefs of Staff/Joint

Secretariat Historical Division, Entry UD 104, History of the Joint Chiefs of Staff in World War II: Organizational Development (vols. 1 and 2), Container 1, National Archives and Records Administration, College Park, MD, 119; Maurice Matloff and Edwin Snell, *Strategic Planning for Coalition Warfare, 1941–1942* (Washington, DC: US Army Center of Military History, 1999), 41–42.

70. Quotation from Dykes Diary, 12 and 13 January 1942, in Danchev, *Establishing the Anglo-American Alliance*, 89; "Memorandum by British Chiefs of Staff on Post-Arcadia Collaboration," 8 January 1942, Document 116, in FRUS.

71. Vernon Davis, *The History of the Joint Chiefs of Staff: Organizational Development*, vol. 1, *Origin of the Joint and Combined Chiefs of Staff* (Historical Division Joint Secretariat Joint Chiefs of Staff, 1972), Record Group 218, US Joint Chiefs of Staff, Office of the Director of the Joint Chiefs of Staff/Joint Secretariat Historical Division, Entry UD 104, History of the Joint Chiefs of Staff in World War II: Organizational Development (vols. 1 and 2), Container 1, National Archives and Records Administration, College Park, MD, 166–67.

72. Proceedings of the American British Joint Chiefs of Staff Conferences, Held in Washington, DC, On Twelve Occasions Between December 24, 1941, and January 14, 1942, "Minutes from the Chiefs of Staff Conference, Federal Reserve Building, Washington, DC, 4:00 P.M., January 13, 1942," in Joint Chiefs of Staff files; "Meeting of the United States and British Chiefs of Staff, 4 p.m., 13 January 1942," Document 109, in FRUS.

73. Proceedings of the American British Joint Chiefs of Staff Conferences, Held in Washington, DC, On Twelve Occasions Between December 24, 1941, and January 14, 1942, "Minutes from the Chiefs of Staff Conference, Federal Reserve Building, Washington, DC, 4:00 P.M., January 13, 1942," in Joint Chiefs of Staff files; "Meeting of the United States and British Chiefs of Staff, 4 p.m., 13 January 1942," Document 109, in FRUS.

74. Proceedings of the American British Joint Chiefs of Staff Conferences, Held in Washington, DC, On Twelve Occasions Between December 24, 1941, and January 14, 1942, "Minutes from the Chiefs of Staff Conference, Federal Reserve Building, Washington, DC, 4:00 P.M., January 13, 1942," in Joint Chiefs of Staff files; "Meeting of the United States and British Chiefs of Staff, 4 p.m., 13 January 1942," Document 109, in FRUS.

75. "Minutes of Meeting of Chiefs of Staff Held in the Embassy Annex on Tuesday, 13 January 1942, at 10:30 A.M.," in War Cabinet and Chiefs of Staff Committee, Records of the Proceedings at the Washington War Conference, December 1941–January 1942, in CAB-99/17 Records of the Cabinet, War Cabinet and Cabinet: Commonwealth International Conferences: Minutes and Papers, "Arcadia" Record of Proceedings at Washington Conference, 1941–1942, the National Archives, Kew, Richmond, Surrey, TW94DU, www.nationalarchives.gov.uk (hereafter cited as CAB-99/17 British Archives); quotation from Proceedings of the American British Joint Chiefs of Staff Conferences, Held in Washington, DC, On Twelve Occasions Between December 24, 1941

and January 14, 1942, "Minutes from the Chiefs of Staff Conference, Federal Reserve Building, Washington, DC, 4:00 P.M., January 13, 1942," in Joint Chiefs of Staff files; and "Meeting of the United States and British Chiefs of Staff, 4 p.m., 13 January 1942," Document 109, in FRUS; Vernon Davis, *The History of the Joint Chiefs of Staff: Organizational Development*, vol. 1, *Origin of the Joint And Combined Chiefs of Staff* (Historical Division Joint Secretariat Joint Chiefs of Staff, 1972), Record Group 218, US Joint Chiefs of Staff, Office of the Director of the Joint Chiefs of Staff/Joint Secretariat Historical Division, Entry UD 104, History of the Joint Chiefs of Staff in World War II: Organizational Development (vols. 1 and 2), Container 1, National Archives and Records Administration, College Park, MD, 167–68.

76. Quotation from Proceedings of the American British Joint Chiefs of Staff Conferences, Held in Washington, DC, On Twelve Occasions Between December 24, 1941, and January 14, 1942, "Minutes from the Chiefs of Staff Conference, Federal Reserve Building, Washington, DC, 4:00 P.M., January 13, 1942," in Joint Chiefs of Staff files; and "Meeting of the United States and British Chiefs of Staff, 4 p.m., 13 January 1942," Document 109, in FRUS; Sherwood, *Roosevelt and Hopkins*, 471.

77. Quotation in "Draft Minute for Submission by the United States Chiefs of Staff to the President and by the British Chiefs of Staff to the Prime Minister," 13 January 1942, p. 232, in FRUS; Leighton and Coakley, *Global Logistics and Strategy*, 251; Gwyer and Butler, *Grand Strategy*, 397.

78. Quotation from Proceedings of the American British Joint Chiefs of Staff Conferences, Held in Washington, DC, On Twelve Occasions Between December 24, 1941, and January 14, 1942, "Minutes from the Chiefs of Staff Conference, Federal Reserve Building, Washington, DC, 4:00 P.M., January 13, 1942," in Joint Chiefs of Staff files; and "Meeting of the United States and British Chiefs of Staff, 4 p.m., 13 January 1942," Document 109, in FRUS; Gwyer and Butler, *Grand Strategy*, 397.

79. Vernon Davis, *The History of the Joint Chiefs of Staff: Organizational Development*, vol. 1, *Origin of the Joint And Combined Chiefs of Staff* (Historical Division Joint Secretariat Joint Chiefs of Staff, 1972), Record Group 218, US Joint Chiefs of Staff, Office of the Director of the Joint Chiefs of Staff/Joint Secretariat Historical Division, Entry UD 104, History of the Joint Chiefs of Staff in World War II: Organizational Development (vols. 1 and 2), Container 1, National Archives and Records Administration, College Park, MD, 168–69.

80. Proceedings of the American British Joint Chiefs of Staff Conferences, Held in Washington, DC, On Twelve Occasions Between December 24, 1941, and January 14, 1942, "Minutes from the Chiefs of Staff Conference, Federal Reserve Building, Washington, DC, 4:00 P.M., January 13, 1942," in Joint Chiefs of Staff files; "Meeting of the United States and British Chiefs of Staff, 4 p.m., 13 January 1942," Document 109, in FRUS.

81. Quotation from Richardson, *From Churchill's Secret Circle*, 103; Dykes

Diary, 13 January 1942, in Danchev, *Establishing the Anglo-American Alliance*, 89.

82. Quotation from Danchev, *Very Special Relationship*, 16; Mark Stoler, *Allies and Adversaries: The Joint Chiefs of Staff, The Grand Alliance, and US Strategy in World War II* (Chapel Hill: University of North Carolina Press, 2000), 104.

83. Leighton and Coakley, *Global Logistics and Strategy, 1940–1943*, 251.

84. Leighton and Coakley, *Global Logistics and Strategy, 1940–1943*, 251; Dykes Diary, 13 January 1942, in Danchev, *Establishing the Anglo-American Alliance*, 89.

85. Stimson Diary, 13 January 1942, Reel Seven, Volume 37, Marshall Papers, Marshall Library.

86. Wesley Frank Craven and James Lea Cate, *The Army Air Forces in World War II*, vol. 1, *Plans and Early Operations: January 1939 to August 1942* (Chicago: University of Chicago Press, 1948), 248–49.

87. "Situation Report, January 14, 1942," Franklin Delano Roosevelt, Papers as President: Map Room Papers, 1941–1945, Military Files, Box 38, #41, Franklin Delano Roosevelt Library.

88. Gilbert, *Winston Churchill: Road to Victory*, 41.

89. First quotation from Winston S. Churchill to General Archibald Wavell, 14 January 1942, in Gilbert, *Churchill Documents*, 81; Farrell, *Defence and Fall of Singapore*, 325–26; second quotation in John Connell, *Wavell: Supreme Commander* (London: Collins, 1969), 105.

90. Connell, *Wavell*, 111.

91. "Winston S. Churchill to General Hastings Ismay, for the Chiefs of Staff committee, 19 January 1942," in Gilbert, *Churchill Documents*, 106.

92. Basil Liddell Hart, "The Military Strategist," in Taylor et al., *Churchill: Four Faces and the Man* (London: Allen Lane, 1969), 191.

93. Quotation from D. Clayton James, *The Years of MacArthur*, vol. 2, *1941–1945* (Boston: Houghton Mifflin, 1975), 93; Stimson Diary, 14 January 1942, Reel Seven, Volume 37, Marshall Papers, Marshall Library..

94. Robinett Diary, 14 January 1942, Box 20, Marshall Papers, Marshall Library.

95. Proceedings of the American British Joint Chiefs of Staff Conferences, Held in Washington, DC, On Twelve Occasions Between December 24, 1941, and January 14, 1942, "Minutes from the Chiefs of Staff Conference, Federal Reserve Building, Washington, DC, 3:00 P.M., January 14, 1942," in Joint Chiefs of Staff files; "Meeting of the United States and British Chiefs of Staff, 3 p.m., 14 January 1942," Document 110, in FRUS.

96. Proceedings of the American British Joint Chiefs of Staff Conferences, Held in Washington, DC, On Twelve Occasions Between December 24, 1941, and January 14, 1942, "Minutes from the Chiefs of Staff Conference, Federal Reserve Building, Washington, DC, 3:00 P.M., January 14, 1942," in Joint Chiefs of Staff files; "Meeting of the United States and British Chiefs of Staff, 3 p.m., 14 January 1942," Document 110, in FRUS.

97. Proceedings of the American British Joint Chiefs of Staff Conferences, Held in Washington, DC, On Twelve Occasions Between December 24, 1941,

and January 14, 1942, "Minutes from the Chiefs of Staff Conference, Federal Reserve Building, Washington, DC, 3:00 P.M., January 14, 1942," Annex 1, "Operation Super-Gymnast," in Joint Chiefs of Staff files; "Meeting of the United States and British Chiefs of Staff," 3 p.m., 14 January 1942, Document 110, and "Report by the Planning Committee of the United States and British Chiefs of Staff, Operation Super-Gymnast," 14 January 1942, 262, in FRUS.

98. Proceedings of the American British Joint Chiefs of Staff Conferences, Held in Washington, DC, On Twelve Occasions Between December 24, 1941, and January 14, 1942, "Minutes from the Chiefs of Staff Conference, Federal Reserve Building, Washington, DC, 3:00 P.M., January 14, 1942," in Joint Chiefs of Staff files; "Meeting of the United States and British Chiefs of Staff, 3 p.m., 14 January 1942," Document 110, in FRUS.

99. Dykes Diary, in Danchev, *Establishing the Anglo-American Alliance*, 90.

100. Tuchman, *Stilwell and the American Experience in China*, 313.

101. Proceedings of the American British Joint Chiefs of Staff Conferences, Held in Washington, DC, On Twelve Occasions Between December 24, 1941, and January 14, 1942, "Minutes from the Chiefs of Staff Conference, Federal Reserve Building, Washington, DC, 3:00 P.M., January 14, 1942," Annex 2, "Post-Arcadia Collaboration," in Joint Chiefs of Staff files; "Memorandum by United States Chiefs of Staff, Post-Arcadia Collaboration," 14 January 1942, Document 121, in FRUS.

102. Gwyer and Butler, *Grand Strategy*, 383–84.

103. Proceedings of the American British Joint Chiefs of Staff Conferences, Held in Washington, DC, On Twelve Occasions Between December 24, 1941, and January 14, 1942, "Minutes from the Chiefs of Staff Conference, Federal Reserve Building, Washington, DC, 3:00 P.M., January 14, 1942," Annex 2, "Post-Arcadia Collaboration," in Joint Chiefs of Staff files; "Memorandum by United States Chiefs of Staff, Post-Arcadia Collaboration," 14 January 1942, Document 121, in FRUS.

104. Robinett Diary, 14 January 1942, Box 20, Marshall Papers, Marshall Library.

105. Stimson Diary, 14 January 1942, Reel Seven, Volume 37, Marshall Papers, Marshall Library.

106. Stimson Diary, 14 January 1942, Reel Seven, Volume 37, Marshall Papers, Marshall Library.

107. Stimson Diary, 14 January 1942, Reel Seven, Volume 37, Marshall Papers, Marshall Library.

108. Quotation from Sherwood, *Roosevelt and Hopkins*, 470–71; Leighton and Coakley, *Global Logistics and Strategy, 1940–1943*, 251.

109. Sherwood, *Roosevelt and Hopkins*, 471–72.

110. First quotation from Pogue, *Ordeal and Hope*, 286; second quotation from Sherwood, *Roosevelt and Hopkins*, 472.

111. Sherwood, *Roosevelt and Hopkins*, 472; Vernon Davis, *The History of the*

Joint Chiefs of Staff: Organizational Development, vol. 1, *Origin of the Joint and Combined Chiefs of Staff* (Historical Division Joint Secretariat Joint Chiefs of Staff, 1972), Record Group 218, US Joint Chiefs of Staff, Office of the Director of the Joint Chiefs of Staff/Joint Secretariat Historical Division, Entry UD 104, History of the Joint Chiefs of Staff in World War II: Organizational Development (vols. 1 and 2), Container 1, National Archives and Records Administration, College Park, MD, 174.

112. "Meeting of Roosevelt and Churchill with their military advisors, 5:30 p.m.," 14 January 1942, Document 112, in FRUS.

113. "Meeting of Roosevelt and Churchill with their military advisors, 5:30 p.m.," 14 January 1942, Document 112, in FRUS.

114. "Meeting of Roosevelt and Churchill with their military advisors, 5:30 p.m.," 14 January 1942, Document 112, in FRUS; quotation from postscript to Brooke Diary, 29 December 1941, in Danchev and Todman, *War Diaries*, 216; Andrew Roberts, *Masters and Commanders: How Four Titans Won the War in the West, 1941–1945* (New York: Harper Perennial, 2010), 75.

115. First two quotations cited in Pogue, *Ordeal and Hope*, 265; final quotation in "Meeting of Roosevelt and Churchill with their military advisors, 5:30 p.m.," 14 January 1942, Document 112, in FRUS.

116. Wilson, *Churchill: Taken from the Diaries of Lord Moran*, 23–24.

117. Wilson, *Churchill: Taken from the Diaries of Lord Moran*, 21.

118. "Meeting of Roosevelt and Churchill with their military advisors, 5:30 p.m.," 14 January 1942, Document 112, in FRUS.

119. "Roosevelt-Churchill dinner, evening," 14 January 1942, "Memorandum by the President's Special Assistant (Hopkins), 15 January 1942," Document 113, in FRUS; Churchill, *Grand Alliance*, 707; Itinerary, Franklin D. Roosevelt Papers, 14–15 January 1942, in Gilbert, *Churchill Documents*, 85.

Chapter 7

1. Lord Moran, *Churchill: Taken from the Diaries of Lord Moran; The Struggle for Survival, 1940–1965* (Boston: Houghton Mifflin, 1966), 26.

2. Winston Churchill Speech, 27 January 1942, in Martin Gilbert, *The Churchill Documents*, vol. 17, *Testing Times, 1942* (Hillsdale, MI: Hillsdale College Press, 2014), 153–76.

3. Quotations from Winston Churchill Speech, 27 January 1942, in Gilbert, *Churchill Documents*, 153–76; Winston S. Churchill to Sir Archibald Sinclair, 23 January 1942, in Gilbert, *Churchill Documents*, 133.

4. Harold Nicholson Diary, 29 January 1942, in Gilbert, *Churchill Documents*, 186.

5. Louis Morton, *Strategy and Command: The First Two Years* (Washington, DC: US Army Center of Military History, 1985), 179; Samuel Eliot Morison, *The Two-Ocean War: A Short History of the United States Navy in the Second World War* (Boston: Little, Brown, 1989), 87; quotation from Wavell's exam-

ples on allied coordination from Field Marshal Earl Wavell, *Soldiers and Soldiering*, 88–91, in Robinett Papers, Box 17, File B17/F3, George C. Marshall Library; H. P. Willmott, *Empires in the Balance: Japanese and Allied Pacific Strategies to April 1942* (Annapolis, MD: Naval Institute Press, 1989), 277.

6. Ronald Lewin, *The Chief* (New York: Farrar, Straus, Giroux, 1980), 161.

7. First quotation from Proceedings of the American British Joint Chiefs of Staff Conferences, Held in Washington, DC, On Twelve Occasions Between December 24, 1941, and January 14, 1942, "Minutes from the Chiefs of Staff Conference, Federal Reserve Building, Washington, DC, 4 P.M., December 25, 1941," in Joint History Office, Pentagon (hereafter cited as Joint Chiefs of Staff files); Frederick Aandahl, William M. Franklin, and William Slany, eds., *Foreign Relations of the United States, the Conferences at Washington, 1941–1942, and Casablanca, 1943* (Washington, DC: US Government Printing Office, 1958); "Meeting of the United States and British Chiefs of Staff, 4 p.m., 25 December 1941," Document 54, https://history.state.gov/historicaldocuments/frus1941–43 (hereafter cited as FRUS); second and third quotations from Brooke Diary, 22 February 1942, in Alex Danchev and Daniel Todman, *War Diaries, 1939–1945, Field Marshal Lord Alanbrooke* (Berkeley: University of California Press, 2001), 232–33.

8. Averell Harriman to Franklin Roosevelt, 7 March 1942, in Franklin Roosevelt, Papers as President: 1933–1945, Franklin Roosevelt Library and Museum, President's Secretary Files, Diplomatic Correspondence, Box 37, http://www.fdrlibrary.marist.edu/archives/collections/franklin/ (hereafter cited as Franklin Delano Roosevelt Library).

9. Mary Williams, *The US Army in World War II: Chronology, 1941–1945* (Washington, DC: US Army Center of Military History, 1989), 17, 20–22; William Manchester and Paul Reid, *The Last Lion: Winston Spencer Churchill*, vol. 3, *Defender of the Realm, 1940–1965* (New York: Little, Brown, 2012), 479–80.

10. Arthur Bryant, *The Turn of the Tide: A History of the War Years Based on the Diaries of Field Marshal Lord Alanbrooke, Chief of the Imperial General Staff* (Garden City, NY: Doubleday, 1957), 245; John Kennedy, *The Business of War: The War Narrative of Major-General Sir John Kennedy* (New York: William Morrow, 1958), 196; quotation in Churchill to Roosevelt, 16 December 1941, in Warren Kimball, ed., *Churchill and Roosevelt: The Complete Correspondence*, vol. 1, *Alliance Emerging October 1933–November 1942* (Princeton, NJ: Princeton Legacy Library, 1984), 294; Gilbert, *Churchill Documents*, 283.

11. Quotation in Churchill to Roosevelt on 17 December 1941, in Kimball, *Churchill and Roosevelt*, 299; Churchill to Roosevelt, 7 February 1942, in Kimball, *Churchill and Roosevelt*, 350; Kennedy, *Business of War*, 196.

12. First quotation in Churchill to Wavell, 10 February 1942, in Kimball, *Churchill and Roosevelt*, 360; second quotation in Lord Moran, *Churchill*, 29.

13. Roosevelt to Churchill, 18 February 1942, in Kimball, *Churchill and Roosevelt*, 362–63.

14. Bryant, *Turn of the Tide*, 279 and 296; Charles MacDonald, *The Mighty Endeavor: American Armed Forces in the European Theater in World War II* (New York: Oxford University Press, 1969), 48; quotation from Memorandum by the British and American Chiefs of Staff, United States: ABC–4/CS–1, British: WW–1 (Final), 31 December 1941, Document 115, in FRUS.

15. Forrest Pogue, *George C. Marshall: Ordeal and Hope, 1939–1942* (New York: Viking Press, 1967), 265.

16. Manchester, *Last Lion*, 466.

17. "Meeting of United States and British Chiefs of Staff," 4 p.m., 13 January 1942, United States Minutes, Document 109, in FRUS.

18. Smith would go on to four stars and serve as Eisenhower's chief of staff in Tunisia, Italy, and Western Europe.

19. Combined Chiefs of Staff (C.C.S. 1st Meeting) Minutes of a Meeting held in Room 1202, Federal Reserve Building, on Friday, January 23, 1942, at 3:00 p.m., Joint Staff Historical Archives, Joint History Office, Pentagon (hereafter cited as Joint Chiefs of Staff files); Combined Chiefs of Staff (C.C.S. 3rd Meeting) Minutes of a Meeting held in Room 340, Public Health Building, on Friday, February 3, 1942, at 3:00 p.m., Joint Staff Historical Archives, Joint Chiefs of Staff files; Dykes Diary, 23 January 1942, and 3 February 1942, in Alex Danchev, *Establishing the Anglo-American Alliance: The Second World War Diaries of Brigadier Vivian Dykes* (London: Brassey's, 1990), 95 and 101; quotation from Dykes Diary, 27 January 1942, in Danchev, *Establishing the Anglo-American Alliance*, 98.

20. Brooke Diary, 9 February 1942, in Danchev and Todman, *War Diaries*, 228.

21. Combined Chiefs of Staff (C.C.S. 4th Meeting) Minutes of a Meeting held in Room 340, Public Health Building, on Tuesday, February 10, 1942, at 3:00 p.m., Joint Staff Historical Archives, Joint Chiefs of Staff files; Dykes Diary, 3 February 1942, and 10 February 1942, in Danchev, *Establishing the Anglo-American Alliance*, 101 and 104.

22. Danchev, *Establishing the Anglo-American Alliance*, 71.

23. Dykes Diary, 14 February 1942, in Danchev, *Establishing the Anglo-American Alliance*, 105.

24. Quotations from Danchev, *Establishing the Anglo-American Alliance*, 72; also Dykes Diary, 10 March 1942, in Danchev, *Establishing the Anglo-American Alliance*, 114.

25. Dykes to Hollis, 21 November 1942, in Danchev, *Establishing the Anglo-American Alliance*, 107.

26. Alex Danchev, *Very Special Relationship: Field Marshal Sir John Dill and the Anglo-American Alliance, 1941–1944* (London: Brassey's Defence Publishers, 1986), 136–37; Pogue, *Ordeal and Hope*, 284; George Bernard Shaw is often credited with the humorous remark; for a detailed discussion on his exact words see Quote Investigator (website), "Britain and America Are Two Nations

Divided by a Common Language," https://quoteinvestigator.com/2016/04/03/common/.

27. First three quotations from Danchev, *Very Special Relationship*, 51 and 65; final quotation from Admiral King to Colonel Thomas Dobyns, 22 June 1951, in the Ernest King Papers, Box 35, Library of Congress, Washington, DC.

28. Brooke Diary, 17 August 1943 (postscript), in Danchev and Todman, *War Diaries*, 444.

29. Danchev, *Very Special Relationship*, 60.

30. Forrest Pogue interview with General Hastings L. Ismay, 20 December 1946, in Forrest Pogue interviews, Military History Institute, Army Heritage and Education Center, Carlisle Barracks, PA.

31. Combined Chiefs of Staff Minutes of Meeting held in Room 240, Public Health Building, on Tuesday March 17, 1942, at 2:30 p.m., CCS 12th Meeting, Joint Staff Historical Archives, Joint Chiefs of Staff files; Steven Rearden, *Council of War: A History of the Joint Chiefs of Staff, 1942–1991* (Washington, DC: National Defense University Press, 2012), 9; quotation in Cable R-115, Roosevelt to Churchill, 9 March 1942, in Kimball, *Churchill and Roosevelt*, 399.

32. Bryant, *Turn of the Tide*, 254.

33. First quotation from Danchev, *Very Special Relationship*, 135; second quotation from Robert Sherwood, *Roosevelt and Hopkins: An Intimate History* (New York: Harper, 1948), 499; third quotation from Winston Churchill, *Grand Alliance* (Boston: Houghton Mifflin, 1950), 686.

34. Letter Admiral King to General Marshall and Admiral Stark, 31 January 1942, and quotation from General Marshall to Admiral King, 17 February 1942, in the Ernest King Papers, Box 35, Library of Congress; Rearden, *Council of War*, 5.

35. Thomas Buell, *Master of Seapower: A Biography of Fleet Admiral Ernest J. King* (Boston: Little, Brown, 1980), 181–82.

36. "Fourth Meeting of the Joint US Chiefs of Staff, Minutes of the Meeting Held in Room 336, Public Health Building, on Saturday, March 7, 1942, at 11:00 A.M.," in RG 218, Records of the US Joint Chiefs of Staff, CCS 334, Chiefs of Staff (Meetings 1–10), Box 194, National Archives, College Park, MD.

37. Quotation from Pogue, *Ordeal and Hope*, 298; Admiral Leahy Diary, 12 April 1939, Admiral William Leahy Papers, Reel 2, Library of Congress; Buell, *Master of Seapower*, 184–85.

38. Quotation in Rearden, *Council of War*, 8–10; James F. Schnabel, *History of the Joint Chiefs of Staff*, vol. 1, *The Joint Chiefs of Staff and National Policy, 1945–1947* (Washington, DC: Office of Joint History, Office of the Chairman of the Joint Chiefs of Staff, 1996), 1–3.

39. First quotation in Rearden, *Council of War*, 52; second quotation in William Leahy, *I Was There: The Personal Story of the Chief of Staff to Presidents Roosevelt and Truman Based on His Notes and Diaries Made at the Time*

(New York: Whittlesey House, 1950), 105.

40. Dykes Diary, 31 January and 16 February 1942, in Danchev, *Establishing the Anglo-American Alliance*, 99 and 106; Sherwood, *Roosevelt and Hopkins*, 491; Winston S. Churchill to President Franklin Roosevelt, 8 February 1942, in Gilbert, *Churchill Documents*, 230.

41. Richard M. Leighton and Robert W. Coakley, *Global Logistics and Strategy, 1940–1943* (Washington, DC: United States Army Center of Military History, 1995), 254–55; Wesley Craven and Frank Cate, *The Army Air Forces in World War II*, vol. 6, *Men and Planes* (Chicago: University of Chicago Press, 1955), 293.

42. Lord Moran, *Churchill: Taken from The Diaries of Lord Moran* (Boston: Houghton Mifflin, 1966), 28–30; Oliver Harvey Diary, 22 February 1942, in Gilbert, *Churchill Documents*, 295.

43. First quotation from Ray Cline, *Washington Command Post: The Operations Division* (Washington, DC: US Government Printing Office, 1951), 89; second and third quotations from J. M. A. Gwyer and J. R. M. Butler, *Grand Strategy*, vol. 3, *June 1941–August 1942* (London: Her Majesty's Stationery Office, 1964), 349 and 351.

44. Lieutenant Colonel Edward Knopf interview with General Thomas Handy, Senior Officer Debriefing Program, US Army Military History Research Collection, Army Heritage and Education Collection, Carlisle Barracks, PA.

45. Lieutenant Colonel Edward Knopf interview with General Thomas Handy, Senior Officer Debriefing Program, US Army Military History Research Collection, Army Heritage and Education Collection, Carlisle Barracks, PA.

46. Lieutenant Colonel Edward Knopf interview with General Thomas Handy, Senior Officer Debriefing Program, US Army Military History Research Collection, Army Heritage and Education Collection, Carlisle Barracks, PA; quotation from Pogue, *Ordeal and Hope*, 271; Albert Wedemeyer, *Wedemeyer Reports* (New York: Henry Holt, 1958), 107.

47. Forrest Pogue notes from a manuscript written by Lieutenant General Sir Frederick Morgan written in the six-week period from the end of his assignment to SHAEF and his assumption as head of UNRRA, in the Forrest Pogue interviews, US Army Military History Research Collection, Army Heritage and Education Center, Carlisle Barracks, PA.

48. Forrest Pogue notes from a manuscript written by Lieutenant General Sir Frederick Morgan written in the six-week period from the end of his assignment to SHAEF and his assumption as head of UNRRA, in the Forrest Pogue interviews, US Army Military History Research Collection, Army Heritage and Education Center, Carlisle Barracks, PA; Pogue, *Ordeal and Hope*, 270.

49. Forrest Pogue interview with Marshal of the Royal Air Force Peter Portal, 7 February 1947, in the Forrest Pogue interviews, US Army Military History Research Collection, Army Heritage and Education Center, Carlisle Barracks, PA.

50. Forrest Pogue interview with Marshal of the Royal Air Force Peter Portal, 7 February 1947, in the Forrest Pogue interviews, US Army Military History Research Collection, Army Heritage and Education Center, Carlisle Barracks, PA; quotation from Denis Richards, *Portal of Hungerford* (London: Heinemann, 1977), 214.

51. Robinett Diary, 29 December 1941, Box 20, in George C. Marshall Papers, George C. Marshall Foundation Research Library and Archives, Lexington, VA (hereafter cited as Marshall Papers, Marshall Library); quotation in Forrest Pogue interview with Marshal of the Royal Air Force Peter Portal, 7 February 1947, in the Forrest Pogue interviews, US Army Military History Research Collection, Army Heritage and Education Center, Carlisle Barracks, PA.

52. Lieutenant Colonel Edward Knopf interview with General Thomas Handy, Senior Officer Debriefing Program, US Army Military History Research Collection, Army Heritage and Education Collection, Carlisle Barracks, PA.

53. Forrest Pogue interview with Marshal of the Royal Air Force Peter Portal, 7 February 1947, in the Forrest Pogue interviews, US Army Military History Research Collection, Army Heritage and Education Center, Carlisle Barracks, PA.

54. Roosevelt to Churchill, 31 January 1942, in Kimball, *Churchill and Roosevelt*, 338–39.

55. Lieutenant Colonel Edward Knopf interview with General Thomas Handy, Senior Officer Debriefing Program, US Army Military History Research Collection, Army Heritage and Education Collection, Carlisle Barracks, PA.

56. Lieutenant Colonel Edward Knopf interview with General Thomas Handy, Senior Officer Debriefing Program, US Army Military History Research Collection, Army Heritage and Education Collection, Carlisle Barracks, PA; postscript to Robinett Diary, 14 January 1942, in Marshall Papers, Marshall Library.

57. Churchill, *Grand Alliance*, 662–63.

BIBLIOGRAPHIC ESSAY

My reliance on primary source materials makes a brief note in order. The minutes of the twelve formal meetings of the American and British Chiefs of Staff during the Arcadia Conference are available at several repositories. I used a set at the Joint History Office Archives, Pentagon, "Proceedings of the American-British Joint Chiefs of Staff Conferences, Held in Washington, DC on Twelve Occasions Between December 24, 1941 and January 14, 1942." (The Joint History Office has recently put this document online; it can be accessed at https://www.jcs.mil/Portals/36/Documents/History/WWII/Arcadia3.pdf.) Other sets may be found in the Arnold Papers at the Library of Congress, Washington, DC; the Marshall Papers in the George C. Marshall Foundation Research Library and Archives, Lexington Virginia; the Franklin Delano Roosevelt Library, Hyde Park, New York; the National Archives and Records Administration, College Park, Maryland, and are accessible online by searching for the conference.

The best published documentary collection on the Arcadia Conference is the State Department's official history: Frederick Aandahl, William Franklin, and William Slany, eds., *Foreign Relations of the United States, the Conferences at Washington, 1941–1942, and Casablanca, 1943* (Washington, DC: US Government Printing Office, 1958). It may be found online at https://history.state.gov/historicaldocuments/frus1941-43. This superb study includes a large number of conference papers and supporting documents as well as the minutes of the twelve formal meetings between the American and British Chiefs of Staff. More importantly, it provides a wealth of information on the various informal meetings held between President Roosevelt and his military and economic advisors as well as his discussions with Prime Minister Churchill.

A major flaw in the official minutes of the formal meetings between the American and British Chiefs of Staff is the poor quality of note taking by the American secretaries. The American secretaries, selected on short notice, were untrained and unable to glean and distinguish the important from the mundane. Their handwritten notes are sketchy and inadequate. Admiral King and General Marshall expressed disappointment with the secretariat's work. The note takers submitted glosses of the discussions and failed to record the depth of the disagreement and tension during the deliberations between the Anglo-American Chiefs. A cursory reading of these minutes conveys a misleading portrayal of equanimity and unanimity on all issues when in fact this was not the case.

Personal diaries provided the texture and background to the discussions, frustrations, and decisions of the Arcadia Conference. On the British side the diaries of the British secretary, Colonel, later Lieutenant General, Ian Jacob (Richardson, *From Churchill's Inner Circle to the BBC*); the army planner Brigadier Vivian Dykes (Danchev, *Establishing the Anglo-American Alliance*); and Field Marshal Alanbrooke (Bryant, *The Turn of the Tide, 1939–1943*) were especially useful.

On the US side the diaries of key participants provided insight into the American objectives as well as their frustrations with their counterparts. Especially helpful were the perceptions of army planner Brigadier General, later General of the Army, Dwight Eisenhower (Ferrell, *Eisenhower's Diaries*); army planner Major General, later General, Joseph Stilwell (White, *Stilwell Papers*); the army secretary during the conference Colonel, later Brigadier General, Paul Robinett (Marshall Papers, Marshall Library); and the Secretary of War, Henry Stimson, who participated in many of the informal discussions before and after the official meetings of the American and British Chiefs (the original of this diary is at the Yale University Library, New Haven, Connecticut).

Key Record Groups at the National Archives and Records Administration, College Park, Maryland, included: Record Group 38 (Records of the Office of the Chief of Naval Operations); Record Group 80

(General Records of the Department of the Navy); Record Group 165 (Record of the War Department General and Special Staff); Record Group 218 (Records of the United States Joint Chiefs of Staff); Record Group 225 (Records of the Joint Army and Navy Boards and Committees); Record Group 319 (Records of the Army Staff); Record Group 331 (Records of Allied Operational and Occupational Headquarters, World War II); Record Group 337 (Records of Headquarters Army Ground Forces); Record Group 338 (Records of United States Army Commands, 1942 to present).

Record Group 218 contained two essential manuscripts originally prepared by the Joint History Office. Grace Hayes's superb study on *The History of the Joint Chiefs of Staff in World War II: The War against Japan*, first printed in classified format in 1953, had a very limited distribution (about fifty copies). The Naval Institute Press published the declassified version in 1982, making its available to the wider public. Hayes wrote her study shortly after the war; it benefited from interviews with participants and editorial and review comments by senior leaders at the conference. Vernon Davis's meticulously researched manuscript, *The History of the Joint Chiefs of Staff in World War II: Organizational Development*, printed in 1972, had a limited distribution. This manuscript is the best single source on the creation and evolution of the Joint Chiefs of Staff, which grew out of the Arcadia Conference.

The Manuscript Division of the Library of Congress, in Washington, DC, has the papers of two key American participants of the Arcadia Conference, Fleet Admiral Ernest King and General of the Air Force Henry Arnold. The Library of Congress also houses the papers of the Secretary of War, Henry Stimson; Secretary of the Navy Frank Knox; Presidential Envoy to Europe on Lend-Lease Averell Harriman; Secretary of the Treasury Henry Morgenthau; Vice President Henry Wallace; Secretary of State Cordell Hull; and the US Ambassador to Great Britain, John Winant.

The Franklin Delano Roosevelt Library and Museum, Hyde Park, New York, has President Roosevelt's Master Speech File, Map Room Papers (Messages and Military Files), Presidential Secretary's files (Safe Files, Confidential Files, Diplomatic Correspondence, and

Departmental Correspondence), Executive Orders and Proclamations, Presidential Press Conferences, Franklin Roosevelt Significant Documents 1932–1945, and the Henry Morgenthau Diaries. It can be accessed online at http://www.fdrlibrary.marist.edu/archives/collections/franklin/.

The George C. Marshall Foundation Research Library and Archives, Lexington, Virginia, has a wealth of material on the accomplishments and innovations of the Army Chief of Staff. In addition to General Marshall's correspondence, this library holds the diary of Brigadier General Paul Robinett, the army secretary during the Arcadia Conference. Robinett's candid insights into the army's positions and goals, as well as his frustrations with both the navy and the British, remain extraordinary. The library also possesses a copy of Secretary of War Henry Stimson's diary and many informative interviews by General Marshall's official biographer, Forrest Pogue.

The army's Heritage and Education Center at Carlisle Barracks, Pennsylvania, has the General Officer Oral Histories/Senior Officer Debriefings conducted by the army's Military History Institute. These interviews with key army staff officers such as Thomas Handy, John Hull, Paul Carraway, Albert Wedemeyer, and Joseph McNarney were crucial to understanding American perceptions during the conference. The Military History Institute likewise has Forrest Pogue's postwar interviews with senior British officers, which provide insight into their perceptions and frustrations with their American counterparts.

The US Army's Center of Military History produced the army's green book series, the *US Army in World War II*. The center's archives include biographies of all US Army general officers and excellent historical geographic files on Japan and Great Britain.

Martin Gilbert's extensive research in the published *Churchill War Papers* and *Churchill Documents* are an invaluable resource.

In Great Britain, the Records of the Cabinet, War Cabinet Chiefs of Staff Committee, "Arcadia," Record of Proceedings at Washington Conference 1941–1942, CAB-99/17, the National Archives, Kew, Richmond, Surrey TW9 4DU, provided excellent insight into British staff meetings, goals, and objectives.

BIBLIOGRAPHY

Aandahl, Frederick, William M. Franklin, and William Slany, eds. *Foreign Relations of the United States, the Conferences at Washington, 1941–1942, and Casablanca, 1943*. Washington, DC: US Government Printing Office, 1958.

Ambrose, Stephen. *Eisenhower: Soldier, General of the Army, President-Elect, 1890–1952*. New York: Simon and Schuster, 1983.

Andrews, Robert. *Masters and Commanders*. New York: HarperCollins, 2008.

Arnold, Henry. *Global Mission*. New York: Harper and Brothers, 1949.

Atkinson, Rick. *Army at Dawn*. New York: Henry Holt, 2002.

Barnett, Correlli. *The Audit of War: The Illusion and Reality of Britain as a Great Nation*. London: Faber and Faber, 2011.

———. *The Desert Generals*. New York: Viking Press, 1960.

Bercuson, David, and Holger Herwig. *One Christmas in Washington: The Secret Meeting between Roosevelt and Churchill That Changed the World*. New York: Overlook Press, 2005.

Bland, Larry, and Sharon Ritenour Stevens, eds. *The Papers of George C. Marshall.* Vol. 3, *The Right Man for the Job*. Baltimore: Johns Hopkins University Press, 1991.

Borg, Dorothy, and Shumpei Okamoto, eds. *Pearl Harbor as History: Japanese-American Relations, 1931–1941*. New York: Columbia University Press, 1973.

Bryant, Arthur. *The Turn of the Tide, 1939–1943: A History of the War Years Based on the Diaries of Field-Marshal Lord Alanbrooke, Chief of the Imperial General Staff*. Garden City, NY: Doubleday, 1957.

Buell, Thomas. *Master of Seapower: A Biography of Fleet Admiral Ernest J. King*. Boston: Little, Brown, 1980.

Burns, James MacGregor. *Roosevelt: The Soldier of Freedom*. New York: Harcourt Brace Jovanovich, 1970.

Churchill, Winston, *The Grand Alliance*. Boston: Houghton Mifflin, 1950.

Cline, Ray. *Washington Command Post: The Operations Division*. Washington, DC: US Government Printing Office, 1951.

Connally, Tom, and Alfred Steinberg. *My Name Is Tom Connally*. New York: Thomas Y. Crowell, 1954.

Connell, John, and Michael Roberts. *Wavell: Supreme Commander*. London: Collins, 1969.

Craven, Wesley, and James Cate. *The Army Air Forces in World War II*. Vol. 1, *Plans and Early Operations: January 1939 to August 1942*. Chicago: University of Chicago Press, 1948.

Crosswell, D. K. R. *Beetle: The Life of Walter Bedell Smith*. Lexington: University Press of Kentucky, 2010.

Dallek, Robert. *Franklin D. Roosevelt: A Political Life*. New York: Viking, 2017.

———. *Franklin Delano Roosevelt and American Foreign Policy, 1932–1945*. New York: Oxford University Press, 1979.

Danchev, Alex. *Establishing the Anglo-American Alliance: The Second World War Diaries of Brigadier Vivian Dykes*. London: Brassey's, 1991.

———. *Very Special Relationship: Field Marshal Sir John Dill and the Anglo-American Alliance, 1941–1944*. London: Brassey's Defence Publishers, 1986.

———. *War Diaries, 1939–1945: Field Marshal Lord Alanbrooke*. Berkeley: University of California Press, 2001.

Dear, I. C. B., and M. R. D. Foot, eds. *The Oxford Companion to World War II*. New York: Oxford University Press, 1995.

Drea, Edward. "Japan's Diplomatic and Military Strategy between the Two World Wars." In *Asian Shadows: The Hidden History of World War Two in the Pacific*, edited by Arthur Herman. Washington, DC: Hudson Institute, April 2017. https://www.youtube.com/watch?v=3gnJe_XpvfE.

Dyer, George. *The Amphibians Came to Conquer*. 2 vols. Washington, DC: US Government Printing Office, 1972.

Eade, Charles, ed. *The End of the Beginning: War Speeches by the Right Honorable Winston S. Churchill, C.H., M.P., 1942*. London: Cassell, 1943).

———. *Secret Session Speeches Delivered by the Right Hon. Winston S. Churchill*. London: Cassell, 1946.

Eisenhower, Dwight D. *Crusade in Europe*. New York: Doubleday, 1949.

Esposito, Vincent, ed. *The West Point Atlas of American Wars*. Vol. 2, *1900–1953*. New York: Praeger, 1959.

Farrell, Brian. *The Defence and Fall of Singapore, 1940–1942*. Singapore: Monsoon Books, 2017.

Feis, Herbert. *The Road to Pearl Harbor*. Princeton, NJ: Princeton University Press, 1950.

Ferrell, Robert, ed. *The Eisenhower Diaries*. New York: W. W. Norton, 1981.

Fraser, David. *Knights Cross: A Life of Field Marshal Erwin Rommel*. New York: Harper Collins, 1993.

Gilbert, Martin. *Churchill: A Life*. New York: Henry Holt, 1991.

———. *The Churchill Documents: Testing Times, 1942*. Hillsdale, MI: Hillsdale College Press, 2014.

———. *The Churchill War Papers: The Ever-Widening War*. Vol. 3, *1941*. New York: W. W. Norton, 2000.

———. *Winston S. Churchill: Road to Victory, 1941–1945*. Vol. 7. Hillsdale, MI: Hillsdale College Press, 1986.

Greenfield, Kent Roberts, ed. *Command Decisions*. Washington, DC: US Government Printing Office, 1960.

Gwyer, J. M. A., and J. R. M. Butler. *Grand Strategy*. Vol. 3, *June 1941–August 1942*. London: Her Majesty's Stationery Office, 1964.

Hamilton, Nigel. *The Mantle of Command: FDR at War, 1941–1942*. New York: Houghton Mifflin Harcourt, 2014.

Hastings, Max. *Winston's War: Churchill, 1940–1945*. New York: Alfred A. Knopf, 2010.

Hayes, Grace. *The History of the Joint Chiefs of Staff in World War II: The War against Japan*. Annapolis, MD: Naval Institute Press, 1982.

Heinrichs, Waldo. *Threshold of War*. New York: Oxford University Press, 1988.

Herman, Arthur. *Freedom's Forge*. New York: Random House, 2013.

Hinsley, Francis Harry. *British Intelligence in the Second World War: Its Influence on Strategy and Operations*. Vol. 2. London: Her Majesty's Stationery Office, 1981.

Hull, Cordell. *The Memoirs of Cordell Hull*. New York: Macmillan, 1948.

Ismay, General Lord Hastings. *The Memoirs of Lord Ismay*. New York: Viking Press, 1960.

James, D. Clayton. *The Years of MacArthur*. Vol. 2, *1941–1945*. Boston: Houghton Mifflin, 1975.

Keegan, John. *Churchill's Generals*. London: Weidenfeld and Nicholson, 1991.

Kennedy, John. *The Business of War*. New York: William Morrow, 1958.

Kimball, Warren, ed. *Churchill and Roosevelt: The Complete Correspondence*. Vol. 1, *Alliance Emerging, October 1933–November 1942*. Princeton, NJ: Princeton Legacy Library, 2008.

King Ernest J., and Walter Muir Whitehall. *Fleet Admiral King: A Naval Record*. London: Eyre and Spottiswoode, 1953.

Kirkpatrick, Charles. *An Unknown Future and Doubtful Future: Writing the Victory Plan of 1941*. Washington, DC: US Government Printing Office, 1989.

Lacey, James, *The Washington War: FDR's Inner Circle and the Politics of Power That Won World War II*. New York: Bantam Books, 2019.

Larrabee, Eric. *Commander in Chief: Franklin Delano Roosevelt, His Lieutenants, and Their War*. New York: Harper and Row, 1987.

Lash, Joseph. *Roosevelt and Churchill: The Partnership That Saved the West*. New York: Norton, 1976.

Leahy, William. *I Was There: The Personal Story of the Chief of Staff to Presidents Roosevelt and Truman Based on His Notes and Diaries Made at the Time*. New York: Whittlesey House, 1950.

Leasor, James. *War at the Top: The Experiences of General Sir Leslie Hollis*. London: Michael Joseph, 1959.

Leighton, Richard, and Robert W. Coakley. *Global Logistics and Strategy, 1940–1943*. Washington, DC: US Army Center of Military History, 1995.

Lewin, Ronald. *The Chief: Field Marshal Lord Wavell, Commander-in-Chief and Viceroy, 1939–1947*. New York: Farrar, Straus, Giroux, 1980.

MacArthur, Douglas. *Reminiscences*. New York: McGraw-Hill, 1964.

MacDonald, Charles. *The Mighty Endeavor: American Armed Forces in the European Theater in World War II*. New York: Oxford University Press, 1969.

Manchester, William, and Paul Reid. *The Last Lion: Winston Spencer Churchill*. Vol. 3, *Defender of the Realm, 1940–1965*. New York: Little, Brown, 2012.

Matloff, Maurice, and Edwin M. Snell. *Strategic Planning for Coalition Warfare, 1941–1942*. Washington, DC: US Government Printing Office, 1990.

McCrea, John, *Captain McCrea's War: The World War II Memoir of Franklin D. Roosevelt's Naval Aide and USS* Iowa*'s First Commanding Officer*. Edited by Julia C. Tobey. New York: Skyhouse Publishing, 2016.

McCullough, David. *In The Dark Streets Shineth*. Stevens Point, WI: Shadow Mountain Press, 2010.

McHenry, Robert, ed. *Webster's American Military Biographies*. New York: Dover, 1978.

Miller, Edward, *War Plan Orange: The US Strategy to Defeat Japan, 1897–1945*. Annapolis, MD: Naval Institute Press, 1991.

Millett, Allan, and Peter Maslowski. *For the Common Defense: A Military History of the United States of America*. New York: Free Press, 1984.

Moran, Lord Charles Wilson. *Churchill: Taken from the Diaries of Lord Moran; The Struggle for Survival, 1945–1960*. Boston: Houghton Mifflin, 1966.

Morison, Samuel Eliot. *The Battle of the Atlantic: September 1939–May 1943*. Boston: Little, Brown, 1947.

———. *The Two-Ocean War: A Short History of the United States Navy in the Second World War*. Boston: Little Brown, 1963.

Morton, Louis, *The Fall of the Philippines*. Washington, DC: US Army Center of Military History, 1985.

———. "Japan's Decision for War." *United States Naval Institute Press*, vol. 80, no. 12 (December 1944).

———. *Strategy and Command: The First Two Years*. Washington, DC: US Government Printing Office, 1962.

Murphy, Robert. *A Diplomat among Warriors*. New York: Doubleday, 1964.

Pogue, Forrest. *George C. Marshall: Ordeal and Hope, 1939–1942*. New York: Viking Press, 1967.

———. *The Supreme Command*. Washington, DC: Government Printing Office, 1954.

Prange, Gordon. *At Dawn We Slept: The Untold Story of Pearl Harbor*. New York: Penguin Books, 1981.

Rearden, Steven. *Council of War: A History of the Joint Chiefs of Staff, 1942–1991*. Washington, DC: National Defense University Press, 2012.

Richards, Denis. *Portal of Hungerford: The Life of Marshal of the Royal Air Force, Viscount Portal of Hungerford*. London: Heinemann, 1977.

Richardson, Charles. *From Churchill's Secret Circle to the BBC: The Biography of Lieutenant General Sir Ian Jacob*. London: Brassey's, 1991.

Roberts, Andrew. *Masters and Commanders: How Four Titans Won The War in the West, 1941-1945*. New York: HarperCollins, 2009.

Romanus, Charles, and Riley Sunderland. *Stilwell's Mission to China*. Washington, DC: US Army Center of Military History, 1987.

Schnabel, James. *The Joint Chiefs of Staff and National Policy, 1945–1947*. Vol. 1. Washington, DC: Office of Joint History, Office of the Chairman of the Joint Chiefs of Staff, 1996.

Schofield, Victoria. *Wavell: Soldier and Statesman*. London: John Murray, 2006.

Sherwood, Robert. *Roosevelt and Hopkins: An Intimate History*. New York: Harper and Brothers, 1948.

Spector, Ronald. *Eagle against the Sun: The American War with Japan*. New York: Vintage Books, 1985.

Stokesbury, James. *A Short History of World War II*. New York: William Morrow, 1980.

Stoler, Mark. *Allies and Adversaries: The Joint Chiefs of Staff, the Grand Alliance, and US Strategy in World War II*. Chapel Hill: University of North Carolina Press, 2000.

———. *George C. Marshall: Soldier-Statesman of the American Century*. Boston: Twayne, 1989.

Taylor, A. J. P., Robert Rhodes, J. H. Plumb, Basil Liddell Hart, and Anthony Storr. *Churchill: Four Faces and the Man*. London: Allen Lane, 1969.

Thompson, Rachel. *Marshall: A Statesman Shaped in the Crucible of War*. Leesburg: George C. Marshall International Center, 2014.

Toll, Ian. *Pacific Crucible: War at Sea in the Pacific, 1941–1942*. New York: W. W. Norton, 2012.

Tuchman, Barbara. *Stilwell and the American Experience in China, 1911–1945*. New York: Macmillan, 1971.

Wedemeyer, Albert. *Wedemeyer Reports*. New York: Henry Holt, 1958.

Weigley, Russell. *The American Way of War: A History of United States Military Strategy and Policy*. New York: Macmillan, 1973.

———. *Eisenhower's Lieutenants: The Campaigns of France and Germany, 1944–1945*. Bloomington: Indiana University Press, 1981.

White, Theodore. *The Stilwell Papers*. New York: DaCapo Press, 1948.

Williams, Mary. *The US Army in World War II: Chronology, 1941–1945*. Washington, DC: US Army Center of Military History, 1989.

Willmott, H. P. *Empires in the Balance: Japanese and Allied Pacific Strategies to April 1942*. Annapolis, MD: Naval Institute Press, 1982.

Wohlstetter, Roberta. *Pearl Harbor: Warning and Decision*. Stanford, CA: Stanford University Press, 1962.

INDEX

CPSIA information can be obtained
at www.ICGtesting.com
Printed in the USA
LVHW081912260221
680067LV00002B/3

9 781623 499327